Management Across Cultures

Challenges and Strategies

Management practices and processes frequently differ across national and regional boundaries. What may be acceptable managerial behavior in one culture may be counterproductive or even unacceptable in another. As managers increasingly find themselves working across cultures, the need to understand these differences has become increasingly important. This book examines why these differences exist and how global managers can develop strategies and tactics to deal with them.

Key features:

- Draws on recent research in anthropology, psychology, economics, and management to explain the cultural and psychological underpinnings that shape managerial attitudes and behaviors
- Introduces a learning model to guide in the intellectual and practical development of managers seeking enhanced global expertise
- Offers user-friendly conceptual models to guide understanding and exploration of topics
- Summarizes and integrates the lessons learned in each chapter in application-oriented "Manager's notebooks"

Companion website featuring instructional materials and PowerPoint slides is available at www.cambridge.org/management_across_cultures.

RICHARD M. STEERS is Professor of Organization and Management in the Lundquist College of Business, University of Oregon, USA.

CARLOS J. SANCHEZ-RUNDE is Professor of People Management at IESE Business School, Barcelona, Spain.

LUCIARA NARDON is Assistant Professor of International Business at the Sprott School of Business, Carleton University, Canada.

Management Across Cultures

Challenges and Strategies

RICHARD M. STEERS
CARLOS J. SANCHEZ-RUNDE
LUCIARA NARDON

CAMBRIDGE
UNIVERSITY PRESS

CAMBRIDGE UNIVERSITY PRESS
Cambridge, New York, Melbourne, Madrid, Cape Town, Singapore,
São Paulo, Delhi, Dubai, Tokyo, Mexico City

Cambridge University Press
The Edinburgh Building, Cambridge CB2 8RU, UK

Published in the United States of America by Cambridge University Press, New York

www.cambridge.org
Information on this title: www.cambridge.org/9780521734974

First published 2010
Reprinted 2010

Printed in the United Kingdom at the University Press, Cambridge

A catalogue record for this publication is available from the British Library

ISBN 978-0-521-51343-2 Hardback
ISBN 978-0-521-73497-4 Paperback

Additional resources for this publication at
www.cambridge.org/management_across_cultures

Contents

List of exhibits		*page* viii
Preface		xiii

1 Global realities and management challenges — 1

Globalization, change, and competitiveness — 3
The new global realities — 12
Challenges facing global managers — 17

2 Developing global management skills — 24

Traditional views of management — 26
Global managers: variety of the species — 28
Rethinking managerial roles — 35
Rethinking managerial skills — 36
MANAGER'S NOTEBOOK: Developing global management skills — 39

3 Culture, values, and worldviews — 45

Culture, socialization, and normative behavior — 49
Core cultural dimensions: a starting point — 55
Regional trends and cultural differences — 64
Digging deeper: cultural complexities and contradictions — 66
MANAGER'S NOTEBOOK: Culture, values, and worldviews — 76

4 Inside the managerial mind: culture, cognition, and action — 85

Culture, cognition, and managerial action: a model — 88
Patterns of managerial thinking — 91
The geography of thought — 96
Culture and the managerial role — 102
Management patterns across cultures — 106

Are management patterns converging?   115
MANAGER'S NOTEBOOK: Inside the managerial mind   118

**5 Inside the organizational mind: stakeholders, strategies,
and decision making**   126
Stakeholders and strategic choice: a model   128
The strategy-structure nexus   134
Organizational decision making: a model   137
Decision strategies across cultures   139
MANAGER'S NOTEBOOK: Inside the organizational mind   149

6 Organizing frameworks: a comparative assessment   155
Culture and organization design: a model   157
US corporations   159
Japanese *kaisha* and *keiretsu*   165
Chinese *gong-si*   175
German *konzern*   181
Mexican *grupo*   186
MANAGER'S NOTEBOOK: Organizing frameworks   193

7 Communication across cultures   199
Eye of the beholder   201
Culture and communication: a model   202
Language, logic, and communication   204
Lingua franca and message comprehension   210
Cross-cultural communication strategies   214
Communication on the fly   228
MANAGER'S NOTEBOOK: Communication across cultures   232

8 Leadership and global teams   241
The meaning of leadership   245
GLOBE leadership study   253
Culture and leadership: a model   256
Global teams   261
Working with global teams   262
MANAGER'S NOTEBOOK: Leadership and global teams   270

9 Culture, work, and motivation 279

The world of work 284

Work and leisure 290

Culture, motivation, and work behavior: a model 292

Culture and the psychology of work 295

Incentives and rewards across cultures 299

MANAGER'S NOTEBOOK: Culture, work, and motivation 310

10 Negotiation and global partnerships 317

Seeking common cause 321

Culture and negotiation: a model 328

The negotiation process: strategies, concessions, and contracts 330

Negotiation patterns across cultures 337

Building global partnerships 342

Managing global partnerships 346

MANAGER'S NOTEBOOK: Negotiation and global partnerships 350

11 Managing in an imperfect world 363

Rules of the game 364

Bases of cross-cultural conflicts 367

Ethics, laws, and social control: a model 373

Ethical conflicts and challenges 374

Institutional conflicts and challenges 384

MANAGER'S NOTEBOOK: Managing in an imperfect world 395

12 Epilogue: the journey continues 404

Learning from the past 405

Looking to the future 407

Appendix A Models of national cultures 411

Appendix B OECD guidelines for global managers 421

Index 430

Exhibits

1.1 The globalization enigma: contradictions and challenges — *page* 8

1.2 The changing global economy — 12

2.1 Global managers: expatriates, frequent flyers, and virtual managers — 29

2.2 Building global management skills — 37

2.3 The experiential learning cycle — 40

2.4 A learning strategy for global managers — 42

3.1 Hofstede's culture ratings for Sweden and Bahrain — 49

3.2 Levels of mental programming — 51

3.3 Selected models of cultural dimensions — 56

3.4 Core cultural dimensions — 58

3.5 Anchors for core cultural dimensions — 60

3.6 Central tendencies of core cultural dimensions across regions — 65

3.7 Cultural complexities and contradictions — 69

4.1 Culture, cognition, and managerial action — 90

4.2 Culture and patterns of managerial thinking — 92

4.3 Looking outside: patterns of East-West cognitive differences — 99

4.4 Looking inside: patterns of East-West cognitive differences — 100

4.5 Cultural differences and the ideal managerial role — 103

4.6 Culture and actual managerial characteristics — 104

4.7 Cultural influences on managerial roles — 105

4.8 Culture and management trends: France, Malaysia, and Nigeria — 108

4.9 Convergence and divergence in future management patterns — 117

5.1 The strategic management cycle — 130

5.2 Centralized versus distributed stakeholder models — 131

5.3 Cultural influences on participation in decision-making — 139

5.4 Management challenge: approaches to participation and decision making — 140

5.5 Centralized decision making (e.g., Australia, Canada, UK, US) — 141

5.6 Centralized decision making (e.g., China)   142

5.7 Consultative decision making (e.g., Japan)   143

5.8 Collaborative decision making (e.g., Germany, Netherlands,
     Sweden)   146

6.1 Cultural influences on organization design   158

6.2 Culture and organization design: country examples   159

6.3 Design of a typical US corporation   163

6.4 Design of a typical Japanese horizontal *keiretsu*   169

6.5 *Keiretsu* network for Mitsubishi's Kirin Holdings Company   171

6.6 Design of a typical Japanese vertical *keiretsu*   172

6.7 *Kongfuzi*'s five cardinal virtues   176

6.8 Design of a typical Chinese family-owned *gong-si*   179

6.9 Design of a typical German *konzern*   183

6.10 Germany's dual system of vocational training   186

6.11 Design of a typical Mexican *grupo*   190

6.12 Management challenge: working with different organizing
     frameworks   193

6.13 Patterns of organization design and management practice:
     a summary   194

7.1 Cultural influences on the communication process   202

7.2 Cultural logic in cross-cultural communication   209

7.3 Challenges facing non-native speakers   211

7.4 High-, mid-range, and low-context cultures   218

7.5 Protocols governing appropriate formalities   222

7.6 Protocols governing appropriate behaviors   223

7.7 Interdependent learning   230

7.8 Management challenge: communicating effectively across cultures   232

7.9 Management strategies: improving cross-cultural communication   235

8.1 GLOBE leadership dimensions   255

8.2 Cultural influences on leadership   257

8.3 Global teams: functions, advantages, and drawbacks   262

8.4 Challenges to global team effectiveness   263

8.5 Types of national and global teams   264

8.6 Characteristics of co-located and virtual teams   265

8.7 Special challenges facing virtual global teams   266

8.8 Management challenge: focusing global team efforts   270

8.9 Management strategies for leading global teams 272
8.10 Management strategies for leading virtual global teams 275
9.1 Personal work values and employee behavior 285
9.2 Top four work preferences for employees in select countries 287
9.3 The psychological contract 289
9.4 Vacation policies in select countries 291
9.5 Cultural influences on work motivation and performance 294
9.6 Ratio of average CEO compensation to average employee compensation 303
9.7 Wage gaps between men and women across nations 304
9.8 Expectations, rewards, and job attitudes 307
9.9 Average job satisfaction levels for select countries 308
9.10 Management challenge and strategies: motivating a global workforce 310
10.1 Cultural influences on the negotiation process 329
10.2 Competitive and problem-solving bargaining strategies 331
10.3 Information exchange and initial offers by culture 333
10.4 Sequential and holistic bargaining strategies 334
10.5 Contracts and the doctrine of changed circumstances 336
10.6 Negotiating tactics in Japan, Brazil, and the US 338
10.7 Negotiating strategies in Japan, Brazil, and the US 339
10.8 Management arrangements for global partnerships 347
10.9 Can people be trusted? 352
10.10 Management challenge: developing mutual trust 353
10.11 Management challenge: aligning corporate cultures 356
10.12 Management strategies: conflict resolution in global partnerships 358
11.1 Sources of cross-cultural conflict 368
11.2 Normative beliefs, institutional requirements, and social control 373
11.3 Levels of understanding of cross-cultural ethical conflicts 376
11.4 Universalism, particularism, and truthfulness 379
11.5 Corruption index for various countries 387
11.6 Management challenge: OECD bribery and corruption guidelines 389
11.7 Management challenge: OECD employee relations guidelines 391
11.8 Management challenge: OECD environmental stewardship guidelines 393

A.1 Kluckholn and Strodtbecks' cultural dimensions   412

A.2 Hofstede's cultural dimensions   413

A.3 Hall's cultural dimensions   413

A.4 Trompenaar's cultural dimensions   414

A.5 Schwartz's cultural dimensions   415

A.6 GLOBE project's cultural dimensions   416

A.7 Common themes across models of national cultures   418

B.1 OECD guidelines for global managers   422

Preface

We live in a turbulent and contradictory world, where there are few certainties and change is constant. In addition, over time we increasingly come to realize that much of what we think we see around us can, in reality, be something entirely different. We require greater perceptual accuracy just as the horizons become increasingly cloudy. Business cycles are becoming more dynamic and unpredictable, and companies, institutions, and employees come and go with increasingly regularity. Much of this uncertainty is the result of economic forces that are beyond the control of individuals and major corporations. Much results from recent waves of technological change that resist pressures for stability or predictability. And much results from individual and corporate failures to understand the realities on the ground when they pit themselves against local institutions, competitors, and cultures. Knowledge is definitely power when it comes to global business and, as our knowledge base becomes more uncertain, companies and their managers seek help wherever they can find it. It is the thesis of this book that a major part of this knowledge base for managers rests on developing a fundamental, yet flexible, understanding of how business management works in different regions of the world. More specifically, our aim is to develop information and learning models that global managers can build upon to pursue their careers and corporate missions.

As managers increasingly find themselves working across borders, their list of cultural lessons – do's and don'ts, must's and must not's – continues to grow. Consider just a few examples: most French and Germans refer to the EU as "we," while most British refer to it as "they"; all are members. While criticizing heads of state is a favorite pastime in many countries around the world, criticizing the king in Thailand is a felony punishable by fifteen years in jail. Every time Nigerian-born oncologist Nkechi Mba fills in her name on a form somewhere, she is told that she should write her name, not her degree. In Russia, companies frequently pay public officials to raid business rivals and subject them to criminal investigations. In Korea, a world leader in flexible IT networks, supervisors often assume employees are not working unless they are sitting at their desks in the office. And in a recent marketing survey among US college students, only 7 percent on average could identify the national origins of many of their favorite brands, including Adidas, Samsung, Nokia, Lego, and Ericsson. In particular, quality ratings of Nokia cell phones soared when students believed (incorrectly) that they were made in Japan.

And there is more: Germany's Bavarian Radio Symphony recently deleted part of its musical repertoire from a concert tour because it violated the European Union's new noise-at-work limitations. US telecommunications giant AT&T has been successfully sued in class action suits for gender discrimination against both its female and male employees. When you sink a hole-in-one while playing golf with friends in North America and Europe, it is often customary for your partners to pay you a cash prize; in Japan, you pay them. The head of Nigeria's Niger Delta Development Corporation was recently fired from his job after it was discovered that he had paid millions of dollars of public money to a local witch doctor to vanquish a rival. The penalty for a first offense of smuggling a small quantity of recreational drugs into Western Europe is usually a stern lecture or a warning; in Singapore, it is death. Finally, dressing for global business meetings can be challenging: wearing anything made of leather can be offensive to many Hindus in India; wearing yellow is reserved for the royal family in Malaysia; and white is the color of mourning in many parts of Asia.

Serious? Silly? Absurd? Perhaps the correct answer (or answers) here is in the eye of the beholder. When confronted by such examples, many observers are dismissive, suggesting that the world is getting smaller and that many of these troublesome habits and customs will likely disappear over time as globalization pressures work to homogenize how business is done – properly, they believe – across national boundaries. But the world is not getting smaller; it is getting faster. And many globalization pressures are currently bypassing – and, indeed, in some cases actually accentuating – divergent local customs, conventions, and business practices, if for no other reason than to protect local societies from the ravages of economic warfare. What this means for managers is that many of these and other local customs will likely be around for a long time, and wise managers will prepare themselves in order capitalize on these differences, not ignore them.

In view of the myriad of challenges such as these, managers viewing global assignments – or even global travel – would do well to learn as much as they can about the world in which they will work. And the same holds true for local managers working in their home countries, where the global business world is increasingly challenging them on their own turf. Like it or not, with both globalization and competition increasing almost everywhere, the challenge for managers is to outperform their competitors, either individually of collectively. This can be attempted either by focusing exclusively on one's own self-interests or by building mutually beneficial strategic alliances with global partners. Either way, the challenges and pitfalls can be significant.

Another important factor to take into consideration here is a fundamental shift in the nature of geopolitics. The days of hegemony – East or West – are over. No longer will global business leaders focus on one or two stock markets, currencies, economies, or political leaders. Today's business environment is far too complex and interrelated for that. Contrary to some predictions, nation-states and multinational corporations will remain both powerful and important; we are not, in fact, moving towards a "borderless society." And global networks, comprising technological, entrepreneurial, social welfare, and environmental interest groups, will also remain powerful. Indeed, networks and relationships will increasingly represent power, not traditional or historic institutions. And future economic and business endeavors, like future political, social, and environmental endeavors, will be increasingly characterized by a search for common ground, productive partnerships, and mutual benefit.

When faced with this increasing global challenge, managers have two choices. First, in international transactions, they can assume that they are who they are and the world should adapt to them. ("I am a Dutch manager with Dutch traits, and everyone understands this and will make allowances.") Or, second, they can work to develop greater multicultural competencies that allow them to either adapt to others where possible or at least understand why others behave as they do. ("I am a Dutch manager who is working to understand the cultural context in which my counterparts operate.") While both approaches can work (especially if these managers and their firms possess critical resources, such as money), the second strategy of working to develop increased multicultural competencies clearly offers greater potential benefits in the long run.

In this endeavor, managers cannot find help by simply reaching for a book called "Global Management for Dummies." Indeed, if it existed, such a book title would be an oxymoron. Global managers cannot afford to be "dummies" – perhaps "uneducated" is a better word here. Simply put, they and their companies would fail if such were the case, full stop. Instead, successful managers view working across borders as a long-term developmental process requiring intelligence and insight, not just a fancy title. It is a strategic process, not a tactical one.

As a result, this book focuses on developing a deeper understanding of how management practices and processes can often differ around the world, and why. It draws heavily on recent research in cultural anthropology, psychology, and management as they relate to how managers structure their enterprises and pursue the day-to-day work necessary to make a venture succeed. It emphasizes both differences and similarities across cultures, since we believe that this mirrors reality. It attempts to explore the psychological underpinnings that help shape managerial attitudes and behaviors, as well as their approaches to people from other regions of the world. But most of all, this book is about learning. It introduces a learning model early in the text to guide in the intellectual and practical development of managers seeking global experience. It further assumes a lifelong learning approach to global encounters, managerial performance, and career success.

The title of this book, *Management Across Cultures: Challenges and Strategies*, reflects our two goals in writing it. First, we wanted to examine how management practices and processes can frequently differ – often significantly – across national and regional boundaries. Managers in different cultures often see their roles and responsibilities in different ways. They often organize themselves and make decisions differently. And they often communicate, negotiate, and motivate in different ways. Understanding these differences is the first step in developing global management capabilities. And second, we wanted to identify and discuss strategies and tactics that can be used by global managers as they work to succeed across cultures. That is, we wanted to explore how people can work and manage across cultures – and how they can overcome many of the hurdles along the way. We see these two goals as both mutually compatible and indispensable for meeting the business challenges ahead.

Like most authors who seek an interested audience, we wrote this book primarily to express our own views, ideas, and frustrations. As both teachers and researchers in the field, we have grown increasingly impatient with books in this general area that seem to have aimed somewhat below the readers' intelligence in the presentation of materials. In our view, both managers and would-be managers are intelligent consumers of behavioral information. To do their job better, they are seeking useful information and dialogue about the uncertain environment in which they work; they are not seeking unwarranted or simplistic conclusions or narrow rulebooks. In our view, managers are looking for learning strategies, not prescriptions, and understand that becoming a global manager is a long-term pursuit – a marathon, not a sprint.

We have likewise been dismayed with books that assume one worldview – whether it is British, American, French, or whatever – in interpreting both global business challenges and managerial behavior. Instead, we have tried diligently to cast our net a bit wider and incorporate divergent viewpoints when exploring various topics, such as communication, negotiation, and leadership. For example, asking how Chinese or Indian management practices differ from American or Canadian practices assumes a largely Western bias as a starting point ("How are *they* different from us?"). Instead, why not ask a simpler and more useful question like "How do Chinese, Indian, American, and Canadian management styles in general differ?" ("How are we *all* different from each another?"). Moreover, we might add a further, also useful, question concerning managerial similarities across cultures ("How are we *all* similar to each other?"). To achieve this, we have resisted a "one-size-fits-all" approach to management, locally or globally, in the belief that such an approach limits both understanding and success in the field. Instead, our goal here is to develop multicultural competence through the development of learning strategies in which managers can draw on their own personal experiences, combined with outside information such as that provided in this book and elsewhere, to develop cross-cultural understanding and theories-in-use that can guide them in the pursuit of their managerial pursuits.

Throughout the process of researching and writing this book, the three authors were fortunate in having an opportunity to create our own "global team," consisting of management researchers from Brazil, Spain, and the US. This combination opened up numerous opportunities for taking multiple, and not necessarily congruent, perspectives on various topics. The lessons were many. First and foremost, we learned that facts and realities often have transient meanings, and can change both across time and borders. We learned that neither individualism nor collectivism is inherently good; that mastery and harmony can at times work in tandem; and that time has many different definitions and applications. Calendars and stopwatches do not necessarily lead to meaningful progress. Goal-directed behavior is often complemented, not displaced, by the more jumbled intersections of multiple simultaneous activities. Chaos theory probably has merit in joint intellectual pursuits. We learned that both rules and relationships could create a vibrant and committed multicultural team that works closely together in a spirit of both flexibility and goal orientation. We learned that non-linear systems could often trump linearity in both quality and completeness. We learned that cultural friction between partners is often a desirable quality, not something to be avoided. In our case, it led to greater creativity and a more realistic view – or, more accurately, views – of the world of work. We learned that assuming a leadership role can be both loud and assertive or quiet and subtle, but both approaches involve manipulation. Finally, we learned that working in a global team can be a great deal of fun, and can create an environment in which much can be learned and shared. We would like to believe that each of us has grown and developed as a result of this team collaboration.

In writing this book, we were also able to draw on our research and teaching experiences in various countries and regions of the world, including Argentina,

Belgium, Brazil, Canada, Chile, China, Denmark, Germany, Japan, Mexico, Norway, the Netherlands, Peru, South Africa, South Korea, Spain, the UK, the US, and Uruguay. In doing so, we learned from our colleagues and students in various parts of the world and believe these experiences made for a far better book than it might otherwise have been. Our aim here is not to write a bias-free book, as we believe this would have been an impossible task. Indeed, the decision to write this book in English, largely for reasons of audience, market, and personal competence, did itself introduce some bias into the end result. Rather, our intent was to write a book that simultaneously reflected differing national, cultural, and personal viewpoints, where biases are identified and discussed openly instead of being hidden or rationalized. As a result, this book contains few certainties and many contradictions, reflecting our views on the life of global managers.

Any book is a joint endeavor between authors and publishers. The people at Cambridge University Press lived up to their reputation as a first-class group of people to work with. In particular, we wish to thank Paula Parish, Philip Good, and Liz Davey for their advice, patience, and support through the project.

Finally, few book projects can be successful without the support of families. This is particularly true in our case, where all three of our families joined together to help make this project a reality. In particular, Richard would like to thank the four generations of women that surround and support him: Pat, Sheila, Kathleen, and Allison. Carlos, who also seems to spend all of his time and money on women, would like to thank his wife Carol and daughters Clara and Isabel. And Luciara, the only sane one in the group, would like to thank her mother, Jussara, for her unconditional support, and her son, Caio, for his inspiration. Throughout, our families have been there for us in every way possible, and for this we are grateful.

Richard M. Steers, USA
Carlos J. Sanchez-Runde, Spain
Luciara Nardon, Canada

CHAPTER 1

Global realities and management challenges

■ Globalization, change, and competitiveness   3
■ The new global realities   12
■ Challenges facing global managers   17

A global manager is set apart by more than a worn suitcase and a dog-eared passport.

Thomas A. Stewart[1]
Editor, *Harvard Business Review*, USA

Global managers are made, not born. This is not a natural process. We are herd animals; we like people who are like us.

Percy Barnevik[2]
Former CEO, ABB Group, Switzerland
CEO, Hand-in-Hand International, UK

Twenty-five years ago, two highly respected management consultants published a comprehensive study of *Fortune 500* companies that sought to identify the key management characteristics of the most successful firms in the US.[3] National Public Radio called the book "one of the top three business books of the century."[4] Based on their research, the authors identified what they considered to be the top forty "excellent" companies. These firms shared several common features that clustered around the three themes of people, customers, and action. More specifically, the researchers concluded that success was associated with eight common company characteristics: a bias for action; close customer relations; an entrepreneurial spirit; productivity through people; a hands-on, value-driven management philosophy that guided everyday practice; a focus on core business areas; a flat organization design, including a small headquarters staff; and a combination of shared company values and high degrees of shop floor autonomy.

Five years after this landmark study was published, a *Business Week* investigation found that of the original forty "excellent" firms, a full one-third had experienced either significant financial loss or bankruptcy.[5] These failings were particularly severe in the

1

technology sector of the economy, where companies such as Atari, Data General, DEC, Lanier, NCR, Wang Labs, and others had experienced significant setbacks. Worse still, today nearly a quarter of the original "excellent" companies are no longer in business.

What happened? Did the researchers use poor methodology or personal bias in selecting their top companies? Did business conditions change so rapidly that many winners suddenly became losers, while other former losers (those not initially selected as "excellent") suddenly became winners? In point of fact, a critical common denominator can be found across the less successful and failed firms: They either underestimated or largely ignored the power and presence of the emerging global economy. That is, they routinely exhibited a singular lack of awareness of global markets, geopolitical threats and opportunities, and factors that could facilitate or inhibit global competitiveness. Simply put, their world changed; they did not. While many of the original "excellent" firms were looking primarily within their own national boundaries for results, the business environment had shifted significantly global issues and opportunities. Thus, for many of these firms, the global economy simply left them behind to be replaced by more competitive firms from both the US and beyond. Indeed, it is difficult today to imagine a best-selling business book that does not take a global perspective, instead of a national one, and incorporate global data and companies into its investigation.

Had more of the firms in this and similar studies published around the same time paid more attention to business in the *global* environment, they would have quickly found that a major ingredient in the long-term success of contemporary firms is the quality – including global qualifications and experience – of their employees all the way from the top management team to the field representatives, production supervisors, and rank-and-file employees. This is where the rubber meets the road in global competitiveness. As MIT economist Lester Thurow observed, the future success of companies – and countries – rests largely on the quality of their technology and their people, not necessarily their cost of materials and labor.[6] In our view, principal among the traits of these "quality" people is their global frame of reference as it relates to managerial behavior and performance. And a global frame of reference is not an easy thing to achieve.

On a managerial level, the plight of many of today's failed or mediocre managers is evident from the legion of stories about failures in cross-border enterprise. Managers are responsible for utilizing human, financial, informational, and physical resources in ways that facilitate their organization's overall objectives in turbulent and sometimes hostile environments about which they often understand very little. These challenges can be particularly problematic when operations cross national boundaries. Nonetheless, ignorance or unfamiliarity with local business customs is seldom an acceptable excuse for failure, and with the current global infatuation with a fairly narrow definition of leadership (lead, follow, or get out of the way), there is seldom any room for anything but success. In fact, particularly in many Western cultures, lack of success is more often attributed to personal failure than external considerations beyond management's control.

As globalization pressures increase and managers spend more time crossing borders to conduct business, the training and development community has increasingly advocated more intensive analyses of the criteria for managerial success in the global economy. As more attention is focused on this challenge, an increasing cadre of management experts are zeroing in on the need for managers to develop perspectives that stretch beyond domestic borders. This concept is identified in many ways (e.g., global mindset, cultural intelligence), but we refer to it simply as *multicultural competence*. Whatever it is called, its characteristics and skills are in increasing demand as large and small, established and entrepreneurial firms strive for global competitiveness.

The challenge of managing successfully in an increasingly complex and global environment is the topic of this book. While the concept of globalization has clearly caught on, and while these challenges are very real, we will suggest in this volume that working to meet these challenges is far more the result of hard work, thinking, reflection, and attentive behavior than any of the quick fixes that are so readily available. We will suggest further that to accomplish this, managers will need to develop some degree of multicultural competency as an important tool to guide their social interactions and business decisions and prevent themselves from repeating the intercultural and strategic mistakes made by so many of their predecessors.

Clearly, working and managing in the global economy requires more than cross-cultural understanding and skills, but we argue that without such skills the manager's job is all the more difficult to accomplish. If the world is truly moving towards greater complexity, interconnections, and corporate interrelationships, the new global manager will obviously need to play a role in order for organizations and their stakeholders to succeed.

Globalization, change, and competitiveness

Although there are many ways to conceptualize globalization, most definitions share common roots. For our purposes here, and following the work of *New York Times* columnist Thomas Friedman, we define *globalization* as the inexorable integration of markets, capital, nation-states, and technologies in ways that allow individuals, groups, corporations, and countries to reach around the world farther, faster, deeper, and cheaper than ever before.[7] In essence, this new global reality represents a major paradigm shift in international politics, economics, and business that impacts corporations and their managers, as well as society-at-large. And, as experience teaches us, few such changes occur without winners and losers. This process is increasingly creating a powerful backlash from those left behind by the new economic and political system.

Economic historians have suggested that, as a world-changing phenomenon, globalization has passed through three reasonably distinct phases.[8] Phase one involved the globalization of countries and ran roughly from the 1400s through to the early 1900s. In this phase, nations tried with varying degree of success to define their relationships with other nations. The Age of Imperialism of the seventeenth and eighteenth centuries, when several of Europe's largest countries tried to divide up much of the rest of the world as colonies, provides a good example of this. Phase two involved the globalization of companies and ran throughout most of the twentieth century. This was the age when many well-known multinational corporations were born and companies began seeing their markets in global terms. Phase three – the current phase – began roughly with the twenty-first century and involves the globalization of individuals. This is when globalization is experienced on a personal level; it affects individuals, for example when an Indian entrepreneur hires young people trained in Hindu temple art to make computer-assisted character designs for global computer game companies. This is a global application of a traditional Hindu art form, and it indicates just how personal globalization can become. Globalization can also be felt on a personal level when outsourced or imported products, ranging from automobiles to toothpaste, lead to downsizing and job losses for individuals in the local economies. The recent economic meltdown has only added to these troubles.

Moreover, because of a decline in the cost of both transportation and telecommunications, combined with the proliferation of personal computers and the bandwidth and common software applications that connect them, global companies are now able to build global workflow platforms. These platforms can divide up almost any job and, with scanning and digitization, outsource each of its components to teams of skilled knowledge workers around the globe, based on which team can perform the function with the highest skill at the lowest cost. Jobs ranging from clothing manufacturing to accounting to radiology are examples of this. Thus, the advice to large and small countries alike around the world seems to be to get on board the global train and find a place to add value; otherwise you risk being left behind.

Globalization drivers

Many factors account for this new global economy. We refer to these as *globalization drivers*. These include the various forces emerging from the global environment that essentially force countries, institutions, and companies to adapt or fail. Consider the following drivers:

- *Increased customer demands and access to competing products and services.* Customers around the world are increasingly demanding more for less. They are putting increased pressure on both the price and quality of products and services that various firms offer. Customers increasingly prefer global brands over local products; they want Blackberries, iPhones, or BMWs, not because they are Canadian, American, or German, but because they are "branded." They see themselves as pacesetters, demanding only the latest in technologies, luxuries, products, and services. Moreover, customers increasingly have greater access to products and services that go beyond local distributors (e.g., internet and television shopping).

- *Increased technological innovation and application.* Improved telecommunications and information technology facilitate increased access to global networks, markets, partners, and customers. Basic and applied research, often conducted by global strategic alliances or international joint ventures, is increasingly generating new products and services (e.g., new technologies, new medicines, new DNA or genetic applications), thereby creating new markets.

- *Increased power and influence of emerging markets and economies.* As many economic forces continue to globalize, differences between haves and have-nots have tended to accentuate. Emerging markets present traditional corporations with a particular challenge, while many emerging economies are demanding greater respect and greater access to global markets. Meanwhile, some economies and societies fall further into poverty and despair. Consider: Zimbabwe continues to sink in a world of official corruption and violence in which its 2008 inflation rate exceeded 250 million percent and expiration dates are now printed on its national currency.

- *Shared R&D and global sourcing.* Many companies are going global in order to spread their research and product development costs across multiple regional markets. Outsourcing is now the rule, not the exception. Consider: 70 percent of the components used to manufacture Boeing's 787 Dreamliner are sourced from foreign suppliers.[9] Global supply chains are becoming increasingly efficient, while transportation and logistical costs are often declining.

- *Increased globalization of financial markets.* Global economies and financial markets have become increasingly interdependent. Access to capital markets is becoming increasingly globalized. This trend has proven catastrophic in some cases where these intertwined markets have collapsed simultaneously.
- *Evolving government trade policies.* Governments are increasingly supporting local economic development initiatives to lure new (and often foreign) investments and create local employment. They are also increasingly supporting aggressive trade initiatives to support global expansion of local companies. Trade barriers are being systematically reduced across much of the world through multilateral trade agreements (e.g., NAFTA, WTO). However, with increased recessionary pressures, it is anyone's guess whether this trend will continue or reverse itself.

Taken together, the results of these globalization drivers represent a sea change in the challenges facing businesses and the way in which they conduct themselves in the global economy, and they have a direct influence on the quality and effectiveness of management. Companies are under increasing pressures for greater efficiencies and economies of scale. Local firms have no place to hide.

Globalization presents companies with both challenges and opportunities, however. The manner in which they respond – or fail to respond – to such challenges will in large measure determine who wins and who loses. Those that succeed will need to have sufficient managers with economic grounding, political and legal skills, and cultural awareness to decipher the complexities that characterize their surrounding environment. And tying this all together will be the management know-how to outsmart, outperform, or outlast the competition on a continuing basis. However, while globalization seems to be inevitable, not all cultures and countries will react in the same way, and therein lies one of the principal challenges for both corporate strategy and national policy.

And looking to the future, what new and different globalization pressures will likely emerge to challenge international (and national) companies and their managers? How will these new pressures affect the opportunities and threats faced by firms? And how will these new pressures affect the management skills that will be required to succeed in the future?

The globalization enigma

Increasingly today, there is an ongoing – and often heated – debate over the merits or demerits of globalization. Some people, including many economists, argue that globalization represents a major instrument of change that can help solve many of today's economic development challenges around the world. It provides a vehicle by which less developed nations can acquire the technology, foreign investment, and training necessary to compete head-on in the future. It represents a ladder to development and prosperity. Other people, including many sociologists, argue the reverse – that globalization represents the exploitation of the weak by the strong, and in doing so threatens the cultural viability of many regions of the earth. It is a mechanism used by multinationals and their governments to oppress and destabilize the workers and governments of weaker nations.

In point of fact, both arguments have merit, due in part to the intricacies and contradictions inherent in the concept itself. In other words, globalization is not exactly what it seems to be to the casual – or even the dedicated – observer. It is complex, contradictory, and impossible to manage. Globalization is, in reality, a highly complex social, economic, and technological phenomenon that must be carefully nuanced to be understood. It is neither linear nor monolithic. Efforts to make it exclusively positive or negative are by definition naïve and unhelpful. As such, managers around the world must avoid the temptation to position themselves with a prejudged, clear-cut, black-and-white viewpoint of events on the ground that often ignore the subtle – and sometimes hidden – realities of globalization.

Much of what we know about globalization is still a work-in-progress, and what we do know presents us with apparently opposing and often contradictory forces that require some form of integration in order to achieve meaningful understanding. This presents managers with an enigma that can hamper understanding. Because of this, management analysis and understanding of the complexities of the global environment can be facilitated by focusing on understanding parallel and often competing *globalization dualities*, instead of looking for right or wrong answers. That is, the global environment exists as a series of push-pull realities that can make simple conclusions both inaccurate and risky.

The application of a dualities approach to improve analysis and understanding is not new. Indeed, researchers and scientists from many divergent fields have long used this technique to better understand certain phenomena. For example, researchers in the field of physics stopped arguing long ago over whether light should be considered in particle versus wave modes.[10] Philosophers also realized that traditional debates alternatively stressing objectivism and subjectivism, or realism and idealism, miss the point of the complexity of approximating truth. In sociology, authors acknowledge the intermixing of structure and action to understand group behavior.[11] Psychologists

Exhibit 1.1 The globalization enigma: contradictions and challenges

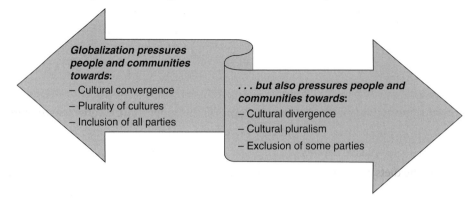

stress the need to consider the interplay of both contextual and intrapersonal variables.[12] Economists, too, are beginning to accept the need to work on assumptions of
both increasing and decreasing returns[13] and multiple versus single equilibrium.[14]
Science seems to march under the banner of integrating knowledge that spans beyond
the simplistic "either-or" logic in favor of a more holistic "both-and" approach. This
approach can also assist with understanding recent globalization effects and
outcomes.

Using a dualities perspective, we can view globalization as existing in a dynamic state
of flux and consisting of multiple processes and forces that flow in different, and often
conflicting, directions.[15] These conflicting forces can often influence how firms organize, people communicate, and managers manage; hence, the enigma. In point of fact, we
can identify three such globalization dualities, each operating in two conceptually
distinct areas. For global managers, this presents three important challenges, as summarized in Exhibit 1.1.

Cultural convergence versus cultural divergence
The first challenge facing managers and their companies in the new global economy
involves the contradiction, or duality, between *cultural convergence* and *cultural divergence*. Simply put, does globalization lead to converging or diverging modes of behavior? That is, does increased globalization cause nation-states to become more similar in
nature and outlook or does it force them to retrench and reinforce their unique beliefs
and value systems? (Consider the ongoing events in the Middle East as an example

here.) This debate can lead managers in circles if questions are considered in terms of discovering a final overall pattern of either convergence or divergence. Rather than force an answer that is only half true, a duality perspective is required to see that globalization in fact leads simultaneously to both increased convergence and increased divergence. Understanding this will make the manager's job in new environments considerably easier.

To see how this works, consider the global fast-food industry. For the past half-century, a few major (mostly American) players in this industry have come to dominate this global market. Concerns about the health implications of fast-food consumption aside, many voices have been raised against the heavy influence of American-based fast foods on the diets and cultures of people around the world. Traditional, non-American eating behaviors are seen as becoming endangered with the corresponding diminution of world cultural diversity. As critics see it, a convergence process is emerging in countries around the world in which brands like McDonald's, KFC, Burger King, and Taco Bell are increasingly and widely recognized. At the same time, however, a divergence process is also operating here. Non-American companies around the world are increasingly adopting the mass-production and mass-distribution approaches of US fast-food firms to provide alternative outlets that emphasize their own culinary traditions. In doing so, far from trying to make all tastes converge toward a unique global standard, fast-food companies typically adapt their menu offerings in foreign countries to match their traditional consumption habits. Big Macs in Israel, for instance, are served without cheese, thereby permitting the separation of meat and dairy products required of kosher restaurants. In India, McDonald's serves vegetarian McNuggets and Maharajah Macs to comply with Hindu and Muslim prohibitions of beef and pork, respectively. It also serves espresso coffee and cold pasta in Italy, McLox (grilled salmon) in Norway, *vin ordinaire* in France, and beer and frankfurters in Germany.[16] As Harvard anthropology professor James Watson observes, "McDonald's restaurants symbolize different things to different people at different times in their lives: predictability, safety, convenience, fun, familiarity, sanctuary, cleanliness, modernity, culinary tourism, and 'connectedness' to the world beyond. Few commodities can match this list of often contradictory attributes. One is tempted to conclude that the primary product is the experience itself."[17] As we have seen, this is an experience that both converges with, and diverges from, the experience of consumers in various parts of the world.

Next, consider a second example dealing with corporate governance across borders.[18] In Germany, labor unions have traditionally held important seats on corporate boards, while in Japan loyal senior managers can cap off careers with a stint in the boardroom. Founding families hold sway on Indian corporate boards, while Communist Party officials dominate corporate boards in China. Just as different nations have developed different languages, foods, and local customs, they have also adapted their own forms of corporate governance. Now, as business continues to globalize, new pressure from international capital markets and government regulators threaten to diminish the local and national flavor of corporate boards. Companies around the world are increasingly being pressured to converge on a model developed largely in the UK and North America in response to the growing power of global capital investors. A central focus of corporate governance is the structure of the corporate board. Many firms are moving to create boards that are more independent from management, populated by non-executive members, and organized around committees overseeing management, compensation, and auditing. In the next fifteen years, it is estimated that corporate boards around the world will move toward a model in which boards typically have ten to fifteen members and three or four major committees. As far back as 1997, Sony rocked Japan Inc. when it reduced the size of its board from thirty-eight to ten and adopted other Western-style characteristics. India, too, has taken steps to increase the independence of its board members with a new law requiring half of all directors to be independent. At the same time, however, despite new regulatory codes and well-meaning attempts at initiating good governance practices, worldwide convergence on one model seems unlikely. Nations and companies will continue to exhibit local characteristics because different countries have followed varying patterns of economic development. A complex mix of historic, legal, political, and economic factors shapes each nation's corporate landscape. As a result, corporate governance and board structures will continue to vary around the world, sometimes significantly.

Thus, the initial fears by business commentators and social critics that globalization would ultimately lead to cultural and business homogenization are clearly unfounded. Indeed, recent experience suggests that cultural differences have not only not been reduced, but, indeed, globalization has made such differences even more salient and pronounced in places. In a swing of the pendulum, some voices are now warning against the excessive proliferation of options and the dangers of social fragmentation brought about by globalization.[19]

Plurality of cultures versus cultural pluralism

The second globalization challenge facing managers and their companies involves the concept of pluralities. Before the current globalization wave, we often heard people talk about a *plurality of cultures* in which organizations needed to compete. For example, Brazil, China, India, and Russia all represent potential markets for an enterprising company, but each has its own unique cultural characteristics that must be accommodated if the venture is to be successful. Indeed, British philosopher Isaiah Berlin once observed, "the plurality of culture is irreducible."[20]

Today, the idea of a plurality of cultures is still valid so long as we add to it the seemingly opposite concept of *cultural pluralism*. Cultural pluralism involves a variety of cultures within a single society (e.g. Australia, Canada, France).[21] As such, our understanding of globalization processes would be incomplete without focusing at least some attention on a duality that helps us understand organizational contexts in terms of both plurality of cultures and cultural pluralism. This duality can have profound implications for managers, especially in terms of the type of knowledge, skills, and abilities that they need to develop. Since we live in a world increasingly characterized by a plurality of cultures, firms that undergo internationalization processes necessarily must face contexts that require cross-cultural management expertise in order to perform across geographic boundaries. But because we also live in a world of cultural pluralism, even firms that remain exclusively local in their scope of operations still need managers who can work effectively across cultures.

Inclusion versus exclusion

Finally, the third globalization challenge facing managers and their companies involves the duality of *inclusion versus exclusion*. This is essentially a question of haves and have-nots, winners and losers in the globalization game. On an individual level, it is well known that globalization can bring extraordinary opportunities to those who can access the education and resources needed to keep pace with global developments. Educated and resourceful elites globalize themselves by successfully managing global challenges, while those lacking education and resources find themselves increasingly marginalized and overwhelmed by the intensity and speed of global changes.[22]

But it is not only individuals. Companies that turn the challenges of globalization to their own advantage also find themselves ahead of those that do not. Similarly, whole societies that lag behind the most advanced economies are also trying to close the gap that separates them from the leaders, and it is not clear that they will all eventually succeed, or at least not easily.

In summary, globalization pressures simultaneously create forces that both drive and constrain belief structures, ideologies, normative patterns of behaviors, and societal goals. Recognition of these forces and counter-forces by managers can go a long way towards facilitating a deeper understanding of how global business works, as well as sensitizing them to identify subtle changes on the horizon that can affect both their and their company's effectiveness in the field. At the same time, however, managers must find ways to accommodate these contradictions and challenges as they move their companies into increasingly turbulent waters.

The new global realities

Much of what is being written today about doing business in the new global economy is characterized by a sense of energy, urgency, and opportunity. We hear about developing transformational leaders, building strategic alliances, launching global product plat-forms, leveraging technological breakthroughs, first-mover advantages, global venturing, outsourcing, sustainable supply chains, and, most of all, making money. Action – and winning – seem to be the operational words. Discussions about global business assume a sense of perpetual dynamic equilibrium. We are told that nothing is certain except change, and that winners are always prepared for change. We are also told that global business is like white water rafting – always on the edge. And so forth. Everything is in motion and opportunities abound (see Exhibit 1.2).

At the same time, however, there is another somewhat more troublesome side to this story of globalization that is discussed far less often yet is equally important. This side is characterized by seemingly endless conflicts with partners, continual misunderstand-ings with suppliers and distributors, mutual distrust, perpetual delays, ongoing cost overruns, political and economic risks and setbacks, personal stress, and, in some cases, lost careers. This downside has several potentially severe consequences for organiza-tional success, especially in the area of building workable global partnerships.

Consider two brief examples here: First, over 50 percent of international joint ventures and strategic alliances fail within the first five years of operation. The principal

Exhibit 1.2 The changing global economy

Current global economy	From intermittent to continual change	**Future global economy**
Broad mixture of local, national, and global markets and organizations.	From isolation to interconnectedness	Greater emphasis on global markets, networks, and organizations over local or national ones.
	From biculturalism to multiculturalism	

reason cited for these failures is cultural differences and conflicts between partners.[23] Why is this? To turn this question around, what does it take to succeed in building successful partnerships in today's increasingly turbulent global business environment?

And second, according to *The Economist*, "the share of non-Americans on the boards of American multinationals is less than 5%."[24] Some Asian and European boards are a bit better, but not by much. If businesses are moving inextricably towards increased interconnectedness and globalization, how will the voices of cultural and national diversity be heard at the highest levels of the organization? And who will recognize and propose solutions that meet both local and global challenges? In other words, if all executives are looking through the same lens, we might question the ability of global firms to compete successfully.

While it is not easy to get a handle on all of the changes occurring in the global environment, three prominent changes stand out: the evolution from intermittent to continual change, from isolation to increasing interconnectedness, and from biculturalism to multiculturalism.

From intermittent to continual change

Change is everywhere. Companies, products, and managers come and go. This turbulence increasingly requires nearly everyone from investors to consumers to pay greater heed to the nature, scope, and speed of world events, both economically and politically. Details have become more important. And while under increasing threat, personal relationships remain one of the last safe havens in an otherwise largely unpredictable world.

Across this changing environment – indeed, as one of the principal causes of these changes – we can see the relentless development and application of new technologies, especially with regard to the digital revolution. The concepts of technology and global economic development are frequently linked in both research and popular discourse. Technology is largely held to be a principal driver of globalization and the key to national economic development and competitiveness. Indeed, global business as we know today would not be possible without technology. It was only with the emergence of affordable and reliable computer and communication technologies that coordination and collaboration across borders became possible. A few years ago, subsidiaries were managed as independent organizations and managers travelled around the globe for coordination purposes. Today, electronic technologies facilitate the transfer of information and makes communication through text, voice, and video simple and affordable.

At the same time, globalization has resulted in an increase in the transfer and diffusion of technological innovation across borders, as well as competition among nations to develop and adopt advanced technologies. As business becomes increasingly global, the need for better and cheaper technology increases, pushing technological development to new heights. Computers are obsolete as soon as they are out of the box, cell phones integrate new functionalities for managers on the move, and we have cell phone coverage and internet access in almost every corner of the world.

Globalization and technology are intertwined, and their evolution goes hand in hand. Global managers can't understand globalization or manage globally without understanding the influence of technology on business. Managers of global corporations must manage the development, adoption, and use of technologies across national divisions. Even managers of organizations based in a single country must be cognizant of the technological choices of their competitors in other countries and the influence of foreign technologies on their operations.

From isolation to interconnectedness

In today's increasingly turbulent and uncertain business environment, major changes occur with increasing regularity. The recent collapse of the global financial markets, accompanied by worldwide recession, has caused hardships around the world and has led to both political and economic changes in both rich and poor countries. The economic and political power of India and China continues to grow exponentially, and both are struggling to manage the positive and negative consequences of growth and development. Russia is trying to reassert itself politically and economically in the world, overcome rampant corruption in its business sector, and reform its economic system in order to build local companies that can compete effectively in the global economy. Japan is trying to rebuild its economy after a decade of stagnation. France is trying to reinvigorate its economy by changing its historically uncompetitive labor policies. Turkey is trying to join the EU so that its companies can gain greater access to world markets. South Africa continues to struggle to shed the vestiges of its old apartheid system and build a new, stronger economy based on more egalitarian principles. And throughout, there is a swelling consumer demand for higher-quality but lower-cost goods and services that challenge most governments and corporations. In a nutshell, welcome to today's increasingly global economy. In this new economy, globalization is not a debate; it is a reality.

Clearly, the degree of economic and political interconnectedness between both countries and companies has increased significantly in recent years – and not always in a positive direction. Consider two recent examples: When the use of ethanol as an additive to gasoline production increased significantly in American and European markets, corn prices around the world skyrocketed, and the price of tortillas in Mexico, a staple food among Mexico's poor, nearly doubled. A short time later, however, the bottom fell out of the ethanol market as oil prices dropped and the price of corn nose-dived. And when tainted consumer products – including milk products, pharmaceuticals, toys, and candy – were seemingly routinely exported from China to world markets, anxieties about buying Chinese-made products increased dramatically and demand for such goods fell. Still today, the image of Chinese-made products remains poor, despite significant quality improvements in many areas. Ironically, in the minds of many global consumers, tainted milk means that Chinese-made televisions, cars, and refrigerators must also be suspect. Unintended, yet nonetheless very real, consequences.

This is not to say that the challenges and potential perils of globalization are a recent phenomenon. Indeed, quite the contrary is true; globalization has always been a major part of commerce. What is new, however, is the magnitude of globalization and its impact on standards of living, international trade, social welfare, and environmental sustainability. In 1975, global foreign direct investment totaled just US$23 billion. By 1998, a little over twenty years later, it totaled US$644 billion. And by 2008, just ten years after that, worldwide foreign direct investment totaled US$1.5 trillion. Despite regional and worldwide recessions and economic setbacks, global foreign direct investment continues to grow at a seemingly uncontrollable rate. What are the ramifications of this increase for organizations and their managers? What are the implications for developed and less developed countries? And is there a role for governments and public policy in this revolution?

From biculturalism to multiculturalism

Developing successful relationships with people from other cultures is challenging by definition for several reasons. People have a tendency to have preconceived ideas about how the world works (or should work), how individuals behave (or should behave), and which behaviors are acceptable or unacceptable. These ideas are largely influenced by our personal experiences and the cultures in which we grew up. As discussed throughout this book, people tend to approach intercultural interactions based on their own perceptions, beliefs, values, biases, and misconceptions about what is likely to happen. As a result, when they engage in exchanges with people from different cultures themselves, they often find that the consequences of their actions are different than what they expected or intended. The results can range from embarrassment to insult to lost business opportunities.

Traditionally, global managers have been advised to deal with such cultural conflicts by adapting to the other culture. In this regard, academic and management training programs have long recognized a fairly typical pattern of behavior and accommodation of people assigned overseas. This is referred to as *culture shock*. That is, managers assigned overseas initially experience stress and anxiety as a result of being immersed in an unfamiliar environment. Over time, they learn new ways of coping and eventually feel more comfortable living in the culture of the host country. They are able to be effective in dealing with people from another country by learning the foreign culture in depth and behaving in ways that are appropriate to that culture. For example, a manager assigned to work in France for several years is advised to study French language and culture and then begin to make French friends upon his or her arrival in the new location.

While this approach to training remains popular, we suggest that the increasing intensity and diversity that characterizes today's global business environment requires a new and broader approach. This new approach is forced upon managers because, unlike in the past, the new global manager must succeed simultaneously in multiple cultures, not just one. Instead of culture shock, we now need to talk in terms of multiple culture shocks. And, unfortunately, at some point this concept becomes either too complex to help managers adapt or, worse still, it becomes meaningless. Gone are the days when a manager prepared for a long-term assignment in France or Germany – or even Europe. Today, this same manager must deal simultaneously with partners from perhaps a dozen or more different cultures around the globe. As a result, learning one language and culture may no longer be enough, as it was in the past. In addition, the timeline for developing these business relationships has declined from years to months – and sometimes to weeks. As the former CEO of BMW remarked, "The world in not getting smaller; it is getting faster."[25] To us, this requires a new approach to developing global managers.

This evolution from a principally bicultural business environment to a more multi-cultural or global environment presents managers with at least three new challenges in attempting to adapt quickly to the new realities on the ground:

(1) *It is sometimes unclear to which culture we should adapt.* Suppose that your company has asked you to join a global project team to work on a six-month R&D project. The team includes one Mexican, one German, one Chinese, and one Russian. Every member of the team has a permanent appointment in their home

country but is temporarily assigned to work at company headquarters in Switzerland for this project. Which culture should team members adapt to? In this case, there is no dominant cultural group to dictate the rules. Considering the multiple cultures involved, and the little exposure each manager has likely had with the other cultures, the traditional approach of adaptation is unlikely to be successful. Nevertheless, the group must be able to work together quickly and effectively to produce results (and protect their careers), despite their differences. What would you do?

(2) *Many intercultural encounters happen on short notice, leaving little time to learn about the other culture.* Imagine that you just returned from a week's stay in India where you were negotiating an outsourcing agreement. As you arrive in your home office, you learn that an incredible acquisition opportunity just turned up in South Africa and that you are supposed to leave in a week to explore the matter further. You have never been to South Africa, nor do you know anybody from there. What do you do?

(3) *Intercultural meetings increasingly occur virtually by way of computers or video conferencing instead of through more traditional face-to-face interactions.* Suppose you were asked to build a partnership with a Korean partner that you have never met and that you know little about Korean culture. Suppose further that this task is to be completed online, without any face-to-face communication or interactions. Your boss is in a hurry for results. What would you do?

Taken together, these three challenges illustrate just how difficult it can be to work or manage across cultures in today's rapidly changing business environment. The old ways of communicating, negotiating, leading, and doing business are simply less effective than they were in the past. As such, the principal focus of this book will be on how to facilitate management success in global environments – how to become a global manager.

Challenges facing global managers

Globalization. Technology. Change. Competitiveness. If this is the new global economy, what are the implications for managers and their organizations? In view of the seismic shifts around the world in terms of how business is now conducted, corporations are scrambling to become more competitive, more market sensitive, more innovative, and more nimble. How is this best accomplished? As they attempt to move ahead, the ground underfoot continues to move.

Success in the global economy requires a number of ingredients, including innovative ideas and products, access to raw materials and competitive labor, savvy marketing strategies, solid financing, sustainable supply chains, and predictable logistical support. However, the central driver in this endeavor – perpetually caught in the middle – is the global manager. Indeed, no one ever said being a manager was easy, but it seems to get more difficult with each passing year. As competitive pressures increase across most industries and services, so too do the pressures on managers to deliver results. Succeeding against the odds often catapults a manager into the higher echelons of the organization, with a concomitant increase in personal rewards. But failure to deliver often slows one's career advancement, if it doesn't stop it altogether. The stakes are very high for both managers and organizations.

With this in mind, what do managers need to know to survive and succeed in this complex and turbulent environment? Certainly they need to understand both micro- and macroeconomics. They need to understand the fundamentals of business practices, including strategy, marketing, operations and logistics, finance, and accounting. And they need to understand issues such as outsourcing, political risk, legal institutions, and the application of emerging technologies to organizational operations. In addition to this knowledge, however, global managers must understand how to work with other people and organizations around the world to get their jobs done. This topic is the focus of this book. In our view, global managers face ten specific people-related challenges that can make the difference between success and failure in the field:

- *Challenge #1: Develop a learning strategy to guide both short- and long-term professional development as a global manager.* Planning is a cornerstone of effective management, and perhaps nowhere is this more important than with regard to professional development. As noted above, global managers are made, not born, and success in the field requires a lifelong perspective on learning and development. In Chapter 2, we address this challenge by first examining new ways of thinking about managerial roles and skills and then by proposing a learning model to aid in this developmental process.

- *Challenge #2: Develop a basic knowledge of how different cultures work, what makes them unique, and how managers can work successfully across such environments.* If culture and cultural differences can play an important role in managerial success in the global arena, it is logical to develop a greater understanding of how cultures differ and how they influence attitudes and behaviors across the globe. This challenge is addressed in Chapter 3, where the concept of culture is discussed, as well as some of the more intractable aspects of culture as they relate to individual and group behavior. Core cultural dimensions are discussed as a way to gain quick conceptual entry into different cultures and organizations. However, constraints and complications surrounding the use of such cultural dimensions is also discussed, making the manager's job all the more challenging.

- *Challenge #3: Develop effective strategies for working with managers from other cultures who may process information differently and view their roles and responsibilities in unfamiliar ways.* Understanding managerial roles and patterns of behavior as they vary across cultures can provide managers with valuable information on how and when to act. In Chapter 4, we examine various patterns of managerial thinking and information processing, and how such differences can affect subsequent behavior. We focus on managerial patterns in three different cultures to provide a comparison here. Moreover, we address the issue of whether management styles are converging or diverging as a result of increased globalization forces.

- *Challenge #4: Develop an understanding of the competing interests and demands of various stakeholders in an organization, as well as the organizational processes necessary for achieving targeted outcomes.* Most organizations consist of several, and often conflicting, stakeholders, including investors, employees, customers, strategic partners, and governments. It is management's responsibility to balance these competing interests and build and operate an organization that best meets these divergent goals. Clearly, this is no easy task, and it is made all the more difficult when we add a cross-cultural component. Chapter 5 explores the relationship between stakeholders, strategy, and structure as they are influenced by cultural and national variations. Based on this, we examine the manner in which organizational decision-making processes can also differ, with a particular emphasis on the role of employee involvement and participation in key decisions.

- *Challenge #5: Develop an understanding of how business enterprise can be organized differently across cultures, as well as the implications of these differences for management, cooperation, and competition.* Managers typically have a pretty good idea of how organizations in their local cultures operate. They understand where power and authority usually reside, as well as the key interrelationships within the organization that must work together to achieve success. What experienced global managers also understand, however, is how organization design can differ around the world, and how such differences can influence this success. Chapter 6 examines this challenge by comparing typical organization designs in five different countries: China, Germany, Japan, Mexico, and the US. Obviously, differences – sometimes substantial – can be found across these structures within each country, but understanding general patterns of organizing should help managers know what to look for in prospective customers, competitors, and partners across borders.

- *Challenge #6: Develop effective cross-cultural communication skills.* It is often said that communication is the glue that holds organizations and inter-organizational relationships together. It is also said that perceptions and patterns of what is being said is in the eye of the beholder. Both the challenges of cross-cultural communication and prospective strategies for improving it are discussed in Chapter 7. Here we discuss the relationship between language, logic, and communication, as well as the challenge of working with colleagues who think and speak in a different language. The issue of message content and message context is also discussed, as is how new technologies are modifying today's communication patterns.

- *Challenge #7: Develop an understanding of leadership processes across cultures, and how managers can work with others to achieve synergistic outcomes.* People often confuse leadership with management, perhaps because of their own culture-based views of what leaders should look like and how they should behave. The key to understanding this topic is recognizing the different meanings of leadership around the world. In point of fact, different cultures place different demands and expectations on their leaders. Thai leaders, for example, often behave very differently than their Australian or Russian counterparts. Moreover, if leaders work through others to achieve results, how are these "others" organized and how can leaders best work with them? A key problem in working across borders lies in understanding how teams consisting of people from different regions of the world work, and how leaders can either support or confront team dynamics and effectiveness. This topic of leadership and global teams is explored in Chapter 8.

- *Challenge #8: Develop a knowledge of how cultural differences can influence the nature and scope of employee motivation, as well as what global managers might do to enhance on-the-job participation and performance.* Managers by definition routinely find themselves responsible for supervising the work of others. In this regard, experienced managers understand that assuming that everyone is motivated by the same incentives and rewards can be shortsighted and a reasonably good recipe for failure. This is one of the principal challenges of managing in the world of work. If this is true for employees in one company or one location, imagine what can happen when supervisory responsibilities cross borders. In Chapter 9, we address the issue of work motivation and job performance across cultures. Included here is a look at personal work values, work-leisure balance, motivational processes, and incentives and rewards. Lessons for global managers are discussed.

- *Challenge #9: Develop effective negotiating skills and an ability to use these skills to build and sustain global partnerships.* If anything best characterizes the new global economy, it is the proliferation of international strategic alliances and joint ventures. Working with global partners is often a requirement for market entry, labor force management, shared costs, venture financing, and so forth. As a result, one of the key challenges facing global managers is, first, how to negotiate with others to create usually beneficial partnerships and, second, how to successfully build and manage such partnerships for the long term. The fundamental challenge here is seeking common cause. This is the subject of Chapter 10. Included here are discussions of trust, aligning corporate cultures, and minimizing cross-cultural conflicts throughout the partnering process.

- *Challenge #10: Develop an understanding of how ethical and legal conflicts relate to managerial and organizational effectiveness, as well as how managers can work and manage in an ethical, fair, and socially responsible manner.* Outside observers frequently remind managers of their ethical and social responsibilities. However, most of these critics have never walked in a manager's shoes. The issue here is not ethical behavior or social responsibility; this is an obvious goal. Instead, the issue is understanding what is "ethical" or "legal," and then navigating through a minefield of contradictions and pressures to achieve these goals. This pursuit is made even more difficult when we recognize that one person's ethics may not coincide with another's. Simply put, ethics often exists in the eye of the beholder. Who gets to choose what is ethical, legal, or socially responsible? Who gets to choose the rules of the game? In point of fact, many of these types of conflict exist in a state of pressures and counter-pressures, and the manager on the scene – not the manager back in corporate headquarters – often finds himself or herself on the hot seat. This conundrum is the topic of Chapter 11. Here we explore the nature of ethical and legal dilemmas, as well as what managers can do to resolve these conflicts in a responsible manner.

Each of these challenges will be discussed sequentially in the chapters that follow. Each chapter presents a model to guide topic exploration and understanding, as well as applied examples to illustrate the points made. Management strategies are also discussed and then summarized at the end of each chapter in a 'Manager's notebook'. Throughout, the emphasis here is on learning and development, not drawing conclusions or selecting favorites. This is done in the belief that successful global managers will focus more on understanding and flexibility than evaluation and dogmatism. This understanding can facilitate a manager's ability to both prepare and act in ways that are more in tune with local environments. As a result, managers who are better prepared for future events are more likely to succeed, full stop. There are fewer surprises and more time to develop winning strategies on the ground. And in the realm of managerial effectiveness, this is crucial. By integrating these two perspectives (explorations into both the cultural drivers underlying managerial action and the common management strategies used in the field), it is our intention to present a more process-oriented look at global managers at work.

This book is aimed at global managers from around the world. It is not intended to be a North American book, a European book, a Latin American book, and so forth. Rather, it aims to explore managerial processes and practices from the standpoint of managers from all regions of the globe – China and India, Denmark and Tunisia, Brazil and Botswana – as they pursue their goals and objectives in the field. This is done in the belief that the fundamental managerial role around the world is a relative constant, even though the details and specifics of managerial cognitions and actions may often vary – sometimes significantly – across cultures. Taken together, our goal in this book is to help global managers develop an enhanced behavioral repertoire of cross-cultural management skills that can be used in a timely fashion by managers when they are confronted with challenging and oftentimes confusing situations. By better understanding cultural realities on the ground and then using this understanding to develop improved coping strategies, it is our hope that future global managers will succeed where many of their predecessors did not.

We begin in Chapter 2 by suggesting a learning model to guide readers throughout this book as we explore the developmental processes of becoming a global manager.

Notes

1 Thomas Stewart, cited in Philip Harris, Robert Moran, and Sarah Moran, *Managing Cultural Differences*, 6th Edition. Amsterdam: Elsevier, 2004, p. 1.
2 David Brindle, "No nonsense: an interview with Percy Barnevik," *The Guardian*, January 23, 2008, p. B1.
3 Tom Peters and Robert Waterman, *In Search of Excellence*. New York, NY: Harper and Row, 1982.
4 National Public Radio, 1983.
5 "Oops. Who's excellent now?," *Business Week*, November 5, 1984, pp. 17–18.
6 Lester Thurow, *Head to Head: The Coming Economic Battle Among Japan, Europe and America*. Cambridge, MA: MIT Press, 1993.
7 Thomas Freidman, *The Lexus and the Olive Tree*. New York, NY: Anchor Books, 2000.

8 Thomas Friedman, *The World is Flat: A Brief History of the Twenty-first Century*. New York, NY: Farrar, Strauss and Giroux, 2005.

9 Keith Epstein and Judith Crown, "Globalization bites Boeing," *Business Week*, March 24, 2008, p. 32.

10 Richard Feynman, *The Character of Physical Law*. Cambridge, MA: MIT Press, 1967.

11 Anthony Giddens, *The Constitution of Society*. Berkeley, CA: University of California Press, 1985.

12 Seymour B. Sarason, *The Making of an American Psychologist: An Autobiography*. San Francisco, CA: Jossey-Bass, 1988.

13 Brian W. Arthur, *Increasing Returns and Path Dependence in the Economy*. Ann Arbor, MI: Michigan University Press, 1994.

14 Mark Blaug, *Economic Theory in Retrospect*. Cambridge, UK: Cambridge University Press, 1997.

15 Carlos J. Sanchez-Runde and Andrew Pettigrew, "Managing dualities," in Andrew Pettigrew, Richard Whittington, Leif Melin, Carlos J. Sanchez-Runde, Frans van den Bosch, Winfred Ruigrok, and Tsuyoshi Numagami (eds.), *Innovative Forms of Organizing: International Perspectives*. London: Sage, 2003, pp. 243–250.

16 James L. Watson, *Golden Arches East: McDonald's in East Asia*. Stanford, CA: Stanford University Press, 1997.

17 Watson, *Golden Arches East*, p. 38.

18 "Is one global model of corporate governance likely, or even desirable?," *Knowledge@Wharton*, January 9, 2008.

19 Néstor G. Canclini, *La Globalización Imaginada*. Mexico City: Paidós, 1999; Jean-Pierre Warnier, *La mondialisation de la culture*. Paris: Editions La découverte et Syros, 1999.

20 Isaiah Berlin, quoted in Richard Hill, *We Europeans*. Brussels: Europublications, 1997, p. 385.

21 Zygmut Bauman, *Culture as Praxis*. London: Sage, 1999, p. xlix.

22 Néstor G. Canclini, *Diferentes, Desiguales y Desconectados: Mapas de la Interculturalidad*. Barcelona: Gedisa, 2004, p. 195.

23 See www.hewitt.com.

24 "The empire strikes back," *The Economist*, September 20, 2008, p. 16.

25 Personal communication, Norbert Reithofer, Munich, Germany, 2004.

CHAPTER 2

Developing global management skills

■ Traditional views of management   26
■ Global managers: variety of the species   28
■ Rethinking managerial roles   35
■ Rethinking managerial skills   36
■ MANAGER'S NOTEBOOK: Developing global management skills   39

Good judgment comes from experience; experience comes from bad judgment.
Mullah Nasrudin[1]
Thirteenth-century Sufi sage, Central Asia

In a time of drastic change, it is the learners who will inherit the future. The learned usually find themselves prepared for a world that no longer exists.
Eric Hoffer[2]
Moral philosopher, USA

From entry-level workers to boardroom executives, everyone seems to be going international these days. In the process, organizations ranging from large multinational corporations to storefront NGOs are seeking people who can successfully work and manage across cultures. And in this endeavor, the capacity to learn and adapt becomes an essential job requirement. Consider recent activities at Google to broaden its employees' global understanding and expertise. To train a new generation of leaders, the search giant is now sending its young "brainiacs" on a worldwide mission.[3]

One recent group of trainees began their journey in a small village outside of Bangalore, India. There were no computers in the tiny village, only unpaved roads surrounded by open fields where elephants roamed and trampled local crops at will. The visit was aimed at educating Google associate product managers about the humble, unwired ways of life experienced by billions of people around the world. Discussions with local villages began awkwardly as the managers discover that villagers have never heard of the company. As one young manager noted, the experience brought a whole new meaning to what's on the back of her shirt, referring to a T-shirt with the company logo in front and, on the back, the now classic phrase from the company's home page: "I'm feeling lucky."

On their first day in Bangalore, the visitors went to the Commercial Street shopping district for a bartering competition. Each Google manager was given 500 rupees (about US$13) to spend on "items that don't suck," with a prize given to the one who attained the highest discount on the purchase. For most, it was the first time they had to bargain with street vendors. "I usually shop at Neiman Marcus," observed one manager, after she bargained the price of a necklace down from 375 rupees to 250. But one of her colleagues won the competition by purchasing a deep-burgundy *sherwani* – a traditional Indian outfit – for one-third of the original asking price.

From India, the group traveled to Japan to visit the company's Shibuya headquarters to network with fellow employees, learn about regional markets, and study the local culture. The visitors shared the product "road map" for the next year with their Japanese colleagues, answered questions, and then heard what the engineers and managers in each location were focusing on. They also got a sense of the local marketplace by talking to local Googlers, customers, and partners. In Tokyo, they learned that Yahoo! Japan is clobbering the competition – it's like Google and AOL and eBay rolled into one – but that Google had captured the imagination of the Japanese people. It was the No. 2 brand in the country, behind Toyota.

Tokyo's legendary electronics district, Akihabara, was chosen for another group competition, ostensibly to sharpen the product knowledge, business skills, and street smarts of the global travelers. They were divided into small teams and given US$100 to buy the strangest gadgets they could find. Diving into stalls full of electronic gizmos, they found items like a USB-powered smoke-removing ashtray and a stubby wand that, when waved back and forth, spells out words in LED lights.

Next, the group traveled to China and came face to face with the realities of doing business there. They immediately recognized the conflict of balancing the company's freewheeling management style with China's rigid government rules – and censorship. At Google headquarters in Beijing, the visiting managers interviewed local English-speaking consumers. Here they learned the stark realities of how effective the Chinese government can be at tilting the playing field to benefit the home team, Baidu.com, by occasionally blocking access to Google's site and by insinuating a nationalistic element into the choice. The lesson was clear to the visiting managers: Baidu knows more about China than Google. The journey continued, as did the learning.

Traditional views of management

Definitions of management abound. What is significant about these definitions, coming from all parts of the world, is their lack of any notable variance. Management is management, or so we are told. Dating from the early writings by Frederick Taylor, Henri Fayol, Max Weber, Mary Parker Follett, and others, in the late nineteenth and early twentieth centuries and continuing through today, most writers have agreed that management involves the coordination and control of people, materiel, and processes to achieve specific organizational objectives as efficiently and effectively as possible. Indeed, business historian Claude George has discovered the roots of such a definition dating back to the ancient Samarians, Egyptians, Hebrews, and Chinese well over 3,000 years ago.[4] Both the concept and the profession of management are not new; indeed, they are widely thought to be a central pillar of organized society: getting things done through coordinated efforts.

While the underlying definition remains the same, variations around this theme can easily be found. Industrial engineers, dating from the time of scientific management proponent Frederick Taylor, have long emphasized production or operations management and the necessity to structure jobs, people, and incentive systems in ways that maximized performance.[5] Similarly, French industrial engineer Henri Fayol, also writing at the beginning of the twentieth century, emphasized the importance of standardized "principles" of management, including division of work, unity of command, unity of direction, and the subordination of individual interests to the general (i.e., organization's) interest.[6] While Taylor focused on workers and Fayol focused on administrative structures, their mantra was the same: Organizations must be managed through strength and logic.

Around this same time, social scientists and other academicians took a different perspective to this same phenomenon. German-born, Harvard-educated psychologist Hugo Munsterberg launched investigations into the application of psychological principles to management and workers. In the process, he created the field of industrial psychology. In his 1913 book, entitled *Psychology and Industrial Efficiency*, he asserted that the aim of this new discipline was "to sketch the outlines of a new science, which is to intermediate between the modern laboratory psychology and the problem of economics."[7] Meanwhile, German sociologist Max Weber wrote extensively about how organizations organize and operate – or, more accurately, should organize and operate.[8] Weber introduced the concept of "bureaucracy" as the most perfect form of organization. (Obviously, this term has taken on very different and negative connotations in recent years, but this was its original meaning.) Rules governed everything and little was left to change. People were hired and promoted based on qualifications, not unlike the ancient Chinese civil service system at the time of Confucius. Power and authority were vested in offices, not individuals. However, even here, the conclusion was the same: Rules and standard operating procedures uniformly enforced by competent managers would lead to efficient operations. The goal remained unchanged.

Now fast-forward 100 years and consider the advice of contemporary writers on management, both east and west. While contemporary writers have added some depth to the ongoing dialog about the nature and role of management, they have not added much breadth. Consider two contemporary definitions of *management*: "Management involves coordinating and overseeing the work activities of others so that their activities are completed efficiently and effectively,"[9] and "Management is the process of assembling and using sets of resources in a goal-directed manner to accomplish tasks in an organizational setting."[10] Once again, the desired end state remains unchanged.

This stability in our conception of management – unchanged over the centuries – implies that all managers do essentially the same work. Indeed, in one of the most frequently cited studies of management, McGill professor Henry Mintzberg concluded that "managers' jobs are remarkably alike," whether we are looking at foremen, company presidents, or government administrators.[11] In the end, "the primary purpose of the manager is to ensure that his or her organization serves its basic purpose – the efficient production of specific goods and services." Mintzberg goes a step further and suggests that all managers serve ten basic *managerial roles* in varying degrees. These are: figurehead, leader, liaison, monitor, disseminator, spokesperson, entrepreneur, disturbance handler, resource allocator, and negotiator.[12] These traits, in turn, can be organized into three clusters: an *interpersonal role*, focusing on building and leading effective groups and organizations; an *informational role*, focusing on collecting, organizing, and disseminating relevant information in a timely fashion; and a *decisional role*, focusing on making creative strategic and tactical decisions on behalf of the organization and securing broad-based support for such actions.

However, while all of this may be correct as far as it goes, this line of reasoning seems to ignore, or at least downplay, the very significant role that cultural differences can play in both the conceptualization and practice of management around the world. In the above example, Google managers learned first hand that people's conception of business management, as well as their application of management principles, often result from a combination of cultural backgrounds, personal experiences, and the situations confronting them. Thus, we must ask if a typical Australian, Czech, or Indonesian manager would approach business decisions and actions in the same way as their Indian, Bolivian, or French counterparts? And if not, how might their approaches be different?

The answer to this question is made all the more difficult by the fact that research and professional studies of management practices over the years have been largely skewed towards some populations but not others. Consider: A Google search of the number of research studies conducted on managers in various parts of the world revealed, not surprisingly, that by far the largest number of studies focused on North American managers (2.7 million), followed by European (1.7 million), Asian (745,000), Middle Eastern (502,000), Latin American (308,000), and Sub-Saharan African (34,000) managers. In view of the disproportionate number of studies focusing on North America and Europe, it is not surprising that we know and understand far less about managerial behavior in other regions of the globe, such as Latin America, Central Asia, and Africa. Even so, there are still sufficient empirical resources in this inventory on which to begin drawing conclusions, as will be done later in the book. First, however, we take a brief look at the variety of global management positions and how they are changing in today's business and social climate.

Global managers: variety of the species

Global managers come in all shapes and sizes, as well as skills and abilities. Indeed, in today's global economy, almost all managers are involved in some form or another with global management. As such, it is difficult – if not impossible – to develop a precise definition that accurately encompasses all of their activities and responsibilities. As a starting point, however, we will define a *global manager* as someone who works with or through people across national boundaries to accomplish global corporate objectives. Inherent in this definition is the assumption that many – if not all – of these managers work with people from differing cultural backgrounds and, as such, must somehow accommodate or respond to these differences. Also inherent in this definition is the recognition that some of these cross-cultural interactions may be across countries with fewer cultural differences than others (e.g., Canada and the US versus Canada and Saudi Arabia). Indeed, some of these cultural differences can often be found within a single country.

Paramount to this definition is the assertion that global managers are – and must be – different than more traditional managers. They must have a worldview, not a national one; they must understand both cultural differences and the ways in which to navigate such differences to achieve corporate objectives; they must seek partnerships, not domination; and, above all, they must have both the competence and confidence to work with colleagues and partners from around the world. Included within this definition are managers who have very different corporate lifestyles. Some live abroad, some live in airplanes, and some live in virtual space. Some do all three.

Exhibit 2.1 Global managers: expatriates, frequent flyers, and virtual managers

Management focus and challenges	Expatriates	Frequent flyers	Virtual managers
Principal management focus	Long-term face-to-face management, where managers are either assigned to reside in a foreign country to oversee company operations or hired to bring special expertise to a foreign firm.	Short-term face-to-face management, where managers with particular expertise (e.g., project management, financial controls) are flown in to plan, implement, or control specific operations.	Virtual (or remote) technical management in specialized areas (e.g., logistics, IT), where managers perform most of their tasks and responsibilities via information networks and digital technologies.
Primary mode of communication and interaction	Largely face-to-face.	Balance of face-to-face and virtual.	Largely virtual.
Key success factors for working across cultures	Typically requires deep knowledge of the culture(s) and culture-business relationships where they live and work; bilingual or multilingual skills important; understanding global issues – not just local ones – is also critical.	Typically requires moderate understanding of cultural differences and dynamics in general and culture business relationships around the globe; multilingual skills important; deep understanding of global issues critical.	Typically requires at least a modest understanding of cultural differences and variations in business practices around the globe, although a deeper understanding is preferred; multilingual skills often useful.
Typical cultural challenge (*global management myopias*)	*Regional myopia*: Overemphasis on local or regional issues and business practices at the expense of global issues and overall corporate objectives.	*Global myopia*: Overemphasis on global issues and overall corporate objectives at the expense of local customs and business practices.	*Technological myopia*: Ignorance of the impact of cultural differences on the local uses, misuses, and applications of information, communication and technology.

Types of global managers

For the sake of parsimony, and while there are obvious risks in categorizations, we suggest that these global managers can be roughly divided into three somewhat overlapping categories: expatriates, frequent flyers, and virtual managers (see Exhibit 2.1). We suggest, further, that the characteristics and cultural challenges of each of these types of managers can be quite different. While *expatriates* typically require deep knowledge of a particular country or region, *frequent flyers* more often require broad knowledge of cultural differences and cultural processes in general. One leads a somewhat stable life, albeit in a foreign country; the other leads a highly mobile existence. This is not to say that one approach is superior to the other, only that they are different and that each plays an important role in global commerce. Added to this is a category of other managers that work largely through computer and information technology and that essentially wander the globe in cyberspace to achieve their results. We refer to these individuals as *virtual managers* in recognition of their basic patterns of collegial and business interaction.

We include *inpatriates* (foreign managers assigned to positions in the parent company's home country) in the same category as expatriates since they share the same kinds of problems and challenges; the only difference is the reverse nature of their assignment. We also lump *telecommuters* (who work largely from home via networks) and *digital nomads* (who work via networks from anywhere in the world, depending upon where they happen to be) into the category of virtual managers, since both manage or do business largely using computer-mediated technologies.

Expatriates: long-term assignments

Traditionally, the most common foreign assignments have involved long-term relocation of parent company managers to various countries where the parent firm does, or wants to do, business. Firms have often preferred to use expatriate managers for a number of reasons, especially when it needed parent company representation and control in a distant location, wanted to provide developmental opportunities for parent company managers, or needed to fill a skills gap where locals do not have the skills to do the job themselves.[13] Today, however, the term "expatriate" has come to describe any person working in residence in a foreign country. This could include a Swiss manager working for a Swiss country in Korea, or a Swiss manager working for a Korean company in Korea. Both face similar challenges of living abroad for lengthy periods.

A good example of expatriate managers can be seen at LG Electronics. Once among the most traditional of Korean *chaebols*, or conglomerates, LG has pushed hard to diversify its top management and become a truly global organization.[14] Irish-born Dermot Boden, chief marketing officer for LG, is one of five Western managers that CEO Nam Yong lured into LG's executive suite. Indeed, foreign managers now represent a quarter of LG's leadership and have taken over key positions in such areas as purchasing, supply-chain management, and human resources.

Nam did not set out to hire a group of aggressive Western-style managers, but he knew LG needed change. The company's Korean management team had built an engineering powerhouse that excelled at manufacturing and high-quality goods, but Nam realized that more than four-fifths of its revenue came from overseas and nearly 60 percent of its manufacturing was done outside of Korea. When he took over LG Electronics' top job in January 2007, the company was coasting. It had become a top-five consumer electronics player globally, but had few hits. Nam believed the company needed to be a trendsetter if it wanted to prosper in the Digital Age. To shake things up, he asked headhunters to find top talent from multinationals worldwide, regardless of nationality.

The foreign managers were asked to standardize the hodgepodge of processes and systems that LG had developed around the world. Purchasing, for example, was done by four different business units and was split among factories and subsidiaries in 110 countries. "I'm like a conductor, getting two thousand purchasing officers to work in concert to make good music," says Tom Linton, a 20-year veteran of IBM who joined LG as its first chief procurement officer in 2008. Nam says Linton's efforts to reshape the purchasing system have already saved the company hundreds of millions of dollars. Meanwhile, LG's supply chain was equally chaotic. Didier Chenneveau, a Swiss who left HP also in 2008 to become LG's Chief Supply-chain Officer, inherited more than ten warehouse-management systems, five transportation operations, and four computer systems to monitor the movement of parts and finished products. His goal: to merge everything into a single global system.

Not unexpectedly, the foreign managers have not been entirely welcomed by local Korean managers. "The biggest worry was the prospect of Western executives imposing a way of thinking that might not work in our Confucian culture," said Marketing Manager Choi Seung Hun. "The prospect of communicating with my boss in English gave me a headache," added Lee Kyo Weon, a purchasing manager. However, over time, both Choi and Lee agreed that the newcomers had made an effort to bridge the cultural gap.

Boden was the first non-Korean to be hired by LG as an internal change agent. In 2007, Nam hired the veteran of Pfizer and Johnson & Johnson to help turn LG into a premium brand. The problem was that LG's marketing was uninspiring. So Boden determined to give the brand a more sophisticated image with high-end products such as a cell phone co-branded with fashion house Prada and washing machines costing US$1,500 or more. He also took a more organized approach to marketing by hiring a single international advertising agency in London to handle advertising worldwide.

Early evidence suggests Nam's globalizing push is paying off. Despite a drop in consumer spending in the wake of the Wall Street meltdown that began in 2008 and 2009, analysts predict that LG should report increased profits in the coming years.

While advantages of expatriate assignments are fairly obvious, finding people who can actually succeed in expatriate assignments can be problematic. While traveling abroad (perhaps on a vacation or business trip) is often seen by people as an enjoyable experience, actually living abroad can be frustrating, stressful, and sometimes very unpleasant. For many, staying in a four-star hotel, eating in fine restaurants, seeing new sights, and knowing that soon they will be back in their own bed is far more preferable to setting up a household in a strange neighborhood where few people speak your language, finding new schools for the kids, shopping in local markets stocked with foods they can't identify, and using public transportation. For others, these same experiences provide a sense of adventure and learning. The challenge for managers – and their companies – is to discover which type of person they are before getting on the airplane.

Many people see an international assignment as a great opportunity. It may be an opportunity to advance one's career, to make more money, or to learn new things. It may represent a personal challenge or a way to a more interesting life. Managers that take international assignments report learning new managerial skills, increasing their tolerance for ambiguity, learning new ways of seeing things, and improving their ability to work with others.[15] However, as noted above, living and working abroad is not easy. Long-term international assignments are particularly challenging for managers with family where a partner may need to give up a career in the home country and may not find suitable employment in the host country, and where children require special attention such as international schooling. A recent survey suggests that 81 percent of workers declining an expatriate assignment cited family reasons.[16]

Frequent flyers: short-term assignments

While extended expatriate assignments are often useful – and sometimes indispensable – for situations where a manager must deal with a limited number of cultures, the increasing intensity and diversity that characterizes today's global business environment often requires a different approach better suited to managers that must succeed immediately and simultaneously in multiple cultures. Indeed, some have suggested that the days when managers prepared for a long-term assignment in Italy, Russia, or Venezuela are rapidly being eclipsed by a new reality where managers sometimes seem to spend more time in the air than on the ground. Today, this same manager may need to deal simultaneously with partners from multiple cultures around the globe. Thus, learning one language and culture may no longer be sufficient. In addition, the timeline for developing business relationships has, in many cases, declined from years to months – and sometimes to weeks.

Consider the example of Adhira Iyengar, an entrepreneur from Delhi, India.[17] Adhira woke up early one recent morning, prepared a cup of tea, and logged onto her PC. As expected, Debra Brown, her business partner in California, was already logged on and asking questions about Adhira's latest report to her. As they finished their online Skype meeting, Adhira looked at her calendar and realized that, again, it was going to be a long day. At 10:00 that morning, she had a conference call with Xiang Bingwei (Mr. Xiang, or "Andrew," for his Westernized name), a client from Shanghai, about some changes in their service contract. At 1:30 in the afternoon, she had a face-to-face meeting with a group of prospective Australian clients in her office in Delhi. Before the end of the day, she had to complete a report and email it to Gabriela Bedoya Cárdenas (Senorita Bedoya, or "Gaby" for short), a prospective partner in Monterrey, Mexico, and she still needed to prepare for her upcoming trip to Oslo the following week.

As illustrated in this example, global assignments of shorter duration – often accompanied by increased intensity – are usually focused on specific tasks or projects and, as such, can often provide easier ways to assess results (see Exhibit 2.1).[18] In addition, there are many managers who would not consider uprooting the family for long-term expatriate assignments, but would be interested in shorter international opportunities. This increases the pool of talent available for such postings, a big plus since the demand for highly qualified international assignees is often higher than the supply.[19] And short-term assignments are often seen by employees as being easier on, their friends and family as well as their home country career opportunities.

The main challenge facing managers on short-term assignments is that they often find themselves in a foreign country without family and friends, and with a very short time to develop relationships and become adjusted.[20] Since the assignee is usually sent abroad for a short period to solve a specific problem or perform a specific task, they are not given the time to learn the ropes and adjust to the new locale, as would be the case in traditional long-term expatriate assignments. Instead, frequent flyers are often expected to perform as soon as they hit the ground, which increases the challenges of the assignment. Strong pressures to perform – quickly – coupled with a limited social and family life, frequently lead assignees to work long hours, enduring high levels of stress and, at times, a poor work-life balance.

Virtual managers: technology-mediated assignments

The same communication technologies that are making globalization a reality and changing the nature of work are also influencing the lives and work habits of global managers. Many of these technologies are not new (e.g., personal computers). However, what is different in recent years is the ways in which these communication technologies have increased both their operating powers and their interactive capabilities. Many of these technologies have merged into more powerful tools for busy managers. As it became possible to access email and the Web through smart phones, it has also become possible to travel light and be constantly connected. It is no longer necessary to carry a laptop and a bag full of cables; it is not even necessary to be in a specific location to connect. Wireless technology makes it possible to perform work anywhere and anytime with minimal equipment, making it possible to be a global manager without leaving one's home base. However, the key issue here is not having access to the technology; rather, it is a manager's ability to use such technology to build workable networks and relationships that collectively serve corporate interests.

Once again, it is important to remember that these three categories of global managers – expatriates, frequent flyers, and virtual managers – represent overlapping categories. Clearly, most expatriates today are heavy users of the Web and other communication technologies, while many virtual managers must travel at times to get their jobs done. Our purpose in differentiating between these three categories, even in terms of general trends, is to highlight differences in managerial responsibilities and challenges in doing business across national borders.

Global management myopia

Finally, we suggest that each type of global manager discussed above (see Exhibit 2.1) carries with it its own particular risk of short-sightedness, whereby managers may fail to see one or more aspects of the company's larger objectives and operations. We refer to this as *global management myopia*. At times, these blinders can be accompanied by an over-protectiveness or advocacy of one's own area of responsibility, often at the expense of the overall success of the firm. These myopias can be summarized as follows:

- *Regional myopia*. Expatriates can run a very real risk of *regional myopia*, where the country or region in which they work overshadows the rest of the world. While this perception may have an upside in terms of genuinely focusing on one country or region and its opportunities and needs, it also risks losing sight of the big picture facing the firm.
- *Global myopia*. At the same time, frequent flyers are often prone to experience *global myopia*, where they focus so intensely on global interconnectedness that they lose sight of the local challenges and opportunities upon which company success is built. In other words, while expatriates may focus too much on the trees, frequent flyers may focus too much on the forest.
- *Technological myopia*. Finally, virtual managers often run a risk of getting so carried away with their advanced technologies that they lose sight of the faces of the people who collectively comprise the enterprise. We refer to this as *technological myopia*. If organizations are comprised of individuals and groups who work together for a collective goal, an overemphasis on remote management through broadband and the internet can at times overlook, ignore, offend, and threaten the organization's most precious resource: its people.

Rethinking managerial roles

Popular slogans nicely illustrate many of the demands currently being increasingly placed on managers and their companies. Consider Intel's "Faster-better-cheaper"; CNN founder Ted Turner's "Lead, follow, or get out of the way"; or Nike's "Just do it."[21] Anyway we look at it, competitive pressures are growing. Why? There are many reasons, but a principal cause can be found within the world's unrelenting drive to build – and capitalize on – a more integrated and more productive global workforce that leads to lower consumer prices and higher corporate profits. When consumers go shopping in any country, most want to buy products or services of the highest possible quality for the lowest possible price. If we are honest, few people enter stores and ask to pay more so that the workers who made the product or provided the service can receive a higher income. Likewise, few people offer to pay more for a product so local firms can remain in business instead of going bankrupt. In the final analysis, from a consumer's standpoint, monetary considerations frequently seem paramount. The more companies satisfy consumer demands, the more likely they are to survive and prosper.

In this cauldron of hyperactivity, increased globalization pressures only add to the turmoil. Like it or not, in today's increasingly turbulent and complex business environment, everyone is (or is rapidly becoming) a global manager, regardless of where they work. Ten years ago, people focused considerable attention on the differences between British managers, Chinese managers, Mexican managers, and so forth. They were relatively comfortable with their well-intentioned cultural stereotypes. Today, these stereotypes have become somewhat blurred as the global economy becomes a reality and most business is international. This is not to say that substantial differences no longer exist between managers from various countries or the ways in which they do business. Of course they do. Rather, it is to say that the very definition of effective management has changed in ways that have little to do with national origin. Today, most managers must engage with customers, business partners, and employees from various regions of the world. Success or failure depends on the manager's ability to communicate, negotiate, contract, lead, organize, coordinate, and control activities across borders.

Indeed, succeeding in today's demanding global economy requires a greater degree of international and cross-cultural communication, collaboration, and cooperation than ever before. Increasingly, companies must think in global terms, as national and even regional companies are increasingly becoming a thing of the past. During the days of the old American frontier in the mid 1800s, there was a popular saying: "Go west, young man." That was where the opportunities were. Today, the advice is very different: "Go global." The future has shifted unequivocally and irreversibly, as have the opportunities, and smart companies and their managers respond accordingly.

The responsibility of managers in all of this is to make things happen – to maximize consumer benefit and the company's bottom line. At the same time, society asks – and often demands – that managers pay fair wages, provide safe and equitable working conditions for their employees, follow the laws and regulations in the countries where they do business, protect the environment, act in socially responsible ways, and abide by ethical norms and professional standards. It is an understatement to point out that accomplishing these often-conflicting goals is no easy task. In view of this, the question for today's managers is how they can best prepare themselves for this brave new world of international business.

Rethinking managerial skills

Becoming a global manager is the result of a process, a career path streaming through different assignments and cultures. It is a journey, not an end state. Indeed, as noted earlier, instead of seeking an ideal (or idealized) global manager, we will consider throughout this book the variety of the species. That is, we will examine various types of international assignments and international managers. This is definitely not a one-size-fits-all paradigm. We will also examine the challenges and opportunities associated with these assignments, and their impact on global managers and organizations. Throughout, we suggest that what differentiates effective global managers is not so much their managerial skills – although this is obviously important – but the combination of these skills with additional multicultural or cross-cultural competencies that allow people to apply their managerial skills across a diverse spectrum of environments. It is this synergistic integration of basic management skills working in tandem with a deep understanding of how organizations and management practices differ across cultures that differentiate the successful from the less successful global managers. This point is illustrated in Exhibit 2.2.

Whether relocating to a foreign country for a long stay, traveling around the world for short stints, or dealing with foreigners in one's home country, managers often face important cultural challenges. As just noted, different cultures have different assumptions, behaviors, communication styles, and expectations about management practice. The ability to deal with these differences in ways that are both appropriate and effective goes by many names, as noted earlier, but we refer to this

Exhibit 2.2 Building global management skills

simply as *multicultural competence*. It represents the capacity to work successfully across cultures. Being multiculturally competent is more than being polite to people from other cultures; it is getting things done through people in other cultures.

Multicultural competence can be seen as a way of viewing the world with a particular emphasis on broadening one's cultural perspective as it relates to cross-cultural behavior.[22] That is, it asks the question: What can we learn from people around us from different cultures that can improve our ability to function effectively in a multicultural world? Multicultural competencies include elements of curiosity, awareness of diversity, and acceptance of complexity.[23] Such people tend to open up themselves by rethinking boundaries and changing their behaviors. They are curious and concerned with context, possessing an ability to place current events and tasks into both historical and probable future contexts. They accept inherent contradictions in everyday life, and have the ability to maintain a comfort level with continual conflict.

In addition, managers who possess multicultural competence have a commitment to diversity, consciousness and sensitivity, as well as valuing diversity itself. They exhibit a willingness to seek opportunities in surprises and uncertainties, including an ability to take moderate risks and make intuitive decisions. They tend to have a strong belief and confidence in organizational processes, possessing an ability to trust subordinates and to minimize control systems. They focus on continuous improvement, including a capacity for self-improvement and helping others develop. They typically take a long-term perspective on activities and plans, focusing on long-term results and not obsessing on short-term problems or results. And finally, they frequently take a systems perspective, including an ability to seek out interdependencies and cause-effect relationships.

So, how can we put all of these diverse skills and abilities into a succinct framework, or set of targets, for furthering the development of global management skills? This can be accomplished by identifying six specific *multicultural competencies* for global managers:[24]

(1) *A cosmopolitan outlook.* Successful global managers tend to be sufficiently flexible to operate comfortably across divergent cultural environments. They understand the dualities, paradoxes, and contradictions that often characterize the global business environment.

(2) *Intercultural communication skills.* Successful global managers typically understand at least one foreign language and certainly understand and appreciate the complexities of interacting with people from other cultures. They understand how to listen as well as talk, and how to interpret the context of messages as well as the content.

(3) *Cultural sensitivity.* Successful global managers have learned to appreciate cultural differences and use experiences in different national, regional, and organizational cultures to build relationships with culturally diverse people. Relationship building is critical.

(4) *Rapid acculturation skills.* Successful global managers have an ability to adjust quickly to strange and different surroundings. This is part of what constitutes a global competency, discussed later. They also understand the risks of insular thinking and action and seek help when needed.

(5) *Flexible management style.* Successful global managers understand how national cultures and social institutions affect the management process. They understand, for example, that a signed contract can mean different things in different places.

(6) *Cultural synergy.* Successful global managers understand how to build cross-cultural teams and capitalize on cultural diversity for the benefit of the organization. They understand the importance of building and using global networks.

Many of these multicultural competencies can be developed through personal initiative and hard work; others probably cannot. Even so, this list nicely summarizes on a general level what companies frequently seek in managerial talent in order to succeed abroad. It seems clear that as the world of business draws closer together, companies in all countries will require managers who can work in a truly global environment. In this environment, successful managers bring a depth and breadth of understanding of how to capitalize on cultural differences in ways that enhance both corporate goals and employee welfare. In large measure, this is what distinguishes between managers who can succeed in their local surroundings and managers who can succeed in the global economy.

Developing global management skills

The above example of Google's traveling managers illustrates how this and many other companies search to find unique ways to educate their managers about both the global challenges facing them and the strategies that can help them succeed. This is not an easy task. Indeed, a pivotal question facing both training directors and managers themselves is exactly how global managers can be developed. Unfortunately, the answer here is not as simple as perhaps it once was. Gone are the days when prospective managers could learn French or German or Italian in college to prepare themselves for their careers and join an international firm. Learning a foreign language or a foreign culture is obviously helpful, but it is at times both insufficient and impractical in view of the rapidity with which business opportunities appear and disappear around the world.

As a result, managers often turn for advice to those who specialize in cross-cultural training and development for help in preparing for foreign assignments. But this over-reliance on others – instead of on oneself – can carry risks. When it comes to global business, it sometimes seems like everyone is an expert. Indeed, when UCLA professor William Ouchi was writing his classic book on what Western managers could learn from Japan, he noted that, in view of the collective lack of expertise on the topic, any Westerner who had flown over Tokyo's Narita Airport could – and often did – claim to be an expert on Japan.[25] In point of fact, what many people fail to understand about being a global manager is that the view from 10,000 meters up is often very different than the view at ground level, where the challenges are immediate and very real.

Much has been written on the topic of developing global management skills, and much of what has been written is contradictory, simplistic, and sometimes simply incorrect. Successful global managers tend to rely on themselves, including their own perceptions and assessments of what is going on in the world. They often require personal insight more than outside advice. Indeed, what often differentiates successful global managers from unsuccessful ones is that they have developed a *way of thinking* about the world that is flexible and inclusive and guides their behavior across cultures and national boundaries.

The experiential learning cycle

Developing global management skills is the central theme of this book. The obvious question here is how these skills are developed and refined and then used effectively in the global arena. To answer this question, we refer back to Nasrudin's observation 700 hundred years ago that people learn and develop based largely on their past experiences and past mistakes. In our view, this is particularly noteworthy with regards to global managers. People try, make mistakes, and learn from those mistakes. This is the essence of experiential learning.

According to experiential learning theory, individual learning occurs over four stages that are collectively and interactively aimed at collecting and transforming knowledge: concrete experience, reflective observation, abstract conceptualization, and active experimentation.[26] This is illustrated in Exhibit 2.3.

In theory, a learning cycle begins with *concrete experiences* – how we feel about things that happen to us in everyday life. For example, imagine we come from a culture that values direct and straightforward communication. We tell things like they are and don't pull our punches. As we engage in conversations with others, we are likely to think that direct questioning is appropriate and will result in a straightforward answer.

Exhibit 2.3 The experiential learning cycle

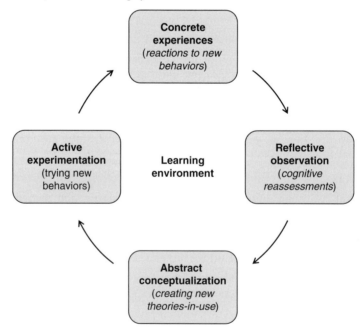

Source: Adapted from Kolb and Kolb, "Learning systems and learning spaces"

Now, imagine that an individual with whom we are communicating comes from a culture that values indirect or subtle communication and the avoidance of public embarrassment. For this person, direct questions may be inappropriate. Finally, consider that neither of us are sufficiently knowledgeable to adapt our communication styles to suit the other's culture. The most likely result of this scenario is that we will ask a direct question and will get what we perceive to be an unsatisfactory or evasive response. At this point, we are likely to experience an emotional reaction – discomfort, perplexity, offense, or surprise. This is our concrete experience.

These experiences or feelings, in turn, may then prompt us to try to understand what is happening. We may engage in *observation and reflection*. That is, once we realize that there is a disconnection between what is happening and what we thought would happen, we observe the other person and try to guess why he or she responded as they did. We may mentally run thorough a list of possible problems: maybe she did not hear you, maybe she did not understand the question, maybe she does not speak English very well, maybe she is shy, maybe she is not comfortable with the question, and so forth. We then search for other clues to her behavior in the context of the situation that can help us understand her behavior. Simply put, we look for additional information that will help us make sense of the situation.

This observation and reflection then forms the basis of *abstract conceptualization and generalizations*. As we think about it, we develop a theory of what is happening. We identify a plausible explanation for her behavior and begin searching for alternative solutions to your problem. Let's suppose that we concluded that our partner is uncomfortable with your question. Her body language suggests that she feels embarrassed to answer. Therefore, we theorize that you should pose the question in a different way.

Finally, this newly developed theory will guide any future actions we take to deal with this individual and others from the same culture. Here, we enter a stage of *active experimentation*. As we practice these new actions, we are developing new theories-in-use and testing the implications of what has been learned. We decide, for example, to formulate our questions in a different way, we observe the results, and start a new learning cycle. The cycle continues until we are able to identify successful behaviors. Learning through experience is a process of trial and error in which we perceive a mismatch, reflect on it, identify solutions, and initiate new behaviors. When we identify successful behaviors, we incorporate them into our theories of how to behave. As such, the next time we engage in a similar situation, we draw upon our latest theory for guidance.[27]

Exhibit 2.4 A learning strategy for global managers

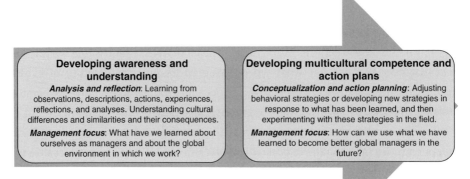

Learning strategies for global managers

This experiential learning model suggests that any developmental strategy for improving global managers' capabilities and skills should incorporate four variables in some form of interactive dynamic:

(1) our actual experiences in the field

(2) the manner in which we try to understand, interpret, and analyze these experiences

(3) the theories-in-use, or action plans, we develop for future action based on our analyses

(4) the attempts we make to try out new behavioral strategies.

Permeating this entire process are two critical learning strategies that aim to make learning and development easier: developing an awareness and understanding of global interdependencies as they relate to cultural influences on human behavior; and developing theories-in-use, or action plans, to prepare for unforeseen events and the unanticipated actions of others (see Exhibit 2.4). Both of these learning strategies have the same goal: developing the multicultural competencies necessary to work successfully across cultures. And both apply to a wide range of global managers, including expatriates, frequent flyers, and virtual managers. While the jobs may be different, the challenges remain the same.

The first learning strategy focuses on developing awareness and understanding. Here we want to learn from our and others' experiences, observations, descriptions, and analyses. We want to process and analyze available information to better understand what occurred and why. What were the consequences? And how could this have been done better? The second learning strategy focuses on developing theories-in-use, or action plans. This includes adjusting our behavioral strategies and creating, and then experimenting with, new action plans in the field.

In the case of Google, both learning strategies were used and both appeared to be successful. Google managers were intentionally placed in unfamiliar circumstances where they quickly had to seek understanding and be aware of their first-hand experiences. They needed to reflect and make sense of these experiences and identify important lessons for the future. At the same time, they had to organize what they saw and develop theories-in-use for future actions that could be tried when they returned to the field. Note that Google went to great lengths to allow their managers to fail as well as succeed. Note, too, that there were few safety nets. Learning strategies such as these have proven to be successful again and again as large and small companies work to improve and internationalize their human resources. With this learning model in mind, we turn now to exploring some of the cultural differences that can at times make working across cultures so problematic, as well as what managers can do to better prepare themselves for success in a turbulent and often contradictory environment.

Notes

1 Cited in Alex E. Bell, "Death by UML fever," *ACM Queue*, March 2004, p. 4. Nasrudin's wisdom is so celebrated that he is claimed as a native son by a number of countries throughout Central and South Asia, including Afghanistan, India, Iran, and Pakistan.
2 Eric Hoffer, *Reflections on the Human Condition*. Titusville, NJ: Hopewell Publications, 1973, p. 32.
3 Steven Levy, "Google goes globe-trotting," *Newsweek*, November 12, 2007, pp. 62–64.
4 Claude S. George, *The History of Management Thought*. Englewood Cliffs, NJ: Prentice Hall, 1972.
5 Frederick Taylor, *Scientific Management*. New York, NY: Harper & Row, 1911.
6 Henri Fayol, *Administration Industrielle et Generale*. Paris: Dunod, 1916.
7 Hugo Munsterberg, *Psychology and Industrial Efficiency*. Cambridge, MA: Riverside Press, 1913.
8 Max Weber, *The Theory of Social and Economic Organization*. New York, NY: Free Press, 1927.
9 Stephen Robbins and Mary Coulter, *Management*. Upper Saddle River, NJ: Pearson – Prentice Hall, 2007, p. 7.
10 Michael Hitt, Stewart Black, and Lyman Porter, *Management*. Upper Saddle River, NJ: Pearson/Prentice Hall, 2005, p. 8

11 Henry Mintzberg, *The Nature of Managerial Work*. New York, NY: Harper & Row, 1973.

12 Henry Mintzberg, *Structure in Fives: Designing Effective Organizations*. Englewood Cliffs, NJ: Prentice Hall, 1993.

13 M. Tahvanainen, D. Welch, and V. Worm, "Implications of short-term international assignments," *European Management Journal*, 2005, 23(6), p. 663.

14 Moon Ihlwan, "The foreigners at the top of LG," *Business Week*, December 11, 2008, p. 35.

15 Nancy Adler, *International Dimensions of Organizational Behavior*. Mason, OH: Thompson, 2008.

16 Martha J. Frase, "International commuters: are your overseas assignments creating risky stealth-pats?," *HR Magazine*, March, 2007, pp. 91–95.

17 Luciara Nardon and Richard M. Steers, "The new global manager: learning cultures on the fly," *Organizational Dynamics*, 2008, 37, pp. 47–59.

18 Carla Joinson, "Cutting down the days: HR can make expat assignments short and sweet," *HR Magazine*, April 2000, pp. 93–97.

19 "Traveling more lightly: staffing globalization," *The Economist*, June 24, 2006, pp. 23–24.

20 H. Mayerhofer, L. C. Hartmann, G. Michelitsch-Riedl, and I. Kollinger, "Flexpatriate assignments: a neglected issue in global staffing," *International Journal of Human Resource Management*, 2004, 15(8), p. 1371.

21 Ken Auletta, *Media Man: Ted Turner's Improbable Empire*. New York, NY: Norton, 2004.

22 Mansour Javidan, Richard M. Steers, and Michael A. Hitt (eds.), *The Global Mindset*. Amsterdam: Elsevier, 2007; Orly Levy, Sully Taylor, Nakiye Boyacigiller, and Schon Beechler, "Global mindset: a review and proposed extensions," in Javidan *et al.*, *The Global Mindset*, pp. 11–41.

23 Kalburgi M. Srinivas, "Globalization of business and the third world," *Journal of Management Development*, 1995, 14(3), pp. 26–49.

24 Phillip Harris, Robert Moran, and Sarah Moran, *Managing Cultural Differences*, 6th Edition. Amsterdam: Elsevier, 2004.

25 William Ouchi, *Theory Z*. Reading MA: Addison-Wesley, 1981.

26 Alice Y. Kolb and David A. Kolb, "Learning styles and learning spaces: enhancing experiential learning in higher education," *Academy of Management Learning and Education*, 2005, 4, pp. 193–212.

27 Robert Hogan and Rodney Warrenfeltz, "Educating the modern manager," *Academy of Management Learning and Education*, 2003, 2(1), pp. 74–84; Kolb and Kolb, "Learning styles and learning spaces."

CHAPTER 3

Culture, values, and worldviews

- Culture, socialization, and normative behavior   49
- Core cultural dimensions: a starting point   55
- Regional trends and cultural differences   64
- Digging deeper: cultural complexities and contradictions   66
- MANAGER'S NOTEBOOK: Culture, values, and worldviews   76

We do not see things as they are; we see things as we are.

Talmud Bavli[1]
Ancient book of wisdom, Babylonia

Ample evidence shows that the cultures of the world are getting more and more interconnected and that the business world is becoming increasingly global. As economic borders come down, cultural barriers will most likely go up and present new challenges and opportunities for business. When cultures come in contact, they may converge in some aspects, but their idiosyncrasies will likely amplify.

Robert J. House[2]
University of Pennsylvania, USA

Grasshoppers are pests in North America, pets in China, and appetizers in Thailand. What does this suggest about the influence of cultural differences on perceptions of even the lowly insect? Indeed, what does this suggest about how and why tastes in general can differ so starkly across nations and regions? If cultures can have such differing views about grasshoppers, imagine what they can do with people. Indeed, philosophers and social scientists have long noted that if you want to understand why people – including managers – behave as they do, a good place to begin is with a serious look at the cultural environment in which they work.

Consider the following three observations. First, Talmudic wisdom dates from over 2,000 years ago, yet is as true today as it was when it was initially written. As noted in the above quotation, culture influences our perceptions of world events and thereby influences our values, attitudes, and behaviors. It tells us what is acceptable and what is not. But if cultures differ, so do our perceptions, values, and judgments. What may be pleasant, attractive, agreeable, or acceptable in one culture may not be in another. Second, more than 700 years ago, Chinese scholar Wang Ying-lin compiled a volume of ancient wisdom thought to be from Confucius and called the *Trimetric Classic* (or *Three Character Classic*), in which he observed that all people are basically the same; it is only their habits and environments that differ.[3] And third, Wharton professor Robert J. House has recently observed that cultures around the world are getting increasingly interconnected and that the business world is becoming increasingly global. When these cultures come in contact, they may converge in some aspects, but their idiosyncrasies will likely amplify.

The *Talmud*, a Confucian scholar, and a modern-day business professor, each coming from a very different time and place in history, all understood what has too frequently eluded many contemporary managers: Culture can make a difference in determining how we think and how we behave. This is equally true in our personal lives and our work lives. Unfortunately, too many managers have ignored even the most rudimentary cross-national differences while working overseas and, as a result, have missed significant opportunities for themselves and their companies.

Culture is both simple and difficult to understand. It is simple because definitions abound that are easily understood by any reader. At the same time, however, culture can be difficult to comprehend because of its subtleties and complexities. The ancient Chinese Taoist philosopher Lao Tzu once observed that "water is the last thing a fish notices," using water as a metaphor for culture.[4] That is, most people are so strongly immersed in their own culture that they often fail to see how it affects their patterns of thinking or their behavior; they are too close to it. It is only when we are "out of the water" that we become aware of our own cultural biases and assumptions. (If you don't believe this, try writing down ten adjectives that best describe your own culture. Then ask some friends from other cultures to write down ten adjectives that describe your culture. Compare the lists.)

In view of this dilemma, consider the challenge faced by Anna Håkansson, a Swedish investment banker from Stockholm, who was informed that she was being sent to the Kingdom of Bahrain to negotiate a contract with Gulf One Investment Bank.[5] How would she prepare herself for the journey? Having never been to the Middle East, she first talked to colleagues who had some experience there. Next, she ran a Google search and discovered that there were over 400,000 hits on Arab culture alone. During this search, she uncovered a number of recent articles in various respected sources that helped her to understand what to expect. For example, an article in the *Washington Post* pointed out that the extended family was the single most important entity of Arab society, playing a pivotal role not only in social life but also in economic and political life as well.[6] Even an individual's self-identity is based on a collective self. Each family member shares a collective ancestry, a collective respect for elders, and a collective obligation and responsibility for the welfare of the other family members. It is to the extended family, not to the government, that a person first turns to for help.

Despite some modernization trends and the adoption of many superficial aspects of Western pop culture, the extended family in the Arab world has been remarkably resilient in the face of Westernization. With the move to the cities, members of Saudi extended families still tend to live in close proximity to one another whenever possible, and when not, they do a great deal of socializing with other members. In addition, many families retain homes in their hometowns as well as their place of work. A major reason for the resilience of the traditional extended family structure, however, is the extraordinary strength of traditional Islamic social, economic, and political values. Although some behavioral patterns have changed over time, Arab society's core values are deeply held and are likely to endure over time.

As Håkansson learned, three characteristics of Arab extended families stand out: gender roles, the role of elders, and the decision-making process. First, Arab societies are typically patriarchal societies, maintaining a respect for age and seniority that has largely disappeared in Western societies. The wisdom and authority of elders is seldom challenged, and younger men and women must wait their turn, often until their sixties or older, before they are accorded the role of family patriarchs and matriarchs.

Second, traditional gender roles in Arab societies share a number of common characteristics with other traditional societies, the most notable of which is that men's roles are outside the home as family providers, protectors, and managers, and women's roles are in the home. Men are predominant outside the home – in business and public affairs – and women are to a large degree predominant within the home, particularly in parental decisions.

And third, Håkansson learned that the traditional method for reaching and legitimizing decisions in Arab society is through consultation (*shura*) among those within the group whose opinions are considered important.[7] From consultation emerges consensus (*ijma`*), which is binding on all members of the group.[8] Within the extended family, the principal consensus makers are senior male members or elders. This ancient process of consultation and consensus was given religious sanction in Islam. From texts in the *Qur'an* and the *Sunna* comes the belief that God would never permit a consensus of the Islamic community to be in error.[9] Consensual decision-making is still the norm in family, government, or business decisions.

Based on what she learned, Håkansson next attempted to find a way to organize everything into a more user-friendly format. She looked for a cultural model she could use to make some comparisons between Swedish and Arab societies to solidify what she had learned. She chose a model developed by Dutch management researcher Geert Hofstede and based on his classic book, *Culture's Consequences*.[10] Hofstede views culture as the "software of the mind" that differentiates one group or society from another (see below for more details). In other words, while people all have the same hardware, their brains and patterns of thinking and behaving can be very different.

Hofstede's assessment of Arab cultures suggests that Arabs as a group tend to value large power distances across populations; that is, it is highly acceptable for people at the top of a social hierarchy to centralize most of the power in their hands. At the same time, Arabs seek to avoid the uncertainties that confront people on an ongoing basis. As a result, these societies are more likely to follow a caste system that does not allow significant upward mobility of its citizens. They are also highly rule-oriented with laws, rules, regulations, and controls in order to reduce the amount of uncertainty, while inequalities of power and wealth have been allowed to grow within these societies. When these two cultural dimensions are combined, it creates a situation where leaders have virtually ultimate power and authority, and the rules, laws, and regulations developed by those in power reinforce their own leadership and control. It is not unusual for new leadership to arise from armed insurrection – the ultimate power – rather than from diplomatic or democratic change.

This high power distance is also indicative of a high level of inequality of power and wealth within the society. These populations have an expectation and acceptance that leaders will separate themselves from the group, and this condition is not necessarily subverted upon the population, but rather accepted by the society as their cultural heritage. Meanwhile, there is high need for predictability in view of the society's low level of tolerance for uncertainty. In an effort to minimize or reduce this level of uncertainty, strict rules, laws, policies, and regulations are adopted and implemented. The ultimate goal of these populations is to control everything in order to eliminate or avoid the unexpected. As a result of this high-uncertainty avoidance characteristic, the society does not readily accept change and is highly risk adverse.

To finish her analysis, Håkansson compared Hofstede's assessment of Arab cultures with his assessment of her native Sweden (see Exhibit 3.1). For Bahrain, she had found that people tend to be high in power distance (PDI), moderately low on individualism

Exhibit 3.1 Hofstede's culture ratings for Sweden and Bahrain

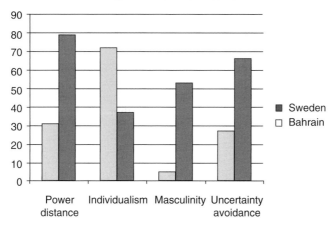

(IND), moderately high on masculinity (MAS), and high on uncertainty avoidance (UAI). For Sweden, by contrast, she found very different scores. Specifically, Hofstede's scale indicates that Swedes tend to be low on power distance, moderately high on individualism, very low on masculinity, and moderately low on uncertainty avoidance. In other words, in Sweden we see a society in which egalitarianism is emphasized, including equality of gender and race. Power is widely shared and uncertainty is tolerated in the belief that it helps facilitate creativity and innovation. Groups, and indeed society itself, is considered to be important by all, but so too is individualism.

Now, Håkansson believed she had a concrete comparative framework on which to compare some of the basic differences between the two countries. Based on what she had learned, she further believed she was now prepared for her business trip to Bahrain. However, what she would learn later, as discussed below, was that she had only scratched the surface in preparing for her global encounter.

Culture, socialization, and normative behavior

A key issue in dealing with culture relates to how we recognize culture when we see it. What do we mean by the term "culture"? One of the main challenges managers face when working across cultures is teasing out cultural influences from other phenomena in the world surrounding us. For example, where does culture end and personality begin? What is universal behavior and what is not? In this regard, finding a suitable working definition of culture can be challenging.

What is culture?

We have already seen that Geert Hofstede defines culture as the collective programming of the mind that distinguishes the members of one human group from another.[11] Meanwhile, cultural anthropologist Clyde Kluckholn defined culture as the collection of beliefs, values, behaviors, customs, and attitudes that distinguish the people of one society from another.[12] The GLOBE researchers defined culture as shared motives, values, beliefs, identities, and interpretations or meanings of significant events that result from common experiences of members of collectives that are transmitted across generations.[13] Fons Trompenaars defined culture as the way in which a group of people solves problems and reconciles dilemmas.[14] Ann Swidler also took a problem-solving approach, viewing culture as a "toolkit" of symbols, stories, rituals, and worldviews that help the people of a culture survive and succeed.[15] Finally, cultural anthropologist Clifford Geertz defined culture as the means by which people communicate, perpetuate, and develop their knowledge about attitudes towards life.[16] Culture is the fabric of meaning in terms of which people interpret their experience and guide their action

While all of these definitions are useful and share a great deal in common, they all have nuanced differences that may have more to say to academicians than managers. From the standpoint of global management, they suggest that culture is perhaps best thought of as addressing three questions: Who are we? How do we live? And how do we approach work? These three questions focus attention on individuals, environments, and work norms and values, and the answers to these questions allow us to draw some inferential conclusions about work and society and how managers in general should behave as they work across cultures.

Three aspects of these definitions are particularly salient for our discussion here:

(1) *Culture is shared by members of a group and, indeed, sometimes defines the membership of the group itself.* As such, cultural preferences are neither universal around the world nor entirely personal; they are preferences that are commonly shared by a group of people, even if not by all members of the group. The fact that most Koreans and Mexicans like spicy food does not require that all of them prefer such cuisine, nor does it require that all Dutch and Canadians avoid them.

(2) *Culture is learned through membership in a group or community.* Cultures, in the form of normative social behavior, are learned from elders, teachers, officials, experiences, and society-at-large. We acquire values, assumptions, and behaviors by seeing how others behave, growing up in a community, going to school, and observing our family.

(3) *Culture influences the attitudes and behaviors of group members.* Many of our innate beliefs, values, and patterns of social behavior can be traced back to our particular cultural training and socialization. After we grow up, culture still tells us what is acceptable and unacceptable behavior, attractive and unattractive, and so forth. As a result, culture heavily influences socialization processes in terms of how we see ourselves and what we believe and hold dear. This, in turn, influences our *normative behavior*, or how we think those around us expect us to behave.

Exhibit 3.2 illustrates the relationship between universal, cultural, and personal preferences. At the bottom of the pyramid is biological programming, characteristics that are part of human nature. At the top of the pyramid are individual characteristics, usually referred to as personality, and made up of a combination of inherited and learned behaviors, preferences, and assumptions. Culture resides between these two and the line that separates them is at best blurred. There are many situations were it is impossible to know for sure why someone is behaving in a certain way. And the reality is, in most instances it does not really matter. Managers need to be effective working across

Exhibit 3.2 Levels of mental programming

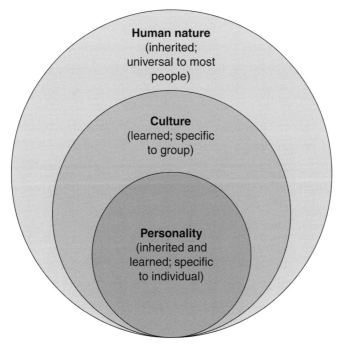

Source: Adapted from Hofstede, *Culture's consequence* and D. Thomas and K. Inkson, *Cultural Intelligence for Global Business: People Skills for Global Business*, San Francisco, CA: Berret-Koehler, 2003.

diversities, which includes culture but is not restricted to it. More important is identifying what is universal and what is not. The erroneous belief that a value, belief, or assumption is universal is likely to bring misunderstandings. For this reason, in this book we will highlight cultural differences in an attempt to bring awareness to non-universal assumptions.

A recent and somewhat intriguing study serves to further illustrate the shared nature of cultures. Apparently, shared values follow people throughout their life.[17] The study found that the anxieties and worries of elderly people were tied very closely to their national origin. That is, aging Germans tend to worry about losing their mental alertness, while their Dutch neighbors worry about gaining weight. Thais worry about losing their eyesight, while the more heterogeneous Americans tend to divide their anxieties between memory loss, weight gain, loss of energy, and an ability to care for themselves. Finally, Egyptians report that they worry about nothing as they age. (The study authors suggested that perhaps the Egyptians concluded that since problems associated with aging are inevitable, there is no need to worry about them – fate happens.) The study concluded that an important aspect of studying aging is developing an understanding of cultural influences.

Culture and normative behavior

In addition, culture often sets the limits on what is considered acceptable and unacceptable behaviors; it pressures individuals and groups into accepting and following *normative behavior*. Culture determines the rules of the road that guide what people can do. Indeed, newspapers and periodicals are filled with examples of people who set out to break a "culture barrier." Rightly or wrongly, these barriers are typically established to ensure uniform practice among members of a society, and, as a result, societies often take a dim view of people who buck the system. Consider two examples.

First, consider the rather unusual profession of debt collection. Debt collectors serve a useful function in societies, however unpleasant the task, but their legitimate (i.e., culturally determined) tools of the trade can differ significantly. In Spain, for example, debt collectors do a thriving business trying to shame or embarrass debtors into paying their bills.[18] When Lian Manuel goes to a house to try and convince someone who is behind in his or her bills to pay up, he dresses in a tuxedo and top hat and carries a brief case with a large sign that reads *El Cobrador del Frac*, or "The Debt Collector in Top Hat and Tails." He then visits the debtor's neighbors to loudly complain about the problem. Other debt collectors wear different uniforms, including the "Scottish collector," who threatens to show up at a debtor's house and play his bagpipes, and the "monastery collector," who shows up dressed as a Franciscan friar. In another case, when a Madrid couple failed to pay for an elaborate wedding reception, the collector obtained the guest list of prominent people and telephoned several of them to ask that they pay €500 for their share of the chicken and cake that were served at the reception. The bill was paid the next day. In such cases, the goal is the same: to embarrass or humiliate the person to clear his or her financial obligations. Why is this done? Largely because Spanish bankruptcy courts have long backlogs and offer little relief, while customers want to be paid, and largely because it is a very effective tool for collection and is culturally acceptable, if disliked, by those being harassed. Meanwhile, in Russia, several debt collectors make their rounds with a leashed black bear at their side. But in the UK, by contrast, publicly humiliating debtors is considered unprofessional and an unfair business practice. And in Canada and the US, it is illegal to harass debtors by publicizing their circumstances to friends and neighbors. Different cultures, different acceptable business practices.

Second, and perhaps more seriously, consider how culture can influence local business practices, like accounting and finance practices. A common example of this involves the financial practices in several Muslim cultures (e.g., Algeria, Saudi Arabia, and Sudan) that follow *sharia*, or Islamic law.[19] Islamic banking and finance practices can be found in over sixty developing countries and fifteen developed ones. Indeed, in many of these countries, Western-style banking practices are prohibited. For example, Islamic law prohibits Muslims from receiving or paying any form of interest, as discussed in Surah II of the *Qur'an*.[20] Interest is seen as taking advantage of others who may not be so fortunate.

As a result, while Western-style lending is based on the concept of interest, Islamic lending is based on the principle of profit sharing. Islamic profit-and-loss plans come in three main forms. First, the *mudaraba* (i.e., trustee finance) consists of entrusting funds for a predetermined share of profit or loss, with investors becoming dormant partners in the project.[21] This is generally used for short-term transactions and mostly in trade and commerce. Most bank customers, for instance, make their deposits under these types of agreements. Second, the *musharaka* (i.e., equity participation) consists of multiple partners who provide funds in varying proportions for long-term projects. The profit or loss is then shared according to participation.[22] Management and participation rights are afforded to all parties, even to those who do not actually participate in the management of the project. And third, mark-up arrangements represent assets that are acquired for later resale or lease, with a mark-up on the price of the purchase.

In addition, in Muslim countries stock market transactions are only allowed if the companies involved only deal in *halal* (or approved) commodities.[23] Moreover, people who can afford it are expected to provide a religious-based annual levy of almsgiving (known as *zakāh*) of approximately 2.5 percent of their holdings.[24] Under the guidance and interpretation of company-based religious supervisory boards, there is a ban on all economic activities related to goods and services that contradict the values of Islam (e.g., alcoholic beverages, pork products, or luxury goods). Gambling and speculation, or blindly undertaking a venture without sufficient knowledge of the risk, is also to be avoided, as are insurance policies (unless organized under mutual ownership), currency hedging, futures contracts, and credit cards. According to Islamic beliefs, these practices require people to look into the future and only God can do this. Certainly, Anna Håkansson would understand this (see above).

Turning to other countries, when analyzing investment alternatives, firms in the US tend to favor discounted cash flow techniques, whereas German companies rely on payback methods and the Japanese prefer return on capital approaches. Also, time horizons for investment decisions tend to be systematically longer for Japanese firms, followed by German and American firms in that order.[25] There is also evidence that corporate financial objectives can vary across countries. Companies in the UK and the US, for instance, tend to favor financial measures such as profits, return on investment, and shareholder value, while Japanese firms tend to emphasize non-financial measures, such as market share and sales growth. Naturally, this makes for difficult evaluations of the comparative success or failure of corporations in international contexts.

Cultural differences can also be found in financial reporting practices, both in terms of performance measurement and information disclosure.[26] More conservative countries, like Germany and Japan, display more conservative accounting practices in terms of the profit recognition patterns of national companies, while less-conservative countries, like the UK and the US, favor less-conservative profit reporting practices. Disclosure practices, as seen in a continuum from transparency to secrecy, are more open and extensive in countries like the Netherlands, the UK and the US than in Switzerland, Germany, and Japan.[27] This is largely because individualist societies (like Australia, the US, and the UK) demand more disclosure and stronger independent auditors to protect the rights of individual investors, while countries high in universalism and uncertainty avoidance (like Sweden, Denmark, Germany, and Japan) instead opt for more uniform accounting rules.[28]

Overall, then, available evidence demonstrates that cultural differences can at times play an important role in accounting and financial practices in different regions of the world. Why is this important? Because global managers that do business across borders and understand how accounting and finance practices differ – or simply know that they do differ – are in a far better position to negotiate contracts, manage partnerships, and build working relationships with both customers and partners around the world.

Core cultural dimensions: a starting point

To understand the changes and challenges around the world, many researchers suggest we need some kind of a tool or mechanism with which to compare cultural differences and similarities. Such a mechanism can provide a heuristic to gain conceptual entry into why some people think and act differently from others. Many researchers – and many global managers – begin by comparing cultures on various cultural dimensions, such as hierarchical or equalitarian, individualistic or collectivistic, and so forth. Indeed, this is exactly what Anna Håkansson did prior to her departure for the Middle East. While comparing cultural dimensions may only provide a thumbnail sketch of some general trends between two or more cultures, it can be useful as a starting point for cross-cultural understanding.

But even this simple strategy is not without its problems. As noted cultural anthropologist Edward T. Hall once observed,

> I have come to the conclusion that the analysis of culture could be likened to the task of identifying mushrooms. Because of the nature of the mushrooms, no two experts describe them in precisely the same way, which creates a problem for the rest of us when we are trying to decide whether the specimen in our hands is edible.[29]

Hall makes an important point here. While the success of global managers frequently rests on their knowledge and understanding of cultures and cultural differences, the experts who advise them are not always in agreement. Indeed, sometimes they are in stark disagreement. What, then, can managers do? Without accurate knowledge concerning cultural beliefs, values, traditions, and customs, managers are left to take their chances in a new, ambiguous, and sometimes threatening environment. Turning in one direction can lead to success; turning in the other can lead to failure. To apply Hall's metaphor, managers must decide which mushrooms are edible and which are not. They need to know which practices or behaviors will create barriers to conducting business and which will open a path to partnership.

Culture theory jungle

A number of attempts have been made to capture the essence of cultural differences – and similarities – across borders. Each offers a different way to understand and measure culture. Four currently popular models are shown in Exhibit 3.3. (A more

Exhibit 3.3 Selected models of cultural dimensions

Hall	Hofstede	Trompenaars	GLOBE project
Context: Extent to which the context of a message is as important as the message itself. *Space*: Extent to which people are comfortable sharing physical space with others. *Time*: Extent to which people approach one task at a time or multiple tasks simultaneously.	*Power distance*: Beliefs about the appropriate distribution of power in society. *Uncertainty avoidance*: Extent to which people feel threatened by uncertain or unknown situations. *Individualism-collectivism*: Relative importance of individual vs. group interests in society. *Masculinity-femininity*: Assertiveness vs. passivity; material possessions vs. quality of life. *Time orientation*: Long-term vs. short-term outlook on work, life, and relationships.	*Universalism-particularism*: The degree to which rules are uniformly or situationally applied. *Individualism-collectivism*: Do people derive their identity from within themselves or their group? *Specific vs. diffuse*: Are an individual's various roles compartmentalized or integrated? *Neutral vs. affective*: Are people free to express their emotions or are they restrained. *Achievement vs. ascription*: How are people accorded respect and social status? *Time perspective*: Do people focus on the past or the future? *Relationship with the environment*: Do people control the environment or does it control them?	*Power distance*: Degree to which people expect power to be distributed equally. *Uncertainty avoidance*: Extent to which people rely on norms, rules, and procedures to reduce the unpredictability of future events. *Humane orientation*: Extent to which people reward fairness, altruism, and generosity. *Institutional collectivism*: Extent to which society encourages collective distribution of resources and collective action. *In-group collectivism*: Extent to which individuals express pride, loyalty, and cohesiveness in their organizations and families. *Assertiveness*: Degree to which people are assertive, confrontational, and aggressive in relationships with others. *Gender egalitarianism*: Degree to which gender differences are minimized. *Future orientation*: Extent to which people engage in future-oriented behaviors such as planning, investing, and delayed gratification. *Performance orientation*: Degree to which high performance is encouraged and rewarded.

Source: Based on Edward T. Hall, *The Silent Language,* New York, NY: Anchor Books, 1981; Edward T. Hall and Mildred R. Hall, *Understanding Cultural Differences*, Yarmouth, ME: Intercultural Press, 1990; Hofstede, *Culture's Consequence*; Fons Trompenaars, *Riding the Waves of Culture: Understanding Cultural Diversity in Global Business*, London: McGraw-Hill, 1993; House *et al.*, *Culture, Leadership, and Organizations*.

detailed description of the various models of cultural dimensions can be found in Appendix A.)

Taken together, these models attempt to accomplish two things. First, each model offers a well-reasoned set of dimensions along which various cultures can be compared. It offers us a form of shorthand for cultural analysis. We can break down assessments of various cultures into power distance, uncertainty avoidance, and so forth, allowing us to organize our thoughts and focus our attention on what otherwise would be a monumental task. Second, some of the models offer numeric scores for rating various cultures. For example, we can use Hofstede's measures to say that Germany is more egalitarian than France. Regardless of whether these ratings are highly precise or only generally indicative of these countries, they nonetheless force managers to confront cultural differences and consider the managerial implications.

Unfortunately, these models frequently focus on different aspects of societal beliefs, norms, and values and, as such, convergence across the models is limited. From a managerial standpoint, questions are logically raised concerning which model best suits the needs of organizations and their managers. This lack of agreement presents managers with a dilemma in terms of managerial understanding and action, which we refer to as the *culture theory jungle*. That is, which model best serves managers' needs in the real world? For example, is it more important for managers to compare cultures based on achievement versus ascription as one model suggests, masculinity versus femininity as another model suggests, or the use of time and space as still another model suggests?

In addition, critics of this research point out with some justification that both the theory and the research underlying the creation and use of such models focuses too much on comparing central tendencies between cultures and not enough on comparing the differences within each culture. In other words, are all Indonesians or Kenyans or Bulgarians alike? Obviously not. Moreover, it is inaccurate to suggest that there are few differences between the peoples of either East Asia (Chinese, Korean, Japanese) or Western Europe (Dutch, French, Germans, Italians). Again, the answer is no. Do these criticisms hold up? Do they change the basic argument about cultural differences influencing the way people see the world and respond to it? Probably not. However, as already noted, while the use of cultural dimensions is certainly useful, it should only be considered the beginning of a more detailed study.

Core cultural dimensions

Even so, while each of these models focus on different aspects of culture, we believe that, taken together, they serve to amplify one another and reinforce their utility as critical

Exhibit 3.4 Core cultural dimensions

Hierarchical	**Power distribution**	Egalitarian
Individualistic	**Social relationships**	Collectivistic
Mastery	**Environmental relationships**	Harmony
Monochronic	**Time/work patterns**	Polychronic
Rule-based	**Uncertainty and social control**	Relationship-based

evaluative components in better understanding global management and the world of international business. Each model has added something of value to this endeavor. With this in mind, if we compare the various models of cultural dimensions, five dimensions emerge as being the most commonly used both by researchers and managers (again, see Appendix A for details).[30] We refer to these as *core cultural dimensions* (see Exhibit 3.4). Each focuses on one of five fundamental questions about cultures as they relate to social interaction and management practices in the global economy:

(1) *How are power and authority distributed in a society?* Is this distribution based on concepts of hierarchy or egalitarianism? What are societal beliefs concerning equality or privilege?

(2) *What is the fundamental building block of a society: individuals or groups?* How does a society organize for collective action?

(3) *On a societal level, how do people view their relationship with their surrounding environment?* Is their goal to control or master their surroundings or to live in harmony with it?

(4) *How do people in a society organize their time to carry out their work and non-work activities?* Do people approach work in a linear (i.e., one thing at a time) or a nonlinear (i.e., everything at once) fashion?

(5) *How do societies try to reduce uncertainties and control the behavior of their members?* Do they focus primarily on rules or relationships? That is, do they work to control people through rules, policies, laws, and social norms that are uniformly applied across society, or do they attempt to control people through relationship and rules often tempered by personal relationships, in-group values, or unique circumstances?

The five core cultural dimensions that emerge from integrating existing models include the following: hierarchical and egalitarian, individualistic and collectivistic, mastery-oriented and harmony-oriented, monochronic and polychronic, and rule-based and relationship-based (also called universalism-particularism). Taken together, these dimensions help build a broad-based portrait of how management and business practices in one culture differ from those in another. Specific definitions guiding our approach to applying these dimensions are discussed below (see Exhibit 3.5). In reviewing these dimensions, it is important to remember that country placement on dimensions is relative. For example, on the hierarchy-equality dimension, while all cultures use hierarchies in various forms, some cultures make greater use of them than others and, as such, would rank higher on this dimension than would other cultures. Dimensions are thus viewed in terms of relative comparisons across cultures, not as metrics or absolute values.[31]

Approach to power distribution
All societies have normative beliefs governing how power and influence should be distributed and used. Typically, these norms are expressed in terms of whether power should be clustered at or near the top of a hierarchy or distributed in a more egalitarian fashion. In other words, is the culture more *hierarchical* or *egalitarian*? Questions pertaining to this dimension include the following: Should authority ultimately reside in strong centralized governments or in the people themselves? Should organizations be structured vertically (e.g., tall organization structures) or horizontally (e.g., flat organization structures or even networked structures)? Is decision making largely autocratic or participatory? Are leaders chosen because they are the most qualified for a job or because they already have standing in the community? Are leaders elected or appointed? Are people willing or reluctant to question authority?

A good example of how power orientation works can be found in Finland, a country that stresses egalitarianism with a passion. Many Finnish laws are based on the principle of equity, not equality. For example, traffic fines vary based on personal income; the more you make, the more you can afford to pay. Police departments maintain direct computer access to internal revenue files to calculate the fines on the spot. Hence, when Jaako Rytsola, a young Finnish entrepreneur, was stopped driving his BMW at 43 miles-per-hour in a 25-mile-per hour zone, his speeding ticket cost him US$72,000. And when 27-year-old millionaire Jussi Salonoja was caught doing 40 in a 25-mile-per-hour zone, he was fined US$225,000. A government minister noted that this was a "Nordic tradition." They have both progressive taxation and progressive punishment.[32]

Exhibit 3.5 Anchors for core cultural dimensions

Hierarchical	Egalitarian
Centralized. Belief that power should be distributed hierarchically across society. Belief in ascribed or inherited power with ultimate authority residing in institutions. Emphasis on organizing vertically and autocratic or centralized decision making. Emphasis on who is in charge. Acceptance of authority; reluctance to question authority.	*Decentralized.* Belief that power should be distributed relatively equally across society. Belief in shared or elected power with ultimate authority residing in the people. Emphasis on organizing horizontally and participatory or decentralized decision making. Emphasis on who is best qualified. Rejection or skepticism of authority; willingness to question authority.

Individualistic	Collectivistic
Person-centered. Belief that people achieve self-identity through individual accomplishment. Focus on accomplishing individual goals. Sanctions reinforce independence and personal responsibility. Contract-based agreements. Tendency toward low-context (direct, frank) communication and individual decision making.	*Group-centered.* Belief that people achieve self-identity through group membership. Preference for preserving social harmony over individual rights. Focus on accomplishing group goals. Sanctions reinforce conformity to group norms. Relationship-based agreements. Tendency toward high-context (subtle, indirect) communication and group or participative decision making.

Mastery-oriented	Harmony-oriented
Dominance over nature. Focus on changing or controlling one's natural and social environment. Achievement valued over relationships. Emphasis on competition in the pursuit of personal or group goals. Embraces change and unquestioned innovation. Emphasis on material possessions as symbols of achievement. Emphasis on assertive, proactive, "masculine" approach. Preference for performance-based extrinsic rewards.	*Accommodation with nature.* Focus on living in harmony with nature and adjusting to the natural and social environment. Relationships valued over achievement. Emphasis on social progress, quality of life, and the welfare of others. Defends traditions; skepticism towards change. Emphasis on economy, harmony, and modesty. Emphasis on passive, reactive, "feminine" approach. Preference for seniority-based intrinsic rewards.

Monochronic	Polychronic
Linear. Sequential attention to individual tasks. Single-minded approach to work, planning, and implementation. Precise concept of time; punctual. Job-centered; commitment to the job and often to the organization. Separation of work and personal life. Approach to work is focused and impatient.	*Non-linear.* Simultaneous attention to multiple tasks. Interactive approach to work, planning, and implementation. Flexible concept of time; often late. People-centered; commitment to people and human relationships. Integration of work and personal life. Approach to work is at times unfocused and patient.

Rule-based	Relationship-based
Rule-based (or universalistic). Individual behavior should be largely regulated by rules, laws, formal policies, standard operating procedures, and social norms that are widely supported by societal members and applied uniformly to everyone. Emphasis on legal contracts and meticulous record keeping. Low tolerance for rule breaking. Decisions based largely on objective criteria (e.g., legal constraints, data, policies).	*Relationship-based (or particularistic).* While rules and laws are important, they often require flexibility in their application or enforcement by influential people (e.g., parents, peers, superiors, government officials) or unique circumstances. Emphasis on interpersonal relationships and trust; less emphasis on record keeping. Moderate tolerance for rule breaking. Decisions often based on subjective criteria (e.g., hunches, personal connections).

Approach to social relationships and organization

The nature of social relationships and perceptions of self-identity have been widely identified in various models of culture as representing a key variable in understanding what differentiates one society from another. This is usually expressed in terms of cultures being more *individualistic* and *collectivistic*. At issue here is whether members of a society see themselves first and foremost as individuals or members of a group. Do they achieve self-identity through their own efforts or through group endeavors? Are individual goals or group goals more important? Do group sanctions reinforce personal responsibility or conformity to group norms? Is individual or group decision making preferred? Is business done primarily based on written contracts or on personal relationships? Is communication characterized primarily by low context (where the message contains all or almost all of the intended message) or by high context (where the context surrounding the message also carries significant information – see Chapter 7)?

An understanding of this dimension is critical for managers to succeed overseas. For example, initiating performance-based incentive systems that reward individual performance will likely have a difficult time succeeding in highly collectivistic cultures. Group-based rewards and incentives will likely be more successful in such circumstances. Likewise, over-emphasizing participatory decision making in a highly individualistic culture may also be problematic (see Chapter 5). Again, the challenge for global managers is to develop administrative practices that support, not contradict, local customs and social norms.

Approach to the surrounding environment

Most societies have a reasonably widely shared view with respect to their relationship to their surroundings. We refer to this as the distinction between *mastery-oriented* and *harmony-oriented*. This relationship often represents an underlying motive structure or goal for the society. That is, on a fundamental level some societies seek to control their surrounding environment, while others seek to live in relative harmony with it. Does a society emphasize competition in the pursuit of personal or group goals or striving for social progress, quality of life, and the welfare of others? Does a society attempt to bend nature to its will or conform to nature as much as possible? Is a society assertive, proactive, and "masculine" (to use Hofstede's term) or passive, reactive, and "feminine?" Does a society tend to emphasize extrinsic rewards based on job performance or intrinsic rewards based on seniority or on one's position in the organization? Is there an emphasis on material possessions as symbols of achievement or on economy, harmony, and societal sustainability? Finally, do people tend to engage in conspicuous consumption or do they tend to be more modest and unpretentious?

An understanding of this dimension can help managers determine how to structure work plans, incentive plans, and may even influence leadership style. For example, most employees in a mastery-oriented culture will respond to challenges and personal incentives; they will strive for success. Employees in more harmony-oriented cultures will more likely focus their attention on building or maintaining group welfare, personal relationships, and environmental sustainability. They tend to be more committed to social progress. As such, they will likely be more responsive to participative leadership and be more skeptical of proposed change. Managers who understand this are in a position to tailor their leadership style to fit the situation.

Approach to work patterns and the use of time

A fourth major difference across cultures is people's approaches to time and tasks. Here we distinguish between *monochronic* and *polychronic*. As illustrated in Exhibit 3.5 above, people in more monochronic cultures tend to be somewhat methodical in their use of time and their approaches to tasks. They see time as a commodity that can be measured, used, and sometimes sold. They often approach work as a series of tasks or goals that should be tackled sequentially, or one at a time. By contrast, people in more polychronic cultures tend to be more flexible, addressing several problems simultaneously. They are often oblivious to time and resist firm deadlines. And they tend to mix work and personal lives in a more fluid fashion that their monochronic counterparts, who stress a clear separation between work and family.

Logical questions to ask here include the following: Do people have a precise concept of time and tend to be very punctual or do they have a relative concept and tend to be late? Do they need a steady flow of information to do their job or does their culture already provide them with this information? Are people more committed to their jobs or to family and friends? Do they separate work and family life or see them as an integrated whole? Do they take a linear or nonlinear approach to planning? And, finally, are they focused and impatient or unfocused and patient?

Approach to uncertainty, predictability, and social control

A final dimension used by managers to differentiate across cultures involves the issue of rules versus relationships as a means of reducing uncertainty in society. That is, how is social behavior best controlled? This distinction is referred to here as *rule-based* and *relationship-based*, although it is also referred to as *universalistic* and *particularistic* (see Chapter 11).[33] In essence, this issue focuses on the means of social control.

Rule-based (or universalistic) cultures believe that social values and standards take precedence over individual needs or claims by friends and relations; rules are intended to apply equally to the whole "universe" of members. Exceptions only serve to weaken the rule of law. For example, a rule that people should bear truthful witness in a court of law, or give their honest judgment to an insurance company concerning a payment it is about to make, is more important than particular family or friendship ties. This is not to say that "particular" ties are unimportant in universalistic cultures; rather, universal truth as embodied in the law is believed to be more important than these relationships. By contrast, particularistic cultures see the ideal culture in terms of human friendship, extraordinary achievement, unique situations, and close personal relationships. The spirit of the law is deemed to be more important than the letter of the law. Clearly, there are rules and laws in particularistic cultures, but these are designed to simply codify how people relate to one another. Rules are needed (if only to be able to make exceptions to them for particular cases), but people need to be able to count on their friends.

As a result, in rule-based cultures there is a tendency to promulgate a multitude of laws, rules, regulations, bureaucratic procedures, and strict social norms in an attempt to control as many unanticipated events or behaviors as possible. People tend to conform to officially sanctioned constraints because of a moral belief in the virtue of the rule of law, and will often obey directives even if they know violations will not be detected. Waiting for a red light in the absence of any traffic is a good example here. Rules and laws are universally applied (at least in theory), with few exceptions for extenuating circumstances or personal connections. There is a strong belief in the use of formal contracts and rigorous record keeping in business dealings. Things are done "by the book" and infractions often bring immediate sanctions or consequences. Finally, decisions tend to be made based on objective criteria to the extent possible. All of this is aimed at creating a society with no surprises.

By contrast, relationship-based (or particularistic) cultures tend to use influential people more than abstract or objective rules and regulations as a means of social control.[34] This personal control can come from parents, peers, superiors, supervisors, government officials, and so forth – anyone with influence over the individual. In this sense, relationship-based cultures tend to be particularistic, and individual circumstances often influence the manner in which formal rules are applied. In addition, greater emphasis is placed on developing mutually beneficial interpersonal relationships and trust as a substitute for strict rules and procedures. There is generally less record keeping and things tend to be done on an informal basis. There is also greater tolerance for non-compliance with bureaucratic rules in the belief that formal rules cannot cover all contingencies and that some flexibility is often required. Finally, decisions tend to be made based on a combination of objective and subjective criteria and with less formality.

This is not to say that relationship-based cultures do not value laws and official procedures; they do. Rather, laws and procedures are often followed only to the extent that one's social network embraces them and sees either the virtue or necessity of following them, not because of some innate belief in their moral correctness, as is the case with universalistic cultures. Where predictability of behavior is important, it is motivated largely through contacts, not contracts, and interpersonal trust and mutual support between partners is critical.

Taken together, these five core cultural dimensions highlight key aspects of cultural differences that can have a bearing on how business and management is conducted – or not conducted – around the world. Like the other models on which it is based, the core cultural dimensions described here provide only a quick cultural snapshot of the central tendencies in one country. They are a good starting point to investigate cultural differences between countries, but their utility will vary depending on countries involved and the particular situation.

Regional trends and cultural differences

In order to operationalize the core cultural dimensions discussed here, it is helpful to have a means of classifying cultures so that country – or at least regional – comparisons can be made. Mindful of the limitations discussed above, we chose to estimate cultural differences within *country clusters* (as opposed to individual countries) by adapting a framework originally proposed by Simcha Ronan and Oded Shenkar,[35] and subsequently used by others with some modifications.[36] This framework focuses on identifying regions where ample anthropological data were available, and our use of these clusters reflects this imbalance. Because of this, some regions (e.g., Central Asia, Polynesia) are not included, while others (e.g., Europe) are covered in considerable detail. In addition, according to these efforts, several countries (e.g., Brazil, India, and Israel) do not easily fit into such a framework, so again some caution is in order.

Based on this research, we can use this framework to identify nine country clusters for which sufficient data were available to estimate central tendencies in cultural characteristics: Anglo cluster (e.g., Australia, Canada, the UK, the US); Arab cluster

Exhibit 3.6 Central tendencies of core cultural dimensions across regions

Country clusters	Power distribution	Social relationships	Environmental relationships	Time/work patterns	Uncertainty and social control
Anglo	Moderately egalitarian	Strongly individualistic	Strongly mastery-oriented	Strongly monochronic	Moderately rule-based
Arab	Strongly hierarchical	Strongly collectivistic	Moderately harmony-oriented	Strongly polychronic	Strongly relationship-based
East European	Moderately hierarchical	Moderately collectivistic	Moderately mastery-oriented	Moderately monochronic	Moderately relationship-based
East/Southeast Asian	Strongly hierarchical	Strongly collectivistic	Strongly harmony-oriented	Moderately monochronic	Strongly relationship-based
Germanic	Moderately egalitarian	Moderately individualistic	Moderately mastery-oriented	Moderately monochronic	Strongly rule-based
Latin American	Moderately hierarchical	Moderately collectivistic	Moderately harmony-oriented	Strongly polychronic	Strongly relationship-based
Latin European	Moderately hierarchical	Moderately collectivistic	Moderately harmony-oriented	Moderately polychronic	Moderately relationship-based
Nordic	Strongly egalitarian	Moderately individualistic	Moderately harmony-oriented	Moderately monochronic	Strongly rule-based
Sub-Sahara African	Moderately hierarchical	Strongly collectivistic	Strongly harmony-oriented	Moderately polychronic	Strongly relationship-based

Note: The country cluster categories used here are adapted from Ronan and Shenkar, "Clustering cultures or attitudinal dimensions" and House *et al.*, Culture, Leadership, and Organizations. The core cultural dimension (CCD) ratings represent central tendencies for selected country clusters (see text for details). Variations, sometimes substantial, around these central tendencies can be found in all clusters and countries. Also note that some regions of the globe (e.g., Central Asia) are not included here due to an absence of substantive data, while others (e.g., Europe) are represented in some detail due to the availability of sufficient data.

(e.g., Dubai, Egypt, Saudi Arabia); Eastern European cluster (e.g., Czech Republic, Hungary, Poland); East/Southeast Asian cluster (e.g., China, Japan, Korea, Singapore, Thailand); Germanic cluster (e.g., Austria, Germany); Latin American cluster (e.g., Argentina, Costa Rica, Mexico); Latin European cluster (e.g., France, Italy, Spain); Nordic cluster (e.g., Denmark, Norway, Sweden); and Sub-Saharan African cluster (e.g., Ghana, Kenya, Nigeria). Culture ratings for regions were then estimated.[37]

The results are shown in Exhibit 3.6. Note that these are only rough estimates based on available research. Moreover, in making use of the information presented here, it is important to recognize that no point on any assessment scale is preferred over any other; they are simply different, and that significant within-cluster variance can often be found.

While it is sometimes necessary to focus on central tendencies between cultures for purposes of general comparisons, the role of individual and regional differences in determining attitudes and behaviors should not be overlooked. Still, it should not be surprising that cultural ratings for countries in the same cluster of the world (e.g., Denmark, Norway, and Sweden) tend to be closer than ratings for countries located in a different cluster of the world (e.g., Italy, Spain, France). This is a natural consequence of contiguous countries in various regions living side-by-side with their neighbors over centuries and sometimes millennia. Still, important cultural differences can be found across peoples inhabiting a particular region. Finally, it is important to remember that, while these cultural dimensions may be a useful shortcut for gaining conceptual entry into general cultural trends across countries and regions, they are in no way a substitute for more-systematic in-depth analyses as they relate to the study of culture, work, and organizations.

Digging deeper: cultural complexities and contradictions

The related concepts of culture and cultural differences were introduced above as a means of seeing beyond overt behaviors and better understanding why and how some people act differently than others. What is often missed in these generalizations, however, is that individuals within the same society may use different strategies to deal with identical challenges. As a result, it is often unwise to stereotype an entire culture. Instead, we look for nuances and counter-trends, not just the principal trends themselves. Failure to recognize this often leads to failed personal and business opportunities.

Consider the concept of equal opportunity in the workplace. The fight for equal opportunity has been a long and difficult struggle in many nations of the world, north, south, east, and west. For many, this struggle has been quite vociferous because the underlying beliefs are so strong. What people often fail to recognize here, however, is that to a large extent societal and corporate practices regarding equal rights are embedded in our core beliefs and values. Hence, it is important to be able to compare such beliefs and practices across cultures, as well as within them. For example, some cultures stress sex role differentiation. That is, men and women are expected to play different roles in society and, as such, should be treated differently. Other cultures have increasingly stressed minimizing sex role differentiation, believing that both men and women should share both home and work responsibilities. Still other cultures strive for flexibility and tolerance. As a result of these cultural differences, many people are quick to criticize the beliefs of others as being either overly paternalistic or overly indulgent. But, for the keen observer, differences can often be found just under the surface.

To see how this works, we revisit Anna Håkansson as she arrives in Bahrain for her negotiations. Her first surprise is meeting her counterpart at Gulf One Investment Bank in Bahrain: Nahed Taher, the first woman CEO of the bank.[38] A former senior economist at the National Commercial Bank, Taher has been immersed in plans for financing public-sector projects, including expansion of the terminal that handles Mecca pilgrims at Jeddah's King Abdulaziz International Airport. She also oversees financing for a water desalination plant for Saudi Arabian Airlines, as well as Saudi copper, zinc, and gold mines. Taher may be an unusual example of an Arab executive, but she is increasingly becoming a common one. In fact, business leaders like Nahed Taher are gaining power despite the odds – ten women executives from the Middle East made the *Forbes* "World's 100 Most Powerful Women" list.

How are these women managing to break through the global glass ceiling? In many cases, the increasing globalization of the world's economy has played an important role. The economic liberalization of several Muslim countries in recent years, along with the privatization of large parts of government-run companies, has helped Muslim business-women get a greater foothold. "Now opportunities are open to everyone," says Laura Osman, the first female president of the Arab Bankers Association of North America. "The private sector runs on meritocracy." In fact, banking in the Muslim world is populated by a growing number of women, even in the historically all-male executive suite. Sahar El-Sallab is second in command at Commercial International Bank, one of Egypt's largest private banks. Indeed, four out of ten Commercial International Bank employees and 70 percent of its management staff are women. Similarly, Maha Al-Ghunaim, Chairman of Kuwait's Global Investment House, has steadily grown the investment bank she founded into more than US$7 billion in assets. It recently won permission to operate in Qatar and next wants to establish a presence in Saudi Arabia.

Muslim businesswomen also sit in the top ranks of mega-conglomerates. Imre Barmanbek runs one of Turkey's largest multinationals, Dogan Holding, which recently went through a shift in operational focus from finance to media and energy. Lubna Olayan helps oversee the Olayan Group of Saudi Arabia, one of the biggest multina-tionals in the Middle East with investments in more than forty companies. And the top ranks of the conglomerate run by the Khamis family of Egypt include several women. Originally from India, Vidya Chhabria is chairman of the United Arab Emirates' Jumbo Group, a US$2 billion multinational that operates in fifty countries, with interests in durables, chemicals, and machinery products. It also owns Jumbo Electronics, one of the Middle East's largest Sony distributors of consumer electronics, as well as worldwide brands in information technology and telecom products. Thus, while Muslim women may still have a long way to go to reach "equality" in the business world, progress can be seen. For a lucky and determined few, opportunities do exist. "Just being a woman in our part of the world is quite difficult," says El-Sallab of Egypt's Commercial

International Bank. "But if you have the proper education, credibility, and integrity in the way you handle your job, intelligent men will always give you your due."

The example of Nahed Taher and these other women managers raises an old dilemma. Even though cultural differences have been acknowledged across nation-states and regions for centuries, there is no consensus regarding the role of cultural differences in global business. Do cultural constraints really matter if people operating in a global arena are able to overcome them? When dealing with this question, most people fall into one of two groups: believers and non-believers. Believers argue that, based on available research evidence and practical experience, culture does matter because what works in London will likely not work Guangzhou, Bangalore, or Moscow. They point out that people who have worked abroad are well aware how different things can be in places around the world, and that much of this difference can only be explained by cultural characteristics. Non-believers, in turn, argue that people are different in general, and that no two Indians (or Chinese or Russians or Saudis) behave in exactly the same way. They argue further that organizations in one country can – and often must – operate very differently from those in another country. Finally, they argue that from the standpoint of research, the variance explained by culture is often small, and numerous other factors may be equally (or perhaps more) important in explaining behavioral differences across borders, including legal, political, economic differences, and available technologies.

Which of these positions is a more accurate reflection of reality, and what are the implications for global managers? While both research and practical experience suggest that culture does matter, research and practical experience also suggests that culture alone is not sufficient to explain the behavior of our foreign counterparts.[39] Otherwise, how can we explain the success of Nahed Taher in a male-dominated culture?

For this reason, we must be cautious in our interpretation of cultural phenomena. Strong preconceptions about the role (or lack thereof) of culture may blind us to the ways in which culture often does matter. Understanding the role of culture in management practice requires a way of thinking about culture that will help to identify cultural influences and inform the best course of action to deal with them. In other words, we need to understand what culture is and what it does, how our own culture has influenced our way of thinking in terms of working assumptions and personal and group biases, and how to acquire a sufficient understanding of how culture works to be able to tease out cultural influences on various situations in which we find ourselves. This is clearly no easy task, but it may nonetheless be an important one for global managers.

Exhibit 3.7 Cultural complexities and contradictions

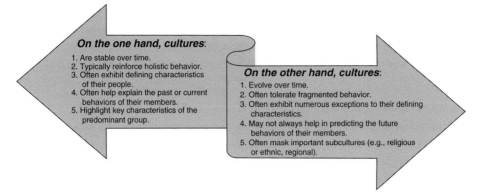

On the one hand, cultures:
1. Are stable over time.
2. Typically reinforce holistic behavior.
3. Often exhibit defining characteristics of their people.
4. Often help explain the past or current behaviors of their members.
5. Highlight key characteristics of the predominant group.

On the other hand, cultures:
1. Evolve over time.
2. Often tolerate fragmented behavior.
3. Often exhibit numerous exceptions to their defining characteristics.
4. May not always help in predicting the future behaviors of their members.
5. Often mask important subcultures (e.g., religious or ethnic, regional).

Our two examples – Sweden's Anna Håkansson and Bahrain's Nahed Tahler – highlight some important limitations of applying simplistic models to complex phenomena. On the one hand, such models provide a good starting point to understanding the influence of culture and the challenges posed by cultural differences. On the other hand, they focus our attention to a limited set of parameters and may mislead our interpretation of reality.

The *dualities perspective* – using a "both/and" logic in which both alternatives or paths have merit for purposes of analysis, rather than an "either/or" logic that forces analysts to choose between alternatives that are simultaneously worth pursuing – was introduced in Chapter 1 as a tool that often proves useful in understanding complex issues. This concept can also be applied here in regards to understanding how culture works in and across various societies. In particular, taking such an approach highlights the fact that cultures often influence attitudes and behaviors in opposites ways. This forces us to delve deeper into our study of cultures in ways that go beyond simply comparing cultural dimensions. Instead, it requires us to seek out underlying complexities and contradictions that ultimately aid in our ability to act successfully in or across very different environments. We suggest five cultural complexities and contradictions worthy of note (see Exhibit 3.7).

Cultural stability and change

One of the dangers in any attempt to categorize cultures into a set of fixed dimensions is that this implies that cultures are stable and remain unchanged. However, while some aspects of culture are indeed stable and persistent, others evolve and change over time.

That is, at the same time that groups of people strive to remain faithful to what and who they are, they simultaneously accommodate change and evolve where necessary or desirable.

Cultures change and evolve over time in response to pressures both outside and inside of society. Because cultures are learned, they are also adaptive and evolve over time in response to a myriad of external forces that can affect society. For example, Saudi women are now being allowed to drive cars – a sign, however small, that things are changing in the Middle East as they are in other parts of the world. Germany offers another example. Following the Second World War, Germany was divided into eastern and western sectors. East Germany was transformed into an authoritarian communist state, while West Germany supported democracy, individualism, and capitalism. Contacts across borders were highly restricted, particularly after the Berlin Wall was erected in the early 1960s. Over time, despite a common heritage dating back centuries, this absolute division created major cultural differences between *Ossies* (East Germans) and *Wessies* (West Germans). Following reunification almost fifty years later, both sides realized that they had grown apart culturally as well as economically. This schism still adversely affects Germany today through differences in work ethics, entrepreneurial drive, economic prosperity, and political beliefs.

On the other hand, some assumptions and beliefs are fairly stable and resist change. We may notice changes in behaviors, but the meanings and assumptions behind these behaviors are often deeply rooted in cultural values that are fairly stable. A good example of this can be found in studies of the impact of television broadcasting around the world. Television series that are aired worldwide are supposed to influence the lives of large populations across cultures with dominant Western, principally American, values. One particular study is interesting in this regard. When it was first released, the mini-series *Dallas* reached hundreds of millions of people in almost ninety countries. As a result, the annual migration of the *tuareg* in the Sahara Dessert was postponed for ten days so that local people could watch the final episodes.[40] Still, the migration occurred anyway and little changed after that.[41] People in different cultures also seek – and often find – different meanings in the same reality. Continuing with the *Dallas* example, researchers found that Dutch audiences saw not so much the pleasures of conspicuous consumption, but a reminder that money and power do not protect people from tragedy. Israeli Arabs saw confirmation that women abused by their husbands should return to their fathers. Black South Africans focused on the risks associated with sexual encounters during the late teens, while Ghanian women confirmed that men are not to be trusted.[42] One mini-series, but many different interpretations.

The implication for managers is that the cultures they must work with – including their own – are in a constant state of flux. As they come in contact with other cultures (perhaps through global organization networks), they face new problems, apply their cultural frames in different ways, negotiate new behaviors, and change important aspects of their culture, leading to behaviors that may seem contradictory. On the other hand, these changes take place within a cultural context, and the outcomes may be different than originally anticipated. Take, for example, the implementation of performance-based rewards. In many Western countries, merit pay and bonuses are (at least in theory) based largely on individual performance, while in many Asian countries they are often distributed equally to an entire group or department. It is largely a matter of equity as opposed to equality.

Scientific and technological advances in foreign cultures is another case in point. When injected with operational meaning within the framework of the culture introducing them, technical and scientific advancements preserve the original distinctiveness of the culture that adopts them. Therefore, technological diffusion does not necessarily lead to a convergence of cultures adopting the new ways. In Israel, for instance, orthodox Jews instal elevators in buildings that automatically stop on all floors during the Sabbath, so that its members do not have to press the floor keys and thereby break traditional Sabbath rules prohibiting any form of work. The technology is not only used; it is also adapted. Similarly, it is the experience of many managers in Asian countries that the adoption and diffusion of Western managerial techniques do not necessarily lead companies to adopt overall Western approaches. Instead, these innovations become new elements within their traditional overall cultural system.

Holistic and fragmented behavior

Another fundamental problem of trying to categorize cultures is that it implies a degree of homogeneity. When describing individual cultures (whether through simplified dimensions or deep descriptive analysis), we focus on shared aspects that are frequently found across the cultural group. Since cultures are shared, by definition culture includes what is common among members of a group. Members of a cultural group invest considerable time and effort in tying together the various strands that collectively represent and define social behavior.

However, cultures are also fragmented in the sense that they often allow for internal variations, and even significant discrepancies, in their midst. Despite people's tendency to stereotype, logic and personal experience suggest that variations – sometimes significant – can be found in all cultures. For example, while people often describe

Australia as a highly individualistic culture and China as a highly collectivistic culture, there are, in fact, many collectivistic Australians and many individualistic Chinese. In fact, many cultures overlap considerably with those of their neighbors, having more in common than not. These differences – and similarities – must be clearly recognized when trying to make comparisons across cultures or nations. While people often generalize about various cultures in order to facilitate a basic understanding of cultural trends, it would be highly inaccurate to conclude that all members of any culture behave in the same way.

Cultural fragmentation, however, does not lead to a complete disintegration of a society. Cultures still remain overall systems of meanings that can help us make sense of experienced variations. The behavior of cultural outliers, for example, remains largely unexplainable except against the backdrop of their own cultural backgrounds. In the end, because cultures are simultaneously fragmented and systemic, holistic and heterogeneous, even the extreme behaviors of outliers can be explained by the fact that such individuals are simultaneously reacting against and within their own cultures.

Consider Commercial International Bank's Sahar El-Sallab's observation (above) that "if you have the proper education, credibility, and integrity in the way you handle your job, intelligent men will always give you your due."[43] That is, within a cultural context there are ways – perhaps only transparent to people within that culture – in which cultural constraints can be overcome. Only by understanding the cultural context in which behaviors occur can outsiders understand the behaviors that will be considered proper or acceptable across nation-states and those that are likely to be very different in Cairo, London, and New York. In other words, we may find fragmentation of behaviors within cultures, but even these behaviors are imbued with cultural meaning.

Universal and idiosyncratic characteristics

Descriptions of culture using a limited set of dimensions may lead to the impression that this limited set of adjectives can capture the essence of culture. However, experience and observation tells us that culture is more complex and paradoxical, with many exceptions and qualifications to any general classification.[44] All cultures contain defining elements that defy universal qualifications. Examples include the Latino notion of *orgullo*, or pride for the accomplishments of their people; the Brazilian *jeitinho*, or flexible adaptability; and the Japanese *kao*, or face (*kao o tateru* for saving face). These unique aspects of culture are enmeshed in and derived from unique historical experiences and responses and are not fully captured by general categories and descriptions, which fail to acknowledge the intricacies of the meaning of the concepts.

For example, while most people would agree that US culture is largely individualistic, the general classification of individualism versus collectivism fails to capture important nuances underlying this defining characteristic that is often captured in the American vernacular by the term "pioneering spirit." For example, consider George Washington's fabled boyhood response when questioned regarding his responsibility for the felling of a cherry tree, "I cannot tell a lie." This response and the actions that preceded it highlight not only the value of truthfulness that American parents attempt to impart to their children, but also a strong pattern of individual choice and action characteristic of the culture. The parable does not indicate that one should consider other's feelings, ask before taking action, or apologize for past actions taken. Rather, it suggests, as does a well-known American axiom, that it is acceptable to "act first, and ask questions later" as long as one takes individual responsibility for one's actions. It is this individual initiative, decisiveness, risk-taking, and responsibility that are conveyed by the term "pioneer spirit", not just individualism.

Going one step further, the conception of individualism as active initiative and responsibility is much more nuanced than the conception portrayed by the general categories of individualism and collectivism, which also cannot explain apparent con-tradictions. For example, American pop and media culture is rife with admiring stories of those who sacrifice for others, such as a soldier who falls on a grenade to save his comrades. While such self-sacrificial action is at odds with a global value of the individual over the group, it is highly consistent with the pattern of individual initiative, decision making, action, and responsibility that is, again, incorporated into the American concept of pioneer spirit. Hence, intelligent managers will avoid simple solutions and look for the nuances underlying categorizations, not just the rhetoric.

Explanatory and predicative powers

A discussion of culture frequently leads to an exaggerated assumption of causality and determinism. It is easy to make connections between general cultural characteristics and actions, such as "People from collectivistic cultures will prefer team work" or "Hierarchical cultures prefer authoritarian leaders." However, these types of conclusions are problematic for several reasons. To begin with, as it was discussed above, fragmenta-tion can result from the acceptance of cultural values within cultures. Second, cultures are composed of idiosyncratic elements that can be combined in unique ways leading to unpredictable consequences. And third, culture both constrains and enables behavior.

Culture provides frameworks for making sense of the world around us, for learning and expanding our horizons. These frameworks are important for interpreting phenomena around us, communicating with others, and organizing social and psycho-logical processes.[45] These cultural frameworks limit the array of alternatives considered by members. In the words of Yi-Fu Tuan, a founding figure of the field of human geography, "all cultures are flawed blinders as well as the source of unique illumina-tions; they deserve affection rather than idolatry; they are our first home rather than the last."[46] Simply put, culture is an important source of biases in the way we interpret the world and choose to act. Understanding these biases may help us explain why people in different places make different decisions. This may help explain, for example, why women in the Arab world are less active in the workplace than Western women.

However, cultural biases may be overcome either by individual effort, such as the example of Nahed Taher and other Arab women who were able to succeed in a male-dominated environment. Similarly, changes in the environment may lead to different behaviors. Personal computers are a wonderful tool for engineers exploring for minerals and oil, unless the engineers find themselves in a region of the globe that does not support such technology. Similarly, culture provides us with guidelines to help us navigate situations, but these situations themselves will often influence the choice of behavior. In other words, the way a person communicates may change significantly when this person is communicating with a boss or a friend, or just by a change in the context around her, such as finding herself in a foreign culture.

Furthermore, these biases are not necessarily a bad thing. In some situations, they may be an asset and an important source of creativity for global companies. As different cultures come in contact with different perspectives, novel solutions may emerge. When combined, the dynamism of cultural frames and their interaction with the environment may lead to apparently paradoxical behaviors. In short, it is very difficult for managers to predict the behavior of their foreign counterparts. Anna Håkansson's efforts as described in the beginning of this chapter may have helped her understand the general-ities of the culture, but they did not provide any guidance in how to deal with Nahed Taher. As such, culture influences, rather than determines, action. Individuals within cultures are able to "use" cultural elements strategically and "negotiate" new cultural arrangements.[47]

Cultures and subcultures

Finally, as noted earlier, a key characteristic of culture is that it is learned. People acquire values, assumptions, and behaviors by seeing how others around us behave and by observing their families. However, herein lies a major source for over-generalizations and stereotypes about national cultures. This is because most people within one culture belong to multiple, and often conflicting, subcultures. Subcultures can include levels of education (intellectual culture), professions or specializations (professional culture), normative beliefs about right and wrong and organized religion (religious culture), places of work (organizational culture), geographic locations within a country (regional culture), and so forth. What this means is that people can also acquire additional cultural tools from the various subcultures to which we belong. Culture is a collective, socially constructed phenomenon that exists or emerges whenever a set of basic assumptions or beliefs is commonly held by a group of people.[48] Thus, multiple subcultures co-exist within organizations, industries, and nations.[49] Cultural makeup is thus layered and influenced by varied group memberships. These subcultures may be overlapping, superimposed, or nested, and may interact with each other. These multiple layers of culture shape individuals' attention, interpretations, and actions, and the cultural layer that is salient can vary over time.[50] As such, in a single point in time, people simultaneously belong to one culture and many cultures, making the study of cultural differences even more problematic.

Culture, values, and worldviews

We have now come full circle from looking for general dimensions with which to compare cultures to understanding that cultures are indeed complex and at times contradictory. Cultures are not easily pigeonholed into groups and categories. And as Edward Hall notes, "culture hides much more than it reveals, and strangely enough what it hides, it hides most effectively from its own participants."[51] Caution is certainly in order.

Added to this is an understanding of the important role that culture and context play in influencing managerial action. These complexities and contradictions raise the intriguing question of how managers should act or react when they find themselves in the middle of cultural tension or change. A major challenge here is that different cultures often require very different behaviors from their managers, and what is acceptable in one country may be offensive in another. This is not surprising, but it nevertheless presents real challenges for managers when interacting with – and sometimes managing – a global workforce (see Chapter 9). How should managers behave, and will they be accepted when they are charged with accomplishing corporate objectives in a foreign culture? Should managers be themselves or try to adapt their management style to fit local customs and expectations? And, fundamentally, how can they survive and succeed when they don't understand the rules of the game, and the rules that they do understand are often changing or do not apply to the specific individuals or contexts they are dealing with?

To aid in this understanding, we can summarize several coping strategies that may help managers as they try and make sense out of the "strange" behaviors of others. More specifically, we discuss three challenges: avoiding cultural stereotyping, seeing cultures in neutral terms, and preparing for the unexpected.

Avoiding cultural stereotypes

To this end, understanding the influence of culture on management practices is an important first step. One wonders what perceptions Anna Håkansson and Nahed Taher may have had of each other. Managers that are able to understand the ways that culture can influence behavior and have the knowledge of how cultures differ are better able to identify cultural phenomena and identify solutions to deal with it. In this regard, the role of *cultural stereotypes* is clearly relevant.

McGill professor Nancy Adler offers some sound advice on how to avoid making over-generalizations or cultural stereotypes about the people from any culture.[52] First, cultural descriptions by their very nature contain limited information. Keep in mind that such generalizations often mask other useful information about cultural diversity. Second, cultural descriptions should be limited to describing members of various groups as objectively as possible and should not include an evaluative component (e.g., this is good, that is bad). Third, cultural descriptions should provide an accurate description of the beliefs, values, and social norms of a group. Fourth, cultural descriptions should be considered a first best guess about the behaviors of a cultural group prior to developing more specific information about individual members of the group. Finally, cultural descriptions should be modified over time, based on new information gained through observation or experience.

When describing cultures and identifying cultural differences between two or more groups, some caution may be in order for at least two reasons. First, while common sense would suggest that bigger cultural differences are harder to deal with than smaller ones, experience suggests that this is not always the case. In some cases, managers moving between countries perceived as culturally similar (e.g., the Netherlands and Belgium) frequently find that "small" differences are just as hard to deal with as big ones. Worse, such small differences are frequently overlooked and not dealt with until some damage is done. On the other hand, what may initially seem like a large cultural difference may be overcome by some smaller similarities. For instance, in a recent joint venture between a Brazilian and a Chinese company (two very different cultures), members found sources of similarity that facilitated the relationship, such as the similar levels of development and the importance of context and relationships in partnerships. In the words of one Brazilian managing director, "The Chinese are the Brazilians of Asia."[53]

Seeing cultural differences in neutral terms

In addition, cultural differences are not a bad thing in the managerial world; they just require a bit more work at times. In many cases, depending on the task at hand, a degree of cultural difference is often seen as leading to improved managerial decision making and action. For example, a recent study found that Portuguese managers perceived business activities with Brazilians and Spaniards (with whom they are culturally more similar) to be riskier and more difficult than with Scandinavians (culturally very different). However, the same managers felt more "at home" and preferred to socialize and make friends with Brazilians and Spaniards.[54]

What this suggests is that cultural differences are not inherently good or bad, but they can be perceived positively or negatively depending on the situation. Additionally, sometimes differences are not perceived the same way by both ends. A manager from Portugal may appreciate Danish punctuality, while the Danish manager may find Portuguese tardiness annoying. On the other hand, the Danish manager may appreciate Portuguese flexibility (particularistic or low rule orientation), while the Portuguese manager may find the Danish obsession with rules frustrating.

Most importantly, it is difficult to predict how these identifiable differences will play out when two cultures meet. As a starting point, cultural frameworks create limitations on our ability to think and perceive the environment, suggesting that individuals from different cultures will have different understandings of the situation, and will likely act differently. However, as individuals interact with each other and the new environment around them, new understandings may emerge and new behaviors may be called for. It would be naïve to think that in a cross-cultural situation, individuals would continue behaving in the same way they would at home for a long period of time. Overtime, either they will negotiate a new way to relate or the relationship will not continue. Unfortunately, it is impossible to predict what will work for a particular context and relationship, since several other factors besides culture come into play. For example, who has power? Who is the majority? Who has the money? What is the personality of the ones in power? What is the goal of the relationship? Are there historical issues as well between both cultural groups that may lead to predispositions, perceptions of superiority, inferiority, or sameness? Referring to the Chinese-Brazilian partnership above, a Chinese manager noted,

> My opinion is that working with Brazilians is easier than working with North Americans, with French, or even with people from Singapore. It's amazing because people from Singapore have the same cultural roots that we have. But with Brazilians, it's easier because we treat each other as being on the same level. This may be more important than having the same cultural roots or speaking the same language.[55]

Simply put, when two or more cultures come in contact, the starting point for interaction is usually what these cultures bring to the table. But the end result will more likely depend on their interactions, the actors and organizations involved, the power differential, and the exchanges that take place. Management researchers Oded Shenkar, Yadong Lou, and Orly Yeheskel, coming from three very different cultures themselves, call this process *cultural friction*, referring to the resistances and conflicts that need to be dealt with as two cultures come into contact, including issues of organizational identities, national identities, differences in resources and interests, and asymmetry in power and hierarchy.[56] These issues are dealt with and negotiated in a process of response and counter-response that will shape the relationship between the parties.

Preparing for the unexpected

Finally, when facing the complexities of cultural influences and the unpredictability of cultural encounters, an obvious question emerges: What can global managers do? An often overlooked response to this difficult question rests on the speed with which managers can learn and adjust their behavior to fit each unique situation. Here, we do not mean adjusting the behavior to fit the other culture; we mean adjusting the behavior to fit the situation. Sometimes, what is in order is adjusting to the other culture as closely as possible. But at other times, this behavior would be counterproductive (e.g., perhaps we really should avoid considering Nahed Taher as a traditional Arab woman). Knowing the difference is what separates successful global managers from the rest. To this end, several important learning skills can be suggested for global managers:[57]

- *Self-awareness*. Global mangers must understand that they are complex cultural beings and that their values, beliefs, assumptions, and communication preferences are a product of their cultural heritage.
- *Empathy*. Global managers must understand that others are also complex cultural beings whose actions are a product of deep-seated cultural values and beliefs. When misunderstandings occur, competent global managers will search for cultural explanations of confusing or offensive behavior, before judging it.
- *Information gathering and analysis*. Managers must uncover hidden cultural assumptions to become aware of how culture is shaping the perceptions, expectations, and behaviors of all involved parties.
- *Information integration and transformation*. Managers must assimilate the information gathered into a coherent theory of action.
- *Behavioral flexibility*. Managers need the ability to engage in different behaviors, to switch styles, and to accomplish tasks in more than one way.
- *Mindfulness*. Global managers must be mindful of themselves, the other, and the interaction. They must pay close attention to their feelings and actions, and others' actions and reactions.

In summary, managers must be keenly aware of their biases (and the biases of others) in their ways of looking at the world. This is not easy because it requires a continual effort to move from our own perspective to the perspectives of others – or, at least, to try to do so). Understanding others requires and allows us to de-center our points of views, thereby expanding our personal worldviews. French philosopher Gilles Deleuze refers to this concept as "being another thought in my thoughts, another possession in my possessions."[58] Throughout the remainder of the book, we will discuss in detail several ways in which culture matters, highlighting how culture leads to different perspectives and understandings, and their implication for management practice. It is our hope that these discussions will help managers identify their own biases in management understanding and facilitate the recognition of potential cultural problems on the ground.

Notes

1 The *Talmud* is a record of rabbinical discussions pertaining to Jewish law, ethics, customs, and history. Two versions exist from the two ancient centers of Jewish scholarship, Palestine and Babylonia. Correspondingly, two bodies of analysis developed, and two works of the *Talmud* were created. The older compilation is called the Jerusalem Talmud (*Talmud Yerushalmi*) and was compiled sometime during the fourth century BCE in the land of Israel. The Babylonian Talmud (*Talmud Bavli*) was compiled about the year 500 CE, although it continued to be edited over time. The word *Talmud*, when used without qualification, usually refers to the Babylonian Talmud.

2 Robert J. House, "Introduction," in Robert J. House, Paul J. Hanges, Mansour Javidan, Peter W. Dorfman, and Vipin Gupta, *Culture, Leadership, and Organizations: The GLOBE Study of 62 Societies*. Thousand Oaks, CA: Sage, 2004, p. 1.

3 Herbert Giles, translation of Wang Ying-lin, *Trimetric Classic*. Shanghai: Kelly & Walsh, 1910. The *Three Character Classic, Trimetric Classic* or *San Zi Jing* (traditional Chinese: 三字經; simplified Chinese: 三字经) is one of the classic Chinese texts. It was probably written in the thirteenth century and attributed to Wang Yinglin (王應麟, 1223–1296) during the Song Dynasty, but has also been attributed to Ou Shizi (區適子, 1234–1324). Some writers have attributed the original wisdom collected in this volume to Confucius, although there is no conclusive evidence on this.

4 Lao-Tzu, or Laozi (Chinese: 老子; pinyin: *Lǎozǐ*), was a philosopher of ancient China and is a central figure in Taoism. *Laozi* literally means "Old Master" and is generally considered an honorific. Laozi is revered as a god in religious forms of Taoism. *Taishang Laojun* is a title for Laozi in the Taoist religion, which refers to him as "One of the Three Pure Ones."

5 Elizabeth MacDonald and Megha Bahree, "Muslim women in charge," *Forbes*, July 30, 2008.

6 Faiza Saleh Ambah, "Saudi women rise in defense of the veil," *The Washington Post*, June 1, 2006, p. A12.

7 *Shura* is Arabic for consultation. It is believed to be the method by which pre-Islamic Arabian tribes selected leaders and made major decisions. *Shura* is mentioned twice in the Qur'an as a praiseworthy activity, and is a word often used in the name of parliaments in Muslim-majority countries.

8 "*Ijma`*" is an Arabic term referring ideally to the consensus of the *ummah*, the community of Muslims or followers of Islam.

9 The *Qur'an*, literally "the recitation" in Arabic and sometimes transliterated as *Quran*, *Qur'ān*, *Koran*, *Alcoran* or *Al-Qur'ān`*, is the central religious text of Islam. Muslims believe the *Qur'an* to be the book of divine guidance and direction for mankind, and consider the original Arabic text to be the final revelation of God. *Sunnah* literally means "trodden path," and therefore, the *sunnah* of the prophet means "the way and the manners of the prophet." The word in Sunni Islam means those religious achievements that were instituted by the Islamic prophet Muhammad during the twenty-three years of his ministry and which Muslims initially obtained through consensus of companions of Muhammad, and further through generation-to-generation transmission.

10 Geert Hofstede, *Culture's Consequence: International Differences in Work Related Values*. Thousand Oaks, CA: Sage, 2001.

11 *Ibid.*

12 Clyde Kluckholn, "Culture and behavior," in Grahm Lindzey (ed.), *Handbook of Social Psychology*. New York, NY: McGraw-Hill, 1951, pp. 921–976.

13 House, *et al.*, *Culture, Leadership, and Organizations*.

14 Fons Trompenaars and Charles Hampden-Turner, *Riding the Waves of Culture: Understanding Cultural Diversity in Global Business*. London: McGraw-Hill, 1998.

15 Ann Swidler, "Culture in action: symbols and strategies," *American Sociological Review*, 1986, 51(2), p. 273.

16 Clifford Geertz, *The Interpretation of Cultures*. New York, NY: Basic Books, 1973.

17 Alice Dembner, "Fears of aging vary by nation," *Register-Guard*, November 6, 2007, p. A12.

18 Thomas Catan, "Spain's showy debt collectors wear tux, collect the bucks," *The Wall Street Journal*, October 11, 2008, p. 1.

19 Our account of Islamic banking and finance follows Mervyn Lewis and Latifa Algaoud, *Islamic Banking*. Cheltenham, UK: Edward Elgar, 2001.

20 We follow the electronic version of Mohammed H. Shakir's *Koran* translation here, available from the Library of the University of Virginia, at http://etext.virginia.edu/koran.html.

21 *Mudaraba* refers to an investment on a person's behalf by someone skilled in finance. It typically takes the form of a contract between two parties, one who provides the funds and the other who provides the expertise, and who agree to the division of any profits made in advance. In other words, banks such as the Islamic Bank of Britain would make *Sharia*-compliant investments and share the profits with the customer, in effect charging for the time and effort. If no profit is made, the loss is borne by the customer and the Islamic Bank of Britain would take no fee.

22 *Musharaka* means partnership. It involves a person placing their capital with another person and both sharing the risk and reward. The difference between *musharaka* arrangements and normal banking is that the person with the capital can set any kind of profit-sharing ratio, but losses must be proportionate to the amount invested.

23 "*Halal*" (also *halāl* or *Halaal*) is an Arabic term designating any object or action is permissible to use or engage in, according to Islamic law and custom. It is the opposite of

haraam. The term is widely used to designate food seen as permissible according to Islamic law. It is estimated that 70 percent of Muslims worldwide follow *halal* food standards and that the global *halal* market is currently a US$580 billion industry.

24 *Zakāh* means "alms for the poor" in Arabic, and represents the Islamic principle of giving a percentage of one's income to charity. It is often compared to the system of tithing and alms, but unlike these other systems it serves principally as the welfare contribution to poor and deprived people in the Muslim lands, although others may have a rightful share. It is the duty of the state not just to collect it, but to distribute it to the needy as fairly as possible. *Zakāh* is one of the Five Pillars of Islam.

25 Chris Carr and Markus Pudelko, "Convergence of management practices in strategy, finance, and HRM between the USA, Japan, and Germany," *International Journal of Cross Cultural Management*, 2006, 6(1), pp. 75–100.

26 Sidney J. Gray, "Cultural perspective on the measurement of corporate success," *European Management Journal*, 1995, 13(3), pp. 269–275.

27 Sidney J. Gray, "Towards a theory of cultural influence on the development of accounting systems internationally," *Abacus*, March 1988.

28 Sidney J. Gray, Stephen B. Salter, and Lee H. Radebaugh, *Global Accounting and Control: A Managerial Emphasis*. New York, NY: John Wiley, p. 121.

29 Edward T. Hall, *An Anthropology of Everyday Life: An Autobiography*. New York, NY: Anchor, 1992, p. 210.

30 See Luciara Nardon and Richard M. Steers, "The culture theory jungle: divergence and convergence in models of national culture," in Rabi S. Bhagat and Richard M. Steers (eds.), *Cambridge Handbook of Culture, Organizations, and Work*. Cambridge, UK: Cambridge University Press, 2009.

31 Nardon and Steers, "The culture theory jungle."

32 Steve Stecklow, "Helsinki on wheels: fast Finns find fines fit their finances," *The Wall Street Journal*, January 2, 2001, p. A1; "Rich Finn gets hefty fine for speeding," *Register-Guard*, February 11, 2004, p. A3.

33 John Hooker, *Working Across Cultures*. Stanford, CA: Stanford Business Books, 2003.

34 *Ibid.*

35 Simcha Ronan and Oded Shenkar, "Clustering cultures on attitudinal dimensions: a review and synthesis," *Academy of Management Review*, 1985, 10, pp. 435–454.

36 House *et al.*, *Culture, Leadership, and Organizations*.

37 Based on the country clusters, and using multiple measures and multiple methods to the extent possible, we assessed and then integrated a combination of quantitative and qualitative measures from available research in order to categorize cultures along the five dimensions. First, existing quantitative measures from such researchers as Hofstede, Trompenaars, and House and his GLOBE associates were examined and compared. Next, ethnographic data compiled largely from cultural anthropology focusing on specific cultures or geographic regions were incorporated into the analysis and compared against the quantitative findings. Finally, remaining points of disagreement were discussed between the co-authors and other researchers in an effort to reach a consensus on the final ratings. While it is not claimed that

this procedure eliminated all errors, it is felt it represents a superior method to the previous reliance on single-source data. Still, room for error persists, in particular due to the potential rater bias of the authors, and readers are cautioned to use their own judgment in interpreting results. In making our assessments, we chose to develop a more conservative ordinal rating scale, clustering cultures into four categories (e.g., strongly individualistic, moderately individualistic, moderately collectivistic, and strongly collectivistic) based on the relative strength of the various dimensions compared to other cultures, instead of attempting to calculate specific numeric (or cardinal) ratings that may appear to be more precise than they actually are.

38 MacDonald and Bahree, "Muslim women in charge."

39 Kwok Leung, Rabi Bhagat, Nancy Buchan, Miliam Erez, and Christine Gibson, "Culture and international business: recent advances and their implications for future research," *Journal of International Business Studies*, 2005, 36(4), p. 357.

40 The *Tuareg* are a nomadic pastoralist people, and are the principal inhabitants of the Saharan interior of North Africa. They call themselves "the free people" or the "people of the veil." They are found mostly today in West Africa, but, like many in Northern Africa, were once nomads throughout the Sahara. They have a little-used but ancient script known as the *tifina*.

41 H. R. Sontag and N. Arenas, "Lo global, lo local, lo híbrido: aproximaciones a una discusión que comienza," in R. Pajuelo and P. Sandoval (eds.), *Globalización y Diversidad Cultural*. Lima: Instituto de Estudios Peruanos, 2004, p. 71.

42 Kwame A. Appiah, *Cosmopolitanism: Ethics in a World of Strangers*. New York, NY: Norton, 2006, pp. 109–111.

43 McDonald and Bahree, "Muslim women in charge."

44 Alan Bird and Joyce S. Osland, "Teaching cultural sense-making", in Nakiye Boyacigiller, Richard Goodman, and Margaret Phillips (eds.), *Crossing Cultures: Insights from Master Teachers*. London: Routledge, 2003, pp. 89–100.

45 Seyla Benhabib, *The Claims of Culture: Equality and Diversity in the Global Era*. Princeton, NJ: Princeton University Press, 2002, p. 15.

46 Yi-Fu Tuan, *Cosmos and Hearth: A Cosmopolite's Viewpoint*. Minneapolis, MN: University of Minnesota Press, 1996, p. 132.

47 Luciara Nardon and Richard M. Steers, "The new global manager: learning cultures on the fly," *Organizational Dynamics*, 2008, 37, pp. 47–59.

48 Edgar Schein, *Organizational Culture and Leadership*. San Francisco, CA: Jossey-Bass, 2004.

49 Sonja Sackmann and Margaret E. Phillips, "Contextual influences on culture research," *International Journal of Cross Cultural Management*, 2004, 4(3), pp. 370–390.

50 Susan Schneider and Jean-Louis Barsoux, *Managing Across Cultures*. London: Financial Times/Prentice Hall, 2003.

51 Edward T. Hall, *The Silent Language*. New York: Anchor, 1990, p. 29.

52 Nancy Adler, *International Dimensions of Organizational Behavior*. Mason, OH: Thompson, 2008.

53 Guilherme Azevedo, "Brazilian management in China and a theory of the formation of hybrid organizational cultures," paper presented at the European Group of Organizations Studies (EGOS) conference, Amsterdam, the Netherlands, 2008.

54 Susana Costa e Silva and Luciara Nardon, "An exploratory study of cultural differences and perceptions of relational risk," paper presented at the European International Business Academy conference, Catania, Italy, 2007.

55 Azevedo, "Brazilian management in China."

56 Oded Shenkar, Yadong Luo, and Orly Yeheskel, "From distance to friction: substituting metaphors and redirecting intercultural research," *Academy of Management Review*, 2008, 33, pp. 905–922

57 Nardon and Steers, "The new global manager."

58 M. Hopenhayn, "La aldea global entre la utopía transcultural y el ratio mercantil: Paradojas de la globalización cultural," in Pajuelo and Sandoval, *Globalización y Diversidad Cultural*, pp. 423–424.

CHAPTER 4

Inside the managerial mind: culture, cognition, and action

- Culture, cognition, and managerial action: a model   88
- Patterns of managerial thinking   91
- The geography of thought   96
- Culture and the managerial role   102
- Management patterns across cultures   106
- Are management patterns converging?   115
- MANAGER'S NOTEBOOK: Inside the managerial mind   118

You get very different thinking if you sit in Shanghai or São Paulo or Dubai than if you sit in New York.

Michael Cannon-Brookes[1]
Vice President, Business Development – India and China, IBM Corporation

Much of management theory is based on the writings of 20th century Western scholars whose disciplinary orientations were heavily grounded in economics and classical sociology. Their writings depict people as being individualistic, utility maximizing, transaction-oriented. In point of fact, people are social and communal beings. Along with rationality, they are also guided by emotions. By acknowledging this, global management discourse can evolve more holistic and inclusive theories.

Mzamo P. Mangaliso[2]
President, National Research Foundation, South Africa

This chapter addresses a simple question: What do managers do – and why? As we shall see, while this question may be simple and straightforward, the answer is far more complex. On the surface, most managers look pretty much alike. Some are Asian, some are Anglo, some are Latino, and so forth. Some are men; some are women. Yet regardless of their outward appearance, we often assume – incorrectly, as Mzamo Mangaliso points out – that these people are basically the same on the inside when they manage. A manager is a manager is a manager. Indeed, we often believe that we can define the roles of managers in ways that transcend cultural differences.

Such is not the case, as noted by Honda Motor Company co-founder Takeo Fujisawa, who points out that "Japanese and American management is 95% the same, and differs in all important respects."[3] And Michael Cannon-Brookes, IBM's Vice President for business development for China and India, reinforces this conclusion with his observation that patterns of managerial thinking often differ across borders. Cultural patterns and belief structures frequently influence managerial perceptions (what managers see), managerial cognitions (what they think), and managerial actions (what they do). And if this is correct, then it necessarily follows that prepared managers understand how such differences can affect their relationships – and success – with partners and competitors sitting on the other side of the global table. To see how this works, consider Kia Motors America.

On a chilly winter morning, senior executives at the California-based headquarters of Kia left their warm offices to stand outside in near-freezing cold to await the arrival of Byung Mo Ahn, the President of Korea-based Kia Motors. The group organized itself into a receiving line and stayed in formation until Ahn arrived in a chauffeur-driven Kia Amanti. Although some of the executives were shivering, it would have been impolite to return inside. Standing to greet top brass has always been an important ritual for Kia, and its parent company Hyundai Motors, even in the US. Upon his arrival, Ahn thanked the executives for their excellent work and for Kia's recent successes. Three day's later, at the end of his visit, Ahn performed another ritual that has become commonplace at Kia and Hyundai: he fired the entire American leadership team.[4]

This marked the fourth major shake-up of Kia's US operations in three years – and the fourth in five years for its sister company, Hyundai Motors. Each time, the pattern is the same: executives are fired either en route to or during the company's annual meeting with its dealers. Context is as important as content, and few people miss the message.

In addition to the myriad of former executives, many Americans who stay often complain that Hyundai's (and Kia's) corporate culture is suffocating. According to several current and former managers, Hyundai Chairman Chung Mong Koo, Kia's President Ahn, and other top executives run the company in a far more authoritarian way than do most American CEOs. These critics add that their Korean overseers micromanage too many details, rarely listen to advice from local managers, and display little tolerance for disagreement. "It's a very feudal approach to management," noted one former Hyundai sales executive. "There's a king, he rules, and everyone curries his favor. It's very militaristic."

However, while Chung's top-down management style rubs many Americans the wrong way, his long-term track record in the US is impressive. Under his leadership, Hyundai

Motors has nearly doubled its sales in the recent years, as has Kia. Chung has won considerable praise for creating a highly disciplined company. When quality complaints began to plague Hyundai several years ago, he ordered engineers to attack the problem with vigor. Within four years, the company had soared from the bottom to the top of US national automobile rankings in quality and customer satisfaction surveys, like J. D. Powers. Unlike Detroit's Big Three, Hyundai and Kia have fewer management layers to hold up decisions. "I can see where Americans would feel uncomfortable," says MIT economics professor Alice Amsden. "American management is used to a different style, but Hyundai deserves a lot of credit for what they have accomplished."[5]

Indeed, boldness is an integral part of Hyundai Motor's DNA. From its beginning in 1947, Hyundai's owners have followed a simple strategy: Build factories first, worry about sales later. In the US, Kia and Hyundai Motors establish sales targets based on what their auto plants can produce, not what the market wants – a persistent source of tension with local managers. At its core, Hyundai has always had the mindset of a manufacturer, not a marketer. As one Hyundai critic observed, "What they need in the US is to let American executives implement marketing strategy in a sustainable way."[6]

US managers have also expressed resentment towards the so-called coordinators, Korean overseers whose job it is to keep an eye on US managers. Culled from the ranks of up-and-coming stars in Seoul, they sit alongside US managers, monitoring decision making and results. They must agree to all major decisions – and sometimes even minor ones, such as whether to award vacations to dealers who hit sales goals. (Japanese automakers also have coordinators in their US operations, but they play more of an advisory role while the US executives typically have free reign to make major decisions.) A Kia spokesperson responded to this criticism by noting that the coordinators serve a valuable purpose: bringing the corporate vision from Seoul to the US, then relaying the needs of the local market back to headquarters. Since few American employees speak Korean, the coordinators also act as translators. While acknowledging that Kia has a Confucian-influenced corporate culture in which "father knows best," the company spokesperson argued that coordinators were not the principal source of conflict with US executives. Instead, he attributed the tension to Korean managers' greater comfort with "stretch goals" than their American counterparts. At the moment, the stretch goals seem to be stressing the US managers to the breaking point.

The example of Kia illustrates several points. Perhaps above all else, it illustrates how assumptions about management, management responsibilities, and management prerogatives can differ significantly across national borders. As such, while it may be easy to gain agreement on a definition of management as a general concept, agreeing on the details can be quite another matter. As is often said in such situations, the devil is in the details. In other words, management on the ground is not always the management we anticipate or expect to see.

This example also raises a number of questions about the nature, scope, and style of management. Specifically, who is doing a better job building a North American automobile market: the Koreans or the Americans? Beyond Kia, and looking to managers more generally, are there specific managerial characteristics that transcend most borders? Do most managers basically perform the same tasks, or do these tasks vary across nationalities and cultures. If they do vary, how does the work get done? Finally, in the face of increased globalization, is the world moving towards a relatively common (or "globalized") management style that will ultimately transcend most cultures, or will cultural differences continue to play a major role in determining managerial behavior? Questions such as these get to the heart of the meaning of management.

Culture, cognition, and managerial action: a model

People learn a great deal from their histories and traditions. Old accounts from settlers and explorers, immigrants and slaves, historians and public figures illustrate earlier incarnations of local cultures and inform current generations about what differentiates one culture from another. One such account from Spain illustrates nicely the relationship between culture and cognition. The story goes that in 1526, an Aztec scribe was told by a Spanish colonial official to keep a record of all of the items collected in tribute for the King of Spain. The scribe carefully entered each item he inventoried into its appropriate category: gold quills, cotton and feathered robes, fine and coarse stones, cacao beans, and so forth. After several weeks, the Spanish official visited the scribe to check his progress. He examined the long lists with increasing perplexity, commenting in anger that all the record keeping was worthless since he could not find the amounts of gold, silver, or precious stones. The scribe answered that he had kept the records the way they always had, up to the smallest item, in clear categories: all the durable items were listed first, followed by round objects, flat objects, cylindrical objects, and hard objects. The official did not know how to react to such a curious (and, in his view, obviously useless) explanation. He personally knew the scribe to be an honest and intelligent man, but the result was completely out of line with the whole purpose of the assignment.[7]

Global managers often find themselves in situations similar to those of the Spanish official or the Aztec scribe when dealing with people from other cultures. There is something in how many "foreigners" make sense of reality that can easily interfere with both our understanding of what is going on, as well as any possible collaboration across cultures. Despite the oft cited commonalities in mental capability and functioning among all humans, all too often our mental processes seem to work towards separating rather than uniting people. Experienced managers have learned that unless they can make sense of the *mental screens* that separate people from different cultures, their work is likely going to be painful, ineffective, and time-consuming. To get beyond these screens, managers need to understand how culture can influence the actual functioning of the managerial mind.

If we ask psychology and management experts to identify the process by which people acquire, transform, and utilize information about the world in order to achieve their goals, it is likely that psychologists will call it cognition, while managers will call it management. And both would be right. Management requires an understanding of what lies behind action. More specifically, it requires knowledge about how our minds function, how the minds of others function, and how can we relate our mental patterns to the patterns of others within an organizational context. This is an important point. We cannot deal successfully with others if we do not understand them. As such, here we begin to see how and why the minds of managers and employees in different cultures work in ways that are simultaneously similar and dissimilar.

The existence of cultural variations in *cognitive processes* may sound a bit strange to people who have given the topic little thought. However, to put this topic into perspective, consider that the human brain at birth weighs only about one-fourth of what it does when people reach young adulthood, when the physical maturation of the brain is complete. As a result, three-quarters of the human brain – including almost all of its cognitive development – occurs outside the womb and in contact with its surrounding external environment, in culturally influenced and constrained settings.[8] As such, culture and cognition can be seen – and perhaps best understood – in terms of an interactive relationship between thought and action in which culturally determined thought processes influence our behaviors, which, in turn, often reinforce or challenge our thoughts and beliefs. Individuals cannot be fully understood in isolation from their environments, and culture and cognition go hand in hand in any effort to understand how people think and behave in organizational settings.

Culture and cognition affect each other both through time and contact with other people, and both ultimately affect employee attitudes and behaviors. Our knowledge about the world is not just pure knowledge of something outside ourselves, but rather knowledge of something outside ourselves as related to something else. It is both objective and subjective – and certainly relative. In this regard, it is easy to understand the famous paradox suggested by British philosopher George Berkeley concerning how something can simultaneously appear to our senses to be both cold and warm depending on whether we touch it with a warm or a cold hand.

This interplay between the objective "out-there" and the subjective "in-here" can be linked to culturally learned behaviors that lead us to choose one way of viewing and evaluating something over another. Simple activities in life assume a culturally acceptable approach of thinking about them, and departures from this approach are often not without risk. Working in an investment bank in London and New York, for example, can be both frustrating and career limiting for employees who reject beliefs in open markets and capitalism. The work cultures of both The City and Wall Street would tend to force such individuals out instead of tolerating attitudes or behaviors that run contrary to the prevailing norms and values. The same can be seen in national cultures, where outliers are routinely ostracized, punished, or worse.

In trying to understand how this works in social situations, including in the business world, we can identify at least three cognitive processes at play in even very simple situations (see Exhibit 4.1). First, we experience events in the external world; we choose what to see and what not to see. This is called *perceptual selection*. Second, we categorize or classify what we have seen or experienced according to some relational comparative guideline; we consider what is important or unimportant, what is good or bad. This is referred to as *cognitive evaluation*. And third, based on these cognitive evaluations, we determine whether what is happening is consistent with what we believe should happen. This is referred to as *cognitive consistency*, and can affect both attitudes and behaviors (e.g., you like your job and your intend to remain with it). On the

Exhibit 4.1 Culture, cognition, and managerial action

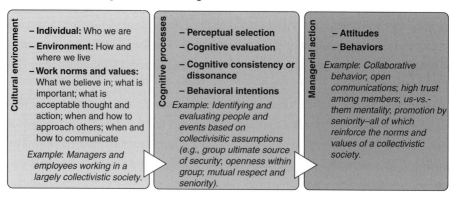

other hand, when attitudes and behaviors are not aligned (e.g., you hate your job but you do not quit), *cognitive dissonance* results. In these cases, those that experience the inconsistencies are likely to be motivated to reconcile their opposing thoughts and actions (e.g., either quitting your job or convincing yourself that there are good reasons to remain).

These cognitive processes, in turn, ultimately influence both our attitudes and behaviors inside the workplace and out, largely through behavioral intentions, or the immediate actions we plan to take as a result of our cognitive evaluations (and possible dissonance). Finally, a feedback loop must be recognized here in that when people follow their socially dictated norms and values and think and make decisions in ways that are cognitively consistent with them, the resulting attitudes and behaviors serve to reinforce the initial norms and values. This is one reason why many societies work so diligently to punish or purge outliers; they threaten the very cultural stability and continuity of the society.

Consider the example of menial work. Many people in many societies have it clearly positioned in their heads that they are "too good" to do low-level, physically demanding, or demeaning jobs. Should they find themselves in such positions (perhaps due to a lost job or a lack of education), they will often complain that they are "better than this" or that life has treated them unfairly. If they can find a way to escape the drudgery of the job, they likely will. Meanwhile, many other people in these same societies see work as a means to an end (e.g., money) and are not resentful about performing such "demeaning" work; in fact, many of these people will argue that there is no such thing as demeaning work, only lazy people. Work has inherent value. In addition, when people find themselves in such low-status jobs, some will often go to great lengths to change the job title and hence raise its status. Thus, garbage collectors or dustmen have become sanitation engineers or recycling technicians. Same job, different status, and a significant move towards achieving greater cognitive consistency.

Patterns of managerial thinking

Based on this introduction, we can now enter more deeply into the managerial world and consider how cultural differences can influence how managers access, organize, and transform information into patterns of meaning – in short, how managers think. Indeed, culturally influenced cognitive patterns can affect a wide variety of managerial behaviors, from leadership and decision making to motivation and negotiation. This is

Exhibit 4.2 Culture and patterns of managerial thinking

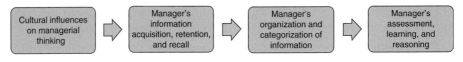

done through the ways in which information is acquired and retained, organized and categorized, and evaluated, learned and utilized (see Exhibit 4.2).

Information acquisition, retention, and recall

The mental representations of time and space that are embedded in particular cultures affect attention processes and memory for temporal information, with direct implications for encoding and retrieval of information, as well as memory and learning.[9] In a series of experiments in Mexico and Morocco, psychologist Daniel Wagner found substantive evidence that the structure of memory is universal across cultures, but that its associated control processes for information acquisition and retrieval are culturally influenced.[10] That is, people memorize things in the same way regardless of where they live, but their cultural background can influence what information they choose to acquire and remember. Moreover, people tend to have better recall of information when it is consistent with their cultural knowledge and values.[11] For example, many managers from mastery-oriented cultures tend to recall the specific successes of their subordinates that involved sales or financial achievements, but not their interpersonal or team-building successes. Meanwhile, in more harmony-oriented cultures, managers tend to recall more about their subordinates, interpersonal or team-building successes, regardless of their sales or financial successes. In addition, when facing the possibility of alternative interpretations of specific events (such as a team success), managers will almost uniformly choose the interpretation that is most consistent with their cultural outlook.[12] That is, managers from highly individualistic cultures will typically ascribe team success to the team leader's skills and efforts, while managers from more collectivistic cultures will typically ascribe it to the skills and efforts of the entire team.

Categorization of information

Societies define different traits in their environment as being disproportionately meaningful and worthy of attention for their assumed practical importance to their culture.[13]

It is not surprising, therefore, that mechanical skills are highly prized in Germany and Scandinavia, where large economic sectors are based on engineering, while financial and legal skills are highly prized in the UK, the US, and Canada, where so much of the economy is based on initial public offerings (IPOs), stock transfers, and leveraged buy-outs.

At the same time, cultures vary in the manner in which they develop categories for purposes of classification. For example, many Chinese raised in a collectivist environment classify people based on criteria that emphasize relationships and contexts. As a result, a woman and a child are often seen as belonging together (as opposed to a man and a woman), because the child needs the woman and the woman takes care of the child. By contrast, Americans raised in more individualistic contexts rely more on isolated properties of the objects in the classification. As a result, a woman and man belong together, rather than with the child, because they both are adults of similar ages.[14] This same pattern can be seen in managers who are likely to work and socialize with people of similar training (accountants with accountants, sales people with sales people, etc.), compared to Chinese managers who more frequently work and socialize with people with highly diverse training.

Researchers have also studied how different people describe themselves and categorize the idea of *self*. On the one hand, many managers from Australia, Canada, and the US, for example, hold an independent concept of self, seeing it as bound, concrete, and comprising mostly fixed and enduring qualities. On the other hand, many managers from China, Japan, and Korea, for example, maintain a concept of self that is more interdependent, socially diffused, relational, context-bound, changing, and malleable. American managers, for instance, describe themselves in abstract and fixed ways ("I am a good boss."), whereas Chinese, Japanese, and Korean managers refer more often to their social roles and relationships ("I work for Samsung" or "I am a Hitachi salaryman").[15] Similar dynamics were found in a comparison of the concept of self of Americans (independent), Southeast Asians (interdependent), and Hindu Indians (the self as religiously defined by invoking notions of reincarnation, karma, and the interconnectedness of all living beings, including multiple lifetimes and forms).[16]

Assessment, learning, and reasoning

Before the idea of intelligence as being multidimensional in nature and scope gained currency, experts recognized that the concept of intelligent behavior varies widely across cultures and, accordingly, that cultures require different skills to cope with their unique environments.[17] As a result, cultural factors often influence what will be learned in a given environment and at what age, leading to different patterns of general ability among people.[18] For example, due to a particular (but not universal) interpretation of the *Qur'an*, Kuwaiti women were only recently educated about local politics and allowed to vote in regional elections.

When inferring mental states of other people, research indicates that several cultures in North America and Western Europe emphasize a *norm of authenticity* (i.e., external actions and emotional displays are seen as consistent with internal states), while East and Southeast Asian societies often tend to consider such manifestations as immature, impolite, and sometimes bizarre. For example, "speaking one's mind" or "telling it like it is" often appear in a positive light among Australians and Americans, but not to the Japanese or Malaysians. Moreover, some Koreans, Japanese, and Thais may give more importance in communication processes to what is left unsaid instead of what is said in open and direct ways, while the opposite applies in many Western societies.[19]

Reasoning processes also play out differently across cultures. Attributions of causality (i.e., what caused something to occur) differentially focus on either the personal characteristics of the individual in more individualistic societies or the overall social circumstances surrounding the events among more collectivist peoples. In this sense, attributions in contexts as varied as the explanation for mass murders, success in sports, and managerial behavior in the workplace all follow a similar pattern that is largely culturally determined.[20]

To see how this works, consider how cognitive processes can influence a manager's approach to marketing and customer relations in Japan.[21] Marketing in Japan is typically seen as an application of common sense, not a "science." In fact, many Japanese managers see themselves as amateurs compared to their Western counterparts. Inside Japanese firms, for example, marketing departments are either relatively small or do not even exist. Instead, marketing is seen as everyone's responsibility rather than the responsibility of specialists. Only when managers require idiosyncratic knowledge or specialty resources, such as market research for new products or technologies, will they go outside the firm.

The purpose of marketing as a tool to influence consumer behavior is also understood differently in Japan and the West. If people believe in the existence of laws of human nature, as many in the West do, it is logical to think in terms of a science of marketing. Many Japanese, however, are far less convinced about the possibility of laws governing human behavior, and, as such, marketing becomes more of a matter of intuition and experience concerning what customers might or might not want. Marketing in Japan resembles more of a craft or art than a science, as it is often seen in the West. Japanese marketing also includes more of an intuitive understanding of the imperfectly understood variability of human behavior than standardized techniques based on systematic data by experts. Because of this, Japanese managers tend to prefer everyday words to specialized jargon in their advertising campaigns, synthesizing over analyzing, and simplicity over sophistication. All of these efforts derive from, and in turn reinforce, an underlying reticence to establish formal departments.

Western and Japanese approaches to marketing strategy can also differ. Japanese managers tend to follow an incrementalist approach to marketing problem solving, with an emphasis on implementation (rather than formulation), and developmental and evolutionary (rather than creational and revolutionary) product strategies aimed at more conservative and cautious product followership positioning, in contrast with a more risk-oriented and product leadership positioning of many American, Australian, British, and Canadian companies.

Differences can be found between typical Japanese firms and their Western counterparts in terms of how sales representatives deal with customers. Foreign observers have noted how naïve Western customers frequently are in responding favorably to widespread promises of customer satisfaction.[22] Many Japanese sales representatives are especially sensitive to this issue and do not guarantee customer satisfaction; instead, they will frequently aim at doing their best and hope that it happens. For many Japanese managers, a guarantee of satisfaction sounds too pretentious, almost like an invasion of privacy. Who are we to judge whether customers will really be satisfied?, the logic goes. This is related to the idea of the relationship between buyer and seller in the West in terms of a horizontal exchange among equals. Some Japanese, however, tend to view this notion as too balanced, and instead see the relationship with customers in more hierarchical terms, where the buyer is more like a master and the seller like a servant. Expressions often heard in the West like "the customer is always right" make little sense within a hierarchical framework, because the very assessment of right and wrong implies a position of superiority by those making the assessment. Ironically, a "customer is always right" attitude actually reinforces the position of the seller, who is willing to concede even if customers are actually wrong. If customers are always right in the West, they are beyond right and wrong in Japan. As a consequence, commercial relationships in the West focus on the transaction and its balance for both buyers and sellers, while caring for the relationship and a mixture of loyalty and interdependence is generally stressed in Japan.

Finally, sales representatives in Japan typically take buyers' complaints, remarks, and requests at face value, while trying to understand exactly what they want. This is done with a lack of personal involvement that Westerners often see as too cold or lacking in emotion. The Japanese salesperson presents product information without drawing conclusions for the customer, unlike Western tactics where, in what often resembles a contest of wills, sellers try to convince customers of the need to purchase the product – preferably immediately because it is "on sale." In Japan, sales representatives who interject themselves into the sale too much lead to customer doubts about the quality of the product or service. Instead, they will frequently take themselves out of the buyer's equation and let the product speak for itself.

In conclusion, cultural differences and their associated social norms and values influence how people think and process information, which, in turn, influences their subsequent attitudes and behaviors, both on the job and off. These attitudes and behaviors then feed back to reinforce the original norms and values. As a result, considerable attention is paid in most societies to reinforcing their basic cultural patterns and obligations so as to stabilize their cultural integrity over the long term. This, in turn, has implications for managers who must somehow make connections with businesses in other cultures in ways that develop and sustain long-term relationships and partnerships.

The geography of thought

If cultural differences influence patterns of managerial thinking, which, in turn, influence subsequent managerial behaviors and attitudes, what can we say about how each group can better understand the other? While little substantive research has been done on this topic in many regions of the world, there is an exception with regard to East Asia (e.g., China and Japan) and some North American and European countries (most notably the US and the UK). Much of this work has been conducted by University of Michigan psychologist Richard E. Nisbett and his colleagues, who offer a wealth of empirical studies and a controversial theory to tie these findings together.[23]

Before we begin this discussion, however, it is important to recognize that the narrow geographic focus on these studies raises at least two concerns for our purposes here. First, are we to ignore the rest of the world in our analyses and, if so, what are the implications for managers working elsewhere? And second, to what extent can we generalize about the people in any given region of the world? Terms like "Western" and "Eastern" that are used in Nisbett's research run a very real risk of creating significant over-generalizations that can be both inaccurate and misinterpreted. For example, who is included in the term "Western?" Does it include all of Europe, part of Europe, or none of Europe? (By the way, what are the boundaries of Europe itself?) Similarly, who is "Asian?" Does everyone included in each of these two groups think alike? Obviously not. Despite these limitations, however, such research can serve as a point of departure for understanding and exploring how cognitive processes can at times be influenced by cultural differences. As such, we will report these findings as they were reported by the initial investigators.

Nisbett's research suggests that cognitive processes can develop in somewhat different ways in so-called "Eastern" and "Western" societies, beginning from infancy. For example, a comparison of language acquisition patterns in the US and Japan found that, when talking to their children, American mothers tend to direct their children's attention to the objects they refer to, while Japanese mothers direct their children's attention alternatively to the objects and to the mother's face. Japanese mothers emphasize personal interactions in their speech ("Here! It's a car. I give it to you. Now give this to me. Yes! Thank you") and engage their children in empathy routines and the showing of positive feelings ("Here! It's a dog. Give it a love. Love, love, love."). In contrast, American mothers directly focus on the object of the conversation ("That's a car. See the car? You like it? It has nice wheels").[24] Furthermore, Japanese mothers expect their children to master such social exchanges at earlier ages than do American mothers.[25] It has also been found that American mothers show a primary interest in the achievement of their children's linguistic competence with an ultimate goal of individual self-reliance and independence, while the priority of Japanese mothers tends to rest on the establishment of affective communication patterns aimed at interdependence and harmonious interactions.[26]

School-age children in Asia are also reared in ways that differ from those in the West. Take, for instance, a classroom with young children in Japan. The kids are asked to work with coloring books around a table. In a typical sequence, the children will first look around at the others and point at the part of the picture that each wants to color. Silently, and after a few glances, they will quickly agree on what to color first. Next, they will point at their boxes of coloring pencils and agree on the color they will use. In the end, they will all paint the same section of the picture with the same color. The final result will be completely different from what you can find in an American or British classroom, where children are encouraged to show their own peculiar tendencies, in distinctively creative ways, and avoiding behaviors that might signal that they copied somebody else's work.[27]

As people mature, they increasingly differentiate between cognitions about external objects and events (i.e., looking outside) and cognitions about the self (i.e., looking inside).

Looking outside: categorization and network maps

Nisbett's findings suggest that Western patterns of thought can be best understood in terms of the use of relatively simple rules in which *categorization processes* help decide where and when such rules should be applied. By contrast, Eastern patterns of thought tend to be more complex and difficult to understand, and without simple rules that can be directly applied to situations. This difference is not unlike the dichotomy between rule-based (universalism) and relationship-based (particularism) that was discussed earlier in the book. Western tendencies towards categorization is often seen in some Asian cultures as being unduly abstract and dismissive of the complexity of the environment, while true understanding requires a consideration of multiple and inter-related factors that cannot be subsumed into processes of formal logic. In other words, what is required is not categorization, but rather *network maps.*

Put another way, Westerners often place a high value on using formal logic to determine cause-effect relationships, while Asians often see this approach as being somewhat naïve for a world full of contradictions that can only be understood through principles of dualism and dialectics that can simultaneously balance each state (*yin*) and its opposite state (*yang*) into a state of harmony.[28] Asians tend to think more holisti-cally, paying greater attention to context and relationships, and valuing experiential knowledge above formal abstraction. Western thinking is far more analytical, focusing on salient objects (e.g., a strategic partner, a leader) and the characteristics of these objects rather than the relationships between the objects in the field, thereby favoring abstraction and formalism.[29] As a result of this, Westerners often tend to think in more simplistic and linear patterns ("Let's see the big picture," "Who is right?") that at times can delude managers into believing that they control the objects and events around them when, in fact, they do not (see Exhibit 4.3).

To see how this works in the world of global business, consider strategic decision making. The strategy-making process in traditional Asian thought is not based on executives acting in one way or another, but rather on a relatively permanent, incre-mental adaptation to the natural flux of things.[30] In the Western tradition, however, this evolutionary, incremental approach would often be seen as indecisive and slow. Western managers tend to emphasize the need for decisive and strong action that breaks the status quo and opens up new venues for entrepreneurs. These different patterns can also be seen, for instance, when comparing American and Japanese busi-ness growth models (see Chapter 5). Japanese firms follow what has been called an *evolutionary* approach, while American companies adopt a *strategic* approach.[31]

Exhibit 4.3 Looking outside: patterns of East-West cognitive differences

Cognitions about external objects and events	"Western" patterns	"Asian" patterns
Mental processing	Seeks to classify objects and events into organized categories so they can be dealt with separately.	Seeks to create network maps incorporating multiple objects and events.
Primary focus of attention	Understanding individual objects and events.	Understanding relationships between objects and events.
Keys to understanding	Identify key variables, often in a sequential manner.	Identify interrelationships in a holistic fashion.
Patterns of evolution	Seeks stability.	Recognizes change.
Relation to environment	Mastery-oriented; control it.	Harmony-oriented; adapt to it.
Modes of thought	Applies formal logic or analytic powers.	Applies a dualistic perspective; accepts contradictions.
Problem-solving criteria	Seeks correctness and truth.	Seeks reasonableness.

Japanese evolutionary firms grow steadily by first exporting its products to neighboring geographical markets. When successful, the next step is the introduction of sales and distribution facilities in the new territories. Building a production plant where the sales and distribution facilities are integrated completes the cycle.[32] The more typically American strategic approach, by contrast, consists of moving through discontinuous steps between analyzing new market entry potential and building up an integrated production and distribution system.

As such, the application of formal logic in the West tends to prefer thought processes that lead into problem-solving processes and are anchored on the concept of what is true and correct. This is consistent with the philosophical traditions in the Western world, whereas Eastern philosophy has usually been more concerned with criteria of reasonableness and pragmatism at lower levels of abstraction. For this reason, it is common for Westerners to incorrectly consider Eastern thinking more in terms of helping individuals to become wise than rationally enlightened. Indeed, this relative lack of concern in traditional Chinese thought with the ideas of truth, being, or ethics (for which there was not even a specific word in the traditional Chinese language), despite their centrality to Western thinking, has led some to even doubt the existence of a Chinese philosophy proper.[33]

The Western focus on particular objects (e.g., people, events, plans, etc.) is also related in Western thinking to assumptions of stability because change is normally more salient when multiple objects are put in relation to each other than when they are individually considered. Westerners see congruence in their trying to control the

Exhibit 4.4 Looking inside: patterns of East-West cognitive differences

Cognitions about self	"Western" patterns	"Asian" patterns
Concept of self	Independent	Interdependent
Focus of attribution	Individual	Situation
Attribution of success	Personal merit	Group merit
Social goals	Fairness or equality	Harmony
Individual goals	Self-knowledge and achievement	Fitting in and acceptance
Overall values	Equality and freedom	Hierarchy and group control
Conflict resolution	Debate and argument (win or lose)	Compromise and face-saving (seeking a middle way)

environments surrounding them, to the extent that they are seen as more stable than in the everything-is-in-flux of Asian tradition. These differing views on stability and change can be found in the ways firms build corporate strategies, hire and develop their employees, and even negotiate contracts, as will be seen later.

Looking inside: independent and interdependent

Up to this point, we have focused on "Western" and "Asian" differences in understanding things outside the individual as he or she tries to make sense of the world (i.e., looking outside). Now we shift our attention to how Asians and Westerners look into themselves and their ways of behaving and dealing with others (i.e., looking inside). Here, too, differences can be found that can have an impact on organizational life (see Exhibit 4.4). And here, too, some caution is in order about over-generalizations.

When drawing comparisons between the east and the west, some researchers – and some managers – tend to note that Westerners and Asians can often hold different self-concepts (*independent* versus *interdependent*). These concepts are related to the points already made about how many Westerners tend to focus their attention primarily on specific objects (i.e., the individual as the principal focus of attention), while many Asians tend to focus more broadly on interrelationships between several objects and their overall standing in a given field or environment (i.e., interrelationships as the principal focus of attention). Since Asians tend to make comparatively broad, complex causal attributions of the antecedents of behavior while their Western counterparts tend to ascribe narrower causal attributions, it has been observed that Westerners tend to explain behavior in terms of the performance of individuals, while Asians are more inclined to explain behavior in terms of the overall set of situational variables influencing the individuals that directly intervene in the chain of events.[34] Asians, then, are more likely to hold groups of people accountable for performance instead of specific individuals, as is common in the West.[35] These patterns go beyond the causes or antecedents of behavior, and also hold true for perceptions of the consequences of events. Here, too, Asians have been shown to be more conscious than Westerners of the downstream effects of actions and events, particularly in regard to effects that are more distant and indirectly related to the focal events. This last point also implies a more complex characterization of reality by Asians *vis-à-vis* Westerners.[36]

Given the emphasis of Westerners on individualism, it makes sense to center the establishment of personal goals on individuals in terms of self-knowledge, self-achievement, and so on. For many Asians, however, since the explanation of events and performance is based more on the overall effort of the group, the goals for the individuals focus more around getting along and fitting-in with other members of the group than with individual achievement. Socially, these different goal orientations translate into the development of dual systems that focus on the preservation of fairness or equity at the individual level in the West and the preservation of harmony in Asia. Independent individuals, seeking their own goals and interests and convinced of their own direct capabilities in the attainment of performance, as is typical in the West, demand freedom and equality of opportunities in order to maximize opportunities of individual achievement. In the East, by contrast, social values stress the establishment of hierarchical and control patterns that stress group goals and motives above individual claims. And, whenever conflicts arise, traditions will also diverge in the West in a preference for debate and argument to validate one's claims or for a middle way or compromising solutions that reinforce group harmony and face-saving for the parties involved (see Chapter 11).

Consider: Does this mean that Western thinking patterns are more "rational" than Eastern patterns? To answer this question as posed would force us to fall into the mental trap we have just been discussing. That is, an overall characterization of one style or the other as more rational (or perhaps "better") would validate the simplification that is involved in the question itself. Does this question refer to such a simple and one-dimensional reality to which a simple "yes" or "no" will suffice for an answer? Isn't reality much more complex than that? In other words, such questions make sense only within a framework that simplifies the complexity of individual judgments that are involved in information-processing activities. As such, they actually follow a Western way of framing issues, regardless of what the actual answers to the questions are. In this sense, these are not valid questions from a multicultural standpoint; instead, they are, indeed, culturally loaded. Rationality in the West tends to seek correct answers; it streamlines information in search of linear models that explain or predict behavior. By contrast, rationality in the East tends to seek models of understanding that are complex and multidimensional. As Chinese philosopher S. H. Liu observes, "it is precisely because the Chinese mind is so rational that it refuses to become rationalistic and refuses to separate form from content."[37]

In summary, what should we make of these differences between "Western" and "Eastern" cognitive approaches as suggested by Nisbett and others? First of all, we need to be cautious because we are on the frontier of today's knowledge in this field. Traditionally, people have believed in universal (or standard) cognitive processes around the world. That view is now being challenged in the light of new evidence, such as the findings presented here. But much remains unknown, especially in terms of a clear understanding of what all humans universally share and what is cultural-specific.[38]

Culture and the managerial role

If managerial cognitions can vary across cultures, so too can the expectations people have concerning appropriate managerial roles. Two related issues are relevant here: first, what is the ideal managerial role – the role people say they prefer to see in good managers?; and second, what is the "real" managerial role – the everyday roles that managers play out in real life, warts and all? Theoretically, these two roles should be highly correlated, but in reality significant differences are often found. And, not surprising, taking these comparisons across borders only adds to the ambiguity.

First, consider how people in various cultures describe their ideal manager. INSEAD professor Andre Laurent conducted one of the more interesting studies on this topic.[39] He focused his attention on understanding the normative managerial role (that is, what is expected of managers) and discovered significant differences across cultures. He asked managers from different cultures a series of questions dealing with effective management. His results demonstrate wide variations in responses across cultures, as shown in Exhibit 4.5. For each set of responses, note how far apart typical managers are in responding to rather simple statements about appropriate managerial behavior. For each of the three questions, the percentage of managers in agreement ranges from 10 to 78%, 17 to 83%, and 26 to 74% respectively. These percentages aren't even close. If managers from different countries differ so much in their descriptions of the correct managerial role, it is no wonder that significant differences can be found in actual management style across national boundaries.

Exhibit 4.5 Cultural differences and the ideal managerial role

Country	Percentage of managers who agreed with each statement		
	"Managers must have the answers to most questions asked by subordinates."	"The main reason for a chain of command is so people know who has authority."	"It is OK to bypass chain of command to get something done efficiently."
China	74	70	59
France	53	43	43
Germany	46	26	45
Indonesia	73	83	51
Italy	66	NA	56
Japan	78	50	NA
Netherlands	17	31	44
Spain	NA	34	74
Sweden	10	30	26
United Kingdom	27	34	35
United States	18	17	32

Source: Data from Andre Laurent reported in John Saee, *Managing Organizations in a Global Economy*. Mason, OH: Thompson/Southwestern, 2005, pp. 39–42.

Second, consider perceptions of actual managers. A similar study conducted by Cambridge University professor Charles Hampden-Turner and Dutch management consultant Fons Trompenaars also found significant differences across managers based on culture, as shown in Exhibit 4.6. For example, managers in the US, Sweden, Japan, Finland, and Korea showed more overall drive and initiative than leaders in Portugal, Norway, Greece, and the UK. Also note that Canadian managers placed less emphasis on managerial drive and initiative than their US counterparts. At the same time, managers in Sweden, Japan, Norway, Canada, and the US tended to be more willing to delegate authority than leaders in Greece, Portugal, Spain, and Italy. These findings, along with those of Andre Laurent, suggest clearly that effective managerial behavior can easily vary across cultures.

Other studies confirm this conclusion. For example, one study found that British managers were more participative than their French or German counterparts.[40] Two possible reasons were suggested for this. First, England is more egalitarian than France, and the political environment supports this approach. And second, top British managers tend not to be involved in the day-to-day affairs of the business, and delegate many key decisions to middle and lower-level managers. The French and Germans, by contrast, tend to prefer a more work-centered, authoritarian approach. While it is true

Exhibit 4.6 Culture and actual managerial characteristics

Country	Manager's sense of drive and initiative (percentage of agreement by managers)	Country	Manager's willingness to delegate authority (percentage of agreement by managers)
United States	74	Sweden	76
Sweden	72	Japan	69
Japan	72	Norway	69
Finland	70	United States	66
Korea	68	Singapore	65
Netherlands	67	Denmark	65
Singapore	66	Canada	64
Switzerland	66	Finland	63
Belgium	65	Switzerland	62
Ireland	65	Netherlands	61
France	65	Australia	61
Austria	63	Germany	61
Denmark	63	New Zealand	61
Italy	62	Ireland	60
Australia	62	United Kingdom	59
Canada	62	Belgium	55
Spain	62	Austria	54
New Zealand	59	France	54
Greece	59	Italy	47
United Kingdom	58	Spain	44
Norway	55	Portugal	43
Portugal	49	Greece	38

Source: Data from Charles Hampden-Turner and Fons Trompenaars, *The Seven Cultures of Capitalism*. New York, NY: Doubleday, 1993.

that German codetermination leads to power sharing with employees throughout the organization, some have argued that this has resulted not from German culture but rather from German laws. By contrast, Scandinavian countries make wide use of participative leadership approaches, again following from their somewhat more egalitarian culture.

On the other side of the world, Japanese managers tend to be somewhat authoritarian but at the same time listen to the opinions of their subordinates. One study found that Japanese managers place greater confidence in the skills and capabilities of their subordinates than their counterparts in other cultures.[41] Another feature of

Exhibit 4.7 Cultural influences on managerial roles

Managerial roles	Differences across cultures
Interpersonal roles	
Figurehead	Figureheads have considerable symbolic value in some cultures; in others, being described as a figurehead is not seen as a compliment.
Leader	Individualistic cultures prefer highly visible "take charge" leaders; collectivistic cultures prefer more consultative leaders.
Liaison	Some cultures prefer informal contacts based on long-standing personal relationships; others prefer to use official representatives.
Informational roles	
Monitor	Culture often influences both the extent of information monitoring and which specific information sources receive greatest attention.
Disseminator	In some cultures, the context surrounding a message is more important than the message itself; in others, the reverse is true.
Spokesperson	Culture often influences who is respected and seen as a legitimate spokesperson for an organization.
Decisional roles	
Entrepreneur	Some cultures are highly supportive of innovation and change; others prefer the status quo and resist change.
Disturbance handler	Some cultures resolve conflict quietly; others accept and at times encourage a more public approach.
Resource allocator	Hierarchical cultures support differential resource allocations; egalitarian cultures prefer greater equality or equity in distributions.
Negotiator	Some cultures negotiate all items in a proposed contract simultaneously; others negotiate each item sequentially.

Source: Based on Henry Mintzberg, *The Nature of Managerial Work*. New York, NY: Harper and Row, 1972, pp. 54–94.

Japanese leadership is an inclination to give subordinates ambiguous goals instead of highly specific ones. That is, many Japanese managers tell their workers what they want in a general way, but leave it to the workers to determine the details and the work plan. This contrasts sharply with typical US managers who like to take a hands-on management-by-objectives approach to project management.

To illustrate this point, let us return to Mintzberg's ten managerial roles. Although this model was designed around North American managers, it can also be useful in exploring on a conceptual level how culture and managerial roles can intersect. For the sake of example, Exhibit 4.7 illustrates how each of the ten managerial roles can be influenced by cultural differences. For example, considerable research has indicated that most people in individualistic cultures prefer managers who take charge, while most people in collectivistic cultures prefer managers who are more consultative. Similarly, managers in high-context cultures frequently make extensive use of the context sur-rounding a message to get their point across, while managers in low-context cultures tend to rely almost exclusively on specific and detailed messages and ignore much of the message context. In short, the managerial role keeps changing – not necessarily in major ways, but certainly in important ways – as we move across borders.

Management patterns across cultures

So what have we learned so far? Managers come in all shapes and sizes, and managerial thinking and managerial roles can be influenced by numerous factors. In this section, we shift focus to examine how cultural differences, in concert with cognitive patterns, can affect managerial behavior. That is, it is argued here that culture and cognitive differences represent an important influence on how managers approach their work, individually and collectively. With this in mind, and based on the earlier discussions on managerial cognitions across cultures, we turn now to a comparison of distinct management styles – or more accurately, management patterns – in three very different cultures, beginning with France.

Management patterns in France

When a senior executive from a major Japanese manufacturing conglomerate was asked where he would prefer to locate a manufacturing facility in Europe, he responded, "Anywhere but France. The French are just too hard to get along with."[42] What is the basis for this comment? To say that the French may be difficult to work with tells us very little. The question is how and why are they different? And who is making the comparison?

As with any culture, it is difficult to capture the essence of a people in a few phrases. People tend to vary considerably within particular cultures, not just between cultures. Perhaps nowhere is this truer than with respect to the French. Even the French will point to sizable differences between Parisians and provincials and between the peoples of the various provinces.[43] Even so, it is possible, on a general level, to develop a thumbnail sketch of trends in French culture using the core cultural dimensions discussed in Chapter 3, where we find that the French are often seen as being moderately hierarchical, moderately collectivistic, moderately harmony-oriented, moderately polychromic, and moderately particularistic. Perhaps the key word here is "moderate." That is, French culture contains a dynamic – a push-pull – which includes numerous opposing beliefs, values, attitudes, and behaviors.

In such an environment, extremes tend to give way to a blend of tolerance, patience, and flexibility.

Going one step further, according to noted anthropologists Edward and Mildred Hall, the French tend to be friendly, humorous, and frequently sarcastic.[44] They admire people who have strong opinions and openly disagree with them, in contrast with many Americans who often prefer people who agree with them. As a result, the French are accustomed to conflict, and will frequently assume in negotiations that many issues simply cannot be reconciled. (*C'est la vie!* or "Such is life!") Many Anglo-Americans, by contrast, tend to believe that conflicts can frequently be resolved if both parties make the effort and are willing to compromise. Perhaps Americans are more optimistic, while the French are more fatalistic.

In addition, personal relationships are very important to the French, and can take considerable time to develop. The French tend to evaluate a person's trustworthiness based on first-hand experiences, while many Anglo-Americans tend to base such assessments on past achievements, reputation, or the evaluation of others.

In France, one's social class – aristocracy, upper bourgeoisie, upper-middle bourgeoisie, middle class, lower-middle class, and lower class – is important, and social interactions are frequently influenced by stereotypes. Moreover, most French can expect little change in their social class, regardless of their accomplishments. It is difficult, if not impossible, to climb the social ladder. To make matters worse for some Americans in the US, the French tend to be very status conscious, and sometimes enjoy showing off their status and culture to friends and strangers alike. As one French MBA student replied when asked about the primary difference between the French and Americans, "The French have more culture."[45] While many Americans may reject this assertion, or even question what it means to have "more" culture, they too are sometimes seen bragging about their own cultural superiority.

Within this cultural environment, French companies, referred to as *Société Anonyme*, tend to be highly centralized with fairly rigid structures and reporting channels (see Exhibit 4.8). As a result, decisions frequently take considerable time both to make and to implement. Foreigners frequently complain about encountering excessive bureaucratic red tape when dealing with French companies.[46] In addition, many French managers are sometimes seen as being fairly autocratic and often more interested in protecting their personal turf than in working with others in the organization to achieve significant results. French managers sometimes refuse to share information with subordinates in the belief that knowledge is power.

Exhibit 4.8 Culture and management trends: France, Malaysia, and Nigeria

Country	Trends in management patterns
France	Top-down and somewhat autocratic management; status-conscious; clear differentiation between management and workers; supervisory role focuses on direction and control; somewhat relationship-based management, but in a hierarchical fashion; somewhat collectivistic and harmony-oriented; polychronic; slow and centralized decision making with slow implementation.
Malaysia	Formal organizations consisting of multicultural and family-based networks; status-oriented; strongly hierarchical; collectivistic; supervisory role focuses on paternalism and support; patriarchal; relationship-based management; stresses harmony and respect; emphasis on trust and personal relationships; slow autocratic decision making with slow implementation.
Nigeria	Autocratic bureaucracies; hierarchical and patriarchal; somewhat collectivistic; supervisory role focuses on direction and control; relationship-based management; autocratic; centralized; resistant to change; close work-family integration; weak work ethic.

Note: This exhibit illustrates general trends in management practice. Clearly, within-culture differences (oftentimes significant) can be found along with the between-culture differences that are summarized here.

Reflecting a tradition of class-consciousness, there is often a large class distinction made at work between managers (or *cadre*) and workers.[47] In the past, most senior executives of France's leading companies (as well as most of France's top political leaders) graduated from a small set of elite polytechnic universities called *grandes écoles*, although more and more are now completing European-based MBA programs. The program of study at these schools historically emphasized engineering and mathematics over business in the belief that anyone who can master mathematics can accomplish almost anything. However, this focus is now changing, and these institutions are globalizing at a rapid pace. School ties are routinely maintained and exploited throughout one's career.

On the job, French leaders are often formal, impersonal, and authoritarian. In interpersonal relations, they can be critical of individuals and institutions alike. A French schoolteacher observed, "The operating principle of French education is negative reinforcement."[48] This tendency carries over to the workplace, where subordinates are routinely criticized. By contrast, Americans tend to believe a bit more in the value of positive reinforcement and incentives over punishment.

Rules and regulations proliferate in French organizations, much like they do in German firms. However, their use and implementation can be quite different. While many Germans use policies and procedures to improve the efficiency of operations, the French prefer *savoir faire* (a certain way of doing something with style) as a substitute for following structured procedures. Cultural expectations require German managers to remain on schedule, maintain commitments, and deal with problems as they arise. By contrast, the more individualistic French are more likely to be concerned with following proper professional protocol. Even so, unlike the Germans, they will often ignore rules when they interfere with the attainment of a key goal.[49]

In the workplace (and in contrast to the corporate cultures in many US and British firms), many French employees are not motivated by competition or the desire to emulate their colleagues. Outsiders frequently claim that they don't have the same work ethic that many Americans and Asians have. French workers avoid overtime work, work an average (and legally mandated) thirty-five-hour workweek, and receive one of the longest statutory vacation periods in the world. While the French admire the industriousness of Americans and Asians, for example, they believe that quality of life is often more important than success at work, and attach great importance to their leisure time. However, few would argue that they work hard during scheduled hours and have a reputation for high productivity. This reputation results in part from a French tradition of craftsmanship and in part from the fact that a high percentage of French workers are employed in small, independent businesses where quality is respected.

Not unlike the comments of the Japanese executive above, many US managers believe that it is more difficult to get along with the French than any other European country. Not surprisingly, many French managers feel the same about Americans. Consider the following examples. According to Hall and Hall, many US managers criticize their French managerial counterparts for a number of reasons:[50] they won't delegate; they won't keep their subordinates informed; they don't feel a sense of responsibility towards their subordinates; they refuse to accept responsibility for things; they are not team players; they are overly sensitive to hierarchy and status; they are highly authoritarian; they are not interested in improving their job skills or knowledge; they are primarily concerned with their own self-interest; and they are less mobile than Americans. Obviously, there are variations in such observations, but, according to these noted anthropologies, this is the gist of American opinion.

At the same time, Hall and Hall quote several French managers who hold similarly negative opinions about their US counterparts:[51] American managers in Europe are not creative – they are too tied to their checklists; success is not achieved by logic and procedure alone; American executives are reliable and hardworking, and often charming and innocent, but they are too narrow in their focus – they are not well rounded; they have no time for cultural interests and lack appreciation for art, music, and philosophy; too many American executives are preoccupied with financial reporting – this syndrome produces people who avoid decisions; and Americans don't know how to present themselves – they sprawl and slouch and have no finesse.

Who is right here? Perhaps perceptions by both sides are correct to some extent. Clearly, one factor that may help explain these differing perceptions is the fundamental difference between French and American cultures in terms of their time orientation. As noted above, most American are decidedly monochronic, meaning that they tend to stress a high degree of scheduling in their lives, with concentration of effort being on one activity at a time, and elaborate codes of behavior built around promptness in meeting obligations and appointments. Put more simply, many Americans tend to be a bit linear in their thinking and behavior, always focusing on the ultimate goal. By contrast, most French are polychronic, stressing human relationships and social inter-action over arbitrary schedules and appointments, and engaging in several activities simultaneously with frequent interruptions. To the French, the journey is probably more important than the ultimate destination.

Management patterns in Malaysia

Imagine the challenges of trying to do business in a culture that is itself highly multi-cultural, consisting primarily of Malays, Indians, and Chinese, along with many others. Among other things, the challenge for global managers here is to understand which cultural norms are applicable to any given interaction and then navigate one's business in ways that do not hit any given cultural minefield. This is clearly no easy task.

Malaysia is a nation of 21 million people situated in Southeast Asia – 59 percent of the population is native Malay, often called *bumiputras* (or "sons of the soil").[52] Another 32 percent of the population is ethnic Chinese, and 9 percent are of Indian origin. Islam is the official religion of Malaysia and nearly all Malays are Muslim. Non-Malays are free to choose other religions. The Chinese are largely Buddhist, with some Taoists, Christians, and Confucianists. In fact, many Chinese practice multiple religions. Indians tend to be Hindu or Sikh, but some are Christian.

A person's ancestral background is often important in determining social status and future opportunities.[53] Wealth is highly admired, and many *bumiputra* Malaysians believe that success or failure is the result of fate or the will of God. Others, like the Chinese, have a somewhat greater tendency to believe that people control their own destiny. Malaysians from all three cultural backgrounds value the family above all else and often use family connections to gain employment and other advantages. Families, in turn, place a high value on personal loyalty and education as a means to get ahead. While all people identify with being Malaysians, they will often identify more strongly with their ethnic background than with their national citizenship. From a culinary standpoint, Muslims do not eat pork, Hindus do not eat beef, and the Chinese eat everything.

Working with Malaysians can require a considerable degree of cultural sensitivity. Not only are one's status and position in the organizational hierarchy important, but also power distances tend to be very high. In business transactions, this means sending business representatives who are of at least an equivalent rank to one's prospective customers. Sending someone of lower rank can be deemed insulting. In the workplace, respecting older workers is important, even by managers who have greater authority. As in many Asian countries, age is highly respected and conveys a sense of both wisdom and authority over others.

Maintaining politeness and harmony are also important, and open conflict is avoided at any cost. Above all, visitors must not cause others to lose face in any of the three ethnic groups. Preserving respect and dignity, even in the face of disagreement, is fundamental to understanding all Malaysians. Family relationships are important, as families form the basis of this highly collectivistic society among all ethnic groups, Malays, Chinese, and Indians. Participative decision making is commonplace, so long as group elders allow it. In negotiations, compromise and collaboration are preferred over confrontation, competition, or a winner-takes-all approach.[54] This emphasis on moderation reflects both Chinese and Malay teachings. As such, listening carefully to one's partners and watching for body language becomes critical in this high-context culture.

Within this cultural milieu, *bumiputra* firms tend to be run based on principles that are consistent with the Malaysian cultures. Organizations tend to be somewhat flat, with power centered at the top. Many businesses are family-owned and family-run. Communication both within an organization and between organizations and their customers is often subtle and generally transmitted in an indirect style. Maintaining one's humility and modesty is crucial. Strong emotions are seldom exhibited, work activities tend to be polychronic, and work goals are modest. Managers are often hired based on family connections, although competence is also important. Status is important at all levels of the hierarchy.

While differences can obviously be found across Malaysia's *bumiputra* firms, common characteristics include the following: managers place a high value on protocol, rank, and status (see Exhibit 4.8 above); self-confidence and the ability to be sensitive to the needs of others are valued managerial qualities; managerial legitimacy is based on education and family background; social relationships are based on collectivist principles; business is largely based on long-term mutual trust; high-context communication is important; employee selection is based on a combination of family connections, cultural grouping, and skills and abilities; managers must show concern for a subordinate's welfare; it is acceptable to terminate employees for poor performance; and, finally, Malaysian firms are reluctant to lay off employees during difficult economic times.

For many years, the government has supported an affirmative action program in hiring and promotion that favors the majority *bumiputras* over ethnic Chinese and Indians, arguing that such a program is necessary to overcome traditional Chinese dominance in business. *Bumiputra* employees are generally thought to be less aggressive and less experienced in business, and can be both humble and shy with strangers compared to the Chinese and Indians. *Bumiputra* firms often enjoy special access to government funding and government contracts.

Among ethnic Chinese, their cultural tendency towards collectivism often extends beyond the family into something called a *pok chow*.[55] This translates roughly as *gang contracting*, and exists when groups of workers band together to seek and conduct work as a team. (Indeed, it represents an ancient Chinese version of the contemporary self-managing team.) Members join together by mutual consent and determine their own work rules, division of labor, and procedures for dividing up their compensation. They frequently even elect their own leaders. They then sell their services to firms or other employers looking for work to be done. *Pok chow* crews are especially popular in the construction industry in Malaysia, where employers only have to deal with crew leaders and can dispense with other complicated organizational procedures or requirements.

Management patterns in Nigeria

The sub-Saharan region of Africa is vast, and wide variations can be found across its various countries and cultures. Even so, as noted in Chapter 3, some notable general cultural trends can be identified. Perhaps the strongest cultural trends include a strong belief in hierarchy and collectivism, as well as a moderate belief in harmony and polychronic communication and time patterns. In addition, a strong particularistic orientation to rules, laws, and polices can also be found. Having said this, it is still useful to drill down a bit and focus on the cultural similarities and differences within a single country like the West African nation of Nigeria.

Nigeria consists of three principal ethnic groups – the Hausa-Fulani, Yoruba, and Igbo – who collectively represent about 70 percent of the population. Another 10 percent of the population consists of groups numbering more than 1 million members each, including the Kanuri, Tiv, and Ibibio. More than 300 smaller ethnic groups account for the remaining 20 percent of the population. As a nation, Nigeria's official language is English. This derives from the many years of British colonial rule, but is also used by the government to provide one unifying language. In addition, over 400 different dialects can be found across the country.

Nigeria is also a land of religious diversity, with Muslims living predominantly in the north and Christians predominantly in the south. Native religions, in which people believe in deities, spirits, and ancestor worship, are spread throughout the country. Many Muslims and Christians may also intertwine their beliefs with more unorthodox indigenous ones.

Along with South Africa, Nigeria is considered a super-power in the African continent, and consequently Nigerians are generally proud of their country. It has the largest population in Africa, and the land is endowed with vast quantities of natural resources. It is the sixth largest oil-producing nation and has a well-educated and industrious society. At the same time, however, Nigeria consistently ranks very high on experts' lists of corrupt countries in which to do business. Bribery is epidemic. Indeed, Transparency International, an organization dedicated to eliminating corruption in international business, ranked Nigeria as the world's most corrupt nation in its study of eighty-five countries.[56]

Extended families are the norm in Nigeria and are, in fact, the backbone of the social system. Grandparents, cousins, aunts, uncles, sisters, brothers and in-laws all work as a unit through life. Hierarchy and seniority guide family relationships. Social standing and recognition is achieved through extended families. Similarly, a family's honor is influenced by the actions of its members. Individuals turn to members of the extended family for financial aid and guidance, and the family is expected to provide for the welfare of every member. Although the role of the extended family is diminishing somewhat in urban areas, there remains a strong tradition of mutual caring and responsibility among the members.

Nigeria is a hierarchical society. Age and position earns, even demands, respect. Age is believed to confer wisdom, so older people are granted respect. The oldest person in a group is revered and honored. In a social situation, they are greeted and served first. In return, the most senior person has the responsibility to make decisions that are in the best interest of the group.

Due to the diverse ethnic makeup of the country, communication styles vary. In the southwest, where the people are from the Yoruba tribe, people's communication employs proverbs, sayings, and songs to enrich the meaning of what they say. This is especially true when speaking their native language, although many of the same characteristics have been carried into their English language usage. The Yoruba often use humor to prevent boredom during long meetings or serious discussions. They believe that embedding humor in their message guarantees that what they say is not readily forgotten. Meanwhile, Nigerians living in the south of the country tend to speak more directly. Nigerians also make extensive use of non-verbal behavior (e.g., facial expressions) to communicate their views.

In discussions, Nigerians frequently begin with a general idea and then slowly move to the specific, often using a somewhat circuitous route. Their logic is often contextual. That is, they tend to look for the rationale behind behavior and attempt to understand the context. Thus, behavior is viewed in terms of its surrounding context, and not simply in terms of what has been observed. As a result, what is not said is often more important than what is.

Management in Nigeria – at least in medium and large-scale firms – has been heavily influenced by British practices, although these practices have been modified to suit local cultures (see Exhibit 4.8 above). Many observers have agreed with Professor Sanjay Choudhary that "the general tone of management is prescriptive, often authoritarian, inflexible, and insensitive."[57] Bureaucracy and hierarchy seem to rule. Some have suggested that these characteristics can be traced to Nigeria's colonial past, where foreign administrators had little faith in the abilities of local employees and hence retained managerial authority at the top of the organization. The menial work that was assigned to subordinates was closely supervised, and no real authority was delegated. However, this is likely only part of the explanation, as Nigerian cultural trends also reinforce this approach to management style.[58] In any case, we frequently find situations in African firms where subordinates have little to do while their supervisors are overworked – a typical indication that managers are reluctant to delegate much autonomy. In this regard, Carleton University professor Moses Kiggundu concludes that this form of organization often results in "a debilitating unwillingness to take independent action."[59]

Another characteristic here is perhaps more directly influenced by local cultures. As Kiggundu also observes in his study of African organizations,

> There would be an atmosphere of management by crisis as events would seem to take everybody by surprise. Conflicts would tend to be avoided, smoothed over rather than directly confronted. Although there would be a lot of activities in these organizations, very few people would be able to assess how well or badly they or the organization as a whole was performing.[60]

Nigerian professor C. G. Obeleagu-Nzelibe adds that we must remember that there may, indeed, be a fundamental conflict between Western and African trends in management thought. Specifically, he observes, "Whereas Western management thought advocates euro-centrism, individualism, and modernity, African management thought emphasizes ethnocentrism, traditionalism, communalism, and cooperative teamwork."[61]

In any case, most local and foreign researchers agree that the typical power structure and workflows lead to chronic inefficiencies. Top managers are authoritarian, paternalistic, over-worked, highly educated, articulate, and widely traveled. However, they seldom provide much in the way of visionary leadership. Organizations frequently do not have clearly stated or widely understood goals and objectives. They tend to be heavily politicized and have weak executive and management systems. Senior executives are often frequently seen as spending too much time outside the organization working on political, religious, and family issues.[62]

On the other hand, middle managers often lack critical managerial skills and knowledge about the industry in which they are working. At the same time, according to Kiggundu, many mid-level managers exhibit low levels of motivation, tend to be risk averse, are often unwilling to take independent action or show initiative, seem to prefer (or are at least used to) close supervision, and are unwilling to delegate.[63] He goes on to point out that mid-level managers in a wide range of developing countries (i.e., not just in Africa) are frequently understaffed and are characterized by weak and/or inappropriate management systems and organizational controls.

Finally, lower-level employees in Nigeria (and Africa more generally) are often described as being over-staffed and inefficient. Operators tend to be under-utilized, underpaid, resistant to change, and rewarded based on factors unrelated to actual job performance. As a result, we often see low morale, lack of commitment, high turnover, and high absenteeism. Communication up and down the hierarchy tends to be poor.

In all, then, Nigeria as a developing country faces a number of challenges, as do global managers who do business there. Global partnerships are encouraged by the local government, making it increasingly important for global managers to understand the culture, politics, and local laws governing commerce.

Are management patterns converging?

About ten years ago, the *Asahi Shimbun*, Japan's second largest newspaper, published a reader's survey about age, status, and importance in families. Specifically, journalists from the newspaper traveled to Newport Beach, California, and talked with a number of men sitting along the beach. They asked each of them a hypothetical question: Suppose you were sitting on the beach and your mother, wife, and daughter were swimming in the ocean just in front of you. Suddenly you see a huge wave coming towards shore and realize the situation has become very dangerous for all swimmers. You have time to swim out and save one of your family members. Who would you save? The results are telling. About half of the men said they would save their wife and half would save their daughter. No one saved their mother. She had had a good life, so it was reasoned, but we have to think of the future, and the future lay with the young. Armed with these findings, the journalists raced back to Tokyo and headed for the local beach. They followed the same routine and asked the same question to a group of middle-aged men. However, in this case, everyone said they would save their mothers. You can always replace a wife or a daughter, so it was reasoned, but you can't replace your mother. Silly survey? Probably. Interesting survey? Possibly. What the journalists found with their less-than-rigorous study was that age and seniority was probably far more important (and hence more respected) in Japan than in the US – or at least in California.

Commenting on this story recently, Rikkyo University professor Junya Ishikawa pointed out that what the journalists had found in Japan might have been accurate ten years ago, but it was certainly not true today.[64] Instead, younger people in Japan today are losing their respect for a rigid seniority system and are turning increasingly towards a youth culture – just like their American counterparts. Question: Are Japanese and American cultures moving increasingly towards convergence? If so, what is happening in the world of management?

In Chapter 3, Robert J. House noted that when cultures increasingly come in contact with one another, they may converge in some respects but their idiosyncrasies may also become accentuated. In this regard, several researchers have suggested that management styles around the world – especially in the industrialized world – are beginning to converge, and that this convergence will likely increase over time as a result of increased globalization pressures. Some support for this comes from HEC-Geneva professor Susan Schneider, who observed that over a twenty-year period, the managerial values of successive MBA classes attending the Swiss business school converged somewhat over time.[65] Did this convergence result from a global trend towards a single management style or was it the result of exposure to Western management-techniques education? Either way, a change was observed.

Other researchers suggest, equally strongly, that a convergence of management styles across various national cultures will never occur. Instead, management styles around

Exhibit 4.9 Convergence and divergence in future management patterns

Local/regional management model	Dual-track management model	Global management model
Continuation of multiple sets of acceptable management behaviors based on local or regional cultures; rejection of any movement towards one homogeneous or transcultural management style.	Movement by some of the more industrialized and "globalized" cultures towards variations around a central set of acceptable management behaviors; reticence among less industrialized, more ideological, or more isolated cultures to abandon enduring local management models.	Emergence of an increasingly narrow set of acceptable management behaviors; movement towards one "global" management style with minor adaptations to fit local conditions.

Greater heterogeneity   Greater homogeneity

the world will remain culturally distinct, requiring global managers to adapt to various local conditions if they are to succeed. Either way (convergence or non-convergence), this is both an intriguing and important question for future managers. Will the future see a continuation of various local or regional management models or a movement towards a single global model, as illustrated in Exhibit 4.9? Or will the future see some sort of a dual-track system in which the management styles in some (perhaps more industrialized) countries will begin to converge, while styles in other (perhaps less developed or more isolated) countries will carry on with little change?

With these conflicting positions in mind, is it likely that management styles around the world will begin to converge in the future as a result of globalization pressures, or that cultural differences will override globalization pressures and make such convergence very difficult, if not impossible? If management styles around the world in fact converge in the future, what will this convergence look like? What will characterize this new "globalized" management style? On the other hand, if management styles around the world do not converge over time, what can global managers do to prepare themselves for a career that involves doing business in various countries that are characterized by highly diverse cultures?

Inside the managerial mind

The opening example of Kia Motors America illustrates the potential challenges that can emerge when managers from one country are sent to another to take charge of operations. In this case, the Korean executive saw his role as CEO quite differently than his Anglo-American predecessor and, while these differences may have made perfect sense in Seoul, they worked less well in California. Moreover, these changes in managerial role behavior were not without their consequences. This example raises three basic issues for global managers. First, how can cultural variations influence managerial cognitions and analyses? Second, how can cultural variations influence the ways in which thoughts are translated into actions? And third, how can cultural variations influence how employees at all levels of an organization see ideal and actual managerial behavior? All three of these issues raise potentially serious concerns about managing across cultures.

Managerial information processing

Research has shown that national and regional cultures can influence the manner and scope of managerial information processing. This can be seen in perceptual selection, where people experience events in the external world and choose what to see and what not to see; cognitive evaluation, where people categorize or classify what we have seen or experienced according to some relational comparative guideline; cognitive consistency or dissonance, where people identify, interpret, and explain perceived inequities where they see them – especially as they relate to inconsistencies between one's attitudes and behaviors; and behavioral intentions, where people create action plans that will frequently guide their subsequent behaviors.

The differing results from these cognitive processes can influence how managers access, organize, and transform information into patterns of meaning. This can be seen in at least three ways:

(1) Culture can influence cognitive patterns that can affect information acquisition, retention, and recall.

(2) Culture can influence the classification and structure of information and knowledge in peoples' minds.

(3) Culture can influence intelligence, learning, and reasoning. To the extent that these influences are significant (and they typically are between highly divergent cultures), differences in managerial perceptions, attitudes, and actions are also likely to be significant. These influences operate through at least four cognitive processes: perceptual perception, cognitive evaluation, cognitive dissonance, and the creation of behavioral intentions. This was illustrated in a comparison of traditional Chinese and traditional Western patterns of thinking.

Managerial thinking and action

A central theme of this chapter has been the interrelationship between culture, management thinking, and managerial action. In fact, culture can influence this process in at least two different ways. First, culture shapes the context in which managerial action occurs (e.g., what is acceptable managerial behavior?). Second, culture influences the ways in which managers think and reason prior to action (e.g., what is the correct managerial role?). This dual effect of culture, both as an external and internal influence on managerial action, helps to explain part of the difficulties in understanding management differences across cultures. Even so, managers can still learn and benefit from a better understanding of these processes. Specifically, three management implications can be identified:

(1) Knowing that culture shapes people's cognitions implies a need to gather multiple inputs from various divergent sources or people to try and understand the process. For example, we know that diverse teams of managers – with alternative views on how things work and with complementary experiences in different parts of world – can provide a range of available responses that is richer than the set of alternatives provided by people with similar backgrounds and experiences. Beyond this, however, the variation in the makeup of such teams can also provide its members with first-hand insights into the actual workings of managerial thought processes that evolved under different cultural constraints, thus allowing for improved awareness and understanding of both other ways of understanding and our own. They provide variation in the content of alternatives, but they also behave as mirrors where we can see the contrast with our own cultural make-ups, which is even more enriching.

(2) Managers need to keep asking themselves not only which alternative courses of action they might be taking when confronting an issue, but also how the thinking about the issue can be approached in a different way. This is virtually impossible when remaining within a single culture, but access to other cultures, we have seen,

provides access to other ways of sensing, classifying, organizing, and retrieving information, as well as alternative paths to intelligence, learning, and reasoning.

(3) Managers can use the core cultural dimensions introduced earlier in the book to map the access that they may already have to alternative cultural approaches, as well as identifying those they are still lacking and which may complement their current talent pool.

Actual versus idealized managerial roles

A final issue of concern to global managers relates to trends in ideal and real managerial roles. It was noted above that both managers and subordinates often have two perceptions of the managerial role: ideal and actual. For example, research has indicated that most people in individualistic cultures prefer managers who take charge, while most people in collectivistic cultures prefer managers who are more consultative (see Chapter 8). Similarly, managers in high-context cultures frequently make extensive use of the context surrounding a message to get their point across, while managers in low-context cultures tend to rely on specific and detailed messages and ignore much of the message context (see Chapter 7). Differences can also be found within single cultures between general perceptions of ideal and real managers, as noted previously. But even this can get a bit murky, since there are clearly individual differences both within cultures and between them.

Being conscious of cognitive differences across cultures is important for global managers for several reasons:

■ A better understanding of social dynamics in international and culturally diverse business contexts allows managers to take a broader view in such managerial activities as international negotiations or team decision making. Managers who cannot read the minds of their international business associates run the very real risk of managing blindly. While this discussion has focused on East–West cognitive differences, since this is where current research has been focused, it is highly likely that such differences also exist in other parts of the world, including Africa, Latin America, Eastern Europe, and so forth. Hence, it is probably desirable for managers to continually be on the lookout for such differences in business transactions across borders.

■ Understanding that different people can contribute different thinking patterns and styles can prove helpful in organizational staffing decisions. For example, when people from around the globe who may think differently are involved in new product decisions, a broader array of ideas (and criticisms) emerge concerning global market potential of the new products.

■ As we will see later in this book, accounting for cultural differences in the design and implementation – and management – of most organizational activities can become critically important where employees and colleagues, with their culturally specific cognitive endowments, are involved. Global organizations require global employees, and there is no cookie-cutter that turns out homogeneous people for such endeavors.

So, what lessons can be found here? Perhaps the most direct lesson is the need for managers from all nations to be on the lookout for different patterns of managerial and employee behavior. Moreover, managers should be prepared to accommodate or in some way deal with these differences in ways that do not jeopardize what they believe in. And, they should remain flexible at the same time as being focused on their goals and responsibilities. Understanding, not acquiescence, is the name of the game here.

Notes

1 Michael Cannon-Brookes, "The empire strikes back," *The Economist*, September 20, 2008, p. 12.
2 Mzamo P. Mangaliso, "Building competitive advantage from *ubuntu*: management lessons from South Africa," *Academy of Management Executive*, 2001, 15(3), p. 23.
3 Takeo Fujisawa, cited in David Thomas, *Cross-cultural Management*. Thousand Oaks, CA: Sage, 2008, p. 145.
4 David Welch, David Kiley, and Moon Ihlwan, "My way or the highway at Hyundai," *Business Week*, March 6, 2008.
5 *Ibid.*
6 *Ibid.*
7 Richard A. Thompson, *Psychology and Culture*. Dubuque, IA: W. C. Brown, 1975, p. 10.
8 Bradd Shore, *Culture in Mind: Cognition, Culture and the Problem of Meaning*. New York, NY: Oxford University Press, 1996, p. 1.
9 Adesh Agarwal, "Time, memory, and knowledge representation: the Indian perspective," in Jeanette Altarriba (ed.), *Cognition and Culture: A Cross-cultural Approach to Psychology*. Amsterdam: North-Holland, 1993, pp. 44–55.
10 Daniel Wagner, cited in Marshall Segall, Pierre Dasen, John Berry, and Ype Poortinga, *Human Behavior in Global Perspective: An Introduction to Cross-Cultural Psychology*. New York, NY: Pergamon, 1990, p. 171.
11 Richard Harris, Lawrence Schoen, and Deana Hensley, "A cross-cultural story of story memory," *Journal of Cross-Cultural Psychology*, 1992, 23, pp. 133–147.
12 Ralph Reynold, Marsha Taylor, Margaret Steffensen, Larry Shirley, and Richard Anderson, "Cultural schemata and reading comprehension," *Reading Research Quarterly*, 1982, 3, pp. 353–366.

13 Ben Blount and Paula Schwanenflugel, "Cultural bases, for folk classification systems," in
    Altarriba, *Cognition and Culture*, pp. 3–22; Pei-Jung Lin and Paula Schwanenflugel, "Cultural
    familiarity and language factors in the structure of category knowledge," *Journal of Cross-
    Cultural Psychology*, 1995, 23, pp. 153–168; Barbara Malt, "Category coherence in cross-
    cultural perspective," *Cognitive Psychology*, 1995, 29, pp. 85–148.

14 Chi-Yue Chiu, "A cross-cultural comparison of cognitive styles in Chinese and American
    children," *International Journal of Psychology*, 1972, 7, pp. 235–242; Alejandro López, Scott
    Atran, John D. Coley, Douglas L. Medinn, and Edward E. Smith, "The tree of life: universal
    and cultural features of folkbiological taxonomies and inductions," *Cognitive Psychology*,
    1997, 32, pp. 251–295.

15 Chi-Yue Chiu, Ting-Yi Hong, and Carol Dweck, "Lay dispositionism and implicit theories of
    personality," *Journal of Personality and Social Psychology*, 1997, 73, pp. 19–30; A. Fiske,
    S. Kitayama, H. Markus, and R. Nisbett, "The cultural matrix of social psychology," in
    D. T. Gilbert, S. T. Fiske, and G. Lindzey (eds.), *Handbook of Social Psychology*. New York,
    NY: McGraw-Hill, 1998, pp. 915–981.

16 Richard Shweder, "Cultural psychology: what is it?," in Nancy R. Goldberger and Jody
    B. Veroff (eds.), *The Culture and Psychology Reader*. New York, NY: New York University
    Press, 1995, pp. 41–86.

17 Howard Gardner, *Frames of Mind: The Theory of Multiple Intelligences*. New York, NY: Basic
    Books, 1983; Daniel Coleman, *Emotional Intelligence*. NY: Bantam Books, 1995; John Berry,
    "On cross-cultural comparability," *International Journal of Psychology*, 1969, 4, pp. 119–128;
    Philip Vernon, *Intelligence and Cultural Environment*. London: Methuen, 1969.

18 Gail Ferguson, "On transfer and the abilities of man," *Canadian Journal of Psychology*, 1956,
    10, pp. 121–131.

19 Kaiping Peng, Daniel Ames, and Eric Knowles, "Culture and human inference: perspectives
    from three traditions," in David Matsumoto (ed.), *Handbook of Culture and Psychology*.
    Oxford, UK: Oxford University Press, 2001, pp. 245–264.

20 Inchoel Choi, Richard Nisbett, and Ara Norenzayan, "Causal attribution across cultures,"
    Psychological Bulletin, 1999, 125, pp. 47–63; Fiona Lee, Mark Hallahan, and Thaddeus
    Herzog, "Explaining real life events: how culture and domains shape attributions,"
    Personality and Social Psychology Bulletin, 1996, 22, pp. 732–741; Michael Morris and
    Kaiping Peng, "Culture and cause: American and Chinese attributions for social and physical
    events," *Journal of Personality and Social Psychology*, 1994, 67, pp. 949–971.

21 Johnny K. Johanson and Ikujiro Nonaka, *Relentless: The Japanese Way of Marketing*.
    New York, NY: Basic Books, 1996.

22 It is easy to attribute manipulative motivations to slogans of the "satisfaction guaranteed"
    type, and some of that will likely be at play in at least some instances. But note that when
    marketing is seen as a *science* based on the *laws* of human behavior, as we have mentioned is
    typical in Western countries, customer satisfaction is something that can be reasonably
    promised on the premise that the relevant variables (regarding what customers need and the
    characteristics of the products offered) have been scientifically pondered. The problem lies
    more with the premise than with the promise.

23 Richard E. Nisbett, *The Geography of Thought: How Asians and Westerners Think Differently … and Why*. New York, NY: Free Press, 2003.

24 Anne Fernald and Hiromi Morikawa, "Common themes and cultural variations in Japanese and American mothers' speech to infants," *Child Development*, 1993, 64, pp. 637–656.

25 Robert Hess, Keiko Kashiwagi, Hiroshi Azuma, Gary Price, and W. Patrick Dickson, "Maternal expectations for mastery of developmental tasks in Japan and the United States," *International Journal of Psychology*, 1980, 15, pp. 259–271.

26 J. Fischer, "Linguistic socialization: Japan and the United States," in R. Hill and R. Koning (eds.), *Families in East and West: Socialization Patterns and Kinship Ties*. The Hague: Mouton, 1970.

27 Brooks Peterson, *Cultural Intelligence*. Yarmouth, ME: Intercultural Press, 2004, p. 3.

28 In Chinese philosophy, the concept of *yin yang* often referred to in the west as "yin *and* yang," is used to describe how seemingly disjunctive or opposing forces are interconnected and interdependent in the natural world, giving rise to each other in turn. The concept lies at the heart of many branches of classical Chinese science and philosophy, as well as being a primary guideline of traditional Chinese medicine and a central principle of different forms of Chinese martial arts and exercise, such as *baguazhang, taijiquan*, and *qigong*. Many natural dualities (e.g., dark and light, female and male, low and high) are cast in Chinese thought as *yin yang*. The relationship between *yin* and *yang* is often described in terms of sunlight playing over a mountain and in the valley. *Yin* (literally the "shady place" or "north slope") is the dark area occluded by the mountain's bulk, while *yang* (literally the "sunny place" or "south slope") is the brightly lit portion. As the sun moves across the sky, *yin* and *yang* gradually trade places with each other, revealing what was obscured and obscuring what was revealed. *Yin* is usually characterized as slow, soft, insubstantial, diffuse, cold, wet, and tranquil. It is generally associated with the feminine, birth, and generation, and with the night. By contrast, *yang* is typically characterized as hard, fast, solid, dry, focused, hot, and aggressive. It is associated with masculinity and daytime. *Yin* and *yang* are complementary opposites within a greater whole. Everything has both *yin* and *yang* properties, which constantly interact, never existing in absolute stasis.

29 Richard Nisbett and Yuri Miyamoto, "The influence of culture: holistic versus analytic perception," *Trends in Cognitive Science*, 2005, 9(10), pp. 467–473; Kaiping Peng and Richard Nisbett, "Culture, dialectics and reasoning about contradiction," *American Psychologist*, 1999, 54, pp. 741–754.

30 François Jullien, *Traité de l'efficacité*. Paris: Grasset, 1997.

31 T. Kagono, I. Nonaka, K. Sakakibara, and A. Okumura, *Strategic vs. Evolutionary Management: A US-Japan Comparison of Strategy and Organization*. Amsterdam: North-Holland Press, 1985.

32 Sea Jin Chang, "International expansion strategy of Japanese firms: capability building through sequential entry," *Academy of Management Journal*, 1995, 38, pp. 383–407.

33 Jesús González Vallés, *Historia de la Filosofía Japonesa*. Madrid: Tecnos, 2007; François Jullien, "Penser d'un dehors (la Chine)," *Entretiens d'Extrême Occident*. Paris: Seuil, 2000.

34 Morris and Peng, "Culture and cause."

35 Chi-Yue Chiu, Michael Morris, Ying-Yi Hong, and Tanya Menon, "Motivated cultural cognition: the impact of implicit cultural theories on dispositional attribution varies as a function of need for closure," *Journal of Personality and Social Psychology*, 2000, 78, pp. 247–259.

36 William Maddux and Yuki Masaki, "The ripple effect: cultural differences in perceptions of the consequences of events," *Personality and Social Psychology Bulletin*, 2006, 32, pp. 669–683.

37 Cited in Peng and Nisbett, "Culture, dialectics and reasoning about contradiction," p. 744.

38 Richard Nisbett, "Cultural influences on cognition: an interview with Richard Nisbett," *Intercultures Magazine*, October–December 2007, pp. 1–5.

39 Andre Laurent, "The cultural diversity of western conceptions of management," *International Studies of Management and Organization*, Spring–Summer 1983, 13 (1–2), pp. 75–96.

40 Richard Hodgetts and Fred Luthans, *International Management: Culture, Strategy, and Behavior*, 5th Edition. New York, NY: McGraw-Hill-Irwin, 2003.

41 James Abbeglen and George Stalk, *Kaisha: The Japanese Corporation*. New York, NY: Harper & Row, 1985.

42 Personal communication, Atsushi Kagayama, Matsushita Business Group, Tokyo, Japan, 2003.

43 Richard Hill, *We Europeans*. Brussels: Europublications, 1997.

44 Edward T. Hall and Mildred R. Hall, *Understanding Cultural Differences: Germans, French, and Americans*. Yarmouth, ME: Intercultural Press, 1990.

45 Cited in John Hooker, *Working Across Cultures*. Stanford, CA: Stanford Business Books, 2003, p. 234.

46 David Hickson (ed.), *Management in Western Europe*. Berlin: Walter de Gruyter, 1993.

47 Jean-Louis Barsoux and Peter Lawrence, "The making of a French manager," *Harvard Business Review*, July–August 1991, pp. 1–8.

48 Hall and Hall, *Understanding Cultural Differences*, p. 99.

49 Ingrid Brunstein (ed.), *Human Resource Management in Western Europe*. Berlin: Walter de Gruyter, 1995.

50 Hall and Hall, *Understanding Cultural Differences*.

51 *Ibid.*

52 "*Bumiputra*" is a Malay term widely used in Malaysia, embracing ethnic Malays, Javanese, Bugis, Minang, and occasionally other indigenous ethnic groups such as the Orang Asli in Peninsular Malaysia and the tribal peoples in Sabah and Sarawak. This term comes from the Sanskrit word *bhumiputra*, which can be translated literally as "son of earth" or "prince of the soil" (*bhumi* = earth, *putra* = prince). Economic policies designed to favor *bumiputras* (including affirmative action in public education) were implemented in the 1970s, purportedly to defuse inter-ethnic tensions. These policies have succeeded in creating a significant urban-Malay middle class, but have been less effective in eradicating poverty among rural communities and have caused a backlash of resentment from excluded groups, including the Chinese and Indian Malaysians.

53 Joseph Putti, *Management: Asian Context*. New York, NY: McGraw-Hill, 1991; Richard Lewis, *When Cultures Collide*. London: Nicholas Brealey, 1999; Martin Gannon, *Understanding Global Cultures*, 2nd Edition. Thousand Oaks, CA: Sage, 2001; Derek Torrington and Chwee Huat Tan, *Human Resources Management for Southeast Asia*. New York, NY: Prentice Hall, 1994.

54 Robert Frank and Phillip Cook, *The Winner-Take-All Society*. New York, NY: Free Press, 1995.

55 Martin Gannon, *Understanding Global Cultures*, 2nd Edition. Thousand Oaks, CA: Sage, 2001.

56 "Out of control," *The Economist*, December 4, 1999, p. 44.

57 Sanjay Choudhary, "The community concept of business: a critique," *International Studies in Management and Organizations*, 1986, 16(2), p. 93.

58 F. Abudu, "Work attitudes of Africans, with special reference to Nigeria," *ISMO*, 1986, 16(2), pp. 17–36.

59 Moses Kiggundu, "Africa," in Ragu Nath (ed.), *Comparative Management: A Regional View*. Cambridge, MA: Ballinger, 1988, p. 225.

60 Kiggundu, "Africa," p. 225.

61 C. G. Obeleagu-Nzelibe, "The evolution of African management thought," *International Studies of Management and Organizations*, 1986, 16(2), p. 11.

62 Peter Blunt and Merrick Jones, *Managing Organizations in Africa*. Berlin: Walter de Gruyter, 1992.

63 Kiggundu, "Africa," p. 225.

64 Personal communication, Junya Ishikawa, Rikkyo University, Tokyo, Japan, 2008.

65 Susan Schneider and Jean-Louis Barsoux, *Managing across Cultures*. London: Financial Times/Prentice Hall, 2003, pp. 112–114.

CHAPTER 5

Inside the organizational mind: stakeholders, strategies, and decision making

- Stakeholders and strategic choice: a model 128
- The strategy-structure nexus 134
- Organizational decision making: a model 137
- Decision strategies across cultures 139
- MANAGER'S NOTEBOOK: Inside the organizational mind 149

There are no universal solutions to organization and management problems ... Organizations are symbolic entities; they function according to implicit models in the minds of their members, and these are culturally determined.

Geert Hofstede[1]
Maastricht University, The Netherlands

Globalization does not mean imposing homogeneous solutions in a pluralistic world. It means having a global vision and strategy, but it also means cultivating roots and individual identities.

Gucharan Das[2]
Former CEO, Procter and Gamble-India

Many years ago (in the late 1930s, to be precise) telecom CEO Chester Barnard defined an *organization* as a system of consciously coordinated activities of two or more persons.[3] In the intervening eight decades, no one has come up with a better definition. Barnard went further to point out that the survival of any organization depends on its members' ability and willingness to cooperate, communicate, and work towards a common objective. In particular, he noted that in any theory of organization or management, communication must play a dominant role. While Barnard was thinking about US firms in the 1930s with a fairly narrow business focus, his observations still apply today when considering both large and small firms doing business around the world. What has changed is not the fundamental challenges facing companies, but rather the magnitude of these challenges, as well as the manner in which firms organize and "think" collectively to accomplish their core mission.

Consider Wipro and Intel, two highly successful IT companies doing business globally, yet headquartered in very different regions of the world. Wipro Technologies is a rapidly growing software-services firm based in Bangalore, India. It is a global services provider delivering technology-driven business solutions that meet the strategic objectives of its clients around the world. The company currently has over forty "centers of excellence" that focus on creating business solutions around the specific needs of various industries. It delivers superior value to business customers through a combination of process excellence, quality frameworks, and service delivery innovations. Indeed, Wipro was the World's first CMMi Level 5 certified software services company, and the first outside the US to receive the IEEE Software Process Award.

Wipro takes a unique approach to both organization and management, largely viewing innovation through the lens of practicality to design unique solutions for its end customers and other stakeholders. It uses applied innovation techniques to infuse newer ideas and newer ways of doing things into all parts of the organization to improve business outcomes – often without major disruptive change. It also uses what it calls a "360-degree business approach," covering process, delivery, business, and technology. As part of this strategy, Wipro Technologies has adapted many principles from the ("lean") Toyota Production System to fundamentally change its operating model in a very different sector from that of Toyota. Throughout, innovation and customer service have been at the root is its business success.

In an era of "faster, better, cheaper" (a company slogan), California-based Intel Corporation also offers a good example of developing a strategy and structure to fit its corporate mission and stakeholder interests. In the final analysis, companies like Intel (and Wipro) live or die based on the quality of their research.[4] In recognition of this challenge, Intel recently reinvented itself again to focus more directly on its R&D environment. This endeavor was called the "Next Generation R&D Model," and was strongly championed by the company's top executives. As Intel CEO Paul S. Otellini noted, "Intel pushes the boundaries of innovation so our work can make people's lives more exciting, fulfilling, and manageable. And our work never stops. We never stop looking for the next leap ahead – in technology, education, culture, manufacturing, and social responsibility. And we never stop striving to deliver solutions with greater benefits for everyone."[5]

The new organizing model began by dividing the company's environment into three interrelated parts. The first component, advanced research and investments, consisted of Intel's many sources for new ideas and products, including universities, government-sponsored research, and new start-ups. The second component focused on Intel's core technologies and proprietary R&D; that is, how the company could capitalize on available research and emerging technologies to develop innovative new products. The final component consisted of technology transfer and "productization" by Intel itself; that is, how to get its new ideas and products to market.

To implement this strategy, Intel selected a network organization design – actually, a new network design since the company has long used this approach. For starters, they implemented a broad reorganization that brought all major product groups in line with the company's strategy to drive development of complete technology platforms based on Intel ingredients. Second, they created two new organizations to address growing opportunities for Intel-based technologies in digital health care and in serving Intel's worldwide distribution channel.

In 2003, Intel began providing customers with full sets of technology ingredients, including microprocessors, chipsets, communications chips, base software capabilities, and other enabling tools that work together as a platform to improve the way technology is used. This coincided with its introduction of the Intel *Centrino* mobile technology. In 2008, Intel continued this trend by more-fully integrating Intel's organizational structure by creating three groups to lead the company's efforts in platforms for mobility, the digital enterprise, and digital home. These platform-based organizations also reflect the company's ongoing convergence of computing and communications by incorporating both capabilities across the new groups. Intel's management anticipated that the new organization would help address growth opportunities by better anticipating and addressing market needs, speeding up decision making, and ensuring world-class operational excellence. Each operating unit has the autonomy to allocate computing and communications resources to be successful, making Intel's entire structure consistent with its platform products strategy.

Reinforcing this organizing strategy is a network of Intel R&D facilities that literally spans the globe. This includes facilities across North and South America, the EU, East and South Asia, Russia, and Israel. Scientific talent is sourced wherever it can be found, and the entire system is coordinated through one of the best computer networking systems available. For Intel, the network organization (in various incarnations over the years) has proven to be a highly successful organizational design in support of their long-term strategy.

Stakeholders and strategic choice: a model

Wipro and Intel have remained competitive through time and economic turbulence by continually evolving as the environment and markets change and develop. In doing so, however, a key responsibility of both companies has been to establish a coherent mission and a strategic plan to guide the firm in the efficient use of its financial, physical, technological, and human resources towards a clearly stated objective. In other words, strategy guides both structure and management, at least in theory. However, as was noted in a previous chapter, other factors, including local beliefs, values, and prevailing social norms, also play a role in the final determination of the outcomes.

The strategic management cycle

Based on available research, it is possible to develop a schematic representation high-lighting the manner in which managers and managerial action interact with several of the more macro aspects of organizations, including their mission and values, strategy and goals, organization structure, and management practices. This can be referred to as the *strategic management cycle*. Historically, the relationships involved in this cycle have been seen largely in terms of a one-way causal relationship. That is, mission determines strategy, which in turn determines structure, which governs management practice, which ultimately determines the extent to which the organization succeeds in achieving its mission. The cyclical nature of this model acknowledges feedback loops throughout the process, but particularly in the same single direction as is suggested for the other factors.

However, more recent evidence, as discussed below, suggests a far more complex and interactive relationship (see Exhibit 5.1). Specifically, while mission and values may help determine an organization's initial strategy and goals (at least in the early years of the venture), organization design and even management practices can also influence strategy in significant ways, especially as the organization matures and is confronted by new challenges and economic realities. Likewise, strategy can influence structure, but so too can management practices. Finally, these interactive relationships are played out in a business environment that is itself multifaceted and interactive. This includes such external factors as geographic location; the cultural milieu(s) in which organizations work; legal conventions and local customs; variations in political and institutional support; a country or region's factor endowments; the specific sector of the economy where the organization does business (e.g., industry versus services); available investments, technologies, and markets; and environmental challenges and goals. In other words (as will be discussed below) the simple strategy-structure-management paradigm is found to be sorely lacking in explanatory power as organization theory crosses borders.

Exhibit 5.1 The strategic management cycle

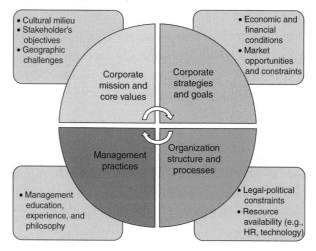

Stakeholder power and influence

Not surprisingly, a company's stakeholders (e.g., investors, customers, employees, etc.) can have a major influence on both the determination of the company's mission and its strategy. Various stakeholders place demands, expectations, and constraints on enterprise activity, and, obviously, these demands frequently differ across the various stakeholders, some wanting better return on their investment and others that want a more socially or environmentally responsible organization. Most strategists understand this. However, what many global managers fail to understand is that the nature and power of a stakeholder group can be influenced by the predominant culture in which the enterprise does business. While, in theory, all stakeholders are created equal, in fact some have far more power than others. We can thus identify two stakeholder models: a *centralized* and a *distributed* stakeholder model.

For example, as shown in Exhibit 5.2, some companies routinely face a stakeholders group where power and influence is fairly centralized. In Korea, Mexico, the UK, and the US, for example, investors, customers, and governments often have considerable influence over enterprise mission and strategy, while employees and the public-at-large do not. At the same time, in Germany, Japan, and Sweden, the opposite situation exists. That is, investors, customers, and governments still have a major influence over missions and strategies, as do employees and the public-at-large. Moreover, American or British firms that do business in Sweden or Germany, for example, face this broader or more distributed stakeholder group and must accommodate these different constituencies

Exhibit 5.2 Centralized versus distributed stakeholder models

To see how variations in the stakeholder model can influence strategy, consider Volkswagen AG.[6] From its corporate headquarters in Wolfsburg, Germany, Volkswagen has consistently tried to accomplish two seemingly contradictory goals: remain a sales leader in the global auto industry while at the same time building and maintaining a "worker's paradise" for its employees. On several occasions over the past decade, however, Volkswagen's twin goals have come under repeated attacks as global car sales plummeted and the survival of the company itself seemed in doubt.

During one of these crises, sales dropped 20 percent in one year, requiring a massive reduction in working hours by company employees. Indeed, the company determined that it had 30,000 more workers than it needed in Germany alone. Its supervisory board concluded that poor economic conditions would likely remain for several years, and that in order to survive, it had to find a way to quickly reduce its operating costs by 20 percent to match the decline in sales.

As Volkswagen faced this challenge, the business and social environment in which key decisions would be made differed sharply from those the company would have faced in the US. For starters, 20 percent of Volkswagen's stock is owned by the state of Lower Saxony, where the company's principle manufacturing facilities are located. In addition, 90 percent of all employees at Volkswagen are unionized. Since the company's union contract required the approval of over 80 percent of the shareholders on all important decisions, any cost-cutting plan that involved large lay-offs was highly problematic. Lower Saxony and the IG-Metall union also had strong representation on the company's supervisory board, where cost reduction strategies would be openly discussed. As a result, major lay-offs were not a viable option.

In addition to its governance structure, Volkswagen had spent decades developing a culture of cooperation and inclusion among all of its employees. Key features of this culture included the widespread dissemination of detailed information on the state of the company to employees, IG-Metall union, and works councils; a receptive climate for unions; informal codetermination in advance of formal decisions; an emphasis on consensus in decision making; and a norm of implementing decisions once they are made.

In creating and supporting this culture, Volkswagen was by no means abandoning its objectives of profitability and shareholder value. Instead, it believed (like many German companies) that all of the principal stakeholders of the company – including employees – should be protected in making major corporate decisions. In other words, capital and labor were seen as joint responsibilities of the company. From the standpoint of top management, Volkswagen had to find a solution that was acceptable to both sides. On the one hand, a reduction in labor costs was required to enhance operating efficiency and competitiveness, particularly in the face of reduced demand for its product. On the other hand, the method of achieving this cost reduction had to be acceptable to rank-and-file employees. Had managers in other countries (e.g., Australia, the UK, the US) faced this dilemma, the decision process would likely have been much simpler due to the fewer powerful stakeholders at the table.

Institutional support

In addition to culture's influence on which stakeholder model is implemented, culture can also influence the scope and nature of a country's institutional support for its industries. That is, how can government actions and institutions support or impede a company's strategic choice and implementation? Consider the case of Korea's Hyundai Motor Company. Hyundai's first entries into the global car markets were disappointing. Product quality was so poor that even low prices could not offset them. Over the years, Hyundai reengineered not just its cars but also the whole company, to the point where its cars are now ranked among the best in the world. Even so, the image of low, or at least mediocre, quality persisted, despite award after award for product quality. The question was repeatedly raised as to how Korean-made cars could possibly be equivalent to upscale German or Japanese cars. Ultimately, the company launched a new advertising campaign aimed at convincing consumers that a Hyundai may not be the high-status choice but it was certainly the intelligent choice (i.e., value for money), a strategy successfully used by Sweden's Volvo many years earlier. Hyundai's strategy was aided in no small way by a long history of government support for the country's heavy industries. This occurred largely through the industrial policy of the Korean Government, which included government financial support, access to emerging technologies, and restricted markets for foreign imports.

Let's go one step further and compare Japan and the US in terms of how their institutional environments may affect a company's strategic choice. If there is a principal difference in the business strategies of Japanese and US firms, it is Japan's preoccupation with gaining market share as opposed to a US preoccupation on short-term net profits or higher stock prices. This fundamental difference results from several differences in the two business environments that allow many Japanese firms to take a longer-term perspective than their US competitors.

First, consider the institutional environment in which most US firms operate. This environment is characterized by the following:

- Distant and oftentimes adversarial business-government relations are common, including government as principal regulator.
- The principal purpose of a company is to maximize stockholder wealth.
- Investors stress short-term transactions and returns on investment.
- A clear link exists between earnings per share and stock price.
- Managers frequently offered stock options and large bonuses for superior performance.
- Finally, undervalued companies frequently subject to hostile takeovers.

Now consider a very different institutional environment found in Japan. This includes the following:

- Strong and relatively permanent cooperative business-government relations permeate the business landscape, including government targeting of strategic industries and support of local industries.
- The principal purpose of a company is to build value over the long-term to benefit investors, employees, and the nation.
- Investors stress long-term stock appreciation instead of earnings per share.
- Dividends are paid at a constant rate as a percent of par value of stock, not as a percentage of profits.
- Managers seldom offered stock options or large bonuses for superior performance.
- Few outside board members are present to defend stockholder interests.
- Finally, undervalued companies typically protected by sister companies from outside takeovers.

As a result of these differences, Japanese firms are better positioned to focus their attention on attaining strategic objectives (such as beating competitors) instead of financial objectives (such as keeping stockholders happy). This competitive advantage occurs for three principal reasons. First, low profits and high retained earnings support growth. Second, close relationships with banks allow the use of heavy debt to support growth. And finally, Japanese stockholders routinely accept low dividends and management's absolute control of the firm.

Within this institutional framework, many Japanese firms are able to develop strategic plans to compete against Western firms by using one or more of the following three strategies. First, compete with high-value products where the company can add value with knowledge instead of some other factor. For example, many Japanese firms tend to compete based on superior technology instead of cost (e.g., cameras). With a highly educated – but also highly paid – workforce, this represents a smart strategy. Second, continually stress productivity improvements to minimize costs and remain ahead of competitors. Japan's use of just-in-time production and total quality management (TQM) quality control systems are legendary. And third, capitalize on the resources of their broad-based business networks, the *keiretsu* (see Chapter 6). For example, Japanese companies routinely get financing from group banks and use group-based trading companies for distribution.

Using these strategies, Japanese firms generally follow an incremental sequence of tactics to capture targeted markets. First, they enter a market at the low end with high-quality products. Through continuous improvement, they then move to penetrate the market and build customer loyalty. Next, they move upscale in the market where profit margins are more substantial. Overseas manufacturing facilities are opened when a sufficient overseas market exists to ensure manufacturing economies of scale. Finally, profits from the venture are re-invested in improving existing products or developing new ones to remain one step ahead of their competitors. The end result of this strategy is to force competitors to play a never-ending game of catch-up until their resources are depleted and they leave the market.

The strategy-structure nexus

Organizations exist in highly complex and conflicting environments, where managers must often act with an absence of critical information. Moreover, as noted above, cultural differences are ever present to confuse things further. The question for the global manager is how to proceed. In the face of this uncertainly, there is often no one best design for any organization. Rather, global companies must find a design that best suits – and supports – their overall global strategy. Fine-tuning a company's overall design so it more carefully responds to and supports corporate strategy is a prerequisite for success in the global marketplace. Unfortunately, this basic paradigm raises a conundrum for many managers.

Logic (and most strategy experts) suggests that there is a rational sequence between strategy and structure in which strategy precedes structure. Hence, a rational company first determines its overall goals and objectives and then designs (or redesigns) its organization structure to support the strategy. Unfortunately, while this practice is common in the West, it is far less common in other parts of the world where local considerations often come into play. To put it another way, the strategy-structure relationship is, to a degree, culture-bound. In many East Asian countries, for example, companies often first consider what resources they currently have – including human resources – and then, and only then, consider what strategies best capitalize on these resources. This may be referred to as *structural determinism*; that is, a strategic management cycle (see Exhibit 5.1, above) in which the quality and positioning (or structuring) of existing key corporate resources – including human resources – influence subsequent strategic decision making to a greater degree than emerging strategies influence organization design. This is a relative, but nonetheless important, difference, since it requires managers to focus more squarely on existing critical corporate resources as a basis for future strategic considerations.

This structural determinism – really an "inverted" tendency when compared with prevailing strategic management theories – can be explained by several factors. First, in many countries (not including the UK or the US), it is sometimes very difficult to offload current employees, so managers are more likely to consider their present employees and how they can best use them. Labor laws and social legislation in the Netherlands, Germany, and the Scandinavian countries make it both difficult and costly to lay employees off, while in Japan, Malaysia, and Thailand, managers can lose face by demonstrating that they cannot make full use of the people they have. (This is the manager's problem, not the employees.) In addition, in countries that use some form of *guānxi* (see Chapter 6) or similar reciprocal exchange relationships that are developed over time, it is not always easy to switch partners and find new ones. This creates organizational inertia that is changed only with great difficulty or crisis.

This "inverted" model can also be seen in the strategic decisions made by Germany's *Mittelstand* firms.[7] Most people are familiar with the names of a number of large and successful German companies, including Siemens, BMW, Volkswagen, Daimler, Beyer, and BASF. What many people fail to realize, however, is that that the real strength of the

German economy actually relies less on these large companies and more on its 2.5 million small and medium-sized firms. These so-called *Mittelstand* (or small to medium-sized) firms account for over two-thirds of the nation's economy and over 80 percent of its private-sector employment. Examples of *Mittelstand* firms include Rational (high-end restaurant ovens), Trumpf (computer-based machine tools), and Playmobil (educational toys).

Germany's *Mittelstand* firms compete in the global marketplace through a global strategy that has served them well for several decades. This strategy can be summarized as follows:

- First, because of their high-cost structure, most *Mittelstand* firms ignore markets characterized by low prices and prefer instead to focus on markets where quality or other product uniqueness can command a high price.
- Within these markets, they focus on making superior products using advanced technologies and/or superior craftsmanship.
- They then compete based on customer satisfaction, not short-term profit maximization.
- To supplement this effort, German firms hire and train the best workers they can find, not the cheapest. They make extensive use of apprenticeship programs as competitive weapons.
- All employees, regardless of level in the organization, are empowered to an extent seldom seen elsewhere to help achieve the firm's mission (see Chapter 6). This is largely done through co-determination and employee involvement.
- Finally, German firms prefer to take a long-term perspective to market development and can be patient when necessary. This is largely possible because most companies have close ties with major German banks, and other financial institutions are patient about getting a return on their investment, unlike North America where investors often require a shorter payback period.

Unfortunately, recent increases in the cost of labor and production in Germany have increasingly threatened the competitiveness of many of these *Mittelstand* firms. As a result, some firms are beginning to curtail many of their German-based operations in favor of manufacturing facilities in other lower-cost countries (notably in Asia and Eastern Europe). Increasing emphasis is being placed on using technology to increase productivity. Even so, the future remains highly uncertain. Despite their current success, many worry that *Mittelstand* firms might eventually price themselves out of global markets in the future because of their high-cost structure. In the final analysis, how much will customers pay for German craftsmanship? On the other hand, if quality has been the long-term basis of a firm's competitiveness, what are the risks of changing (or devaluing) this strategy?

Organizational decision making: a model

As exemplified by the examples of Wipro and Intel above, making timely, relevant, and hopefully wise) decisions concerning the future directions of a firm is clearly a principal function of management. Critical to this process is where, when, and how information is sourced for optimum results. In other words, who has useful and important information or viewpoints that can lead to better decisions and who can be ignored, either for confidentiality or efficiency reasons? Clearly, there are considerable and often heated disagreements on this issue. At the heart of this disagreement is the issue of employee involvement and participation in decision making.

Not surprisingly, participation can take many different forms both within and between cultures. In Japan, for example, culture and traditions dictate that managers consult with their workers on many aspects of individual and departmental performance. Individual employees are encouraged to step forward with ideas to improve operations or product development. As a result, employee suggestion systems abound in Japanese companies. However, organization-wide issues are typically left to senior managers. By contrast, Germany long ago enacted a series of federal laws that mandate employee participation in virtually all key decisions an organization makes (see Chapter 6 for more details). This form of participation normally takes place through elected representatives to management boards, rather than having individual employees step forward with ideas or suggestions. Finally, the situation in countries like Australia, Canada, the UK and the US is somewhat difficult to describe since it is characterized by wide variations in the amount of allowed participation. For example, companies in these countries tend to support broad-based employee participation, while others shy away from it. No cultural or legal mandates require participation, so prevailing organizational norms are set either by corporate culture or senior management.

As we consider these trends, however, two caveats must be kept in mind. First, most of the rigorous studies on the impact of employee participation and involvement were conducted among either English-speaking (typically British and North American) or Scandinavian (e.g., Norwegian, Swedish) employees. As a result, far less is known about the motivational potential of employee participation across other cultural groupings. The obvious unanswered question here is the extent to which theory actually translates into action around the world. Put another way, do employees in countries as diverse as

Costa Rica, Egypt, India, Malaysia, and Nigeria all perform better if allowed high amounts of participation?

A second problem is a bit more esoteric. Specifically, throughout the employee participation movement, the actual concept itself remains only loosely defined. That is, what exactly does "participation" or employee involvement mean? How is the concept operationalized? And how far down the organizational hierarchy does actual participation actually exist? In point of fact, employee participation is operationalized in many different ways in different cultures around the world. Differences can also be found in the extent to which senior managers are actually committed to such participation or just give lip service to it or – worse still – use it as a form of exploitation by creating the impression that "your opinion counts" when in fact it does not.

The intersection of these two problems – the questionable universality of participation as a sound management principle and the variable implementation of participative principles – creates significant challenges for global managers. Simply put, can managers trust what they have been taught about how much they should attempt to involve rank-and-file employees when sent to a new and unfamiliar work environment?

To address this challenge and delve further into the manner in which participation strategies are enacted around the world, we need an analytic framework to further guide our study. This framework must address cultural influences on decision making from the standpoint of both managers and employees (see Exhibit 5.3). Following this approach, cultural environments create and reinforce multiple and often conflicting cultural drivers of decision-making through the culture's prevailing social normative beliefs and values of both managers and employees. These drivers include beliefs and values about who should be involved in the decision, how to approach problem identification and analysis, acceptable or mandated information search procedures, decision rules, by what standards subordinates assess the competence of the decision-maker, and which management skills decision-makers will have to make and implement the decision.

As a result of the interactions of these factors, culture-based decision-making strategies will be developed, as well as preparation to put these strategies to work. These strategies can include many variables but principally affect what kind of decision-making approach will be favored: centralized, consultative, or collaborative (see discussion below). However, at the same time that managers are preparing, employees are also preparing and developing their own strategies. Finally, the mix of cultural drivers, preparedness, and strategies come together at a cultural crossroads to influence decision behavior and outcomes. As noted in Chapter 2, this is where the rubber meets the road. Resulting outcomes can include negative employee reactions to not being included in

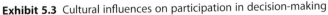

Exhibit 5.3 Cultural influences on participation in decision-making

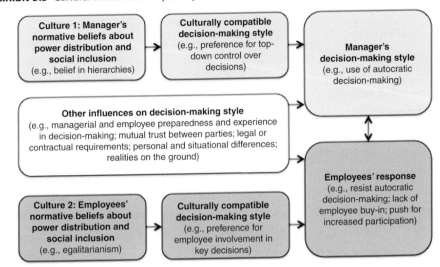

the decisions. Or, alternatively, they can include active behavior by employees with regard to decision quality, timeliness, support and ownership by employees, and the ability of the decision-maker or organization to successfully implement the chosen course of action. These outcomes are then evaluated by both sides to determine their degree of success or failure, and lessons that can be applied to preparations for future decision-making episodes.

Clearly, any model such as this one described here makes the decision-making process appear to be simpler than it really is. That is, in reality, we are likely to find considerably more interactive dynamics between players and factors, as well as other external factors (e.g., institutional factors, respective bargaining positions of each side) in play. Even so, the model does highlight several of the key attributes in the decision-making process. With this in mind, we turn to a more detailed look at decision-maker strategies and behaviors.

Decision strategies across cultures

While many heuristics are available to examine the degree of employee participation allowed or encouraged in organizational decision making, we will make use of a long-standing framework initially developed by Victor Vroom and Phillip Yetton.[8] Their

Exhibit 5.4 Management challenge: approaches to participation and decision making

Centralized decision making	Consultative decision making	Collaborative decision making
Managers may or may not seek advice or input from subordinates and others, and then make the decision largely unilaterally.	Managers actively seek advice and input from subordinates and others, discuss issues, and then make the decision somewhat unilaterally.	Managers work closely and interactively with subordinates and others and seek a consensual or collective decision.

Autocratic and exclusive ◁──────────────▷ Participative and inclusive

"normative decision model" has seen widespread use among scholars and managers, due in part to its strong empirical base and in part to its down-to-earth approach to understanding how decisions up and down the organizational hierarchy are actually made. The part of the model we use here is a classification scheme relating to the amount of participation actually allowed by subordinates. Vroom and Yetton differentiated between three levels of employee participation, allowing for variations around each (see Exhibit 5.4):[9]

(1) *Centralized decisions.* Where the manager-in-charge either makes a decision or solves a problem unilaterally after brief discussions or input from subordinates or others. (Many researchers refer to this as "authoritarian" decision making, but it is more accurate to characterize this approach as being unilateral in nature, and not necessarily autocratic.)

(2) *Consultative decisions.* Where the manager-in-charge actively seeks advice and input from subordinates and others (often working together as a team) but still makes a unilateral decision.

(3) *Collaborative decisions.* Where the manager-in-charge works closely and interactively with subordinates and others and seeks a consensual or collective decision in which everyone has an opportunity to take part.

Centralized decision making

If we look at a typical decision-making process in many of the so-called Anglo countries (e.g., Australia, Canada, the UK, the US), we often find a process much like that shown in Exhibit 5.5 – but with obvious notable variations. Here, problem identification is largely a managerial or supervisory responsibility; workers' opinions are often ignored or not offered in the first place. Once a problem or issue has been identified, it is

Exhibit 5.5 Centralized decision making (e.g., Australia, Canada, UK, US)

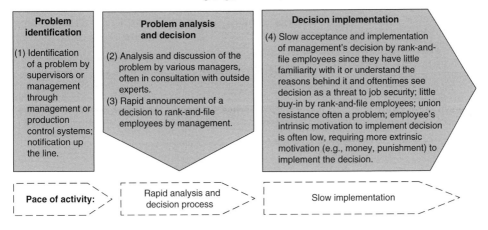

management's responsibility to analyze and resolve it, often with the help of senior managers or outside specialists and consultants. Decisions are then passed down to lower-level employees in the form of changed work procedures. Not surprisingly, since the people at the bottom of the hierarchy often have little understanding of management's conclusions or intents, decision implementation tends to be slow as management now must convince workers to join the decision. Frequently, extrinsic rewards (i.e., externally administered rewards such as pay or bonuses) must be used instead of intrinsic rewards (i.e., internally administered rewards such as pride in accomplishment or job satisfaction) as a result of this process.

To see how this centralized decision process can play itself out in the US, consider the recent example of executive selection at General Motors. For several years, and for a variety of reasons, GM's auto sales had declined precipitously. Despite continual pressure to resign and let someone else take the helm, CEO Rick Wagoner repeatedly sought the support of friendly members of the board of directors to continue in his leadership role. Finally, when annual losses reached US$40 billion in 2008, Wagoner was forced to admit that he was "somewhat stretched" in his job and needed more help. His answer was to divide his current job into two, retaining the CEO and chairman's largely external role while promoting long-term GM executive Frederick Henderson to become the new Chief Operating Officer. Henderson had an established record as a turn-around artist within several of GM's divisions in both Asia and Europe, and Wagoner was convinced he could help with the company's transition into a more competitive organization. But Wagner's decision was taken largely unilaterally. It was "something I'd been thinking about for a while and talking to the board about."[10] In

Exhibit 5.6 Centralized decision making (e.g., China)

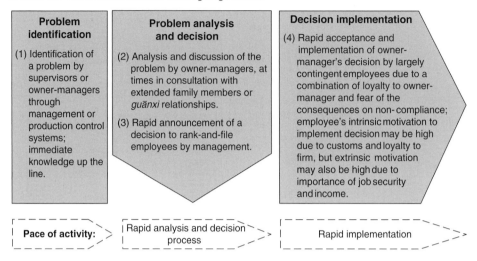

view of the pivotal role played by a COO in any restructuring effort, it is interesting how few of the major stakeholders in GM's future (e.g., alliance partners, unions, division managers, suppliers, distributors, etc.) were actually involved in this decision. Wagoner proposed Henderson, the board agreed, and the decision was announced. At the same time, the board of directors voted to increase Wagoner's salary by 33 percent.[11] (It is interesting to note here that in other Western countries, including Australia, the UK, the Netherlands, and Sweden, it is customary to allow company stockholders to vote on executive compensation; not so in the US.[12]) Within six months, GM was facing bankruptcy and turned to the federal government for a bailout. Shortly thereafter, Wagoner was fired as CEO.

Meanwhile, the decision process described above is not dissimilar from that commonly found in Chinese *gong-si*, or family-based companies (see Chapter 6 for details on this type of organization). Despite being a collectivistic country, China is still hierarchical, leading to centralized power in decision-making. As shown in Exhibit 5.6, problem identification is typically done by either supervisors or owner-managers using fairly rigid management and production control systems. The owner-managers then discuss and analyze the problem, often in consultation with extended family members or *guānxi* relationships. Because of the autocratic decision style, rapid announcement of a decision to rank-and-file employees by management is possible. Rapid acceptance and implementation of an owner-manager's decision by largely contingent employees is also possible due to a combination of loyalty to the owner-manager and fear of the consequences on non-compliance. Employees' intrinsic motivation to implement decisions may be high due to customs and loyalty to the firm, but extrinsic motivation may also be high due to importance of job security and income.

Consultative decision making

Decision making in a typical Japanese *kaisha* (company) reflects Japanese culture and is seen by many observers as being quite distinct from the West (see Chapter 6 for details). Not surprisingly, Japanese firms endorse the concept of decision-making based on consensus up and down the hierarchy.[13] The system by which this is done is usually called *ringi-seido* (often shortened to simply *ringi-sei*), or circle of discussion, as illustrated in Exhibit 5.7.

When a particular problem or opportunity is identified, a group of workers or supervisors will discuss various parameters of the problem and try and identify possible solutions. At times, technical experts will be brought in for assistance. If the initial results are positive, employees will approach their supervisor for more advice and possible support. This entire process is generally referred to in Japan as *nemawashi*. The word *nemawashi* is derived from a description of the process of preparing the roots

Exhibit 5.7 Consultative decision making (e.g., Japan)

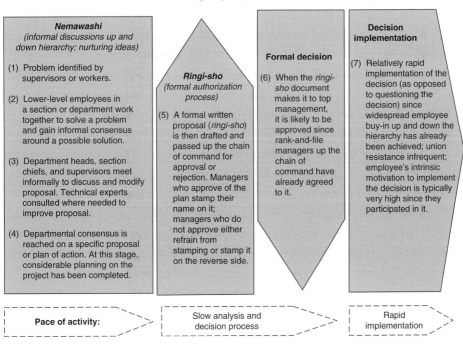

of a tree for planting.[14] The concept here is that if the roots are properly prepared, the tree will survive and prosper. Similarly, if a proposal is properly prepared, it too should survive and prosper.

When a group has achieved informal consensus, a formal proposal is then drafted for submission up the chain of command. This formal document, known as a *ringi-sho*, is reviewed by successively higher levels of management. If a manager agrees with the proposal, he stamps his name on it; if not, he either refrains from stamping it or stamps it on the reverse side. By the time the document reaches upper management, it has become clear whether it has broad-based support or not. If it does enjoy support, in all likelihood top management will formally adopt the proposal. In this way, upper management frequently has little input into the decision-making process. If a proposal has universal support up the chain of command, top managers will be hard-pressed to oppose it.

While discussions concerning a particular decision or course of action are proceeding, two seemingly contradictory processes often occur that tend to confuse many Westerners. In Japan, doing or saying the right thing according to prevailing norms or social custom is referred to as *tatemae*, while doing or saying what one actually prefers to do (which may be difficult) is referred to as *honne*.[15] Thus, in a conversation or meeting, to some Westerners a Japanese manager may speak in contradictions, or worse, speak insincerely. In reality, the manager may simply be saying what he believes he is obliged to say, while hoping that through subtle signals the recipient of the message will discover his true desire or intent. This can be confusing to many Westerners and requires them to listen carefully and observe body language as well as formal speech (e.g., reading someone's face). After all, Japan is a high-context culture, while most Western nations are not.

A key point to remember here: the *ringi-sei* process tends to result in slow decisions, often a disadvantage in a fast-paced competitive global business environment. However, this process yields considerable support for and commitment to the emergent solution when it is achieved. By contrast, many Western decisions are typically made unilaterally much higher up in the management hierarchy but, once made, frequently face considerable opposition or apathy as managers and workers attempt to implement them. As a result, strategic planning is frequently accomplished more quickly in the West, while strategic implementation is frequently accomplished more quickly in Japan.

To see how this process works in practice, consider Toshiba.[16] For several years, Toshiba fought rival Sony over who would control the next-generation DVD format (Toshiba's HD DVD or Sony's Blu-ray). This was a battle of technology, movie studios, merchandisers, and customers. When it finally became painfully clear that Sony's Blu-ray format was going to win the battle, Toshiba's CEO Atsutoshi Nishida initially took no action. Instead, he spent considerable time thinking about both the DVD market in general and Toshiba's role in this changing market in particular. He discussed the matter with numerous colleagues up and down the corporate hierarchy. He talked with his alliance partners outside of Toshiba. Then he held more discussions and floated more proposals. Word came from throughout the organization that the company needed to remain in the DVD market, partly because of pride and partly because people reasoned that the company had the advanced technologies required to compete over the long term. In the end, instead of admitting defeat, Nishida built a consensus within Toshiba and among its partners to cease any further futile competition against Sony. At the same time, he began pushing his researchers to try and leapfrog Blu-ray technology with something even better for the distant future. Consensus was also reached on a decision to push current marketing efforts harder to capture a larger market share for standard-format (or older) DVD players – a much larger market than the anticipated market for Blu-rays. He then announced quietly that Toshiba was yielding to Sony's Blu-ray. Within two months, Toshiba began shipping new models of standard-format DVD players at reduced cost to global markets.

Collaborative decision making

Finally, the decision-making process found in many German, Dutch, and Scandinavian firms tend to be more participative than any country in either the Anglo or the Asian cluster. This is due in large measure due to the presence of codetermination laws and works councils.

Collaborative decision making can be highly complex due to the knowledge and power of the various stakeholders (see Exhibit 5.8). In this process, problems are most frequently identified by either supervisors or workers through a combination of job experience and sophisticated production-control processes. Lower-level employees in a section or department begin by working with supervisors to help identify the underlying causes of the problem, as well as possible solutions. Next, department heads, section chiefs, and supervisors meet to discuss and develop a proposal to remedy the situation. Technical experts and works council members are frequently consulted as needed to achieve the best possible solution. The problem and possible solutions are then passed up the management hierarchy. Management discusses the problem and possible solutions widely and then makes a formal decision, often in consultation and negotiation with works council members and the local industrial union leadership.

Exhibit 5.8 Collaborative decision making (e.g., Germany, Netherlands, Sweden)

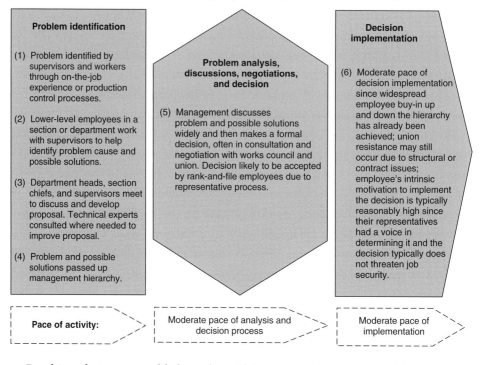

Problem identification

(1) Problem identified by supervisors and workers through on-the-job experience or production control processes.

(2) Lower-level employees in a section or department work with supervisors to help identify problem cause and possible solutions.

(3) Department heads, section chiefs, and supervisors meet to discuss and develop proposal. Technical experts consulted where needed to improve proposal.

(4) Problem and possible solutions passed up management hierarchy.

Problem analysis, discussions, negotiations, and decision

(5) Management discusses problem and possible solutions widely and then makes a formal decision, often in consultation and negotiation with works council and union. Decision likely to be accepted by rank-and-file employees due to representative process.

Decision implementation

(6) Moderate pace of decision implementation since widespread employee buy-in up and down the hierarchy has already been achieved; union resistance may still occur due to structural or contract issues; employee's intrinsic motivation to implement the decision is typically reasonably high since their representatives had a voice in determining it and the decision typically does not threaten job security.

Pace of activity: | Moderate pace of analysis and decision process | Moderate pace of implementation

Resulting decisions are likely to be widely accepted by rank-and-file employees because of the representative process through which they were made; workers at all levels have had a voice throughout the process. As a result, decision implementation typically proceeds at a moderate pace, although union resistance may still occur due to structural or contract issues. Employee's intrinsic motivation to implement the decision is typically reasonably high since their representatives had a voice in determining it and the decision typically does not threaten job security.

To see how collaborative decision making works, let's return one more time to Volkswagen AG. When threatened financially due to declining auto sales (as discussed above), Volkswagen was required to follow a consensual decision-making process as part of Germany's legislated codetermination system (see Chapter 6). As the management and supervisory boards examined the problem, several traditional solutions, like early retirement, temporary reductions in working hours, and consensual termination agreements, were eliminated due primarily to excessive costs associated with their implementation. The only viable solution from management's standpoint was to reduce the workweek of all employees without compensatory payments. The question then was how to gain the support of labor to this course of action.

Volkswagen opened negotiations with its principal union, IG-Metall. At first, union representatives rejected even the basic idea of reducing the workweek without compensation. Over time, however, they became convinced of the necessity for change. From then on, the question was how to achieve the company's goal with the minimum of pain for employees. Union leaders and works council members held focus groups with employees to discuss various options and seek suggestions and ideas. These proposals were summarized and fed back to management.

After thorough negotiations, IG-Metall and the management board agreed on a compromise plan that shortened working hours without compensation while simultaneously increasing worker productivity. Management did not receive the magnitude of working hour reductions they had sought, but the increased productivity agreements were designed to compensate for this loss. The three-part plan was as follows. First, Volkswagen converted its workforce to a four-day workweek, reducing working hours from thirty-six hours to twenty-eight hours and reducing labor costs by 20 percent. However, at the same time, the company and union agreed to eliminate several bonuses, holidays, and other prerequisites that historically had been salary add-ons, and use this money to continue paying workers for a full thirty-six hour week. As a result, workers could receive their full regular pay but could no longer count on as many add-ons during lean times. Second, workers were encouraged to take more time off without pay for holidays or to pursue educational opportunities. Employees could even take blocks of up to three months off at one time without pay, a feature that proved to be particularly popular with younger employees. Finally, it was agreed that the company would increase the working hours of trainees while decreasing the hours for older workers, with obvious implications for reduced costs.

Efforts to increase productivity were also agreed upon. This was accomplished by scheduling manufacturing based more closely on actual customer demand instead of building costly inventories in anticipation of demand; enhancing continuous improvement efforts focusing on reducing the costs and time associated with manufacture; and emphasizing employee training at all levels to improve employee skills and effectiveness.

The plan was implemented with mixed support among employees. Suspicion was high in some areas, but with the strong backing (and buy-in) of the union, most workers complied. Over time, however, most workers finally came to accept the plan. Three years after implementation in an employee survey, 50 percent of the workforce said they were satisfied with the plan (especially the four-day workweek), while 16 percent said they were dissatisfied. In interviews with workers, the union found that the most positive outcomes of the new plan were the four-day workweek, which allowed more free time with friends and family, and the continuous improvement plan, which asked workers for their suggestions, opinions, expectations, and ideas. But above all, Volkswagen workers – a full 75 percent – stressed the importance of protecting the jobs of their fellow workers. In the end, workers kept their jobs (although at reduced income levels), the company reduced its costs sufficiently to meet the realities of the marketplace, and society at large did not experience massive unemployment with its associated social welfare costs.

In summary, as we have seen throughout this discussion on organizational decision making, we hear a lot about the role of employee participation and involvement. In some countries, employee participation is a preciously guarded right; it is assumed. In other countries, workers have no expectations of employee participation; indeed, they often see managers who seek their opinions as being weak. In still other countries (some include Canada and the US in this category), participation is often honored more in rhetoric than in actual practice. That is, while many companies may proclaim their interest in the opinions of subordinates, they are often more interested in results than in process. Consider the following challenge: How does a manager determine how much participation to encourage or allow among his or her subordinates? And what should a manager do if the advice offered by subordinates is self-serving, excessively expensive, or simply unrealistic?

MANAGER'S NOTEBOOK

Inside the organizational mind

This chapter focused on the interrelationships between stakeholder interests, corporate strategies, and organizational decision making. The concept of an "organizational mind" was used as a metaphor here to emphasize how various parties both inside and outside the firm work together – sometimes more successfully than others – in a dynamic fashion to achieve overall objectives. The manner in which these processes operate often resembles "thinking," even though in actuality it is the combined cognitive inputs of a number of members and groups, each thinking independently but hopefully moving in the same direction. In this regard, three key points should be emphasized.

Stakeholders, strategies, and structures

Global managers are well advised to focus on interrelationships, not individual issues, as they attempt to understand the organizational world. That is, instead of simply trying to identify the particular strategies employed by various firms (a naïve endeavor at best) the intelligent manager seeks to understand the cultural and economic milieu in which such strategies are formulated and implemented. The same can be said for organizational structures. That is, why do some firms in some parts of the world organize their financial, physical, and human resources differently than others? Efforts to understand such differences typically begin with an understanding of the cultural bases of organized behavior. For example, why are some firms risk-oriented while others are not? What are the key roles played by various stakeholders in the determination of strategy? As noted above, some companies exist in a fairly centralized stakeholders environment, while others exist in a more centralized one. This can make a significant difference in how corporate strategies, and resulting structures and behaviors, are developed. At the same time, it can be helpful for purposes of understanding to remember the concept of structural determinism; that is, in some cultures, it is structure that determines strategy, not the other way around. This can have a direct impact on international negotiations or partnership building, to take just one example.

By focusing on interrelationships and interactions among these factors, global managers have a better opportunity to understand what they see. This goes back to the learning model discussed in Chapter 2, where it was suggested that awareness and understanding are equally important in learning as experience and action plans. This model cautions against approaching strange or unfamiliar situations with the assumption that we can learn as we go. Rather, when we have a choice, it is more than likely better to learn and understand first, and then, and only then, to initiate action.

Operations and TQM strategies

Following from the above discussion of how culture and strategies can drive structures, it is important to recognize that, at least to some degree, these same forces can influence operational decisions. A good example here is the manner in which the application of manufacturing technologies can vary across cultures. Most discussions about the role of operations management in business organizations focus on the technical challenges facing managers, including instrumentation, machines, operational processes, and gadgets. Far less is mentioned about cultural influences, and yet these too can be important from the standpoint of global management.[17] The transfer and adoption of technology across borders depends in no small way on such cultural characteristics as risk orientation, individualism-collectivism, mastery-harmony, and power distribution (see Chapter 3).[18] Countries are generally expected to favor technological advancement and innovation when they are more egalitarian and individualistic, stress certainty and predictability, and frame their decision-making processes in terms of what the future might bring rather than past experience. Unfortunately, research in this area is scarce to the point that concrete observations are impossible. Still, some evidence does exist, particularly with regard to preferred manufacturing strategies.

Competing with advanced technologies is commonplace in many companies around the world, and no single country has a monopoly on such techniques. Technologically advanced products and processes are highly sought after by customers in markets ranging from automobiles to electronics. Even so, notable trends can be identified across countries that serve to differentiate companies in a very general way in their approaches to using technology as a strategic asset in manufacturing. In much of North America, for example, manufacturing is often characterized by the extensive use of *automation* techniques. The challenge is how best to use automation to manufacture good products at competitive prices. Indeed, these companies frequently use automation as a cost-saving substitute for employees, instead of as a complement to them. In doing so, they often try to compete based on cheap labor, often with mixed results.

Meanwhile, many Japanese companies emphasize *process simplification* to achieve a competitive edge. Process simplification involves finding easier, more efficient ways to manufacture something. This might include reducing cycle times in the manufacturing process or using fewer parts in design and manufacture. For example, when the new 1997 Toyota Camry was introduced, it contained 20 percent fewer parts than its predecessor. As a result, its selling price was actually reduced over the previous year, making it more competitive. Camry sales soon reached number one in the US market. In 2002, an even newer Camry was introduced, again with 20 percent fewer parts than its 1997 predecessor, and again at a lower price. And in 2006, Toyota did it again with its newest model. In doing so, Toyota continued to raise the bar for its competitors, who had to struggle to keep up.

By contrast, German manufacturers seldom use product simplification methods. Instead, they stress *technological complexity* and product superiority. That is, many German firms try and develop the most sophisticated products they can using the latest technologies, even if this leads to higher production costs and higher prices. Technological complexity makes for superior products, it is believed. For example, the new BMW 7 Series has more than 120 electric motors, including 38 motors just to adjust the seats, plus dozens of microprocessors to control everything from the humidity inside the car to the angle at which the wipers rest on the windshield.[19] And at Volkswagen, engineers built a fully integrated electrical system. That is, the starter, horn, lights, stereo system, and security system are all tied to a single wire, instead of separate wires for each system as is found in North American and Japanese cars. It is an engineering masterpiece. However, while German cars may be more technologically sophisticated than their Japanese or American rivals, they can also be more error prone. When something goes wrong, everything can be adversely affected. If the lighting system goes out, the security system also goes out. In Japanese cars, by contrast, where process simplification is stressed, there are actually five wiring systems, each somewhat autonomous from the others. As a result, product assembly is easier and cheaper because it is less complex. Moreover, if the car's lighting system fails, for example, this has less impact on other electrical systems, like the stereo and security system. This is not to say that one system is superior, only that each is based on a different assumption about the best approach to production technologies.[20]

Finally, in the area of TQM, while there is agreement across industries in Germany, Japan, and North America as to how to define TQM, executives in these countries differ in the relative importance of the elements in that definition. Quality standards, technical accuracy, and customer approval receive support in all three countries. However, the Germans also emphasize product standards, while the Japanese emphasize accuracy and precision, and the Americans and Canadians emphasize customer approval and satisfaction.[21] Again, even in something so seemingly generic as TQM, significant differences can be found across cultures in the manner in which such programs are organized and implemented.

Organizational decision-making processes

Finally, considerable differences were found between organizational decision-making processes across national boundaries. These differences typically revolved around the issue of employee involvement and participation in decision-making. Specifically, when and where is high (or low) employee involvement useful – and acceptable – as organizations work to make the right decisions concerning present and future actions? This challenge raises two seemingly unrelated questions. First, is employee input into organizational decisions some form of inalienable right that all employees deserve or is it a practical issue that must be determined on a case-by-case or country-by-country basis? Social scientists frequently take the inclusive approach, arguing that all organizational members have an inherent right to participation because of their membership status. Anything else is inequitable. Others argue just as vociferously that the quality of the decision is what matters, not necessarily who was, or was not, involved in it. Indeed, a common definition of management includes the responsibility of managers (as opposed to "workers") to make timely and relevant decisions affecting the future of the firm. Who is right here? Certainly, culture plays a role here. In some countries, including the US, laws that stipulate that the legal responsibility of members of the boards of directors of firms focus exclusively on the welfare of the stockholders, not others. At the same time, other countries, including Germany, the Netherlands, and the Scandinavian nations, have laws that stipulate the board members must include employee and customer welfare in their strategic decisions. Perhaps the determination of who is right here depends on where the question is asked, as well as whether people believe this is a normative, legal, or practical question.

The second question is equally complicated: Who is best equipped to be involved in organizational decisions? Some argue here that only those who understand the broad goals, tactics, and challenges of a firm should be at the table. These are typically managers; they alone can see the big picture and make "rational" decisions about the firm's future. Others argue that "managers" and "experts" are not necessarily the same people. Perhaps the best decisions come from including a broader base of organizational members, including the shop floor (e.g., assembly line workers) or the field (e.g., sales representatives). This may not be where managerial expertise is, but it is certainly where manufacturing and customer expertise is, it is argued. As noted above, many firms in the US – although certainly not all – take the former position that a more top-down approach to decision making is more efficient and objective, while many firms in Japan – again, not all – take the latter position that, like the bloodstream, quality decisions must serge throughout many parts of a company before they are ready for implementation. Again, who is "right" may depend on local circumstances and customs.

Notes

1 Geert Hofstede, *Culture's Consequences*, 2nd Edition. Thousand Oaks, CA: Sage, 2001, pp. 373, 375.
2 Cited in David Thomas, *Essentials of International Management: A Cross-cultural Perspective*. Thousand Oaks, CA: Sage, 2002, p. 189.
3 Chester I. Barnard, *The Functions of the Executive*. Cambridge, MA: Harvard University Press, 1938.
4 See www.intel.com.
5 *Ibid.*
6 Cornelia Kothen, William McKinley, and Andreas Georg Scherer, "Alternatives to organizational downsizing: a German case study," *M@n@gement*, 1999, 2(3), pp. 263–286.
7 The term "*Mittelstand*" normally refers to German, Austrian, or Swiss small and medium-sized enterprises (SMES). However, precisely defining what constitutes a *Mittelstand* firm is difficult, since the word actually directly translates as "middle class." *Mittelstand* firms are typically owned and managed by a family, owned by family, but run by an outside management team, or partially owned by family but with outside shareholders. German *Mittelstand* firms employ over 70 percent of all employees in private business, according to the Institut für Mittelstandsforschung.
8 Victor Vroom and Philip Yetton, *Leadership and Decision-making*. New York, NY: Wiley, 1973.
9 We use the terms "unilateral" and "collaborative" here instead of Vroom and Yetton's original "autocratic" and "group" in view of the nebulous meanings and normative ascriptions associated with the original terms.
10 John Stoll and Mike Spector, "Wagoner outlines his role in GM's hierarchy," *The Wall Street Journal*, March 5, 2008, p. B1.
11 John Stoll and Nicolas Brulliard, "GM chief Wagoner gets 33% raise," *The Wall Street Journal*, March 7, 2008, p. B6.
12 Joann Lublin, "Say on the boss's pay," *The Wall Street Journal*, March 7, 2008, p. B1.
13 Hiroki Kato and Joan Kato, *Understanding and Working with the Japanese Business World*. Englewood Cliffs, NJ: Prentice Hall, 1992.
14 *Nemawashi* (根回し in Japanese) is an informal process of quietly laying the foundation for some proposed change or project, by talking to the people concerned, gathering support and feedback, and so forth. It is considered an important element in any major change, before any formal steps are taken, and successful *nemawashi* enables changes to be carried out with the consent of all sides. *Nemawashi* literally translates as "going around the roots," from 根 (*ne,*

root) and 回 す (*mawasu*, to go around something). Its original meaning is literal: digging around the roots of a tree, to prepare it for a transplant.

15 *Honne* and *tatemae* are Japanese words used to describe recognized social phenomena. *Honne* (本音) refers to a person's true feelings and desires. These may be contrary to what is expected by society or what is required according to one's position and circumstances, and they are often kept hidden, except with one's closest friends. *Tatemae* (建前), literally meaning "facade," is the behavior and opinions one displays in public. *Tatemae* is what is expected by society and required according to one's position and circumstances, and these may or may not match one's *honne*. This *honne/tatemae* divide is considered to be of paramount importance in Japanese culture. The very fact that the Japanese have single words for these concepts leads some Japanese experts to see this conceptualization as evidence of greater Japanese complexity and rigidity in etiquette and culture. *Honne* and *tatemae* are arguably a cultural necessity, resulting from a large number of people living in a relatively small island nation. Even with modern farming techniques, Japan today domestically produces only 39 percent of the food needed to feed its people, so close-knit cooperation and the avoidance of conflict remain of vital importance today as it did in ancient times. For this reason, the Japanese tend to go to great lengths to avoid conflict, especially within the context of large groups. The conflict between *honne* and *giri* (social obligations) is one of the main topics of Japanese drama throughout the ages. In such dramas, the protagonist would typically have to choose between carrying out his obligations to his family or feudal lord or pursuing a forbidden love affair or other personal interest. In the end, death would often be the only way out of the dilemma.

16 Yukari Iwatani Kane, "Toshiba's plan for life after HD DVD," *The Wall Street Journal*, March 3, 2008, p. B1.

17 Richard M. Steers, Alan D. Meyer, and Carlos J. Sanchez-Runde, "National culture and the adoptation of new technologies," *Journal of World Business*, 2008, 43(3), pp. 255–260.

18 Rabi S. Bhagat and Anne McDevitt, "Cultural variations in creation, diffusion, and absorption of organizational knowledge," in Rabi S. Bhagat and Richard M. Steers (eds.), *Handbook of Culture, Organizations, and Work*. Cambridge, UK: Cambridge University Press, 2009; Geert Hofstede, *Culture's Consequences: Comparing Values, Behaviors, Institutions, and Organizations across Nations*. Thousand Oaks, CA: Sage, 2001.

19 Neal Boudette, "A bad report card for European cars," *The Wall Street Journal*, November 9, 2004, p. D1.

20 *Ibid.*

21 J. Hammond, "An international look at quality practices," *Management Review*, 1991, 80(5), pp. 38–41.

CHAPTER 6

Organizing frameworks:
a comparative assessment

- Culture and organization design: a model   157
- US corporations   159
- Japanese *kaisha* and *keiretsu*   165
- Chinese *gong-si*   175
- German *konzern*   181
- Mexican *grupo*   186
- MANAGER'S NOTEBOOK: **Organizing frameworks**   193

Intuitively, people have always assumed that bureaucratic structures and patterns of action differ in the countries of the Western world and even more markedly between East and West. Practitioners know it and never fail to take it into account.

Michael Crozier[1]
Sociologist, France

Generalizing about organizations is a tricky and not entirely respectable business.

Patricia Morison[2]
Journalist, *Financial Times*, UK

Both French sociologist Michael Crozer and British journalist Patricia Morison make compelling and similar points about efforts to understand organizations around the world. Patterns of organizing clearly differ across borders and cultures, but we run a very real risk of misinterpreting what we see if we push too hard towards sweeping generalizations. Even so, it is sometimes helpful to use broad strokes to paint pictures of what managers can expect to find when they begin to travel.

Consider the East Hope Group of Shanghai, China. Four brothers of the Liu family founded the firm in1982.[3] It was one of the first privately held enterprises (or *gong-si* – see below) allowed to flourish under China's new government policies supporting the development to large-scale privately held companies. To get the business started, the Liu brothers sold their wristwatches and bicycles to raise the necessary US$120 to open a very small agricultural business. Today, the East Hope Group is the largest animal-feed producer – as well as one of the largest private enterprises – in China, with 10,000 employees working in 120 various business enterprises around the country. East Hope has expanded into real estate, heavy industries, financial investments and securities, and construction, and is a major shareholder in Minsheng Bank, the first privately owned bank in China. And it remains family-owned and operated. The four brothers and their families jointly own the East Hope Group Corporation Ltd., while each brother heads one of the firm's four separate and highly diversified divisions. Notably, the "dominant" family head is not the eldest, but the third brother, Liu Yonghao. In addition, Liu family members can be found throughout the key executive and managerial positions in all four divisions. When important decisions arise, family members meet to discuss strategies and tactics and make decisions about future courses of action. These decisions are then relayed to lower-level non-family employees for implementation. The original company motto remains: "Help the farmers succeed, meet the needs of city residents, and contribute to the country's development."

East Hope's national culture – and corporate culture – differs significantly from the typical firm found in the US, the UK, Canada, and so forth, as do its targeted markets. Not surprisingly, this has led to differences in the way this Chinese company approaches strategic and structural decisions. Clearly these differences go a long way towards explaining the differences in their organizing frameworks, but there is something more here. East Hope exists in a predominately Eastern (specifically Chinese) society that stresses collectivism, hierarchy, and family control. Employees do not openly criticize the owner-managers. By contrast, many, although certainly not all, Western firms exists in a culture that predominantly stresses individualism, egalitarianism, and independence. As such, overt conflicts are widespread and seen as facilitating corporate competitiveness. Such is not the case at East Hope.

About the same time as East Hope was founded in China, five brothers emigrated from Vietnam to the US in the early 1980s to seek their fortune.[4] Upon arrival in San Francisco, the brothers and their wives found work at odd jobs and began saving everything they could. Soon, they found an opportunity to buy a failing restaurant that had a sideline of making donuts. They pooled their savings and combined it with investments from other members of their extended family in Vietnam and began a bakery on the site. Sugar Bowl Bakery was born. They learned the business as they went. Family members had no assigned jobs; rather, they split everything up so things were being done twenty-four hours a day, seven days a week. They ran the operation as a genuine family business and achieved considerable success through sacrifice, persistence, vision, hard work, and, perhaps most of all, family unity. Their business plan was simple: Move ahead, step by step.

While growing the business, a family business structure began to develop, with clearly defined roles and accountability. Each member assumed certain responsibilities based on his or her skills and strengths. One took over cash management, another retailing, and still another business development. As with East Hope, Sugar Bowl broke with tradition and chose a younger brother, who was fluent in English and had a business education, to become CEO. Yet it retained a "flat" structure to speed communication, innovation, and response time to customers. The family members worked together to discuss every new idea or strategy, and each new project had to receive the unanimous support of all family members to proceed. As one brother noted, "We don't have to go through layers; it's just one step to the CEO."[5]

Today, the Ly family runs a US$45 million family empire. Its customers include Starbucks, Costco, and a number of five star hotels. In ten of the past eleven years, Sugar Bowl has been identified as the fastest growing private company in the San Francisco Bay area. Now, a new generation of Ly family members is growing into their roles within the firm. Yet, despite running their business in a largely individualistic culture like the US for thirty years, and producing "Western" baked goods, Sugar Bowl continues to use an organizing framework rooted in the cultural traditions of its owners. Perhaps the question here is not so much *whether* culture influences organization design, but *which* culture.

Culture and organization design: a model

The examples of the East Hope Group and the Sugar Bowl Bakery illustrate one particular approach to organizing: the family business. But while family businesses operate around the world, the centrality of family members in managing them can vary considerably. In some cases, the family members decide to run the ventures themselves, while in others the family hires outside "professional" managers. The choice of organizing models here often depends on many things in the business environment. Clearly, economic, political, and market forces play a role here, but so too does culture (see Exhibit 6.1). More specifically, culture can influence organization design through local social pressures and constraints on behavior, as well as through management predispositions, which are also influenced by local social pressures (e.g., family values, educational systems). This can be seen in both of the examples above. However, when we look at other family businesses, such as

Exhibit 6.1 Cultural influences on organization design

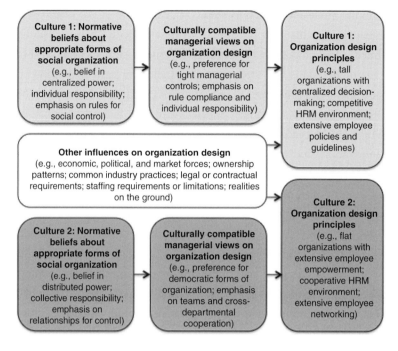

Germany's *Mittelstand* firms, considerable differences begin to emerge, and these differences are the result of both the business environment and the culture.

Understanding these cultural differences can prove useful for working across cultures, particularly in global partnerships. In many ways, a company's unique organization design is like its own personal fingerprint. It can provide insights into a company's character, values, ambitions, management systems, and operating procedures. Comparing these designs can help us understand how cultural differences can influence how businesses operate and how management is conducted. Because of this, we turn now to a comparison of current and future trends in organizing frameworks (or patterns) for five countries: China, Japan, Germany, Mexico, and the US (see Exhibit 6.2). This comparison is done using the core cultural dimensions discussed in Chapter 3 as a starting point.

In this overview, however, some caution is in order. First, space does not permit a detailed examination of companies in each culture; instead, we present overviews by painting with broad strokes. Moreover, while this discussion is aimed at highlighting some organizational differences across the cultures, considerable variations can exist

Exhibit 6.2 Culture and organization design: country examples

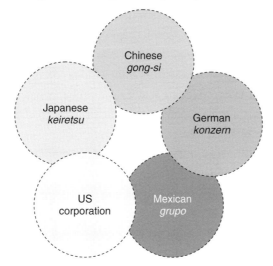

within each country. In other words, these comparisons are intended to illustrate different trends; they are not meant as monolithic descriptions of culture and organization design. And finally, no organizing framework exists in a steady state. That is, as social pressures change, we would expect organization designs and management practices to also evolve over time. Thus, we focus on organizing trends, not principles. We begin with a look inside a typical US business organization.

US corporations

Identifying a "typical" company in any culture is a challenge, but perhaps nowhere is this challenge more acute than with respect to American firms. Like elsewhere, US companies reflect the culture(s) where they do business, and since the US is so strongly multicultural, it is not surprising to find major differences across companies – even in similar industries. Still, it is possible to develop a general portrait of what such a company looks like in terms of its basic organizing structure and management processes. To accomplish this, however, it is useful to first consider how we might describe American culture.

US cultural patterns

Based on the Anglo core cultural dimensions discussed in Chapter 3, we might begin by suggesting that the dominant central tendencies of American culture are moderately egalitarian, strongly individualistic, strongly mastery-oriented, strongly monochromic, and moderately universalistic. This description helps us build a platform – albeit an imprecise one – for further analysis. Now let's go a step further. What happens when we add to this picture the observations of people who have spent considerable time with Americans? Journalists and social scientists from various countries have tried to do this for many years.[6] While acknowledging that the US probably has greater diversity than many other countries, these writers have nonetheless tried to characterize Americans using a small number of adjectives.

For starters, Americans tend to be highly individualistic. Perhaps no other country in the world stresses individual rights and responsibilities more than the US. Here, a "man's home is his castle" and success is determined by personal effort. It is important to be independent and stay out of other people's business. At the same time, Americans tend to be materialistic. As a society that is focused on achievement, material possessions often represent symbols of success, and conspicuous consumption can become a lifestyle. This belief often leads to a short-term focus that requires considerable energy to achieve immediate results. Americans also tend to be informal. Americans tend to be "laid back" and spend their time "hanging out." They are often uncomfortable with formality and are quick to remove their coats, use first names, and discuss personal details with new acquaintances. Many people also feel the typical American is linear. Americans tend to be single-minded in the pursuit of their objectives and often rush headlong towards their goals with a determination that can border on obsession. They do things "24/7" and are never far from their cell phones, laptops, and Blackberries. Work frequently takes precedence over family and friends.

In addition, Americans can at times be a bit impatient. Americans seem to be in a perpetual hurry; they want things done now. Time is seen as a measurable – and sometimes marketable – commodity that should be used wisely in the pursuit of one's objectives, whether business or pleasure. Compared to many other cultures, Americans are risk-oriented. Americans tend to be optimistic and opportunistic, and are often comfortable taking risks in order to achieve desired objectives. They are also superficial. Americans often ignore the details or conflicting positions underlying complex issues and prefer to focus on the "big picture." They enjoy small talk, but have little patience with cultural niceties or ceremonial observances. They sometimes have difficulty building deep or lasting relationships. And they can be blunt. They often like to "put their cards on the table" from the start and are suspicious of anyone who does not reciprocate. Understanding nuances or subtleties in conversations is not their strong suit.

Americans are often described as being overly trusting and friendly towards people they hardly know. They come across to many foreigners as naïve and uninformed on matters of global importance. They are admired for their technical competence, but not their sophistication. However, they can also be very generous. On a per capita basis, Americans give more money to charities than anyone else on the planet. Some say this is because they have more money to give or because of US tax policies that reward charitable contributions, but there is more to it than this. There is a fundamental belief that people have a moral responsibility to support social causes, political causes, local causes, and even sometimes perfect strangers to an extent seldom seen elsewhere. Finally, many Americans tend to be a bit jingoistic and seem convinced that the United States is the greatest country in the world. There is no reason to discuss this; anyone who disagrees is simply wrong.

Do all Americans fit this description? Of course not. For starters, the US is a very heterogeneous society consisting of many strong cultures. Most of its citizens, or their ancestors, migrated to the US from various regions of the world in search of a better life, and brought their cultures with them. It is therefore important to recognize that when people try to describe a "typical" American, they are often focusing on Anglo-Americans or, more accurately, European Americans. Other American cultures, including Asian Americans, African Americans, Native Americans, and so forth, can have very different cultural characteristics. And even among the European American community, stark cultural differences can be found. Indeed, the individualistic nature of the US encourages and supports cultural diversity. Despite all of this, if so many observers from so many different backgrounds come to the same conclusions about the "typical" American, such observations are difficult to ignore.

Even so, a critical question here is not so much how the typical American (or anyone else) is described, but rather against which standards they are judged. That is, what are the characteristics of different cultures and how do these differences affect interpersonal assessments and relations? For example, people from more collectivistic cultures, such as China, Korea, and Japan, often see Americans (as well as some British, Australians, and Canadians) as being highly individualistic, while these "Westerners" often see their "East Asian" counterparts as being highly collectivistic. The point here is not that one orientation is superior to the other. Rather, the point is that if both "Westerners" and "East Asians" can better understand each other, if they can genuinely get inside each other's heads and learn what motivates them, they are far more likely to succeed in forming partnerships or doing business together than if they remain mired in their own cultural crosscurrents.

Organization and management trends in the US

Based on what has been learned so far about prevailing American cultural patterns, consider how the people characterized by this description might build organizations. First, many of these organizations would likely stress individual achievement and responsibility, control over the environment, a linear approach to decision making, respect for rules and policies and a sense of order, and a belief that, at least in theory, anyone can rise to the top. As a result, the typical US organization is perhaps best described as a loosely coupled system with many key parts located outside of the company for purposes of efficiency and flexibility.

In addition, in many US firms, CEOs get most of the credit for company successes and much of the blame for failure; they also get much of the money, regardless. US CEOs tend to have considerable power as decision-makers and leaders so long as they succeed. Indeed, we often hear about the "imperial CEO." If they do not succeed, however, they tend to disappear rather quickly. Partly as a result of this, many US firms tend to have a top-down decision-making style.

Organization design in typical US firms tend to be rather fluid. They tend to have many alliances and partners and frequently reinvent themselves when the need arises (e.g., under conditions of financial exigency). When they need capital to expand the business, market research for a new product, or in-depth legal advice, most US firms typically go outside the company. Likewise, both manufacturing and service companies often rely on outside suppliers and distributors that have only a tenuous relationship to the company.

Inside many American companies, employees on all levels are often viewed as factors of production rather than valued members of the organization. Indeed, in some American companies, "permanent" employees are routinely hired and fired based on variations in workloads. From an accounting perspective, they are considered as part of a firm's variable costs, not fixed costs. And the use of contingent workers is on the rise, partly to save money and partly to increase operating efficiency. Not surprisingly, as a result of this fluidity, employee commitment to organizations is on the wane.

In view of the high levels of individualism across US society (indeed, can we talk in terms of one society?), creating a "typical" organizing framework is imprecise to say the least, Still, it is possible to at least highlight some of the more common trends, as illustrated in Exhibit 6.3.

This exhibit illustrates the general paradigm for US firms. However, in view of the highly individualistic nature of the prevailing culture, it is not surprising to find

Exhibit 6.3 Design of a typical US corporation

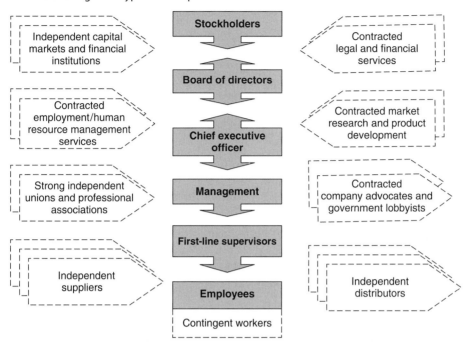

Note: The shaded boxes represent formal parts of the organization. The white boxes represent independent agencies, institutions, service providers, and contingent workers that are largely outside the formal organization design.

a wide variation around this general model. US firms can be highly autocratic or highly participative, mastery-oriented or harmony-oriented, and so forth. Even so, a general model serves a useful purpose as a starting point for cross-cultural comparisons.

Organization and management trends in Canada and the UK

It is clearly a mistake to assume that organization and management practices are identical – or even similar, in some cases – across the broad so-called "Anglo" cluster. For example, when British managers are asked to compare US and British managers and corporations, they typically offer one of two responses: either they are very similar or they are very different. Such is the heterogeneity of corporations on both sides of the Atlantic. Frames of reference, as well as nuances, become both important and ambiguous. At the same time, when Canadians are asked to compare US and Canadian managers and organizations, they, too, can sometimes find sizable differences.

In order to delve a bit deeper here in this comparison, and commenting on British organizational trends, London Business School professor Nigel Nicholson has suggested that the major challenge is to understand how much of an organization's ethos or operating model comes from national cultures, sector cultures, or parent company cultures.[7] At the national level, key inputs are obviously regulatory elements as well as governance norms and cultural factors, such as shared expectations of employees and other stakeholders. On these factors, only a few differences between the two cultures are noted. However, the typical governance rules in the UK are quite different. As a rule, British companies are far less tolerant of power aggregation than are their American counterparts. For example, they tend to oppose unitary boards of directors and strongly prefer the separation of the Chairman and CEO roles between two people, unlike the tendency in the US to integrate these two roles into one person. They also dislike dual-share voting systems, and have rules that prevent banks from owning major shares in companies.

In addition, British firms are also far less encumbered with layers of lawyers, spend far less money on government lobbying, and have generally weak trade associations. Management consultants do have an influence on British firms, but less so than in the US.

In general, then, Nicholson notes that British firms tend to be more liberal than the US and maintain more liquidity and fluidity in ownership. However, if British firms are more liberal in ownership and governance, they tend to be more conservative in management policies and practices. The ethos of British management is highly pragmatic, achievement-oriented, and entrepreneurial, but is often opposed to "out-of-the-box" thinking, weak on leadership, strong on financial management, and frequently poor on vision, community, and integration.

Adding to these observations, University of Birmingham professor John Child cautions against placing too much emphasis on seeing ideal types and archetypes of British (or any other) firms.[8] For example, while many larger UK companies have been acquired by or merged into larger non-British firms, a strong entrepreneurial and SME sector remains. And, as in any country, there are large differences between traditional manufacturing and newer service firms.

Like Nicholson, Child points to differences in ethos as providing particularly significant contrasts between US and British firms. Indeed, he adds to Nicholson's list of features characterizing many larger British firms, including a short-term cost-conscious orientation (hence, a generally low emphasis on personal development and training), poor internal integration (both horizontal and vertical), and a continuing failure to communicate adequately with employees. Finally, although some have suggested that Britain may be losing its individualistic culture to a degree, Child points out that in organizations that continue to use performance-based incentives (see Chapter 10), such as in many financial and consulting services, we still see high levels of initiative and a strong achievement orientation.

Speaking of differences between Canadians and their US counterparts, McGill professor Nancy Adler offers the following observations: Compared to Americans, Canadians tend to understate their strengths and perhaps overstate their weaknesses.[9] They do not usually claim to be the best at something. Canadians strongly believe in collegiality. For example, Canada is one of the leaders in creating middle-country initiatives where a group of countries in the world tries to get something done (instead of trying to go it alone). Canadians tend to be more formal than Americans – titles and family names are important. Canadians are generally more polite and less confrontational than their American counterparts. Canadians are also less explicitly and publicly religious. Finally, Canadians believe in more collective responsibility across society in such areas as education and health care. All of this is not to say that overlaps do not occur; obviously they do. However, assuming that Americans and Canadians live identical life styles or share identical values can only lead to lost opportunities for global managers.

In summary, some might argue that in making comparisons between American and British firms, and, indeed, firms in Australia, Canada, and New Zealand, the key issue is whether within-group variance is larger or smaller than between-group variance. That is, commonalities can be found among all of the countries that comprise the so-called "Anglo" cluster. Part of the reason for these similarities can be found in the historic British influences in all of these cultures. Even so, in recognition of the strong individualism found in this cluster, it is not surprising to find it is difficult to make generalizations about organization design and management practice. At the same time, part of the differences here can be found in the increasing cultural heterogeneity of people inhabiting all of these countries. Diversity is increasing throughout. Indeed, as these two countries, along with their Australian, Canadian, and New Zealand counterparts, become increasingly multicultural, perhaps the term "Anglo" will lose much of its meaning as a descriptor of this cluster of countries.[10] In fact, these countries and cultures may begin evolving in very different directions in the future. For now, however, the evidence suggests that this country cluster retains much of its utility as characterizing central trends in this cluster.

Japanese *kaisha* and *keiretsu*

Japan is often the country of choice when making comparisons with American, British, and other so-called Anglo countries. There are many reasons for this. Many Westerners are somewhat familiar with Japan and its culture. Japan's economy remains strong in many business sectors and most geographical regions. Company names like Mitsubishi, Sumitomo, Mitsui, Toyota, Nissan, Honda, and so forth are household brands, and countless people around the world own products manufactured by them. In view of this, we turn now to a look inside the typical Japanese organization. The first thing to be learned is that, like the situation in the US, there is probably no such thing as a typical Japanese firm, although the variance in Japanese firms is clearly somewhat smaller.

Japanese cultural patterns

Perhaps the best way to understand how Japanese firms work and do business is to begin with some observations on the local culture. As discussed in Chapter 3, an overview of Japanese culture includes a strong belief in hierarchy, strong collectivism, a strong harmony orientation, moderate monochronism, and strong particularism. Hierarchy beliefs in Japan can be seen in the deep respect shown to elders and people in positions of authority. In many circumstances, their directives are to be obeyed immediately and without question. This belief follows from early Confucian teachings (see below). Indeed, the concept of authority in Japan differs from that typically found in the West. Western views of authority see power generally flowing in one direction: down. The supervisor or manager gives directions; those below him or her follow them. Authority is a one-way concept. In Japan and many other Asian countries, by contrast, power still flows downwards but those exercising power must also look after the welfare and well-being of those they manage. In other words, a supervisor expects his or her directives to be followed without question, but will also spend considerable time guiding, coaching, and teaching subordinates so they can progress in their careers. Subordinates – and in many cases their families too – will be looked after. Thus, authority here is seen as a two-way street; both sides (superiors and subordinates) have a role to play. By deferring to those above you, you are in essence asking them to look after you.

Japan is also a highly collectivistic nation. Groups generally take precedence over individuals, and people gain their personal identity through their group membership. An old saying, "The nail that sticks out will be hammered down," best exemplifies the importance of this belief. Contrast this to the old American and British saying, "God helps those who help themselves." Collectivism versus individualism. As a result, employees naturally gravitate towards groups at work, and group achievement surpasses individual achievement on the job. Seniority-based (group) rewards are frequently preferred over performance-based (individual) rewards, particularly among older employees.

Harmony – both with other people and with nature – is also a strong characteristic. Japan's respect for its surrounding environment is legendary. This is not to say they refrain from changing or challenging nature; rather, they typically attempt this in ways that do as little harm as possible to the environment. Likewise, most Japanese will go to great lengths not to offend anyone or create open conflict or argumentation. As a result, communications in Japan tends to emphasize context at least as much as content. Non-verbal signs and signals are frequently used to convey thoughts in cases where words may be inappropriate.

The Japanese are frequently described as being moderately monochromic. That is, they tend to focus on one or only a few tasks at a time and clearly separate work and family issues as they relate to the workplace. And finally, many observers have noted that Japanese society tends to be highly particularistic. That is, while clear rules of law pervade society, exceptions are routinely made for friends and family or for powerful and influential people.

Organization and management trends in Japan

Japan's large vertically integrated *keiretsu* organizations (e.g., Sumitomo, Mitsui, Mitsubishi, Matsushita) represent a unique approach to organization that has served their companies and their country well over the years.[11] The design of these organizations is rooted in Japanese history and is successful largely because it is congruent with the national culture.[12] The effects of this congruence can be seen in the unsuccessful attempts of many Western firms to imitate the basic *keiretsu* design. In contrast to their Anglo-American and even to some extent some European counterparts, Japanese firms tend to treat their employees as a fixed cost, not a variable cost, and relationships with suppliers tend to be closer and more stable over time. Executives have less power and decision making is distributed throughout the firm. Financing is more likely to come from inside the Japanese conglomerate's own financial institutions (e.g., company-owned banks or insurance companies), while marketing research and even legal advice is frequently done within the group. Finally, Japanese unions tend to be company unions (referred to as enterprise unions (see below)) and are more closely associated with company interests than is the case in the West.

To succeed in business, various individual Japanese companies (*kaisha* in Japanese) join together to form a business group, or *keiretsu* network. The *keiretsu* provides financial, organizational, legal, and logistical support for its sister companies. For example, when Mitsubishi Motors (a *kaisha*) needs glass, sheet metal, electrical components, or fabric for its automobile assembly line, it is likely to secure most if not all of these materials from other companies within the Mitsubishi Business Group (a *keiretsu*). Obviously, not being a *keiretsu* member can lead to isolation and missed business opportunities. It is this isolation from the market – not being allowed membership in key business relationships – that many Western companies object to in attempting to conduct business in Japan.

Japanese *keiretsu* can be divided into two basic types: horizontal (*yoko*) and vertical (*tate*). A *horizontal keiretsu* consists of a group of interlocking companies typically clustered around a main bank, a lead manufacturer, and a trading company, and overseen by a President's Council consisting of the presidents of the major group companies. Exhibit 6.4 illustrates how a horizontal *keiretsu* is organized. The "Big Six" horizontal *keiretsu* are Mitsui, Mitsubishi, Sumitomo, Fuyo, Sanwa, and Dai-Ichi Kangyo Bank Group. By contrast, a *vertical keiretsu* consists of a large manufacturing company surrounded by numerous small and subservient suppliers and distributors that keep the operations running smoothly, typically through a just-in-time (or *kanban*) production system. Most Japanese automobile companies (e.g., Toyota, Nissan) are vertical *keiretsu* (see below).

A good example of a horizontal *keiretsu* can be seen in the Mitsubishi Business Group. Mitsubishi has a main bank (Mitsubishi Bank), a trading company (Mitsubishi Shoji), and a flagship manufacturer (Mitsubishi Heavy Industries). In addition, three financial firms are typically clustered around these three key companies: a life insurance company, a non-life insurance company, and a trust bank. Together, these financial firms, the trading company, and the group's key manufacturers give the *keiretsu* its unique identity. Beyond this are hundreds of large and small companies that are associated with the group. Senior managers from the principal companies are frequently assigned to serve in management positions in the smaller firms to assist with inter-company coordination support. Interlocking directorates are common to reinforce this family system.

Within each horizontal *keiretsu*, a *main bank* performs several functions. Its most important role is providing funds for company operations, expansion, and R&D. First, these banks provide more than two-thirds of the financial needs of *keiretsu*-affiliated companies. Second, member companies frequently hold stock in sister companies (known as stable cross-shareholdings). Main banks are among the nation's largest shareholders for such firms, providing considerable stability for company management interested in long-term growth strategies. Third, main banks provide an important

Exhibit 6.4 Design of a typical Japanese horizontal *keiretsu*

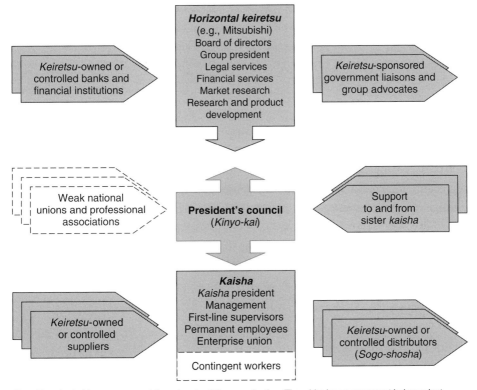

Note: The shaded boxes represent formal parts of the organization. The white boxes represent independent agencies, institutions, service providers, and contingent workers that are largely outside the formal organization design.

audit function for member companies in monitoring corporate performance and evaluating risk. Fourth, main banks provide the best source of venture capital for member companies interested in launching new but risky ventures. For instance, Sumitomo Bank provided massive start-up investments in member company NEC's initiative to capture the semiconductor market. Finally, main banks serve as the "company doctor" in rescuing companies that are facing bankruptcy. Since corporate bankruptcy can threaten public confidence in Japan's economic system, not just a specific business group, main banks often quietly provide financial support to keep ailing companies going until the firm can be re-organized or the problem resolved. This financial commitment to member companies can also create trouble for the *keiretsu*, however, when the main bank is required to bail out a non-competitive company that should perhaps be sold off or dissolved.

The trading company, or *sogo shosha*, provides member companies with ready access to global markets and distribution networks. These companies (e.g., Mitsubishi Shoji, Sumitomo Busan) maintain offices throughout the world and are continually on the lookout for new or expanded markets. At the same time, their field offices collect and analyze market and economic intelligence that can be used by member companies to develop new products or otherwise get a jump on the competition. They frequently assist member companies with various marketing activities as well, and facilitate imports into Japan for their business customers. In fact, historically, Japanese trading companies have been responsible for almost half of Japan's imports and three-fifths of its exports. Finally, the *sogo shosha* often provide significant credit (through the group's main bank) for small and medium-sized companies involved in business activities with member companies, again getting a jump on competitors that operate further from lines of credit.

Finally, although hundreds of companies may be affiliated with one *keiretsu*, only the principal companies are allowed to join the *Presidents' Council* (*shacho-kai*, or *kinyo-kai* in the case of Mitsubishi). This council (typically consisting of the CEOs of the top twenty to thirty group companies) meets monthly to discuss principal strategies for the group, as well as issues of coordination across the various sister companies. Since council meetings are private and no records are maintained, little is understood about how such councils actually work. At the very least, however, these meetings facilitate extensive cooperation across member companies on developing group strategy and group solidarity, as well as mediating disagreements across member companies.

To many observers, the very structure of these conglomerates seems to provide an unfair advantage in global competition. To see how this might work, consider the example of Kirin Holdings Company, a member of the Mitsubishi *keiretsu*. While Kirin produces a wide array of consumer products, including soft drinks, pharmaceutics, and health foods, they are perhaps best known for beer. To produce, bottle, and distribute beer, Kirin needs help from a multitude of sources. In many cases, it can get this help from other sister companies on a long-term reliable manner (see Exhibit 6.5).

When Kirin Holdings Company needs glass for its bottles, it contacts Asahi Glass, a Mitsubishi company. When Kirin needs aluminum for its cans, it contacts Mitsubishi Aluminum. When Kirin needs plastic to bottle its soft drinks, it contacts Mitsubishi Plastics. When Kirin needs paper for labels, it contacts Mitsubishi Paper. When Kirin needs financing for its operations, it contacts Mitsubishi Bank. When Kirin needs to construct new facilities, if contacts Mitsubishi Construction. When Kirin needs cars and trucks to help distribute its products, it contacts Mitsubishi Motors. And when Kirin

Exhibit 6.5 *Keiretsu* network for Mitsubishi's Kirin Holdings Company

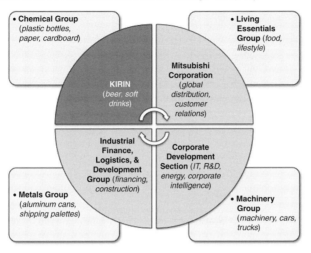

needs global distribution of its products, it contacts Mitsubishi Shoji. Is this smart coordination and control by the *keiretsu* managers or restraint of trade since other (largely foreign) firms oftentimes cannot break through the barriers to seek some of the business? What might foreign firms do to get inside the *keiretsu* network?

This interlocking set of companies that comprise a *keiretsu* like Mitsubishi can create a considerable competitive advantage in the marketplace. While comparable examples of global sourcing, integrated manufacturing, and multinational marketing can be found in the West, it is questionable whether these companies approach the *keiretsu* model in terms of integration and cooperation. What makes the *keiretsu* system unique is that it represents an entire social system in which national culture, government policies, corporate strategies, and management practices are fully integrated, mutually supportive, and reinforced through incentives and rewards that make the entire enterprise run smoothly over the long run. Thus, while some similarities exist, and while Western multinationals frequently pursue vertical integration to achieve operating efficiencies, it would be misleading to claim that Western companies have adopted the Japanese business model as their own. Neither their cultures nor government regulations in many cases would allow it.

When most Westerners think of a *keiretsu*, they have in mind the horizontal variety discussed above. However, the *vertical* (or pyramid) *keiretsu* can be just as powerful, if less well known. Key vertical *keiretsu* include the major Japanese automobile firms such as Toyota, Nissan, and Honda, as well as some of the major electric giants like Sony and Panasonic (including Quasar and National brands). An illustration of the organization

Exhibit 6.6 Design of a typical Japanese vertical *keiretsu*

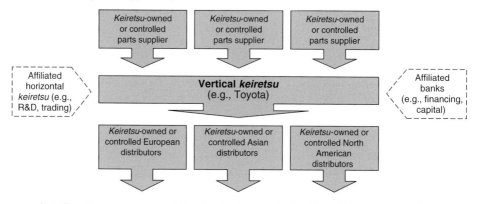

Note: The shaded boxes represent formal parts of the organization. The white boxes represent independent agencies, institutions, service providers, and contingent workers that are largely outside the formal organization design.

structure of a vertical *keiretsu* is shown in Exhibit 6.6. As noted above, a vertical *keiretsu* consists of a major company surrounded by a large number of smaller firms that either act as suppliers or distributors for the big firm.

In point of fact, there are two kinds of vertical *keiretsu*: a *production keiretsu*, in which a myriad of parts suppliers join together to create subassemblies for a single end-product manufacturer (such as Toyota), and a *distribution keiretsu*, in which a single large firm, usually a manufacturer, moves products to market through a network of wholesalers and retailers that depend on the parent company for goods. Since most manufacturers have both *keiretsu* types (production and distribution), we can envision the two like an hourglass: an upside-down (production) pyramid on top, in which individual parts suppliers provide various parts (e.g., fabric for car seats) to subcomponent assembly companies that ultimately provide subassemblies (e.g., completed seats) to the parent company in the center of the hourglass. Here, the parent company assembles the end products and prepares them for market. Next, these products are passed down into another (distribution) pyramid where they are distributed to wholesalers and ultimately to retail consumers.

In some cases, a leading company from a vertical *keiretsu* will form an alliance with a horizontal *keiretsu* to ensure solid financing and improved trading capabilities. Toyota is a member of the Mitsui Group, for example, in addition to running its own vertical *keiretsu*. Finally, numerous small supplier firms become quasi-members of the group and receive long-term purchasing contracts, as well as assistance with financing and sometimes R&D. These suppliers support the famous *kanban* (or just-in-time) inventory system that Japan is noted for and must remain loyal to one group. That is, when supplies on an assembly line get short, suppliers are automatically notified and replenish the factory in short order.

Now, let's turn to human resource management policies in Japan. Japanese *kaisha* tend to view all regular employees (not including continent workers or workers employed by company suppliers) as part of their permanent cost structure. As such, during difficult financial periods, most Japanese companies will go to great lengths to retain their workers. This contrasts with the situation in many Anglo-American firms, where lay-offs are frequently seen as an easy solution to financial exigency. If workers are seen as a fixed cost (instead of a variable cost), it makes sense to invest heavily in their training. Long-term employment will allow for sufficient payback of such training expenses. In this sense, Western observers have suggested that Japanese companies treat their employees more like family members than employees.

Concern has frequently been expressed that employee commitment to their companies in Japan may be too strong. Many Japanese refuse to take all of the vacation time to which they are entitled – a practice seldom witnessed in the West. A commonly used Japanese word, *ganbatte*, typifies this overzealous commitment to work.[13] Indeed, Japanese employees and even school children will often be heard to say to their friends or colleagues, "*ganbatte kudasai*" – "never give up, try harder, do your best." On the positive side, *ganbatte* shows strong commitment to succeed on behalf of one's company or family. On the negative side, it often manifests itself in large numbers of work-related health problems. Health care professionals express concern about the large number of Japanese employees who overwork themselves to the point of becoming ill.

Finally, it is important to note that in view of Japan's long-running economic problems and increased global pressures for efficiency, several Japanese companies (e.g., Hitachi, Toshiba, NEC) have recently begun to back away from their former policies of ironclad job security and lifetime employment.[14] Other companies are beginning to place greater emphasis on individual performance and performance appraisals, referred to as the *nenpo* system.[15]

Even so, the general characteristics of Japanese human resource management systems remain relatively constant. Concern for the group, respect for age and seniority, and devotion to the company remain hallmarks of the typical Japanese firm. Indeed, Fujitsu recently decided to discontinue its much-heralded Western-style performance-based pay system because it proved to be a poor fit with Japanese culture. Fujitsu's new system will emphasize worker enthusiasm and energy in tackling a job instead of actual goal accomplishment in annual performance evaluations.[16] Moreover, when Fujitsu announced that it was laying off 15,000 workers, or 9 percent of its workforce, it made it clear that all involuntary lay-offs would take place in operations outside of Japan. Any Japanese workforce reductions would be accomplished through retirements and normal attrition.

There are over 70,000 labor unions in Japan, most of which are company-specific. These *enterprise unions* tend to include both workers and lower-and middle-level managers. This differs from the situation in Canada and the US, for example, where most unions are industrial unions that cross several companies in the same industry.

Although many enterprise unions affiliate with national labor federations (which facilitate the annual spring wage negotiations, or *shuntō*), these organizations are more decentralized than in the US or Canada.[17] As a result, Japanese workers in enterprise unions typically do not experience the same degree of divided loyalties (union versus company) that are often seen in America and Canadia among unionized workers. In addition, it is not uncommon for union members in Japanese companies to rise through the management ranks – even to the position of company president in some cases. This seldom occurs in the US, where the managerial hierarchy is separate and distinct from the "blue collar" class and where junior managers are typically hired from among recent college graduates, not rank-and-file production workers. Even though enterprise unions are often linked to large nationwide industrial unions, industrial action (e.g., strikes) is rare, and most disputes are settled relatively amicably.

The lack of clear divisions between labor and management in Japanese firms often makes it possible to enlist workers at all levels in efforts to improve productivity and product quality. Quality and service are company-wide concerns from the top to the bottom of the organization, not just management concerns. Japan is noted for its widespread use of *quality circles*, small groups of workers who spend time (frequently their own) trying to improve operational procedures or product quality in their own area.[18] These efforts help Japanese firms with their *kaizen*, a philosophy of continuous improvement that is also a hallmark of Japanese manufacturing firms.[19]

In summary, the typical Japanese approach to organization and management is both different and effective, and represents a formidable threat to global competitors. Japanese firms have found a way to build their organizations in ways that draw support from the local environment and culture and mobilize their resources in ways that many Western firms have difficulty understanding, let alone responding to. It is a model that prizes cooperation and mutual support among friends and all-out competition against all others.

Chinese *gong-si*

More people speak Mandarin Chinese as their first language than any other runner-up language in the world, including (in descending order) Spanish, English, Bengali, and Hindi.[20] Throughout China, the predominant business model is organized around the family and, at least traditionally, is based on so-called Confucian principles. However, Chinese culture is, in fact, far more complex than this. Moreover, it continues to evolve over time to changing circumstances and demands.[21] Hence, we turn to a look inside China's broad-based culture, past, and present.

Chinese cultural patterns

When Westerners attempt to describe Chinese culture, they invariably begin – correctly or incorrectly – with Confucianism. Contrary to popular Western belief, *Confucianism* is a philosophy, not a religion. Kong Qui was a senior civil servant in China in the sixth century BCE. His Western name, Confucius, is actually a Latin form of the title *Kongfuzi*, which means Great Master Kong. Kong Qui was a moral philosopher, best known for his thoughts on correct moral character and personal responsibility. Although he never published his thoughts or philosophy, his disciples collected them and subsequently published them in a classic book called the *Analects*.[22]

Known for his wisdom and insight, Kong Qui promulgated a code of ethical behavior that was meant to guide interpersonal relationships in everyday life. This code was summed up in the so-called *five cardinal virtues* (see Exhibit 6.7). While these principles suggest a way of living in the broader society, they also have implications for business practices today:

- *Filial piety*, which traditionally requires a son to show respect and absolute obedience to his father at all times. From this principle we can also see the origin of the familism that permeates Chinese society to this day. One's family is vitally important because it defines who people are and where they belong in the larger society. The family looks after its own, a factor that often leads to the nepotism that is frequently seen in Chinese companies. As a part of this *familism*, we see too the special emphasis that is placed by the family on education and continual self-improvement as a means of aiding in the development of one's self, family, and community. Each individual has an obligation to maximize his or her contribution to the family.
- *Absolute loyalty* to one's superiors can be seen today in the strong commitment shown by many Chinese employees toward the company and its leader. The president of the company traditionally embodies the essence of the company itself, and as such is to be respected and followed without question.

- *Strict seniority* is a pillar of proper social relationships, with the young showing respect and obedience to the old and the old assuming responsibility for the well-being and future of the young.
- *Subservience*, initially based on gender, required women to obey their husbands in all things. Their role was primarily that of a homemaker, and it was rare to see women in business. They controlled few resources or assets. While sex role stereotyping still exits today, in recent years it has diminished in magnitude and Chinese women are now much more likely to be treated as equals, especially in the more prosperous urbanized areas of the country like Shanghai and Beijing. Indeed, it is very common now to see women running both large and small businesses, and, indeed, observers suggest that women in China now have more equality than in most other Asian countries.
- *Mutual trust between friends and colleagues* must be preserved at all times. This is seen as the key to all human relationships and a major determinant of the humanity and solidarity of the culture. Even today, maintaining harmonious relationships among work associates is a never-ending pursuit for employees at all levels in the organization. Business activity is based more on personal relationships and contacts than on written contracts. Reciprocity and exchange represent an important part of this process.

Exhibit 6.7 *Kongfuzi's* five cardinal virtues

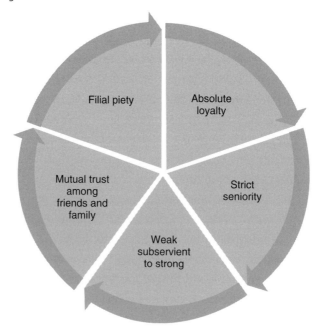

Kong Qui and his followers saw the universe – and hence society – as a hierarchical system ruled by an educated aristocratic elite. Concepts such as democracy and equality were disdained, while learning and education were highly prized. Confucian society stressed the virtues of self-discipline, hard work, diligence, and frugality.[23] Hence, the fundamental nature of human relationships is not interactions among equals, but rather interactions among unequals. That is, correct interpersonal behavior is determined by one's age, gender, and position in society, and a breach in this social etiquette carries with it severe penalties.

These five cardinal virtues are reinforced by five additional characteristics or social patterns of traditional Chinese society. First, consider the concept of *guānxi*. *Guānxi* can be defined as a strong personal relationship between two people with implications of a continual exchange of favors.[24] Others define it simply as good connections or tight social networks based on trust, common background, and experience. Two people have *guānxi* when they can assume that each is conscientiously committed to the other regardless of what happens. This bond is based on the exchange of favors (i.e., social capital), not necessarily friendship or sympathy, and it does not have to involve friends. It is more utilitarian than emotional. It also tends to favor the weaker of the two parties in ongoing exchanges, an outgrowth of the Confucian doctrine of looking after those less fortunate than oneself. Failing to meet one's obligations under this equity arrangement causes severe loss of face and creates the appearance of being untrustworthy.

The second factor in determining social relationships in China (and elsewhere in Asia) is *mien-tzu*, or face (i.e., dignity, self-respect, prestige). A central tenet of Confucianism is to maintain long-term social harmony.[25] This is based both on the maintenance of correct relationships between individuals and on the protection of one's face. All social interactions must be conducted in a manner in which no party loses face. Face can be classified into two types: *lian* and *mianzi*. *Lian* is associated with personal behavior, while *mianzi* is something valuable that can be achieved. Under this system, a Chinese man or woman may be criticized for having no *lian* and will be seen as being unsuccessful if he has no *mianzi*. Normally, people of higher rank possess greater *mianzi*. Together they determine who has face, who gains it, and who loses it. As a result, face represents a key component in the exercise of *guānxi*. If a person has little *mianzi*, he or she has limited social capital with which to cultivate social connections.

Simply put, face represents the confidence society has in one's moral character. It represents one's self-image or reputation. The loss of face makes it impossible for an individual to function properly in the community. This occurs when an individual, either through his own actions or the actions of people close to him, fails to meet essential requirements placed upon him by virtue of his social position. Hence, if an individual cannot keep a commitment, however small, he loses face. Similarly, a person loses face when he or she is not treated in accordance with his or her station or position in society. Thus, a senior manager will lose face if it becomes known that a junior colleague is earning a higher salary or was promoted ahead of him.

The third important factor here is *renqing*, or personal obligations. These personal obligations accrue to individuals as a result of past *guānxi* relationships. That is, it involves unpaid debts or favors that are owed to others as a result of past favors in a continuing exchange relationship between friends and colleagues. In addition to various social expressions (such as offering congratulations or condolences and making gifts on appropriate occasions), *renqing* often includes a display of human empathy and personal sentiments. It focuses on social emotions – emotions played out in public – rather than personal emotions, which are frequently hidden from view. If one fails to follow the rule of equity in the exchange of *renqing*, one loses face, hurts the feelings of others, and looks inconsiderate. This applies even to one's closest friends. As such, some have translated *renqing* as "humanized obligations" instead of personal obligations, which implies that a continued exchange of favors with a sentimental touch is involved.

Fourth, consider the importance of *rank*. Confucian principles were designed to recognize hierarchy and differences between class members. As a result, the behavioral requirements of individuals differed according to who was involved in the relationship. Among equals, certain patterns of prescribed behavior existed. You can see this today when two strangers discover upon meeting for the first time that they both attended the same high school or college. An instant bond emerges and there is a sense of immediate camaraderie. On the other hand, for people from outside this common background or clan, there is frequent hostility or distrust. Foreign observers note that some people can be very blunt and impolite when talking with total strangers, yet very hospitable and generous when dealing with friends or acquaintances. It is a question of belonging.

Finally, within one's broad circle of acquaintances, there is a clear responsibility for maintaining *group harmony*. Again, this principle stresses harmony between unequals. That is, it links persons of unequal rank in power, prestige, or position. Since strong personal relationships outside the family only tend to occur between persons of equal rank, age, or prestige, harmony is the means of defining all other necessarily more formal relationships. It is everyone's responsibility to continually maintain this harmony among one's acquaintances and family members, and considerable effort is invested in doing so, including gift giving.

Organization and management trends in China

In view of China's strong cultural traditions, it is not surprising that its companies, both large and small, reflect this heritage. Chinese companies are generally called *gong-si* (pronounced "gong-suh"). While the term "*gong-si*" originally referred to private family-owned enterprises, recent Chinese corporate law now uses this term to refer to all companies, regardless of whether they are large or small, family-owned or state-owned. To clarify this difference, smaller and medium-sized family-run enterprises are now often called *jia zu gong-si*. An illustration of a typical family-run SME is shown in Exhibit 6.8.

Found throughout China, Taiwan, and elsewhere in the world where overseas Chinese congregate, the Chinese family business tends to be a small entrepreneurial venture owned by family members and typically employing members of the extended family as well as others whom the family feels it can trust.[26] These firms are particularly prevalent in Southern China and among overseas Chinese. As a rule, Chinese family firms are considerably smaller and exhibit greater independence than their Japanese or Korean counterparts.

The dominant management style of the *gong-si* is *patrimonialism*, which includes paternalism, hierarchy, mutual obligation, responsibility, familism, personalism, and connections.[27] As a result, typical Chinese family business are often characterized by power and influence being closely related to ownership, autocratic leadership, and a

Exhibit 6.8 Design of a typical Chinese family-owned *gong-si*

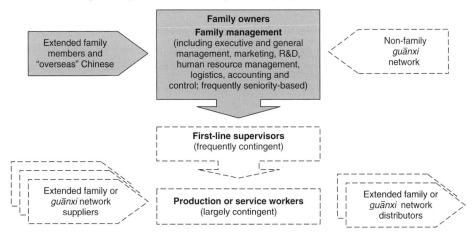

Note: The shaded boxes represent formal parts of the organization. The white boxes represent independent agencies, institutions, service providers, and contingent workers that are largely outside the formal organization design.

personalistic style of management designed in part to pay honor to the founder or leader. This can be seen in the example of the East Hope Group, above.

Following from Confucian thought, the family is the most fundamental revenue and expenditure unit. Within a family, each member contributes his or her income to a common family fund. Each member then has a right to a portion of these funds, while the remainder belongs to the family as a whole. The interests of the entire family take precedence over individual members and others outside the family. As a result, business owners tend to regard the business as the private property of the core family (not an individual), and are therefore reluctant to share ownership with outsiders or to borrow from individuals or organizations unrelated to the family in some way. Top management positions are often filled with family members, sometimes despite a lack of managerial competence. Company size tends to be small. Over 90 percent of these firms employ less than fifty people, including family members, and focus their energies on a small area of business – production, sales, or service.[28]

Gong-si companies have little formal structure, few standard operating procedures, and little specialization.[29] While they lack formal structure and procedures, personal relationships are likely to take precedence over more objectively defined concerns such as organizational efficiency. Who one knows is often more important than what one knows, and employee loyalty is often preferred over actual performance. Decisions are frequently based either on intuition or on long-standing business exchange relationships. According to Ming-Jer Chen, if these family firms have a competitive advantage, it lies in their small size, flexibility, network of connections, and negotiation skills.[30]

As noted in Chapter 3, cultures can sometimes evolve over time in response to external stimuli. China provides a good example of this. Perhaps one reason Chinese culture has endured for so many millennia is that it is at once both strong and flexible. Its roots are very deep, yet it is sufficiently flexible to adapt to shifting political sands (from empire to nationalism to communism to quasi-capitalism). As China has begun to prosper in response to its newfound economic freedoms, and as more young Chinese are exposed to Western thought (e.g., capitalism, democracy, individualism), a clear evolution in management thought can be seen from older managers to younger ones.[31] Many young Chinese managers, with greater educational opportunities and more overseas experience, are beginning to develop their own framework for business management that differs significantly from that of their parents. This new approach can perhaps best be described as a blend of old and new, East and West. The trend in Chinese management philosophy is changing rapidly towards a greater emphasis on competitiveness, innovation, and individual responsibility. These changes are real and widespread. How they will influence future successes or failures of Chinese business-men and women remains to be seen. What is clear, however, is that these changes pose a significant challenge for all partners doing business in the region, regardless of their home country.

German *konzern*

Germany is a country widely known and respected for its cutting-edge technology and craftsmanship. It is also known as a high-cost producer. Combining these two attributes leads to its position in the global marketplace as a producer of innovative, high-quality, and expensive goods and services. However, as globalization pressures continue and price points becomes an increasingly important factor for global consumers, the obvious question is: How can German companies compete now and in the future? To explore this question, it is necessary to examine the unique approach to organization and manage-ment that is found in Germany and its Germanic (and to some extent Nordic) neighbors.

German cultural patterns

A number of social scientists have attempted to describe German culture in general terms. Geert Hofstede, for example, has described the typical German as relatively individualistic (although not so extreme as Americans), high on uncertainty avoidance and masculinity, and relatively low on power distance.[32] Hall and Hall add that Germans tend to be very punctual about time, follow schedules closely, demand order, value their personal space, respect power and position, and seek detailed infor-mation prior to decision making. Indeed, Hall and Hall quote a French executive as saying that "Germans are too busy managing to think creatively."[33] As discussed in Chapter 3, cultural anthropologists suggest that the dominant German culture includes a mastery orientation, moderate individualism and egalitarian, a strong rule-based orientation, and a monochromic approach to time.

To foreign observers, Germans tend to be conservative, formal, and polite.[34] Formal titles are important in conversations, and privacy and protocol are valued. In business, Germans tend to be assertive, but not aggressive. Although firms are often characterized by strict departmentalization, decisions tend to be made based on broad-based dis-cussion and consensus building among key stakeholders. Negotiations are based on extensive assessments of data and plans and, since Germany is a low-context culture (where message clarity counts), communication is explicit and easily understood by foreigners.

Germans tend to be broadly educated, multilingual, and widely traveled. They are highly regarded for being trusted partners, as well as for their forward-looking human resource management policies. In recent years, perhaps because of this informed worldview, Germany has witnessed an increased flexibility in cultural expressions. Still, differences remain.

Organization and management trends in Germany

As with companies in any country, it is difficult to generalize about the nature or structure of the typical German firm (or *Konzern* in German). Like the US, German firms generally take one of two legal forms: a limited partnership designated by a *GmbH* (*Gesellschaft mit beschraenkter Haftung*) following the company name, or a public stock company designated by an *AG* (*Aktiengesellschaft*) following the name. As such, the company Volkswagen AG is a public company with publicly traded stock. In German conglomerates, the parent company is often referred to as the *Muttergesellschaft* (literally "mother company").

From an organizational standpoint, German firms are typically led from the top by two boards. At the very top is the *supervisory board* (or *Aufsichtsrat*), as shown in Exhibit 6.9. This board, much like a board of directors in US firms, is responsible for ensuring that the principal corporate objectives are met over the long term. Its members are typically elected for five years and can only be changed by a vote of 75 percent of the voting shares. A key function of the supervisory board is to oversee the activities of the *management board* (or *Vorstand*), which consists of the top management team of the firm and is responsible for its actual strategic and operational management. These two boards are jointly responsible for the success or failure of German enterprise.

On a company level, a legally binding *codetermination* system (*Mitbestimmung* in German) supports worker rights. This system is based on the belief that both shareholders and employees have a right to influence company policies, and that profit maximization must be tempered with concern for social welfare. Under codetermination, workers may exercise their influence on corporate affairs through representatives on the supervisory board. Typically, one-half to one-third of the members of this board are elected by the workers – normally through their works council – while stockholders elect the remainder. As such, German workers can have a significant influence on strategic decision-making. Moreover, many serious labor problems are discussed and resolved at this executive level before they grow into major conflicts.

Exhibit 6.9 Design of a typical German *konzern*

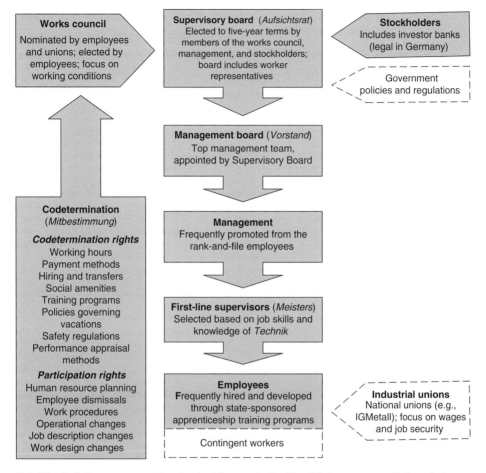

Note: The shaded boxes represent formal parts of the organization. The white boxes represent independent agencies, institutions, service providers, and contingent workers that are largely outside the formal organization design.

On a plant level, workers exercise their influence through *works councils*. Works councils typically have no rights in the economic management of the firm, but have considerable influence in human resource management policies and practices. Their principal task is to ensure that companies follow regulations that exist for the benefit of their employees. As such, works councils have the right to access considerable company information concerning the running of the firm, including economic performance. Rights granted to works councils are divided into *codetermination rights* (the right to approve or reject management decisions) and *participation rights* (the right to be consulted on management decisions).

The German industrial relations system is highly standardized, extensively organized through state regulation, and characterized by formal recognition of employee rights at all levels of the firm.[35] This concept of fostering strong employee participation in corporate decision making is generally referred to (especially in Europe) as industrial democracy. *Industrial democracy* refers to a consensus among national leaders and citizens in a country that employees at all levels of organizations have a right to be involved in decisions affecting their long-term welfare. Nowhere is the concept of industrial democracy better illustrated than in Germany, where strong industrial unions, codetermination, and works councils characterize the workplace environment.

On a national level, the German constitution guarantees all citizens the right to join unions and engage in collective bargaining. It also indirectly guarantees the right of companies to join employer associations. At present, 42 percent of German industrial workers (and 30 percent of all German employees) are members of unions, compared to less than 10 percent in the US. Eighty percent of German employees are members of various branches of Germany's largest trade union, the *Deutsche Gewerkschaftsbund* (or DGB). Moreover, the national government plays a strong role in industrial relations. All political parties have strong factions representing workers' interests, although the Social Democratic Party has the closest links to unions. Extensive legislation covers labor standards, benefits, discrimination, plant closures, and employee rights.

Collective bargaining agreements are negotiated on an industry-wide basis, either nationally or regionally. Little direct bargaining takes place between unions and employers at the plant level. As a result, wage differentials across companies in similar industries are small. Employment disputes are usually settled through labor courts, consisting of three persons: a professional judge who is a specialist in labor law, a union representative, and a representative of the employer's association. These courts have jurisdiction over both individual employment contracts and collective contracts involving industrial disputes.

A hallmark of German firms is the technical competence they bring to the manufacture of so many diverse products. German engineering is world famous. A major reason for this lies in the training of managers and workers. Line managers in German firms are typically better trained technically than their European or American counterparts, with closer relations between them and technical experts in the firm. In contrast to American managers, most German managers are trained as engineers and have completed some form of craft apprenticeship training program. The typical German organization is distinguished by its tightly knit technical staff superstructure, closely linked to supervisory and managerial tasks that, when combined, produce high levels of performance. Compared to French or British industry, German firms have a lower center of gravity; that is, they have less proliferation of administrative and support staff and more hands-on shop floor managers.

From the first-line supervisor (usually held by a *Meister*, or master technician) on up, managers are respected for what they know rather than who they are. They tend to be far less controlling than many of their US counterparts. Instead, it is assumed that workers and supervisors will meet deadlines, guarantee quality and service, and do not require close supervision. Independence within agreed-upon parameters characterizes the working relationship between managers and the managed.

Behind the organizational facade of German firms is a particular notion of technical competence commonly referred to as *Technik*. This describes the knowledge and skills required for work.[36] It is the science and art of manufacturing high-quality and technologically advanced products. The success of *Technik* in German manufacturing is evidenced by the fact that over 40 percent of Germany's gross domestic product is derived from manufacturing. Indeed, Germany is responsible for over half of all EU manufactured exports. It is for this reason that knowledge of *Technik* represents a principal determinant in the selection of supervisors and managers.

A principal method for developing this technical competence in workers begins with widespread and intensive *apprenticeship training programs*.[37] It is estimated that over 65 percent of 15- and 16-year-old Germans enter some form of vocational training program. Apprenticeship programs exist not only for manual occupations, but also for many technical, commercial, and managerial occupations. There are two principal forms of vocational training in Germany. The first consists of general and specialized training programs offered by vocational schools and technical colleges. The second, referred to as the *dual system*, combines in-house apprenticeship training with part-time vocational training leading to a skilled-worker certificate. There are over 400 nationally recognized vocational certificates. Qualifications for each certificate are standardized throughout the country, leading to a well-trained workforce with skills that are not company-specific. This certificated training can be followed by attendance at one of the many *Fachschule*, or advanced vocational colleges. Graduation from a *Fachschule* facilitates the achievement of a *Meister* (or master technician) certification (see Exhibit 6.10).

The dual system of apprenticeship training represents a partnership between employers, unions, and the government. Costs are typically shared between companies

Exhibit 6.10 Germany's dual system of vocational training

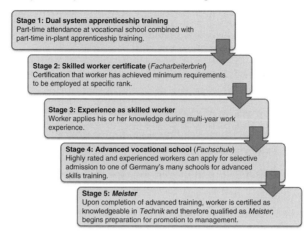

and the government on a two-thirds/one-third basis. Employers are legally required to release young workers for vocational training. German companies are also widely known for their enthusiastic support of company-sponsored training programs. Mercedes-Benz (part of Daimler), for example, regularly offers 180 vocational courses to its employees. Each year, the company has over 600 employees studying in vocational or modular management development courses, as well as over 4,000 employees who participate in some form of formal training at the company's training center.

Before leaving this topic, it should be noted that in recent years some people have criticized the complexity of German apprenticeship programs, as well as the length of time required for certification.[38] It has been argued that this lengthy certification procedure hinders entrepreneurship and Germany's competitive position in the world by limiting access to many professions, inhibiting change in those professions, and stifling creativity and innovation. However, German unions – and many companies – have resisted change.

Mexican *grupo*

Finally, we take a brief look at organization and management in Mexico. Mexico's competitive strength lies in its low-priced workforce and rising manufacturing quality. Individual worker productivity varies widely throughout Mexico. In many key industrial clusters, the country has developed a level of labor productivity that compares favorably with many heavily industrialized countries. In recent years, the Mexican

Government has been active in raising the level of productivity of the Mexican work-force, including the widespread use of government-sponsored training programs and reinvestment programs.

Mexican cultural patterns

Cultural anthropologists and other social scientists tend to describe the Mexican culture as being collectivistic, hierarchical, polychronic, paternalistic, group-centered, security-oriented, somewhat formal, and at times fatalistic.[39] This certainly does not apply to all Mexicans; indeed, it doesn't even recognize that Mexico is a multicultural society with both European and native influences. Even so, foreign visitors frequently observe that Mexicans will at times go to great lengths to protect their dignity, uphold their honor, and maintain their good name. The uniqueness of the individual is honored in Mexico, and people are judged on their individual achievements, demeanor, trust-worthiness, and character. Personal respect is a very important element in any relation-ship. Even a relatively insignificant comment or action can be interpreted in a negative or deprecating manner and can destroy the trust between two people.

Mexican business culture operates under a strict caste system. Most business is conducted between equals, and titles and social position are important. As a result, it is unlikely that a Mexican company president would meet with a mid-level representa-tive of another firm, even an important foreign firm. Thus, smart international com-panies send presidents to meet presidents, vice presidents to meet vice presidents, and so forth. In addition, a personal introduction through a mutual friend is always helpful, as it is in many parts of the world.

Mexicans are polite in formal business situations, but become more relaxed once the parties have established their relative positions within the hierarchy and begin to get to know each other. For this reason, it is crucial for global managers to determine and acknowledge the status of the person they are dealing with when preparing for a face-to-face meeting, as well as to convey their own position. People are also evaluated on their outward displays, their personal image (*imagen*), so they should dress well. In Mexico, formality rules.

Networking is very important in Mexico. Cultivating personal relationships with those who may be in a position to help you is crucial to successful business in Mexico. These relationships are typically built on complex personal ties rather than legal contracts, as is typical in much of the West. Being accepted as part of a network also entails reciprocity. This requires you to use your own contacts and connections (called *palancas*) to help others when called upon for assistance. This is similar to the Chinese concept of *guānxi* that was discussed below. Your success depends in part on who you know. As part of this relationship building, gifts are traditionally exchanged during formal ceremonies, especially during official visits by governmental authorities. For Mexicans, typical gifts include regional handcrafts, books, or pieces of art.

A key issue for success in managing in Mexico is flexibility. Recognizing cultural norms, particularly the importance of holidays and festivals, is essential. In addition, many Mexican companies take a more paternalistic approach in their relations with their employees. This often means providing services that are not traditionally considered the responsibility of employers throughout much of the West. For example, many Mexican employees will expect the company to provide transportation to the work site. This is often accomplished by subcontracting privately owned buses to travel through the neighborhoods of the employees and gather the workers each morning. Many firms also provide cafeterias and feed their employees lunch each day.

In any culture, the use of time can tell us a great deal about how organizations (and societies) work. This is clearly true in Mexico. Time is frequently used intentionally to demonstrate who is more important. Making someone wait shows power, prestige, and status. At the same time, managers must be careful not to offend their counterparts and thereby risk losing business.

Another aspect of time is the sense of urgency with which business is done. Mexico is famous for the concept of *mañana*. The idea here is that there is always another day to complete today's work. While putting things off is commonplace, it would be incorrect to equate this phenomenon with laziness or an unprofessional work attitude. Rather, it represents a different approach to doing business – one that seeks to prioritize conflicting requirements. Mexicans believe that there are other priorities in life than just work and that conditions often conspire to prevent the realization of plans as envisioned. Rather than get unduly stressed about multiple and often conflicting demands, they often take a more relaxed attitude, assuming that things will eventually get done. This is a hard concept for many Anglo-Americans, Asians, and Europeans to comprehend. As such, foreigners must understand that when Mexicans promise that something will be done by a certain time or date, they are often saying this to please the person they are dealing with rather that giving a straightforward appraisal of when the work will be done. In Mexico, unlike many other countries, such promises are not considered a contract or firm obligation. Time commitments are more likely to be made out of politeness and the need for having a ballpark idea of when the work will be completed. Therefore, foreigners should not expect that work would actually be finished when promised, and should plan accordingly.

Organization and management trends in Mexico

When doing business in Mexico, proper contacts with various government departments can be vital for success. Like their American and Canadian counterparts, most Mexican business people tend to be somewhat scornful of the effectiveness of political officials in general, and often claim that they want little to do with them. However, in Mexico (as elsewhere), when a cabinet official, governor, or mayor launches a new program, those same business people often race to see who can be first on the scene to lend a hand and participate in the program. There is a reason for this. No political office in the US can compare in terms of raw power to that wielded by government officials in Mexico. Top government officials preside as if over a fiefdom, and their decisions can have a significant impact on any business. Official contacts are of tremendous help to any business endeavor. Another benefit is that one's credibility within the business community increases proportionally to the depth and breadth of his or her access to government officials.

In recent years, the Mexican Government has taken significant steps to crack down on bribery and corruption at all levels. This is not to say major bribery no longer exists, but it is much more subtle and is less likely to involve visitors from other countries. The tradition of bribery, or *mordida* (the bite), predates the Mexican Republic, and one may still be asked for a "contribution" from time to time. Small-scale bribery often involves minor officials that regularly deal with foreign businesspersons or tourists who expect a small cash payment in return for their providing a service (e.g., extending a tourist card or visa). Paying such bribes is straightforward, but discreet.

Mexico as a nation remains concerned about being economically (or even politically) absorbed into the wealthy and powerful US economy to the north. Indeed, there is an old Mexican saying: "Poor Mexico: so far from God and so near the United States." As a result, national sovereignty remains a critical issue.

According to IPADE professor Carlos Ruiz Gonzalez, a typical Mexican business group (or *grupo*) consists of several highly diverse companies that operate in a climate of familial ties, mutual trust, and overall cooperation.[40] *Grupos* are typically led by strong, powerful CEOs who are often also the principal stockholders (see Exhibit 6.11). Member companies typically share operating philosophies, channels of distribution, marketing intelligence, and efficiencies of scale, even though they are legally separate entities. New acquisitions are quickly integrated into the business group. As Carlos Slim Helu, Chairman of Mexico's Grupo Carsa and one of the richest men in the world, observes, "It's not a question of arriving and putting in a whole new

Exhibit 6.11 Design of a typical Mexican *grupo*

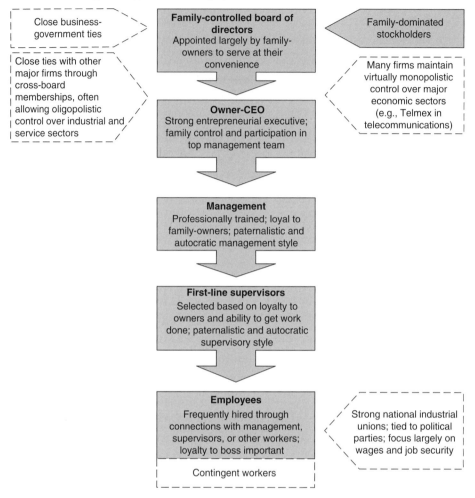

Note: The shaded boxes represent formal parts of the organization. The white boxes represent independent agencies, institutions, service providers, and contingent workers that are largely outside the formal organization design.

administration, but instead, arriving and compacting things as much as possible, reducing management layers. We want as few management layers as possible, so that executives are very close to the operations. We also don't believe in having big corporate infrastructures."

Many Mexicans value strong interpersonal relationships, human dignity, and the full enjoyment of life. There is a strong belief in the importance of achieving a suitable balance between home life and work life. By contrast, many Anglo-Americans seem to value aggressively attacking problems, egalitarian conduct, and accomplishing tasks at almost any price. As such, working long hours is assumed and, for many, a rich family life can be a detriment to career success. This is less important for most Mexicans. Finally, Mexican businesspersons typically negotiate contracts and deals in restaurants, hotels, conference rooms, or other neutral territory. Rarely will a Mexican company conduct extensive negotiations at its own place of business.

Global executives observe that Anglo-American and Mexican managers frequently approach business matters in very different ways. Many of these differences are based on contrasting beliefs concerning what constitutes good management.[41] For starters, consider the following: Many Mexican managers see Anglo-American managers – particularly those from the US – as being too direct, too impatient, and too reticent to accept blame. On the other hand, many Anglo-American managers see Mexican managers as being too polite, too indecisive, and too slow to act. In addition, many Anglo-Americans seek rational, linear decisions based on concrete and business-related evidence. By contrast, many Mexican managers use a more non-linear approach, considering other issues (e.g., personal relationships, traditions, and personal loyalties) and reaching decisions through extended discussions with various parties. Many Anglo-Americans see no problem in criticizing others in public or placing blame or responsibility for failure on specific individuals. By contrast, many Mexicans prefer to avoid placing blame and instead focus on the positive aspects of individual behavior or performance.

Not unlike the general trend in China, foreign observers also suggest that management in Mexico tends to be somewhat more autocratic than is typically found in Anglo-American or European firms. However, while a manager in Mexico must be respected by his or her subordinates for being tough and decisive, he or she must also be seen as *simpatico*, or understanding. Managers in Mexico tend to exhibit a strong sense of paternalism, caring for the personal side of their employees that is often absent and at times even resented north of the border. They must act like a *patron* and treat their subordinates like an extended family, like Japanese managers. Along with this, managers must also treat their employees with a strong sense of respect; personal slights frequently bring strong resentment. Mexican workers often need more communication, relationship building, and reassurance than employees in some Western countries.

As a result of the above, many Mexican firms are characterized by strong, centralized decision making. While the necessity to decentralize many functions and responsibilities is recognized, it is clearly understood that the boss has the final say. Today, particularly in the larger firms, a new generation of younger and highly educated managers is beginning to gain prominence. This new generation is beginning to change corporate cultures to be more receptive to decentralization of decision making.

To see how this works, consider Grupo Carso. Headquartered in Mexico City, Grupo Carso is controlled by Carlos Slim Helú, a Mexican entrepreneur currently ranked as the second richest man in the world with a net worth of around US$60 billion. He and his group of companies have a substantial influence over the telecommunications industry in Mexico, and much of Latin America as well. He controls *Teléfonos de México* (Telmex), Telcel, and *América Móvil*, as well as other companies in heavy industry, services, retail and consumer goods, and banking and finance. In 2009, he bought a major interest in the *New York Times*.[42] He is also one of the world's most generous philanthropists, investing his wealth in infrastructure development, urban redevelopment, and educational projects throughout Mexico and Latin America.

Carlos Slim's leadership style is very practical. Decision making is highly centralized for purposes of developing overall group and company strategy. But at the same time, implementation decisions are fairly decentralized, particularly when compared to other Mexican firms. Grupo Carsa has no corporate staff, and each company has its own structure so that the total organization can be more efficient. Simple structures, organizations with minimal hierarchies, personal development, and internal training for executives – this, along with flexibility and rapid top-down decision making, allows Grupo Carsa to remain one of the world's most nimble entrepreneurial conglomerates.

MANAGER'S NOTEBOOK

Organizing frameworks

So, where does this leave us? From a managerial standpoint, three challenges emerge that must be resolved for managers to successfully work with organizations across cultures (see Exhibit 6.12). First, managers must develop an understanding of cultural trends, organizing patterns, and management styles in their own country. This is often easier said than done. We often assume, incorrectly, that we already know this, but looking deeper might reveal that we have something to learn here. Second, based on this local understanding, and as discussed earlier in the book, managers must develop sufficient insight and understanding of other countries and cultures with which they or their companies do (or wish to do) business. And finally, managers must continue to develop their management and multicultural skills so that they can successfully bridge these two cultures and help meet corporate objectives.

How can we learn these skills? Perhaps a good place to begin is by using a comparative analysis to tease out similarities and differences – large and small – between and across organizations around the globe. This was the goal of this chapter. And what conclusions might such an analysis reveal?

As illustrated in Exhibit 6.13, probably the most obvious conclusion here is that these various organizing frameworks are highly correlated with the cultural traits of their home countries. Japan is a collectivistic society that fosters inclusion and group membership. Not surprisingly, major Japanese *keiretsu* (as well as smaller firms) make use of a group mentality and paternalism in structuring their firms and managing their people. Everyone "belongs" to the company – and the company belongs to them. By contrast, Germany is a more individualistic country but is still largely egalitarian in nature. As such, German firms may be somewhat more bureaucratic, but they still provide a strong

Exhibit 6.12 Management challenge: working with different organizing frameworks

Local understanding:
Understand one's own culture, organization, and management style, as well as corporate mission and objectives

Global understanding:
Understand culture, organization, and management style of global customers, partners, employees, etc.

Global management:
Develop suitable management and multicultural skills to bridge cultural divisions and achieve corporate mission and objectives.

Exhibit 6.13 Patterns of organization design and management practice: a summary

Country	Organization design trends	Management trends
Chinese *gong-si*	Flat, fluid organizations with little structure; power centered in closely-knit family owners; large numbers of non-family contingent workers; hierarchical and autocratic; collectivistic.	Supervisory role focuses on direction and control; patriarchal; relationship-based management; family managers as generalists; emphasis on building trust and personal relationships (*guānxi*); somewhat monochronic; highly centralized and rapid decision making with rapid implementation.
German *konzern*	Formal bureaucratic organizations with strict hierarchies; power dispersed across multiple stakeholders, including works councils and industrial unions.	Supervisory role focuses on technical expertise (*Technik*) and consensus building; rule-based and somewhat linear management; formal; highly participative; slow consensual decision making with moderate pace of implementation; strong apprenticeship training leading to *Meister* status.
Japanese *kaisha* and *keiretsu*	Formal organizations consisting of closely-knit extended networks; hierarchical and autocratic; collectivistic; close affiliation with banks; strong trading companies; company unions.	Supervisory role focuses on paternalism and support, particularly at lower levels of the hierarchy; relationship-based management; strong group orientation; harmony-oriented; emphasis on trust and personal relationships; avoids overt conflict; emphasis on employee development and mutual commitments; employees as fixed cost; slow decision making but rapid implementation.
Mexican *grupo*	Formal and family-owned and controlled organizations; close ties to government and other major firms; hierarchical; somewhat collectivistic.	Supervisory role focuses on direction and control; patriarchal and autocratic; relationship-based and non-linear management; use of connections (*palancas*); emphasis on trust and personal relationships; slow autocratic decision making with slow implementation.
US corporation	Often informal organizations comprising loosely coupled systems; power based in stockholders and executive team; emphasis on efficiency and flexibility; moderately egalitarian; mastery-oriented.	Supervisory role focuses on direction and control; rule-based management; stresses individual achievement and responsibility; imperial CEO; highly trained management cadre; flexible and innovative; respect for rules and policies and a sense of order; extensive use of contingent workers; linear, rapid, and somewhat autocratic decision-making but with slow implementation; employees as variable cost.

Note: This exhibit illustrates general trends in organization design and management practice. Clearly, within-culture differences (oftentimes significant) can be found along with the between-culture differences that are summarized here.

basis for employee participation and involvement at all levels. Thus, while both Japanese and German firms foster employee participation, the basis for such inclusion is very different: participation in Japanese firms is based on societal norms, while in Germany it is based on the prevailing legal system. Meanwhile, non-family employees in a Chinese *gong-si* or a Mexican *grupo* seldom have expectations of participation. And, finally, while terms like employee participation or involvement are frequently heard throughout the corridors and factories of American and Canadian enterprises, such words oftentimes carry little real meaning beyond the rhetoric. The lesson here is simply put: Cultures do matter when attempting to understand or manage organizations around the world.

A second conclusion that emerges from this review is that organization design and management practices frequently interact with one another; each influences the other. Clearly, part of the reason behind this is that cultural differences influence both organization design and management practice. However, it goes beyond this. Regardless of local cultural variations, organizations and their managers comprise learning systems that build on past experiences and future expectations in ways that can change both the structure of the organization and its management strategies and practices.

A third point to note is that these organizing frameworks are continually evolving in varying degrees in response to global and local changes. A major factor here can be found in the various globalization pressures and dualities discussed in Chapter 1. Another influence can be found in the rapid evolution of information and computer-mediated technologies that have the power to change the ways in which fundamental communications occur through the firm and its partners (see Chapter 7).

Finally, it should again be noted that, while the organizing frameworks discussed here may represent central tendencies in various countries, wide variations can obviously be found everywhere. As a result, while these frameworks may be instructive for purposes of general comparisons across cultures, they are not intended to represent universal patterns of organizing.

Notes

1 Michael Crozier, *The Bureaucratic Phenomenon*. Chicago, IL: University of Chicago Press, 1964.

2 Patricia Morison, cited in Richard Hill, *We Europeans*. Brussels: Europublications, 1997, p. 9.

3 *Ibid.*, p. 29.

4 T. Foster Jones, "The family that bakes together," *The Costco Connection*, February 2009, pp. 20–22.

5 *Ibid.*, p. 22.

6 Phillip Harris, Robert Moran, and Sarah Moran, *Managing Cultural Differences*, 6th Edition. Amsterdam: Elsevier, 2004; Peter Lawrence, *Management in the U.S.A*. London: Sage, 1996; Richard Lewis, *When Cultures Collide*. London: Nicholas Brealey, 1999; Edward T. Hall and Mildred R. Hall, *Understanding Cultural Differences: Germans, French, and Americans*. Yarmouth, ME: Intercultural Press, 1990.

7 Personal communication, Nigel Nicholson, London Business School, UK, 2008.

8 Personal communication, John Child, University of Birmingham, UK, 2008.

9 Personal communication, Nancy Adler, McGill University, Montreal, Canada, 2008.

10 It should be remembered that the term "Anglo" came into widespread use by cultural anthropologies and social psychologists in the 1970s and 1980s to describe this cluster, and much has changed in the intervening years.

11 Toyohiro Kono and Stewart Clegg, *Trends in Japanese Management: Continuing Strengths, Current Problems, and Changing Priorities*. London: Palgrave, 2001; Masahiko Aoki and Ronald Dore (eds.), *The Japanese Firm*. Oxford: Oxford University Press, 1994.

12 James Abbeglen and George Stalk, *Kaisha: The Japanese Corporation*. New York, NY: Harper & Row, 1985.

13 Christopher Meek, "*Ganbatte*: understanding the Japanese employee," *Business Horizons*, January–February 1999, pp. 27–36.

14 Kono and Clegg, *Trends in Japanese Management*.

15 John Cullen and K. P. Parboteeah, *Multinational Management: A Strategic Approach*. Cincinnati, OH: Southwestern College Publishing, 2005.

16 Miki Tanikawa, "Fujitsu decides to backtrack on performance-based pay," *The New York Times*, March 22, 2001.

17 "*Shuntō*" (春樗) is a Japanese term, usually translated as "spring (wage) offensive," with the word "wage" sometimes substituted with livelihood, labor, or similar terms. It refers to the annual wage negotiations between enterprise unions and the employers. Many thousands of these unions conduct the negotiations simultaneously from the beginning of March.

18 Kono and Clegg, *Trends in Japanese Management*.

19 Paul Lillrank and Noriaki Kano, *Continuous Improvement: Quality Control Circles in Japanese Industry*. Ann Arbor, MI: Center for Japanese Studies, University of Michigan, 1989.

20 *Language Magazine*, April 2000, 10(3), pp. 3–4.

21 Ming-Jer Chen, *Inside Chinese Business: A Guide for Managers Worldwide*. Boston, MA: Harvard Business School Press, 2001.

22 Confucius (551 BCE–479 CE) (Chinese: 孔夫子; pinyin: *Kǒng Fūzǐ*), literally "Master Kong," was a Chinese thinker and social philosopher, whose teachings and philosophy have deeply influenced Chinese, Korean, Japanese, Taiwanese, and Vietnamese thought and life. His philosophy emphasized personal and governmental morality, correctness of social relationships, justice, and sincerity. These values gained prominence in China over other doctrines, such as Legalism (法家) or Taoism (瀟家), during the Han Dynasty (206 BCE–220 CE). Confucius' thoughts have been developed into a system of philosophy known as *Confucianism* (儒用). It was first introduced into Europe by the Jesuit Matteo Ricci, who was the first to Latinize the name as "Confucius." His teachings may be found in the *Analects of Confucius* (用畢), a collection of "brief aphoristic fragments," which was compiled many years after his death. Modern historians do not believe that any specific documents can be said to have been written by Confucius, but for nearly 2,000 years he was thought to be the editor or author.

23 Wenzhong Hu and Cornelius Grove, *Encountering the Chinese*. Yarmouth, ME: Intercultural Press, 1999.

24 *Guānxi* (traditional Chinese 楙 係; simplified Chinese 关 系) describes the basic dynamic in the complex nature of personalized networks of influence and social relationships, and is a central concept in Chinese society. In Western media, the pinyin romanization of this Chinese word has tended to over-simplify the meaning of this term into "connections" or "relationships." Neither of these terms sufficiently reflect the wide cultural implications that *guānxi* describes. At its most basic, *guānxi* describes a personal connection between two people in which one is able to prevail upon another to perform a favor or service, or be prevailed upon. The two people need not to be of equal social status. *Guānxi* can also be used to describe a network of contacts, which an individual can call upon when something needs to be done, and through which he or she can exert influence on behalf of another. In addition, *guānxi* can describe a state of general understanding between two people, in which both parties are aware of the other's needs and wants, and takes these into account when making decisions or taking action. The term is not generally used to describe relationships within a family, although *guānxi* obligations can sometimes be described in terms of an extended family. The term is also not generally used to describe relationships that fall within other well-defined societal norms (e.g., boss-worker or teacher-student friendship). The relationships formed by *guānxi* are personal and not transferable. When a *guānxi* network violates bureaucratic norms, it can lead to corruption, and *guānxi* can also form the basis of patron-client relations.

25 Christopher Earley, *Face, Harmony, and Social Structure.* New York, NY: Oxford University Press, 1997.

26 Gordon Redding, *The Spirit of Chinese Capitalism.* Berlin: Walter de Gruyter, 1990.

27 John Child, *Management in China During the Age of Reform.* Cambridge, UK: Cambridge University Press, 1994.

28 Redding, *The Spirit of Chinese Capitalism.*

29 Sameena Ahmad, "Behind the mask: a survey of business in China," *The Economist*, March 20, 2004, pp. 3–19.

30 Chen, *Inside Chinese Business.*

31 Ahmad, "Behind the mask."

32 Geert Hofstede, *Culture's Consequence: International Differences in Work Related Values.* Thousand Oaks, CA: Sage, 1980, revised 2001.

33 Hall and Hall, *Understanding Cultural Differences.*

34 Hill, *We Europeans.*

35 "German industrial relations: slowly losing their chains," *The Economist*, February 21, 2004, p. 49; Almut Schoenfeld, "Germany rethinks generous perks for civil servants," *Wall Street Journal*, April 5, 2004, p. A17.

36 Ingrid Brunstein (ed.), *Human Resource Management in Western Europe.* Berlin: Walter de Gruyter, 1995.

37 Cullen and Parboteeah, *Multinational Management.*

38 John Miller, "Employment rules hinder EU," *The Wall Street Journal*, August 16, 2004, p. A11.

39 Christopher Engholm and Scott Grimes, *Doing Business in Mexico*. Upper Saddle, NJ: Prentice Hall, 1997; Eva Kras, *Management in Two Cultures: Bridging the Gap Between US and Mexican Managers*. Yarmouth, ME: Intercultural Press, 1989.

40 Our thanks to Professor Carlos Ruiz Gonzalez, IPADE Business School, Universadad Panamericana, Mexico, for his helpful comments on this section.

41 Engholm and Grimes, *Doing Business in Mexico*.

42 Eric Dash, "Mexican billionaire invests in Times Company," *New York Times*, January 20, 2009, p. A-1.

CHAPTER 7

Communication across cultures

- Eye of the beholder   201
- Culture and communication: a model   202
- Language, logic, and communication   204
- *Lingua franca* and message comprehension   210
- Cross-cultural communication strategies   214
- Communication on the fly   228
- MANAGER'S NOTEBOOK: Communication across cultures   232

A different language is not just a dictionary of words, sounds, and syntax. It is a different way of interpreting reality, refined by the generations that developed the language.

Federico Fellini[1]
Filmmaker and director, Italy

Whatever the culture, there's a tongue in our head. Some use it, some hold it, and some bite it. For the French it is a rapier, thrusting in attack; the English, using it defensively, mumble a vague and confusing reply; for Italians and Spaniards it is an instrument of eloquence; Finns and East Asians throw you with their constructive silence. Silence is a form of speech, so don't interrupt it.

Richard D. Lewis[2]
Communications consultant, UK

Namasté is a common greeting used on the Indian subcontinent. It literally means "I bow to you," and is used as an expression of deep respect in India and Nepal by Hindus, Jains, and Buddhists. In these cultures, the word (from the ancient Sanskrit) is spoken at the beginning of a conversation, accompanied by a slight bow made with hands pressed together, palms touching and fingers pointed upwards, in front of the chest. This silent gesture can also be performed wordlessly and carry the same meaning, as is often done at the close of a conversation. As such, *namasté* is a form of both verbal and non-verbal communication. When used appropriately, it signals parties to a conversation that the people involved likely understand something about prevailing social norms and values. They are one of "us," and a bond is easily formed. It may be only one word, but it carries significant symbolism.

As this example indicates, communication is all about conveying meaning to others. It is the principal way we reach out to others to exchange ideas and commodities, develop and dissolve relationships, and conduct business. Within one culture or language group, communication can often be problematic – particularly across age groups, geographic regions, and gender. However, these problems pale in comparison to the challenges of communicating across cultures. Consider three more examples of communicating across cultures.

First, note how the use of signs, symbols, and colors can carry deep meanings, and how these meanings can vary across cultures. During a meeting in Prague between a Japanese businesswoman and her Czech host, confusion quickly emerged when the Japanese women went off to the restroom. She began to open the door to the Men's Room when her host stopped her. "Don't you see the sign?," she asked. "Of course, I do," the visitor responded, "but it is red. In our country, a red colored sign means it's the Ladies' Room. For men, it should be blue or black." Her Czech host returned to the meeting room remembering that she too had looked at the sign but had focused on what was written, not its color. She wondered how many other things she and her Japanese colleague saw but interpreted differently.[3]

Next, consider non-verbal communication. A British professor of poetry relaxed during one of his lectures at the prestigious Ain Shams University in Cairo.[4] Indeed, he got so comfortable that he inadvertently leaned back in his chair and crossed his legs, thereby revealing the sole of one of his shoes to his students. Obviously, in much of the Muslim world, this is the worst insult anyone can inflict on another. The following morning, the Cairo newspapers carried banner head-lines about the student demonstrations that resulted. They denounced what they saw as British arrogance and demanded that the professor be sent home immediately.

Finally, consider language differences or, more specifically, language competencies. One example here should suffice to make the point. When two US tourists were traveling on a bus in Stuttgart recently, and one of them sneezed, a German passenger turned around and said, "*Gesundheit.*" One visitor looked at the other and noted, "How nice that they speak English here."[5]

Eye of the beholder

Examples such as these – and there are an infinite number of them – illustrate how simple and often unintended words or behaviors can lead to misunderstanding, embarrassment, conflict, and even a loss of business opportunities. At the root of these issues is the topic of cross-cultural communication: the words, messages, formalities, body language, status, and so forth that comprise how we attempt to exchange information and convey meaning. Throughout this process, people often tend to hear what they want to hear. Their frames of reference and individual situations – and even their worldviews – can all work to filter message reception by screening in/out what the receiver will likely attend to and by attaching meanings to how messages are interpreted.

A major filter on message reception lies within our perceptual processes. That is, what people see or hear can be heavily influenced by what recipients are looking to see or hear. Many years ago, a short training video titled the *Eye of the Beholder* followed a scene that was observed by three different people. Based on their own particular frames of reference and different viewing angles, each person saw something entirely different. Message filters can include a number of cognitive processing factors, including *selective perception*, a tendency for people to focus on or pay attention to messages that relate to their immediate problems or needs, and *recency effects*, a tendency for recipients to focus on the most recent message or interaction compared to earlier ones. Both of these filters are embedded in managerial thinking, as discussed in Chapter 4.

Similarly, the manner in which received messages are interpreted can also affect message clarity and saliency. This can be seen in both political and advertising campaigns, where message recipients are often likely to interpret messages (particularly in terms of favorability or unfavorability) based on their predisposition to the candidate or product. Thus, Conservative and Labor Party members in the UK and Democrats and Republicans in the US all tend to be more skeptical or suspicious of information provided by their opponents compared to information provided by their own parties. Similar interpretations can be seen in various parts of the world, especially in Africa and Latin America, when large outside ("foreign") companies seek to create a new venture in their backyard. Can we trust these outsiders? What are their motives? Will they help us or exploit us?

A more personal example of this process can be found when two people either mistrust each other based on past experiences or have not had sufficient opportunity to develop a mutual trusting relationship in the first place (see Chapter 10 for details). In such cases, the other party's comments can often be misconstrued, ignored, or rejected outright. Hence, particularly in some regions of the world (e.g., Asia and Latin America), experts emphasize the need to develop personal relationships prior to opening negotiations or building cross-cultural teams.

Culture and communication: a model

In any cross-cultural exchange between managers from different regions, the principal purpose of communication is to seek common ground – to seek out ideas, information, customers, and sometimes even partnerships between the parties. Both business in general and management in particular rely on people's willingness and ability to convey meaning between managers, employees, partners, suppliers, investors, and customers. Indeed, it can be argued that most efforts to build or to understand organizations begin with an understanding of basic communication and exchange processes.

There are numerous comprehensive models that attempt to capture the various elements of the communication process. Our effort here is more directly focused on the interplay between culture, communication, and exchange in the work environment. According to this model, summarized in Exhibit 7.1, characteristics inherent in the cultural environments of each participant helps determine various common yet

Exhibit 7.1 Cultural influences on the communication process

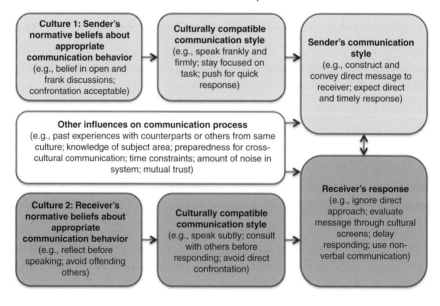

enduring normative beliefs underlying the communication process. In a cross-cultural environment, these cultural drivers often influence the extent to which communication should be open and frank or more subtle, the degree to which confrontation or open conflict is acceptable, and so forth.

As a result of these normative beliefs, certain culturally compatible communication strategies emerge, including people's expectations and objectives in initiating or responding to a message or comment, choice of language and transmission strategies, choice of direct or indirect communication, and status considerations. Three principal communication behaviors can be identified: verbal, non-verbal, and virtual. These strategies are aimed at achieving a number of intended message outcomes. Included here are clear message reception, clear mutual understanding of intended message, agreement with or acquiescence to intended message, and, hopefully, improved mutual trust.

A number of limitations on both message content and the choice of message transmission can be found across cultures. This is largely a challenge for both senders and recipients of messages. Senders must decide (or guess) how to formulate a message so it is culturally consistent with the sender's culture, but hopefully also consistent with the recipient's culture. At the same time, recipients must judge whether the message is appropriate and what kind of response, if any, to make. Typically, most senders pre-screen most messages to ensure (as they see it) that they are culturally consistent, hopefully for both parties. However, what is often acceptable in one culture is not necessarily acceptable in another. Communication patterns to be discussed here include message content, message context, communication protocols, single-language communication, technology-mediated communication, and information-sharing patterns. Taken together, these patterns illustrate many of the challenges faced by global managers when communicating across cultures. However, moderating the conveyance of the sender's message – from drivers to strategies and from strategies to intended outcomes – is the culture and perspectives of the recipient.

Like the sender, the recipient also has normative beliefs that often influence how he or she receives the message. This, in turn, influences how the recipient interprets and responds to the sender's message. Consider a meeting between two managers from New Zealand and Malaysia. While cultural drivers influence how and by what format the New Zealander will choose to send a particular comment or message (e.g., verbal communication, saying what one means, etc.), her Malay counterpart likely sees things very differently (e.g., using body language or silence during the meeting). Because of this, the received message can differ – sometimes substantially – from the original intended message. And the recipient's response will obviously reflect these interpretations. To complicate this a bit further, in actuality both speakers typically engage in two-way communication almost simultaneously, meaning that the relationship, as well as the thoughts, between sender and recipient is interactive and multi-linear in nature, not linear.

As a result of their interactions, these two managers will likely learn whether their targeted outcomes were or were not achieved, or were only partly achieved. In addition, as a result of their learning (assuming they were interested in learning), each manager will come away from the meeting better prepared for the next time, assuming each has closely observed what happened the first time. This might include inferences that the existing communication strategies are either inhibiting message clarity or are somehow inappropriate (e.g., insisting on using English in bilingual environments). This is discussed in greater detail below.

And finally, a number of events and actions that are outside the intended communication channel hang in the air ready to cause message interference with message transmission, message reception, or both. These impediments can include: interruptions; competing messages; distractions; hostilities; status, age, and gender issues; and language or cultural fluency issues. In other words, the simple act of communicating with another person from a different country or culture can quickly morph into a maze or labyrinth with multiple players, multiple channels, and multiple opportunities to miss one's mark. The challenge can seem quite difficult, and, when the stakes are high (brokering a sale), the consequences can be significant for both manager and company.

Language, logic, and communication

Based on this overview, how do communication processes actually work across borders? In order to understand this issue, it is first necessary to understand two fundamental issues: language and logic. More specifically, it is necessary to understand that when other people are speaking "foreign" languages, they are also using different linguistic structures. They use words and grammar in ways that can sometimes provide insight into their patterns of thinking (see Chapter 4). In addition, we need to understand something about cultural logic, or the tendency for people to interpret the expressions and actions of others using their own frames of reference. That is, if a colleague says something to us, we tend to assume that her thoughts behind her message are the same as our own thoughts. These two issues – language and logic – are at the heart of understanding how others communicate and, as a result, how we should communicate with them.

Language and linguistic structures

Language is central to human communication. It plays an important role in initiating conversations and conducting most human affairs, including being socialized into the world, managing organizations, and running countries. Language also allows us to relieve stress by expressing our feelings and facilitate problem solving by thinking out loud. It is also due to language that we are able to preserve our histories, passing knowledge from one generation to the next.

Language and *linguistic structures* (i.e., the manner in which words, grammar, syntax, and the meaning of words are organized and used) are closely linked to cultures because, while culture provides the meaning and meaning-making mechanisms, language provides the symbols to facilitate the expression of such meanings. On one hand, language reflects culture because it describes thoughts, ideas, and artifacts that are relevant to a cultural group. It is through language that we share information, teach, and learn how to behave appropriately.[6] On the other hand, culture reflects language because language provides the means with which we organize our thinking and describe the world around us.

Language is an important channel of cultural information. It provides the means through which we can communicate cultural meaning, but culture provides the key to decoding the meanings underlying language. For example, the word "cat," in English, may mean a domestic pet, a jazz musician, a type of tractor, a type of fish, a kind of sailboat, or a kind of whip. To understand what "cat" means in a particular sentence, we must rely on our experience in the particular context to attach a meaning to the word.

Consider a related challenge in linguistic structures: When communicating within a single culture (e.g., England), the process of abstract meaning is facilitated by commonly shared meanings among group members. Thus, when a group of Brits attends a meeting scheduled on the "fourth" floor of a London business tower, they know that the meeting is actually on the fifth floor of the building, since Brits distinguish between the ground and first floors. On the other hand, when communicating across cultures this process can be challenging, since the link between words and their meanings are not always clear.[7] Thus, when a group of Americans attend a meeting scheduled on the "fourth" floor of a New York high rise, they do, in fact, go to the fourth floor, since Americans typically use ground and first floors interchangeably. Going further with this example, when foreign travelers attend a staff meeting on the "fourth" floor of a Seoul high rise, even the more experienced travelers can become puzzled. While the number four (*sa* in Korean) is not in itself unlucky as many believe, its oral pronunciation sounds identical to the Korean word for death – something that is seldom, if ever, discussed in Korean society. As a result, many Korean buildings either use the English letter "F" ("fourth") for this unnamed floor or simply don't have such floors. (Note that older buildings in the West frequently have omitted the thirteenth floor because this number was widely considered to be unlucky.)

Languages also vary in the categories available to classify objects, in how verb tenses are used, how gender is or is not assigned to things, and how spatial relations are conveyed. These differences influence what speakers must pay attention to and how they classify the external world and express their internal state. In this regard, notable linguists Edward Sapir and Benjamin Whorf argue that people live "at the mercy of the particular language which has become the medium of expression for their society," suggesting that language is not only a way to solve communication problems and reproduce ideas, but is also a way to shape ideas and, hence, worldviews.[8] They argue further that the "worlds in which different societies live are distinct worlds, not merely the same world with different labels attached."[9]

According to Sapir and Whorf's view, the world presents itself in kaleidoscopic ways, waiting for our minds to organize it according to some classification scheme provided by our language. That is, objects are not classified together through language because they are more alike than others; rather, they seem more alike because they have been classified together by a given language. As a result, different languages lead to different worldviews from which one can hardly escape.[10] As such, languages differentially embody specific world experiences, thus predisposing their speakers to see the world accordingly.

In other words, the importance of language to understand different cultures and worldviews goes beyond expressing different thoughts and contexts. Language imposes a structure on our way of thinking that leads to different ways of experiencing the world and, as a consequence, different worldviews. For example, languages can vary in the number and type of forms of address available to people when meeting others. In English, for example, there is typically only one word for "you." Native speakers use this same word when speaking to almost any person (royalty excepted), regardless of age, gender, seniority, or position. On the other hand, romance languages like Spanish and French distinguish between a formal and an informal address ("*usted/tu*" in Spanish, "*vous/tu*" in French). In Japanese, there are, in fact, many equivalent words for "you," depending on someone's age, seniority, gender, family affiliation, and position.

Moreover, each of these distinctions can be subdivided further to signal finer and subtler distinctions. The implication of these linguistic differences is that, depending on the language being spoken, people must pay attention to different cues and focus on different aspects of their context and message. While in Japan deciding if a speaker is younger or older than the other party is always important, this information often has little relevance for many English speakers. Perhaps this is why many Japanese examine business cards very diligently before speaking or bowing, instead of immediately putting them in their pocket or purse as is common in the West. In point of fact, they are simply trying to determine the respective ranks of the two individuals.

Conversely, the lack of a specific linguistic label is also significant of a given world-view. For instance, the fact that in some languages there is no direct translation for "privacy" is likely to indicate that either personal privacy is virtually absent or is held in a quite different regard in that society.[11]

In other words, language shapes ideas by providing the vocabulary and structure to organize the world. What follows is that different observers of the same phenomena, speaking different languages, will come up with different conclusions. Indeed, studies with bilingual and bicultural Chinese Americans and Mexican Americans found that participants responded differently to questions depending on the language they were speaking, which shows how culture and language are closely intertwined. These studies show that when answering in English, participants endorsed American values, and when answering in Cantonese or Spanish, they endorsed Chinese and Mexican values respectively.[12]

Just like culture, these different worldviews and thinking structures provided by language have the potential to influence human behaviors in general and management activities in particular. Language is also a window into different cognitive styles, as discussed in Chapter 4. For example, some researchers argue that the grammar and structure of Chinese languages favor intuitive versus logic reasoning.

Languages provide subtle yet powerful cues on what to account for in our dealings with other people (respect, precedence, social distance, and so on). Those who are not conscious of those differences are bound to lack a precise understanding of the situations they may be facing and make communication mistakes. Needless to say, knowledge of the other's language helps develop understanding that goes beyond the content of the messages exchanged. Indeed, learning the language of the host country is one of the most commonly heard pieces of advice received by expatriates. Besides a deeper understanding of the culture and the ease with which one can communicate with locals, there are other reasons why learning the language of the foreign country is advantageous. First, one has more autonomy and independence, can gain more information about the local environment, and thus adapt more easily. Second, learning the local language builds good will, as the expatriate or inpatriate shows commitment to the local culture, enhancing managerial credibility. And, finally, learning additional languages helps in other foreign situations. The more languages one speaks, the easier it becomes to learn and understand other cultures and languages.

Cultural logic and shared meaning

At its core, interpersonal communication in general – and cross-cultural communication in particular – is an interactive process, requiring two or more people to exchange thoughts, ideas, emotions, questions, proposals, and so forth, in an effort to find common ground. It is at the heart of how we do business, negotiate contracts, lead groups, work with team members, and motivate employees.

One of the most important lessons for global managers is that there is almost always a logic underlying any communication effort. People have goals and reasons behind what is said and how things are said, and these reasons can differ substantially across national borders (just as they can sometimes also vary within national borders). When people talk with one another, they often rely on cultural logic to facilitate the conversation. *Cultural logic* is the process of using our own assumptions to interpret the messages and actions of others, thereby hypothesizing about their motives and intentions.[13] Put another way, cultural logic provides people with a system of assumptions about what is mutually known and understood among individuals (i.e., our common ground). People often rely on cultural logic to facilitate communication and decrease what needs to be said into a manageable amount, since it would be too difficult and time consuming to express all of someone's thoughts and assumptions behind everything they say. A shared cultural logic therefore helps people to fill the gaps left by what is unsaid, thereby facilitating the process of creating a shared meaning.

For example, in the course of a communication with a colleague you may just say "the boss" without further details. You know your colleague knows who your boss is, and you know your colleague knows that you know that she knows who your boss is. This common knowledge allows for simplified communication. When moving across cultures, though, sometimes there is an assumption of a common knowledge that is not real.

To illustrate how this works, consider how two people might approach each other in a conversation. As illustrated in Exhibit 7.2, the person initiating a conversation creates a mental image of an idea he wishes to communicate. He also often has a preference about how he wishes to communicate the message. And he has assumptions about how

Exhibit 7.2 Cultural logic in cross-cultural communication

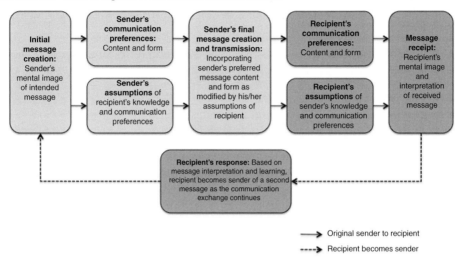

the other person likes to communicate, as well as her knowledge and understanding about the topic being communicated. Taking all of this into account, the message sender will decide on the content and format of the message. That is, he will decide which aspects of the proposal needs to be explained, which aspects are commonly understood and require little or no explanation, and what should be the appropriate context, language, and protocols surrounding the message. At the same time, the recipient of the message also has a preference about how messages should be communicated, as well as assumptions about how the sender communicates. Based on this, the recipient will form a mental image of what the message means and, based on her conclusions, craft her own message in response. Thus, the recipient becomes the sender, and communication cycle begins again. As additional messages are exchanged, both parties learn more about each other's knowledge and communication preferences, and mutual assumptions about each other's knowledge and styles become fine-tuned.

This process of learning is key to the success of the cross-cultural communication. With this in mind, consider the example of a Canadian sales representative trying to establish an appointment with a prospective Brazilian buyer. The Canadian sales representative seeks to meet a Brazilian buyer at 8:00 a.m. on the following morning to discuss her company's products. She therefore creates a mental picture of the message she is trying to convey, using her own cultural logic (in this case, relying heavily on her Canadian emphasis on monochronic time – see Chapter 3). In doing this, however, she needs some form of verbal shorthand; that is, she needs to make some assumptions about what is in the mind of her prospective Brazilian customer or her message will become excessively long and will risk being ignored. To do so, she has to assume that her prospective customer makes the same assumptions about the use of words as she does. For example, she assumes that "8:00" means 8:00 sharp, not later in the morning when she has other appointments. She also has to assume that her counterpart will understand her message and this agreement to the meeting indicates that he will be there at 8:00 a.m. sharp. So far, so good.

However, while the Canadian sales rep is making assumptions, so, too, is her Brazilian counterpart, and his assumptions about the message may differ considerably. Following his own cultural logic (particularly the Brazilian emphasis on polychronic time), the buyer may assume "8:00" is only a targeted or rough time and that slippage in the time schedule is perfectly acceptable, since he has other commitments around the same time. He could then assume that his Canadian counterpart is also flexible and that she agrees with his loose interpretation of when the meeting will begin.

The end result of this episode is predictable. Using straight cultural logic, both sides risk being disappointed or frustrated when they meet, leading possibly to a poor business outcome. Had both (or even one) party understood the variability in cultural logic and had been more flexible or patient, perhaps this result would have turned out differently. Instead, the Canadian risks coming away from the meeting thinking that her prospective partner is too unreliable, while her Brazilian counterpart may conclude that the Canadian is too rigid to base a partnership on.

However, as illustrated in Exhibit 7.2, the communication process is dynamic and interactive, and as individuals' logics interact, a communication pattern will evolve. For example, after a first failed meeting time, the Canadian and Brazilian will develop new ways of communicating, maybe specifying the time expectations as Brazilian time (polychronic) or Canadian time (8:00 sharp).

At the same time that individuals are making assumptions about what the other knows and thinks, they are also making assumptions about how best to deliver a message. As will be discussed later in this chapter, cultural groups develop preferences for communication protocols, behaviors, and even appropriate topics for discussion.

Lingua franca and message comprehension

Language is always a potential impediment to effective cross-cultural communication. In this regard, there are two issues that are worthy of note. First, which language should be used in a conversation? Some argue that English is increasingly becoming the *lingua franca* of global business; as such, everyone should speak English.[14] Or, as a Texas preacher once observed, "If English was good enough for Jesus, it's good enough for me."[15] Not everyone agrees with this, obviously. Indeed, both Mandarin Chinese and Spanish have more native speakers around the world than English. Why shouldn't everyone speak Chinese or Spanish? Others have suggested that the language to be spoken should be determined by who has the money – consistent with the oft-cited phrase "serve the customer." If the French are buying, it is logical for both parties to speak French. This debate may never be resolved since, among other things, mass conversions to a foreign language can threaten the cultural integrity of a country or region. And second, if the sender or recipient of a conversation – written or oral – is using a non-native tongue, message details and message interpretations going both ways can easily get lost. Both of these challenges are illustrated in Exhibit 7.3, and can confront every manager, regardless of his or her native language. (These issues, as well as suggestions for overcoming such impediments and enhancing message clarity, will be discussed later in this chapter.)

For managers living largely in the English-speaking parts of the world, there is an added challenge. Which English are you speaking? Norman Schur has compiled a British-English/American-English dictionary which contains nearly 5,000 entries that are translated from one version of English to the other.[16] We are told that "pass out" in British-English means to graduate in American-English. "Lifts" are elevators, "companies" are corporations, "corporations" are municipalities, "tipping" means dumping (as in trash, which is actually "jumble"), "sheltered trades" are domestic monopolies, "to hire" means to lease; and "roger" is not someone's first name. We are further told that in

Exhibit 7.3 Challenges facing non-native speakers

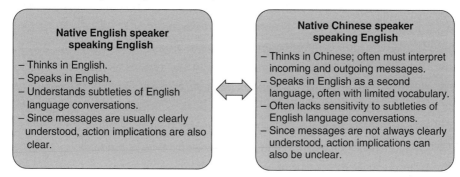

the UK "shares" are stocks and "stocks" are government bonds. We are told that a clerk in the US is pronounced "clark" in the UK, and that schedule is pronounced "shedule." Spellings can also differ (behavior or behaviour). And this is all before we recognize that many sectors of British culture often speak differently and use very different words to communicate. If this were not enough, we must remember that people in Australia, Canada, New Zealand, and other locales are different still in their choice and use of words.

Many of these differences are influenced by local traditions, customs, and local slang, but in some cases cultural differences can also play a major role. Consider the use of English in India. In the past few years, India has emerged as the outsourcing capital of the world. Almost two-thirds of all *Fortune 500* companies currently outsource to India, and this number continues to increase annually. The primary, although not exclusive, focus of this business centers around computer-mediated technologies, including software development, call centers, and similar activities that require highly skilled, English-language proficient, and relatively inexpensive labor. This labor force literally works 24/7 to meet the real-time requirements of its various global customers.

To outsiders, India's offshore industries, as well as its equally successful manufacturing firms, look like the epitome of organizational and managerial efficiency. Under the surface, however, we can see a number of differences in managerial attitudes and behaviors that can present challenges to the uninitiated. In particular, cultural differences between workplace values and cultural contexts make India a living laboratory on how to work across cultures. In this regard, we focus here on the interrelated issues of power, time, and communication as they affect management practice. These variables, in turn, influence perceptions about authority, responsibility and accountability, sense of urgency, and notions of commitment, agreements and contracts, risk-taking, and conflict.

Cultural anthropologists observe that many Indians tend to follow hierarchies fairly rigidly. Orders and information tend to flow from top to bottom, and very little formal communication occurs in the reverse direction. It can therefore be useful at times to use informal channels to pass information and news in all directions and make sure that everyone involved understands the importance of the various aspects of projects or work schedules (e.g., deadlines). Managers and employees in many Western countries tend to work with clear deadlines. By contrast, Indians often tend to value flexibility with a client over the necessity to stick to a firm deadline, especially during projects. Under these circumstances, they may not necessarily view a deadline as imperative unless its importance has been emphasized through back channels.

Communication processes are particularly noteworthy here. Consider: Many Westerners tend to be fairly direct in their communication efforts. However, there are times when these same individuals will shift course and send less-than-clear instructions, perhaps turning a phrase in an attempt to be more polite or less autocratic. As such, they may say to a subordinate something like "It might be a good idea to add more details to this proposal" or "I think this presentation could have more examples." This approach is often considered to be more polite than simply giving orders. However, many Indians might interpret these statements as opinions or suggestion, not directives. As a result, considerable confusion can emerge by one party's attempt to be softer or more egalitarian when speaking to subordinates. In these circumstances, it is important to be aware of the subconscious assumptions being made by others and ensure that possible misinterpretations are avoided. At the same time, Indians can be very direct during discussions and this can cause discomfort for some Westerners.

In contract negotiations, it is important to document all requirements related to a project. Since differences in perceptions can be subtle and ubiquitous, observers note that it is essential that two steps be followed: document all requirements, so that the company has the opportunity to determine exactly what they are required to do; and have Indian business partners reiterate their understanding of the requirements.

Like a number of other countries, Indians oftentimes cannot decline a request, even if they do not have either the desire or the capability to meet the demands of that request. This stems partially from an unwillingness to close a door of opportunity and partly from an unwillingness to be viewed as unable to do something that is asked of them. It is important to probe and make sure that there is both the desire and the ability to fulfill the request, and that, indeed, the work can and will be done. Indians do not see interrupting or being interpreted as rude. If asked not to interrupt, they may interpret it as a sign that their opinions are not respected, and they may not contribute to the conversation even when their opinion is sought. It is necessary to recognize this possibility and explain at the beginning of a meeting or a conversation in a clear, direct, and respectful manner, that each person would like to complete his or her part of the conversation and then would very much welcome (and need) responses and ideas from the other parties to the conversation.

Indians tend to speak at a much more rapid pace than people in Western Europe or North America. The cadence of Indian English is quite different from other forms of English, and it takes some time to tune the ear to a different kind of "music." Many words in Indian English are holdovers from the era of British colonization and may be unfamiliar, especially to Americans who have little experience outside the US. Some words in Indian English are accented on a different syllable than is commonly found in the US or the UK, adding to the confusion. Indian English is also somewhat more formal than American English, but not British English.

While such differences may be understandable, it should be noted that even the British often have trouble understanding the different dialects found across the UK. And this problem is not unique to the English language. Spaniards and Mexicans often find it difficult to understand each other, as do French and French Canadians and Brazilians and Portuguese. And in China, there are several distinct dialects that, while sharing the same written characters, are virtually unrecognizable to other Chinese when spoken. Perhaps the most important lesson here for global managers is that being told that your counterparts "speak" English, Spanish, French, Chinese, and so forth, does not guarantee easy communication. In fact, it may guarantee just the opposite. That is, believing that your counterparts speak your language allow for numerous faulty assumptions, misinterpretations, and confusion. This is particularly true when negotiating contracts, legally binding documents that can cause confusion and financial loss if not clearly understood by all parties.

Cross-cultural communication strategies

Consider the following: You are a partner in a small, but global, electronics firm that does business primarily in Western Europe and East Asia. You are trying to sell your IT services to two small companies, one in Spain and one in Korea. However, when you try to telephone each of the presidents of the two small firms, no one answers. Question: Should you leave a message informing them that you will call back at a particular time? The correct answer is yes and no. Why? In Spain, it is perfectly acceptable to leave a message for others (including more senior people) saying you will call back at a given time. Of course, the person you are calling has no obligation to be there when you call back, but at least you can record your intent. In doing so, you are being polite in saying that you will take the responsibility to link up at a future time. By contrast, leaving such a message on the phone of someone in Korea (particularly if they are older) is often considered rude and inconsiderate, because it obligates the other person to sit by the phone at a specific time waiting for you call. Many Koreans consider constraining the behavior of superiors an offense against social norms. Instead, etiquette requires that you either leave no message or leave a simple message saying that you called but without reference to a possible callback time.

Routine behaviors such as these can have major ramifications for success or failure in social situations around the globe, and, while a lack of understanding here may can be appreciated or even forgiven, it nevertheless seldom leads to positive outcomes. Once again, we return to the inescapable conclusion that global managers must be well prepared for new situations and new contacts if they wish to succeed. And center stage in these preparations is knowing how and when to talk – and what to say.

Thus, continuing with the model introduced above in Exhibit 7.1, as people begin to prepare for an upcoming interaction, assuming they have time to prepare, what types of communication strategies and behaviors are managers likely to see? While numerous options can be identified (this is obviously a complicated process) we focus on four of the more common strategies: message content; message context; communication protocols; and technology-mediated communication.

Message content

Message content describes what a sender attempts to incorporate into his or her message; indeed, it is typically the central point of a message. In the example of our Canadian manager above, she is attempting to establish an 8:00 a.m. appointment with a potential customer. This is her central message. However, in this attempt, she must constrain her message by potential limitations on appropriate or acceptable topics for discussion, her use of affirmations and rejections, and her and her colleague's openness to express opinions.

Appropriate topics for discussion

What people can and cannot talk about varies by culture. Consider just one example that happened to one of the authors recently. When asked by a Korean friend how the family was doing, an American visitor replied that his younger brother had recently died. The Korean friend looked puzzled and there was an awkward moment of silence. Then he responded, "Did you see the baseball game last night?" This was obviously not a subject he wished to discuss.

In some cultures, it is perfectly acceptable to ask about one's family; indeed, it is often considered impolite not to ask. In other cultures, however, this topic is off limits. Likewise, some cultures prefer not to talk about illness or bad fortune, perhaps in the belief that not talking about something will make it less likely to happen. Other cultures talk about health care issues, sometimes including the topic of serious illness or even death; others resist doing so, as just noted. People in some cultures may also brag to anyone who will listen about how much money they've made or how they used questionable tactics to make a sale; others prefer not to discuss this, even if true. It is typically inappropriate to discuss money in France or personal matters in England. Moreover, people are expected to talk about themselves in South Asia and Latin America, but not in Germany or the Netherlands.

When sending a message, individuals are likely to screen the communication to decide what is an appropriate topic for discussion. At the same time, the recipient is likely to do the same. Messages considered inappropriate may be either ignored (e.g., he can't be asking how much money I make) or deemed offensive (e.g., I can't believe she is asking how much money I make!)

Affirmations and rejections

Similarly, the use of affirmations and rejections can be influenced by culture. In this regard, some cultures (e.g., many East and Southeast Asian countries) often prefer to convey messages quietly using silent or hidden communication techniques, while others (e.g., Anglo and Germanic countries) prefer a more direct and verbal communication format. Consider, first, affirmations. Affirmations can be difficult to interpret. For example, in response to a question like, "What do you think of our proposed agreement?," many Japanese managers or negotiators will respond with "*hai*," often misunderstood in the West to mean "Yes, I agree," when it actually means "Yes, I understand." Americans and other Westerners also use terms ambiguously. Consider what the term "sure" means in the US. "Can you deliver the product by tomorrow?" "Sure." This seldom means "yes" in any absolute term; rather, it simply means that the person thinks (or hopes) it can be done. As such, it seldom means that this person will put his or her honor or job on the line in the event of failure. (Ironically, a "yes" from a Japanese manager actually does means "yes"; his or her honor stands behind what is said). And in Mexico, both "sure" and "yes" are often said when the party knows categorically that something probably cannot be done. It is said to please or pacify the other person for the moment; they will deal with it tomorrow.

At the same time, many Japanese managers and negotiators are often reluctant to say "no" to someone, since this infers rejection and loss of face to the other person. They often prefer to say nothing or signal disapproval with body language. By contrast, many Americans, Canadians, and Brits, who often lack the ability to read someone's face, tend to prefer simply saying "no." No rejection or loss of face for the other party is intended – or even considered.

Openness to express opinions

Finally, in some cultures (including Australia, Canada, Denmark, Germany, and the US), people are encouraged to speak up and express their opinions. They are expected to defend both themselves and their principles. Indeed, numerous business managers and executives have ended up in court for their failure to do so. In other cultures, however (including countries in East and Southeast Asian and the Middle East), subordinates are limited in their ability to address superiors for almost any reason, and must rely on silent or non-verbal communication techniques to convey messages. Indeed, in some cultures, subordinates have no opportunity to say anything, only to do what they are told. Likewise, in the UK, subjects are not supposed to address royalty unless they are given permission to speak. And even among "equals," some cultures emphasize silent communication (e.g., Thailand, Malaysia), while others prefer greater use of verbal communication techniques (e.g., Canada and the US).

At the same time, some cultures – and probably all cultures to a degree – encourage speakers to act with deference, humility, and subtlety when speaking to superiors (one's boss, for example), but at the same time act authoritarian, direct, and sometimes dismissive when speaking to subordinates ("inferiors?"). This is particularly noteworthy in Latin America and South Asia (including Mexico, the Central American countries, India, and Pakistan). The presumption here is that there is a natural order of power and privilege and that everyone must somehow fit into this system. Whether this improves communication effectiveness, however, is open to debate.

Message context

Communication is so pervasive in our everyday lives and so intertwined with culture that some researchers argue it is impossible to separate communication from culture. For them, culture *is* communication.[17] For instance, noted anthropologist Edward T. Hall points out that people communicate with each other through behaviors, not just words, suggesting that cultural assumptions in general are often part of a *silent language* used to convey meaning without words. Silent communication is the use of non-verbal or visual communication (e.g., facial expressions, gestures, use of personal space, opulent surroundings, etc.) to convey messages to senders or receivers alike. Such messages are typically subtle in nature and can be difficult to notice unless one is looking for them. However, senders usually intend that such messages will be received or discovered by others. In fact, to someone who can "read" these silent messages, they can sometimes scream very loudly.

The importance of silent, or non-verbal, communication can be found in a recent finding that verbal communication typically carries less than 35 percent of the meaning in two-way communication, suggesting that non-verbal characteristics become extremely important when communicating across cultures. To make matters worse, research suggests that when verbal and non-verbal messages contradict each other, we are more likely to believe the latter.[18] In some cultures, this percentage is even lower.

Exhibit 7.4 High-, mid-range, and low-context cultures

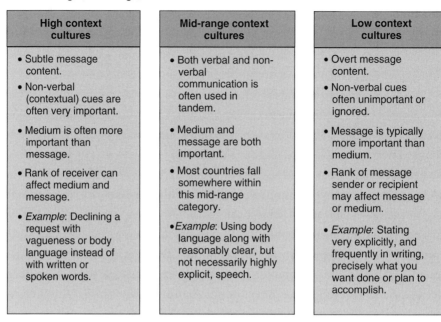

High context cultures	Mid-range context cultures	Low context cultures
• Subtle message content. • Non-verbal (contextual) cues are often very important. • Medium is often more important than message. • Rank of receiver can affect medium and message. • *Example*: Declining a request with vagueness or body language instead of with written or spoken words.	• Both verbal and non-verbal communication is often used in tandem. • Medium and message are both important. • Most countries fall somewhere within this mid-range category. • *Example*: Using body language along with reasonably clear, but not necessarily highly explicit, speech.	• Overt message content. • Non-verbal cues often unimportant or ignored. • Message is typically more important than medium. • Rank of message sender or recipient may affect message or medium. • *Example*: Stating very explicitly, and frequently in writing, precisely what you want done or plan to accomplish.

The meaning of messages is not explicit in the content of the message and must be sought after. As was discussed in Chapter 3, Edward T. Hall suggests that this difference lies in how much *message context* surrounds the *message content*.[19]

Hall distinguishes between high- and low-context cultures, as shown in Exhibit 7.4. In *low-context* cultures, such as Germany, Scandinavia, and the US, the context surrounding the message is far less important than the message itself. The context provides the listener with little information relating to the intended message. As a result, speakers must rely more heavily on providing greater message clarity, as well as other guarantees like written documents and information-rich advertising. Language precision is critical, while assumed understandings, innuendos, and body language frequently count for little.

By contrast, in *high-context* cultures, such as those found in many parts of Asia and the Middle East, the context in which the message is conveyed (that is, the social cues surrounding the message) is often as important as the message itself. Indeed, the way something is said can even be more important in communicating a message than the actual words that are used. Here, communication is based on long-term interpersonal relationships, mutual trust, and personal reputations. People know the people they are talking with, and reading someone's face becomes an important – and necessary – art. As a result, less needs to be said or written down. These subtleties in communication patterns often go unnoticed by many outsiders who are listening very carefully to every word that is spoken – only to miss the real message.

At times, non-verbal communication is the only recourse open to subordinates who are reticent to challenge or contradict their superiors. As noted in Chapter 5, for example, many Japanese employees differentiate between saying what is expected of them according to prevailing norms or social custom (*tatemae*) and saying what they believe to be true but cannot say openly (*honne*). Oftentimes, *honne* is expressed through non-verbal forms, while *tatemae* is expressed verbally.

Non-verbally transmitting context in a message can be accomplished in several ways, including facial expressions, personal space, body language, and secret communication.

Facial expressions

There are many examples where the context of a message can work to complement – or reject or modify – verbal messages. *Facial expressions* are an important component of non-verbal communication. Whereas some facial expressions are fairly universal – a look of happiness, sadness, anger, fear, disgust, and surprise – and typically can be recognized by people from almost all cultures, research has demonstrated that individuals are better able to recognize such emotions in people from their own culture than from other cultures.[20] This is because cultural expectations dictate when, where, how, to what extent, and to whom such facial expressions are displayed. For example, in Mediterranean cultures, it is common to exaggerate signs of grief or sadness, while Chinese and Koreans prefer to conceal emotions and not engage in animated facial expressions. For this reason, the meaning associated with such facial expressions can vary somewhat. While smiling is a ubiquitous trait, culture influences when and how frequently people smile. For example, in Thailand (the "Land of Smiles"), a smile is a sign of friendliness; in Korea and Japan it can be a sign of shallowness.[21] Research comparing Japanese and American interpretions of emotions found that Americans – who tend to express emotions more openly than the Japanese – often focus on the mouth to interpret emotions, while the Japanese often focus on the eyes. Interestingly, this pattern can be noticed in the use of computer emoticons – symbols used to display emotions in electronic communication. In North America, a happy face is depicted as:) or :-), and a sad face as :(or (:-(. In Japan, however, a happy face is typically represented with the symbol ^–^, while a sad face is represented with the symbol ;_;.[22] The same, only different.

Personal space

Oftentimes, *personal space* can also vary across cultures. In some cultures, including those of North America, Northern Europe, and much of Asia, people tend to remain relatively far apart when talking to each other, even among good friends, so as not to invade anyone's personal or private space. In other cultures, such as those in Latin America and many Arab countries, people tend to stand much closer together when talking or doing business, frequently touching one another. This latter practice sometimes makes managers from other regions of the world a bit anxious. Another example of the use of personal space can be seen in some countries where open office architecture is used in office layouts (i.e., when all employees, including managers, sit in the same large room as one community), compared to other countries that stress closed office architecture (i.e., where most managers have their own private offices away from their subordinates – and from each other). Clearly, such structural differences are likely to have an impact on communications and corporate culture. In open architecture arrangements, most communications – including comments from the boss, for example – quickly become common knowledge, whereas this same communication in a closed office layout often remains confidential, even if there is no need for this.

Body language

In addition, *body language* represents the way people move, stand, sit, and walk. This, too, can send important messages to others, whether they intend it or not. Through body movements, individuals communicate their attitudes about others, as well as their emotional state. For example, when individuals are nervous, they have a tendency to fidget, tap on the table, and so forth. Scholars suggest that people can make as many as 700,000 distinct physical signs.[23] Many of these non-verbal messages are easily understood. For instance, if people get lost in a foreign city, the look on their faces as they look at a map is likely to attract the attention of locals, regardless of where this occurs. When identifying where people want to go, the locals are likely to point in that direction. However, pointing can be done in different ways, for example with the index finger in the US and Canada, with the little finger in Germany, and with the entire hand in Japan.[24] Similarly, Italians and Brazilians, for instance, speak with their hands and body with animated – almost theatrical – movements, while by comparison Nordics tend to avoid using their arms as much when conversing with others.[25]

Secret communication

A fourth form of non-verbal communication involves the use of *secret* (or hidden) *communication*. These are messages that are typically aimed exclusively at insiders to a group or organization, and can include the use of protocols, formalities, symbols, or interpersonal "rules" designed to convey messages that are often unknown to outsiders.

They can also include insider rules governing acceptable topics to discuss, when emotional displays are acceptable or welcome, the use of humor in conversations, the use and meaning of code words, and so forth. Such messages are typically difficult for outsiders to understand, and frequently involve hidden meanings behind messages. They can be difficult to observe even if outsiders know what they are looking for. They can also help explain the reasons behind use of certain terms or actions, if only they could be identified.

Communication protocols

In addition, moderating the conveyance of any message is a series of culture-based *communication protocols* that serve to limit boundaries of what is considered acceptable communication. In a sense, these protocols specify the "rules of the road" when communicating with people from other cultures. Acting somewhat like etiquette in social situations, communication protocols encourage speakers to adapt appropriate formalities and behaviors in order to enhance their chances of success in the conversation. Two types of communication protocols can be identified: appropriate formalities and appropriate behaviors.

Appropriate formalities

First of all, communication protocols provide a number of conversational formalities – formal guidelines and sometimes very explicit rules – concerning acceptable or preferred conversational guidelines; that is, relating to how and when messages can be appropriately conveyed. For example, what are the prevailing norms about how individuals start or end a conversation? Who speaks first? Should people be assertive and say "Sorry for interrupting you …" or wait until they are invited to speak? Once the conversation is completed, is it acceptable to leave or should people linger awhile before departing? Similarly, cultural rules inform the way we organize our messages, whether linearly or non-linearly, planned or spontaneous, and even what topics should be discussed first or last. It also suggests when we can speak: is it okay to interrupt others, or should we wait until they finish? Several illustrations of these differences are shown in Exhibit 7.5.

Appropriate behaviors

Communication protocols also guide people in terms of appropriate behaviors that accompany their conversation. People convey meanings based on the way they speak and the tone, speed, and volume of voice they use. However, these verbal variations are used differently in different countries. Sometimes a change in the tone of a voice signals

Exhibit 7.5 Protocols governing appropriate formalities

Formality protocols	Alternative styles	Examples
Opening a conversation	Assertive vs. hesitant	People are typically expected or encouraged to be assertive in Anglo-Saxon countries, taking the initiative to communicate; people are expected to stand silently and wait for an invitation to speak in Japan.
Ending a conversation	Sudden vs. elaborate	People in North America are often allowed to leave a conversation once the main topic is finished; people in Spain are generally expected to linger awhile and talk about other things before departing.
Presenting ideas or proposals	Sequencing vs. integration of information to be presented	Many North Americans tend to communicate linearly, with explicit links between topics and ideas, favoring a planned approach to communication; many Asians prefer a more non-linear approach, following a circular pattern of communication; many people from the Mediterranean tend to favor a zigzag approach where tangential ideas may be explored and elaborated before the speaker returns to the main point.
Interruptions and silence	Wait one's turn vs. interrupt to make a point; short vs. long periods of silence	People in Italy can sometimes be found speaking in a conversation any time they have something to say, and it is not uncommon for more than one person to speak at the same time; people in Northern European countries are more likely to wait until another speaker finishes, even if the shift from one speaker to another happens quickly. Conversations in much of Latin America tend to have very few lapses of silence – indeed, silence or "dead air" often makes such people uncomfortable, forcing them to speak again. By contrast, silence periods are common in Japan.
Vocal characteristics	Rapid vs. slow; loud vs. soft	Indians tend to speak English twice as fast as Americans, Britons, or Canadians; Spaniards tend to speak significantly louder than the French or Belgians.

a change from formality to informality. In American stores, customers are frequently greeted by clerks with a "How are you doing?", which is puzzling for many Europeans who associate such a friendly tone with a personal relationship and genuine interest.

Protocols can limit the appropriateness of emotional displays, such as anger or sadness. Consider the very real example of a Spanish woman assigned to work in Germany for a short period of time. The day after she arrived in Germany, she received a phone call at work informing her that a close relative had suddenly passed away. The woman was emotionally disturbed and burst into tears. She was appalled by the lack of sensitivity of her German colleagues, who did not inquire about what happened nor provide emotional support. On the other hand, her German colleagues were surprised by her reaction and thought she was immature and unprofessional.[26] The issue here is that while in Spain, outward emotional displays are acceptable and even expected at times, in German they are considered inappropriate, and taking interest in a colleague's personal affairs can be deemed rude and unprofessional.

Finally, as illustrated in Exhibit 7.6, protocols often suggest when certain kinds of "functional" communication are appropriate.[27] Included here are issues such as when and where to make apologies or requests, as well as providing feedback or disagreeing with someone. Consider the role of apologies. In some cultures like Indonesia, apologies are used frequently in order to promote social bonding and show empathy. In other cultures, including much of Western European, apologies are used to admit guilt and are used only when there is a real need for it. In some cultures, apologies are a sign of professionalism and politeness; in others, they are a sign of weakness and lack of confidence. Misunderstandings are likely to occur when

Exhibit 7.6 Protocols governing appropriate behaviors

Behavioral protocols	Functions	Examples
Apologies	Acceptance of responsibility; face-saving for self or others; admission of guilt; empathy with others; social bonding.	Apologies in Indonesia are used frequently in order to promote social bonding and show empathy; apologies in western Europe are typically used to admit guilt and used sporadically.
Disagreements	State one's opposition (e.g., for the record); pursue best answer (e.g., constructive criticism), humility (e.g., dismissing accolades) etc.	Disagreements in Japan are often communicated with silence; disagreements in Spain are often communicated through emotional outbursts; disagreements in Northern Europe tend to be clearly, calmly, and directly stated.
Emotional displays	Communicate feelings: express happiness, sadness, anger, etc.	Outward displays of emotions are accepted and sometimes encouraged in Brazil; control over one's emotions is admired in Japan.
Feedback	Express positive or negative opinions; suggest new directions; motivate and build confidence; assertion of power, etc.	Praise is a key motivational strategy in North America and positive feedback is delivered frequently; praise and positive feedback are saved for extraordinary circumstances in Russia, otherwise may be interpreted as hollow and false; positive feedback in both France and Indonesia can sometimes be offensive in that it suggests that the supervisor was surprised that the employee did a good job.
Requests	Seek help with task completion; ask a favor.	In North America, requests are expected to be clear, direct, and precise or they may not be heard; in Brazil, requests are more likely to be made indirectly.

apologies are expected but do not come, or when they are not expected and come as a surprise. For example, in Japan, an apology is considered a lubricant of human life and people are willing to tolerate difficult situations or mistakes, as long as apologies are expressed. However, if an expected apology does not come, they may feel angry and offended, and may feel inclined to break the relationship. Interestingly enough, even though the Japanese communication style tends to be more indirect than that of the Americans, researchers have found that Japanese apologies tend to be more direct and explicit, as well as more elaborated than that of Americans.[28]

Technology-mediated communication

In recent years, cross-cultural communication has become even more complicated and challenging due to the advent of two relatively new features of everyday life: technology and speed. That is, new communications technologies and the increased speed of much of our communication require many managers to work smarter as they work faster. Gone are the days of the leisurely face-to-face conversation over coffee or tea or a two-hour lunch. Instead, in an increasingly crammed schedule, managers must often become more efficient – for better or worse. The question is whether this new technology and speed will lead to better decisions, sales, production, and revenues or to increased opportunities for misunderstanding, damaged relationships, and lost business.

Global managers today rely to a great extent on electronic or technology-mediated communications, such as emails, instant or text messaging, remote team sessions, websites, and other internet-based technologies. While a relatively new – and ever-expanding – technology, this strategy has increasingly replaced face-to-face communication because of its ability to neutralize the distances between people and speed message transmission. Large quantities of data can be easily and quickly exchanged in real time, an important advantage for many types of global business. However, some important challenges face the global manager when relying heavily on technology-mediated communications.

Lack of contextual information

Many global managers in today's virtual business environment face a real challenge: how to work across cultures from afar. While a wealth of academic and practitioner literature recognizes and discusses the challenges of working abroad and working with people from different cultures, much less is known about how we deal with other cultures without the benefit of "seeing" how different things can be in other regions of the world. This lack of contextual information (see above) increases opportunities for misunderstandings, which, in turn, can create interpersonal conflicts and erode trust.

Simply put, the context underlying a message can provide a wealth of information when communicating face to face. It can provide face-saving ways to say "no." It can also serve as a barometer on how a current meeting is going. When this context is absent, as it often is with virtual or computer-mediated communication, both the sender and the recipient lose considerable information behind what is said online. And many of the facts that are received are encrypted in ways that limit their useful interpretations.

For example, when a British manager flies to Thailand for a meeting (or vice versa), he or she is likely to be bombarded with environmental stimuli that are quite different from their home country. This could include different sounds, signs, building architecture, street names, traffic patterns, use of space, and so forth. At the very least, this should sensitize the manager to the fact that he or she is not home and that things may be different here. From this, the manager might go one step further and conclude that business practices may also be somewhat different, thereby requiring increased sensitivity when talking to prospective partners. If this same meeting took place electronically, all of this context would be missing, and the manager – indeed, both managers – might assume that the other party understood what was not said as well as what was. As a result, miscommunications and incorrect or misleading messages can emerge almost from the beginning.

Besides cultural differences, this lack of common context can also make it difficult to interpret information from afar. For example, if our Canadian manager has an on-site meeting at 8:00 a.m., but the local traffic or local weather is very bad and her Brazilian counterpart fails to show up on time, she may quickly infer that he must be stuck in traffic or having difficulties arriving due to icy or stormy road conditions. However, if her Brazilian counterpart was in Sao Paulo and failed to be online at 8:00 a.m., she has no contextual information upon which to infer much of anything. Her counterpart may not have responded at the agreed upon time because he uses polychronic instead of monochronic time, has lost interest in doing business with her company, or is ill or injured. Obviously, her response to the attributions she makes regarding his reason for not making contact can have significant implications for how she will respond. At the same time, while most people do not expect others to be at their computer doing business on important local holiday, they may fail to remember that local holidays can differ across national boundaries.[29] Hence, emailing her Brazilian counterpart with a critical question during spring Carnival, for example, when most Canadians are working but when Brazilians are celebrating a major holiday, may not lead to the quick response she sought.

Assumptions about mutual knowledge

In addition, electronic communications can often result in shorter messages, again possibly losing useful information. Writing down details of a message can sometimes be laborious, leading writers to shorten their messages.[30] (Text messaging makes this even worse.) One study found that in similar circumstances, individuals communicating via text-based virtual technology exchanged an average of 740 words per message, while individuals communicating verbally exchanged an average of 1,702 words – or more than twice as much as virtual communication.[31] This, of course, is understandable since it is often difficult to know what information is most relevant to the exchange and it takes a lot of work to write down details of their everyday reality, not knowing which parts may be relevant to dispersed team members. As a result, an email message to a subordinate to "get this done now" might mean you must complete the job immediately regardless of costs, risks, partner relationships, or even legal constraints. Or it might mean, simply, push as hard as you can but don't ruffle anyone's feathers. To put this another way, adverbs and adjectives are often the first casualties of electronic communication.

This problem is at the core of the concept of mutual knowledge. *Mutual knowledge* represents the knowledge that individuals share and know that they share.[32] That is, mutual knowledge refers to the common basis of information that does not have to be repeated when communicating. To see how this works, consider the difference between two *co-located* employees (i.e., located in the same place) and two dispersed employees (i.e., located in different places, either down the street or across the globe). In the first case, when talking to a colleague at the next desk, a person might point out that "this decision came from the 15th floor," meaning that the general manager made the decision and that you do not feel you have the authority to contest it. Your colleague, working in the same environment, would understand that top management occupies the 15th floor and that in this organization their decision is not easily reversed. This understanding is mutual knowledge. However, your dispersed colleague may not be aware of the office in your locale, and may not understand the power structure of the organization, thereby having a difficult time understanding your apparently lax attitude about the issue.

Because of this, people at all levels of the organization often have a tendency to omit contextual information, erroneously assuming mutual knowledge across different locales. To make matters worse, when contextual information is communicated, it is frequently ignored or forgotten. It is often difficult for dispersed people to imagine their colleague's contexts, and even harder to update their mental picture of these contexts as their situation changes.[33] This difficulty in understanding the other person's situation also hinders people's ability to identify which aspects of their own situation need to be explained. This lack of mutual knowledge frequently creates conflicts, as remote partners fail to understand why others fail to honor deadlines, insist on particular points, or drop out of communication without warning.[34]

Technology breakdowns

Furthermore, even when dispersed members communicate and attend to information, technological breakdowns may cause information leaks that partners may not be aware of. For example, emails may not reach their final destination, attachments may not go through, different versions of documents may be erroneously circulated, and so on. Sometimes members send information to one team member believing that everyone had access to that information. In these cases, members may assume mutual knowledge and not realize the problem, attributing any difficulties to other members. To make matters worse, even when members discover the source of the difficulties, they often do not retrace in their minds the inaccurate assumptions they have drawn.[35]

Asynchronous communication

This problem is accentuated in *asynchronous communication*, or communication across significantly different time zones. Because of these different time zones, many conversations among team members by telephone, video conference, or messaging systems can be difficult to arrange. Communicating asynchronously means that someone has to be available either very early in the morning or very late at night, not always a popular occurrence for the person who must get up very early or go to bed very late. Thus, while it is relatively easy to set up a *synchronous* call between team members or partners in London, Paris, and Rabat, it can be significantly more difficult to set up an *asynchronous* call between the same people in London, Bombay, and Sydney. And if there are transmission problems or delays, this problem gets worse. Moreover, when virtual communication (e.g., email) is relied upon because of these time differences, information can be exchanged but, given the low richness of the medium and the low levels of real-time feedback, little may be achieved in terms of shared understanding. Shared understanding requires more than information exchange; it requires people to learn together, relate to one another, and develop mutual expectations about the nature of the goal, task, and processes to accomplish the goals.[36]

Communication on the fly

As discussed throughout this chapter, cross-cultural communication is a process in which individuals from different cultural backgrounds exchange messages to accomplish something – negotiate a deal, share information, coordinate activities, and so forth. The challenges of such communications are twofold. First, frequently there is little common ground – the knowledge base of both parties is different and it is not clear what is commonly known. Second, the ways in which messages are delivered – topics, protocols, and behaviors – are sometimes dramatically different, making it difficult for parties to interpret messages. If the communication process is successful, individuals will develop a common ground and will learn how to communicate with each other effectively. However, this process can take time and has a degree of risk involved.

Under ideal circumstances, successful global managers will work to establish sound and productive long-term interpersonal relationships with their colleagues and partners around the world. However, in many instances (especially in the case of frequent flyers), time is a luxury they do not have. That is, in many cases global managers find themselves thrown into a new environment where the people and culture are largely unknown to them, yet they are still responsible for accomplishing their mission – and quickly. In such circumstances, successful managers will be those who can learn to accomplish goals while working with others from different cultural backgrounds in the course of minimal interactions and on short notice. In other words, many successful global managers must learn to communicate and work with people from other cultures "on the fly." In these cases, managers can often compensate for a lack of knowledge about a specific culture by developing and drawing on their learning skills. Once managers are able to successfully interact with people from foreign cultures, it will be easier to acquire business and local knowledge. Mastering learning skills is thus possibly the best strategy available to managers who want to succeed in the multicultural reality of today's business environment.

As discussed in Chapter 2, knowledge is typically defined as familiarity that is gained by actual experience. In other words, learning occurs when individuals grasp and transform their experiences into new knowledge. The process of knowledge creation consists of four stages: experience, observation, reflection, and abstract conceptualization. While learning can begin in any of the four stages, learning is, above all else, a process: an individual has an experience, observes and reflects on the experience, develops theories and conceptualizations to explain the experience, and finally tests theories through active experimentation.

To illustrate, consider the following scenario: You come from a culture that values direct, straightforward communication. When you converse with others, you ask direct questions as you have learned from experience that this behavior usually results in straightforward answers. Now, imagine that you engage in a conversation with an individual from a culture that values indirect communication and "saving face." This person has learned through experience that indirect and subtle suggestions yield comfortable interactions allowing all parties to save face. Neither of you are sufficiently knowledgeable to adapt your communication styles to fit the other's culture.

In this scenario, you are likely to ask a direct question and get what you perceive to be an unsatisfactorily vague response. You are then likely to experience an emotional reaction – discomfort, perplexity, offense, or surprise – to the results of your actions. This *concrete experience* will likely prompt you to try to understand what is happening through *observation* and *reflection*. You recognize that there is a mismatch between what is happening and what you thought would happen, and then observe the other person to try to ascertain why she is responding as she is: maybe she did not hear you, maybe she did not understand the question, maybe she does not speak English very well, maybe she is shy, maybe she is not comfortable with the question. You then search for other clues in her behavior and in the context of the situation that can help explain her behavior. Your observation and reflection provides a foundation for *abstract conceptualization* and *generalization*. You develop a theory to explain what is happening: you identify a plausible explanation for her behavior and search for alternative solutions to your communication problem. Let's suppose that you conclude that your partner is uncomfortable with your question. Her body language suggests that she feels embarrassed, so you theorize that you should pose the question in a different way. Your theory will guide your future actions when dealing with this individual and others from similar cultures.

Learning through experience is a process of trial and error in which individuals' experience does not meet expectations, leading to reflection, identification of solutions, and experimentation with new behaviors. Individuals identify successful behaviors and incorporate them into theories of how to behave. When the individual next engages in a similar situation, he draws on his latest theories for guidance. One tests the implication of new concepts by practicing new actions. For instance, in the example above, you might decide to formulate your question in a different way and observe the results, beginning a new learning cycle that continues until you are satisfied that you have identified successful behaviors.

At the same time that one party is reflecting and learning during the interaction, the other party is doing the same, and behaviors on both sides are likely to be adjusted. This

Exhibit 7.7 Interdependent learning

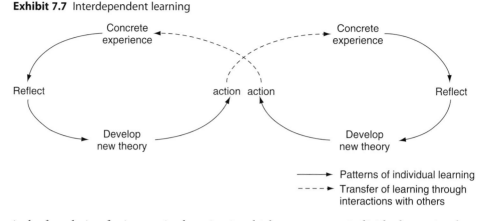

is the foundation for interactive learning in which two or more individuals are simultaneously experiencing problems, reflecting on them, theorizing about them, and engaging in corrective actions. In other words, the learning of one party leads to an action that will influence the learning of the other party in a cycle of interdependent learning. This interdependence is illustrated in Exhibit 7.7.

An intercultural interaction is an opportunity for interdependent learning in which individuals both learn about the other's culture and negotiate effective ways of relating to one another. Ideally, as individuals from different cultures interact, they develop better ways of communicating with each other. However, if learning does not happen, the interaction fails and the relationship suffers. For example, if after asking a question and receiving an unsatisfactory answer the individual does not observe and reflect on the other party's behavior, she may engage in actions that are detrimental to the relationship. An effective intercultural interaction is the result of successful interdependent learning, through which two or more parties negotiate ways of communicating and working together. We can identify at least four steps in this process:

(1) *Negotiating identities.* Identity is the answer to the question "Who am I?", and it is a key mechanism through which individuals create categories and define themselves in relation to others. This categorization process influences one's perception of his or her position in relation to others, as well as how he acts and feels about interactions. When a person engages with another from a different cultural background, her assumptions, values, and beliefs may be questioned, and her perceptions about who she is, her competence, status, and self-worth may be challenged. An intercultural interaction is likely to produce strong feelings about one's identity and expectations. For an interaction to be positive, these feelings must be positive for both parties. For example, to an Australian employee, questioning the boss is

not only natural but expected. However, an Indonesian manager may feel disrespected and threatened when facing such overt questioning. In order for the interaction to succeed, the parties must preserve a satisfactory identity for themselves while respecting and preserving others. That is, the Australian employee must be able to express her opinion without offending the Indonesian manager.

(2) *Negotiating meaning.* Meaning refers to the interpretation individuals assign to their experience and observations. For example, in some cultures questioning the boss means professionalism; in others, lack of respect. When two individuals from different cultures interact, they are likely to have different interpretations of the meaning of what they are discussing. A communication will only be successful if both parties agree on the meaning of what is being talked about.

(3) *Negotiating rules.* Once individuals agree on acceptable identities and meanings, they need to negotiate new rules that will inform their relationship. These rules are akin to theories of action and, over time, create a common context. For example, continuing with the example above, it may be agreed that disagreements will not be made in public. Over time, rules regarding the most important cultural obstacles to the success of a relationship can constitute a newly shared culture for the individuals involved.[37] However, at minimum, even in the time-sensitive situations in which today's global managers operate, recognition of the need to negotiate rules and imperfect attempts to do so supports successful interaction.

(4) *Negotiating behaviors.* Finally, once individuals develop new theories of action and agree on a common set of cultural rules to guide interaction, they must *negotiate new behaviors*, or do things in a different way. Here, the Australian manager will have to control her urge to openly discuss her opinions and save them for private situations in which the Indonesian managers can save face. In these cases, it is important that managers recognize their weaknesses and compensate with other behaviors. For instance, individuals who find it difficult to communicate indirectly may compensate by searching for opportunities to discuss issues one-on-one and by prefacing their direct statements with an apology.

In summary, learning to communicate "on the fly" requires managers to engage with others in an interactive process in which both parties feel comfortable with their position via-à-vis each other (identities), agree on the meaning of what is being communicated, establish some rules to guide their relationship, and engage in behaviors that are in line with such rules and meanings. This is a process of trial and error that can be facilitated by managers' awareness of the process and conscious attempt to learn and improve communication.

Communication across cultures

With increasing globalization and the associated need to communicate with people from different cultures in person or through communications technology, developing the skills to communicate effectively across cultural boundaries is fundamental to any aspiring global manager. To this end, managers are advised to develop communication flexibility, or the ability to say the same thing in several different ways. No communication style is good or bad in itself, but is more or less appropriate to specific situations. Managers that are able to communicate in different ways are more able to solve problems and engage in successful relationships with multiple cultures as they are better able to convey meaning and be understood.

When we are discussing the "rules of the road" in cross-cultural communication, we must remember that different roads have different rules, and that global managers are unwise to ignore these differences. This dilemma was exemplified in the opening example of two company executives reaching out to create a partnership. Whether one side or both sides failed to understand the cultural differences that were involved remains open for question. What is not open for question, however, is that we can all do a better job communicating across cultures. Let's look at three concrete actions that are available to all managers: improving message clarity, improving message comprehension, and recognizing and then minimizing communication breakdowns (see Exhibit 7.8).

Exhibit 7.8 Management challenge: communicating effectively across cultures

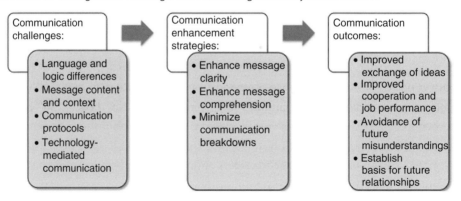

Enhancing message clarity

Regardless of culture, most everyone (except ciphers) seeks to be understood when trying to communicate with others, and failing to do so can often be very frustrating – and non-productive. To a manager (or anyone else), the realization that, despite her best efforts, her message was met with a blank stare, a grimace, inaction, or actions that demonstrate a lack of understanding can be daunting. However, when the same manager does not understand either why the message failed or how to improve future messages, frustration can turn into despair.

While it is difficult to generalize here without more detail, such managers can work on at least three issues that relate to message clarity: message content, language clarity, and communication strategy (delivery style).

Message content

First, even though it may sound obvious, the first step towards successful cross-cultural communication is *message content* – to know what you want to say and saying it clearly, repeating the key message in different ways. Many times we engage in conversations not knowing exactly what our purpose is, and we make up our mind about what we are trying to say in the process of the communication. While this is normal in any communication, and likely to happen in cross-cultural situations, it pays off to pay attention to what you are trying to say and making sure that the important bits of the message are highlighted, reinforced, and repeated in different ways. Sometimes it is helpful to use additional means of communication, such as written materials and visual aids, to facilitate the understanding of the message.

Language clarity

Second, consider *language clarity*. Opportunities for misunderstanding abound in almost any intercultural interaction. In such situations, people often do not share common cultural logics to help them fill the gaps and make sense of missing pieces of information. Moreover, many times they do not have the same command of the language, or maybe know different variations of the same language using expressions that do not carry the meaning we intended. For example, you can buy a 500-page English-English dictionary that translates American into English and back…500 pages! Or, perhaps their communication strategy is not compatible and a message is not received because of the way it was communicated. In any case, dealing with these issues is seldom easy, and even the most experienced global managers are likely to get into trouble from time to time.

At the heart of this challenge is language: which language is used and how it is used. As was discussed above, the language we speak can often constrain our thoughts and limit what we can say. In global business interactions, the chances are that at least one, if not all parties involved, is communicating in a second language, with varying mastery levels. Managers engaged in long-term interactions with a foreign nation, either by moving to the foreign location or periodically engaging with natives from the foreign culture, are advised to acquire a rudimentary understanding of the local language. The ability to communicate simple thoughts and understand the basic logic of the language increases significantly the resources available to communicate and create meaning. Of course, this is not always possible. Many times we are involved with several cultures simultaneously (e.g., frequent flyers), and learning new languages takes time and a significant level of personal investment. In these situations, people tend to prefer to use their own language and strive to achieve clarity by carefully selecting our words.

Delivery style

And third, people use different *delivery styles* to communicate. These styles are influenced by people's cultural backgrounds, personal preferences, and the context of the communication episode. However, delivery styles tend to be very important to us, and abrupt changes in such styles can often lead to confusion and/or discomfort.

The first step in communicating better is to become aware of our own communication style preferences and habits. For example, if you know you have a tendency to communicate indirectly, and many times others do not understand what you are trying to say, you are more likely to check for understanding and re-state your position in a more direct way when you realize your message did not get through. Similarly, if you are aware of your difficulties to apologize when you do not feel it is appropriate to recognize guilt, you may notice when others react to a missing apology and take steps accordingly. Clearly, no particular delivery style is better than another. However, the ability to communicate using more than one style is better than having only one way of saying things. Just as speaking more languages opens up opportunities to communicate with more people, communicating in more than one style creates more communication possibilities.

The second step in effective delivery is observing and deciphering the delivery style of our counterparts. Understanding how others communicate helps us to interpret what they are saying, and gives us insight into how we can adapt our style to be better understood. Or at least it gives us an indication of where communication problems may occur. For instance, imagine one of your team members has a tendency not to speak up

Exhibit 7.9 Management strategies: improving cross-cultural communication

Communication-improvement strategies	Specific tactics for improving communication across cultures
Enhancing message clarity	• State message clearly; slow down. • Repeat message using different words, if possible. • Back up spoken message with written materials. • Speak in the other's language, if possible. • Avoid using idioms, jargon, or ambiguous words. • Convey message in ways that are not offensive or threatening to others.
Enhancing message comprehension	• State your expectations and assumptions clearly. • Restate the positions of all parties during discussions to clarify common understanding. • Deal with questions and concerns as they arise. • Be patient; repeat message as often as needed. • Ask each side to state the other's position as he/she sees it. • Avoid being so polite or subtle that message context gets lost. • Write down any agreements of additional information to be sought.
Recognizing and responding to communication breakdowns	• Observe body language for signs of distress, anger, or confusion. • Be patient and understanding. Take a break when appropriate. • Mentally change places with others, asking yourself how they would respond to what you are saying. • Notice your own reactions to the situation.

and voice her opinion in situations of disagreement. Knowing this, you may strive to get her opinion in private, prior to the meetings, or start the meeting by asking her opinion before any disagreement becomes evident.

These communication strategies are summarized in Exhibit 7.9, along with specific strategies that can be used to help minimize each challenge.

Improving message comprehension

Communication episodes are generally considered to be successful not when everyone agrees to a proposal, request, or demand, but rather when everyone agrees about the meaning of what is being communicated. For example, what does signing a contract mean? For some cultures it means the end of a negotiation; for others it means the beginning of a relationship. As such, when a person says that "I am glad we were able to sign a contract," this may mean "I am glad the negotiations are over and I can go back to business" or it may mean "I am glad we agreed to start a relationship and will continue the negotiations for a long time to come." Unless a common meaning is created, this relationship is likely to run into trouble in the future when one part wants to renegotiate the contract and the other feels cheated (see Chapter 10).

A shared meaning must be constructed through interaction, as individuals exchange information. In other words, a successful communication uncovers hidden cultural assumptions, making parties aware of how culture is shaping perceptions, expectations, and behaviors. Uncovering cultural assumptions involves two behaviors: enquiry and advocacy.[38]

Enquiry

The first such behavior, *enquiry*, refers to exploring and questioning one's own reasoning and the reasoning of others. In other words, individuals strive to create and accept a new common meaning by asking the following questions: How do you and I perceive the situation? What do you and I wish to achieve in this situation? Which actions are you and I willing to take to achieve this goal? Enquiry requires suspending judgment, letting go of a previous understanding, and tolerating uncertainty until a new understanding may be created. We like to be right, but in a cross-cultural situation, what is right is relative. Arriving at a common meaning requires dealing with the ambiguity of not knowing what right is – at least for the time being.

Advocacy

The second behavior, *advocacy*, refers to expressing and standing up for what one thinks and desires. Advocacy suggests stating clearly what you think and want, and explaining the reasoning behind your view. In other words, it requires knowing yourself and understanding what your assumptions and points of view are. It also requires taking responsibility for how you feel about things. For example, if you are frustrated because your counterpart always comes late to meetings (something perhaps acceptable in her culture), you may say, "I prefer it when I do not have to wait for you, because for me it is very stressful not knowing what time you will arrive." This is very different than saying, "I am a busy person and it is inconsiderate when you fail to keep your appointments." The first statement is about you and how you feel about the interaction, and opens up the possibility for the other person to understand your point of view and to respond. The second can easily be construed as a personal attack that is likely to be taken personally. After all, she will likely provide a reason for her tardiness and the problem remains unsolved.

When individuals combine enquiry with advocacy, they share information about their cultural assumptions, the meanings they associate with the issue, and the reasoning for their thinking. This sharing of assumptions and interpretations creates the basis for a new, mutually acceptable meaning to emerge. Engaging in enquiry and advocacy is challenging because it requires uncovering our own perceptions, exposing ourselves, being open to listen to the other's perception, and being willing to give up the safety of our own previous interpretations in order for a new culture-free interpretation to emerge. To make matters worse, cultural-based preferences can also influence how individuals may go about doing this. For example, in some cultures, individuals prefer to express themselves using open and direct communication, whereas in other cultures individuals are likely to share their assumptions indirectly, making it difficult for direct communicators to fully understand. Some indirect communicators may even feel uncomfortable with direct questioning of their assumptions, which could potentially close communication even further.

Additionally, cultural-based preferences may suggest circumstances in which enquiry and advocacy are more likely to be successful. For instance, in some cultures it may be during formal meetings, in other cultures it may be late at night over drinks, and in still others it may be through informal one-on-one conversations. As a result, in order to negotiate meaning, individuals must gather information in several different ways, relying on the context, body language, subtle cues, and messages.

Minimizing communication breakdowns

Finally, even when we strive to be clear and are careful to express our assumptions, there are times were a communication just doesn't work. In these situations, it is important to notice – as quickly as possible – that there is a problem so that we can take measures to remediate it. Many times the signs that a communicated message is not working are there from early on, but none of the parties notice it. And when they notice it, it is usually too late as the damage caused is already too big to be bridged. It may be that someone is deeply upset, or that the business deal did not go through and a competitor has won the contract.

To see how this problem can manifest itself, consider three examples.[39] First, when someone fails to stop talking about something and keeps repeating it again and again, our first tendency is to label the person or situation as extremely annoying. Instead, we would likely do better if we stop and think what he or she is really trying to say. If the same issue or topic keeps coming up, it is probably because our communication counterpart feels the message is not getting through to us – and it probably isn't. Try asking questions to clarify the point and state clearly what you have understood so far. Second, if someone who was friendly and informal suddenly becomes formal and "official," or someone that was very talkative suddenly becomes silent, this may be a sign that the other person felt her style was not welcome or understood. If this was not the case, it is worthwhile to investigate what may have caused the change. And third, sometimes two individuals are in agreement on something, but they don't recognize it. This frequently happens in multicultural teams, where two individuals argue for hours about something they actually agree on, but do not realize. Using different ways of saying the same thing may help.

In addition to these cues, there are other red flags that may be noteworthy throughout the conversation. For example, if you find yourself thinking that people from other cultures are backward, uneducated, or the like, consider how communication styles may be affecting your perception. It may be that you simply do not understand one another. It may also be that you are not listening. As the thirteenth-century Venetian explorer Marco Polo once observed, "It is not the voice that commands the story; it is the ear".[40]

Notes

1 Cited in Richard Hill, *We Europeans*. Brussels: Europublications, 1997, p. 345.
2 Richard Lewis, *When Cultures Collide*. London: Nicholas Brealey, 1999, p. 94.
3 Xiaohong He, Mohammad Elahee, Robert Engle, Chadwick Nehrt, and Farid Sadrieh, *Globalization and International Business*. Garfield Heights, OH: NCP, 2007, p. 54.
4 Gary Ferraro, *The Cultural Dimension of International Business*. Upper Saddle River, NJ: Pearson/Prentice Hall, 2006, p. 80.
5 *Ibid.*, p. 36.
6 Larry Samovar, Richard Porter, and Edwin McDaniel, *Communication Between Cultures*. Belmont, CA: Thomson/Wadsworth, 2007, pp. 165–167.
7 Samovar *et al.*, *Communication Between Cultures*, p. 172.
8 Edward Sapir, *Selected Writings in Language, Culture, and Personality*, edited by D. V. Mandelbaum. Berkeley, CA: University of California Press, 1949, p. 162.
9 *Ibid.*
10 Richard A. Shweder, "Anthropology's romantic rebellion against the enlightment, or there is more to thinking than reason and evidence," in Richard A. Shweder and Robert A. LeVine (eds.), *Culture Theory: Essays on Mind, Self, and Emotion*. Cambridge, UK: Cambridge University Press, 1984, p. 44–45.
11 Alessandro Duranti, *Linguistic Anthropology*. Cambridge, UK: Cambridge University Press, 1997, p. 26.
12 Sapir, *Selected Writings*, p. 162; Donnel Briley, Michael Morris, and Itamar Simonson, "Cultural chameleons: biculturals, conformity motives, and decision making," *Journal of Consumer Psychology*, 2005, 15(4), p. 351; Lauren Aaronson, "My Spanish side," *Psychology Today*, 2005, 38(4), p. 26.

13 Nick J. Enfield, "The theory of cultural logic," *Cultural Dynamics*, 2000, 12(1), pp. 35–64.

14 *Lingua franca* (from Italian, literally meaning "the Frankish language") is a language that is systematically used to communicate between persons not sharing a mother tongue, in particular when it is a third language, distinct from both persons' mother tongues. "*Lingua franca*" is a functionally defined term, independent of the linguistic history or structure of the language. It may also refer to the *de facto* language within a more or less specialized field. A synonym for *lingua franca* is "vehicular language." Whereas a *vernacular* language is used as a native language in a single speaker community, a *vehicular* language goes beyond the boundaries of its original community, and is used as a second language for communication between communities. For example, English is a vernacular in England, but is used as a vehicular language (that is, a *lingua franca*) in the Philippines.

15 Private communication to authors, 2007.

16 Norman Schur, *British English: A to Zed*. New York, NY: HarperCollins, 1991.

17 Edward T. Hall and Mildred R. Hall, *Understanding Cultural Differences: Germans, French and Americans*. Yarmouth, ME: Intercultural Press, 1990.

18 Samovar *et al.*, *Communication Between Cultures*.

19 Edward T. Hall, *The Silent Language*. New York, NY: Anchor Books, 1981.

20 University of Alberta, "Culture is key to interpreting facial emotions," *Science Daily*, April 5 2007 (www.sciencedaily.com/releases/2007/04/070404162321.htm).

21 Samovar *et al.*, *Communication Between Cultures*.

22 University of Alberta, "Culture is Key."

23 Samovar *et al.*, *Communication Between Cultures*.

24 *Ibid*.

25 *Ibid*.

26 Private communication to authors, 2008.

27 Diane M. Saphiere, Barbara K. Mikk, and Basma I. DeVries, *Communication Highwire: Leveraging the Power of Diverse Communication Styles*. Yarmouth, ME: Intercultural Press, 2005.

28 Toru Kiyomiya, "Japanese corporate apology: critical perspectives to Japanese formality of apology," paper presented at the EGOS conference, Vienna, Austria, 2007.

29 Catherine D. Cramton, "Finding common ground in dispersed collaboration," *Organizational Dynamics*, 2002, 30(4), p. 356.

30 Catherine D. Cramton and Kara L. Orvis, "Overcoming barriers to information sharing in virtual teams," in C. B. Gibson, and S. G. Cohen (eds.), *Virtual Teams that Work: Creating Conditions for Virtual Team Effectiveness*. San Francisco, CA: Jossey-Bass, 2003, pp. 214–232.

31 Susan G. Strauss, "Getting a clue: the effects of communication media and information distribution on participation and performance in computer mediated and face-to-face groups," *Small Group Research*, 1996, 27, pp. 115–142; Cramton and Orvis, "Overcoming barriers to information sharing."

32 Catherine D. Cramton, "The mutual knowledge problem and its consequences for dispersed collaboration," *Organization Science*, 2001, 12(3), p. 346.

33 Cramton, "The mutual knowledge problem," p. 356.

34 *Ibid.*

35 *Ibid.*

36 Pamela J. Hinds and Suzame P. Weisband, "Knowledge sharing and shared understanding in virtual teams," in Gibson and Cohen, *Virtual Teams that Work*, pp. 21–36.

37 P. Christopher Earley and Elaine Mosakowski, "Creating hybrid team cultures: an empirical test of transnational team functioning," *Academy of Management Journal*, 2000, 43(1), pp. 26–49.

38 Victor Friedman and Ariane Berthoin Antal, "Negotiating reality: a theory of action approach to intercultural competence," *Management Learning*, 2005, 36(1), p. 69.

39 Adapted from Saphiere *et al.*, *Communication Highwire*, pp. 224–225.

40 Marco Polo, cited in Laurence Bergreen, *Marco Polo: From Venice to Xanadu*. New York, NY: Vintage Books, 2007, p. i.

CHAPTER 8

Leadership and global teams

- The meaning of leadership   245
- GLOBE leadership study   253
- Culture and leadership: a model   256
- Global teams   261
- Working with global teams   262
- MANAGER'S NOTEBOOK: Leadership and global teams   270

Human values, integrity, and innovation drive us … I win when my team wins; my team wins when Wipro wins; Wipro wins when its customers and stakeholders win.

Azim H. Premji[1]
CEO, Wipro Technologies, India

Getting Americans and Japanese to work together is like mixing hamburger with sushi.

Atsushi Kagayama[2]
Vice President, Panasonic Corporation, Japan
President, American Kotobuki, USA

If we collected all of the truly great business leaders of the world in one place, who would be their leader? Could they even choose a leader? Would everyone else become a follower or would we see the creation of a hierarchy of leaders? Can we say that there are leaders of leaders? If so, there must be leaders of leaders of leaders, and so forth, to the point that the concept of leadership itself becomes almost meaningless. Clearly, leadership is far more complex than simply saying that leaders boast certain characteristics or other qualities that make them stand out.

Leadership expert Warren Bennis has tried to capture this essence of leadership by noting that "leadership is like beauty; it's hard to define, but you know it when you see it."[3] Well, maybe. Research suggests that some cultures value leaders who take charge, are visible, and are assertive, while others want leaders who are essentially invisible and move behind the scenes (see discussion below). Some cultures want leaders who stand

241

above the crowd and demand respect, while others want leaders who are humble and remain part of the crowd. In point of fact, the variety that can be found in some of the best-known leaders in the world, business or otherwise, mirrors the variety that can be found across all peoples and societies.

What many leadership experts, both in the classroom and in the field, fail to do is pay sufficient attention to the context in which leadership is exercised. And located dead center within context is culture and cultural differences. In fact, a good way to get a more solid grasp on how leadership operates – or fails to operate – across cultures is to consider how leadership styles can vary across countries and regions. More specifically, what does organizational research have to say about systematic variations in cultures as they relate to leadership style?

Consider what happened when a Brazilian of Lebanese decent with a French passport was sent to Japan to turn around an ailing company. When the Japanese economy went into an economic tailspin several years ago in response to increasing competitive pressures and declining corporate revenues, economic growth slowed to a crawl as numerous local companies and industries faltered. Corporate growth rates slowed, the stock market stagnated, and many Japanese industrialists began to lose confidence in the formerly successful Japanese economic model. Among the corporate elite, venerable automobile maker Nissan suffered one of the greatest falls.[4] Significant expansion of its domestic markets had left the company with too many factories and workers as it was forced to battle for market share in the crowded Japanese auto market by keeping its prices down. Nissan also suffered from excess capacity in its European markets, while the high value of the yen made it difficult to export its way out of trouble. Meanwhile, an unexpected Asian currency crisis dried up demand for its cars throughout much of East and Southeast Asia. As a result, the company quickly found itself operating in the red.

In an effort to turn the company around, Nissan executives initiated a cost-cutting program and announced that it would cut the number of suppliers it would use in the future, thereby increasing the size and reducing the cost of orders from the remaining suppliers. The company also decided to trim its workforce and reduce the number of parts used in manufacturing to simplify its procurement procedures and reduce its inventory costs. Unfortunately, these efforts were implemented with only modest enthusiasm and failed to reduce costs significantly or return Nissan to profitability. Unable to overcome its mounting problems, Nissan finally suffered the ultimate indignity for a Japanese company; it was essentially taken over by a foreign company. Renault bought 37 percent of Nissan's common stock, thereby transferring control of Japan's second-largest automobile company to a French firm.

Shortly thereafter, Renault sent one of its most highly respected executives, Carlos Ghosn, to Tokyo to assume control over the ailing company as its new CEO. After spending several months reviewing Nissan operations, Ghosn announced a revival plan for the company that was designed to reduce annual operating costs by nearly US $10 billion. To accomplish this goal, Ghosn planned to close five Japanese factories and eliminate 16,000 jobs in Nissan's domestic operations. Mindful of Japan's distaste for layoffs and labor laws that make firing employees expensive, Ghosn decided that employment reductions would be achieved largely through attrition, which averaged close to 2,000 domestic employees per year. Early retirements were also considered, but were ruled out when local labor unions objected.

Other cost reductions included closing regional offices in New York and Washington, DC, and reducing the number of models produced. To reinforce the critical challenges facing the company, Ghosn announced that no one in purchasing, engineering, or administration would receive a pay raise until they could show what their contribution was to cost cutting. To cut Nissan's massive debt, Ghosn also began efforts to streamline the company's dealership networks in Japan, North America, and Europe. In Japan, one-half of the dealerships were closed, leading to considerable local protests.

Another problem emerged when Ghosn realized that Nissan had a product image that differed across countries, thereby making it difficult to launch cost-effective cross-border advertising campaigns. Worse still, he discovered that Nissan suffered from a brand deficiency, leading customers to value rival products more highly than his company's products. Ghosn responded by giving one firm exclusive worldwide advertising rights for Nissan in an effort to build a more unified brand image.

Ghosn then turned his attention to Nissan's supply chain. He estimated that Nissan's parts procurement costs were 10% higher than Renault's, and that by combining, centralizing, and globalizing Renault's and Nissan's parts procurement, he could achieve a cost reduction of 20%. To do so, however, he had to confront the very *keiretsu* system on which Nissan and other major Japanese conglomerates were built (see Chapter 6). This represented a major risk in view of the financial stake Nissan held in most of its *keiretsu* partners. His criticism of the *keiretsu* system was blunt: the purchase of parts through this antiquated system promoted inefficiency and mediocrity. Since supplier partners were guaranteed business, they often failed to innovate or cut costs. Nissan needed suppliers that were innovative, and Ghosn concluded that this would not happen with the current system. To this end, he announced that Nissan would liquidate its holdings in all but 4 of its 1,400 partners. In addition, Nissan would cut the number of its suppliers in half. Instead of purchasing the same part from several suppliers, the company would henceforth concentrate its purchases among a smaller number of suppliers, allowing them to achieve greater economies of scale and reduce their costs. Suppliers that could cut their costs by at least 20 percent would be guaranteed orders; others would not. The Japanese Government, as well as many labor unions, were alarmed. It was predicted that Ghosn's controversial plan would lead to tens of thousands of job losses as smaller inefficient suppliers closed their doors. Others predicted that Ghosn himself would be gone within a year; traditional Japanese business culture would force him out.

Still in control, however, Ghosn next addressed Nissan's traditional inward-looking corporate culture. After concluding that many executives were more interested in protecting their own departments than promoting overall corporate objectives, and that communication across divisions was poor, he set about initiating major changes in the way Nissan ran itself as a corporation. To accomplish this, he moved swiftly to redirect company managers' attention by refocusing their efforts on improving profits and enhancing customer satisfaction. He established a network of multinational, cross-functional teams to reexamine and reinvigorate each of the firm's principal activities, ranging from R&D to purchasing to manufacturing to distribution. These teams were also charged with the responsibility of reducing divisional barriers and building a global partnership for the future. Ghosn even began openly discussing a Western-style pay-for-performance compensation system for managerial and non-managerial employees alike to replace the existing seniority system that was so deeply entrenched in Japanese work culture. And to drive the point home that Nissan would become a truly global firm, not just a Japanese firm operating internationally, Ghosn suggested that henceforth the company's official language should be English, not Japanese.

While all of this was going on, and despite an incredibly busy work schedule, Ghosn began studying the Japanese language, never becoming proficient but learning enough to converse in simple ways and show employees his commitment to the firm and its Japanese culture. This also aided in his efforts to better understand local customs and practices.

Looking back on his efforts, what Ghosn had done in short order was to challenge the traditional Japanese approach to organization and management and force employees at all levels not to Westernize but to globalize – to build a new management system that focused more on the global than the local. The result was a new way of managing that ultimately led the company to record profits and an enhanced reputation around the world for quality and innovative products.

Despite this record of success, some critics suggest Carlos Ghosn's organizational changes will be transitory and that Japanese culture will eventually reassert control over the firm after he leaves. Others suggest that any outsider like Ghosn will never understand the Japanese business culture or have sufficient credibility to motivate Japanese managers and workers. Still others are not so sure, suggesting that it may indeed be easier for an outsider to effect genuine change in a large and complex organization than for a Japanese insider who is closely tied to the local culture. Despite such questions, Carlos Ghosn and Nissan continue to move forward.[5]

Today, the Nissan-Renault alliance is expanding into Russia and India, and more expansion and partnerships are envisioned. Carlos Ghosn was subsequently promoted to become the new CEO of Renault, but in the process opted to continue his role as CEO of Nissan at the same time. As a result, Ghosn has begun a dialogue about possibly moving himself upstairs (to something approaching a group chairman) and appointing two new and separate CEOs for Renault and Nissan. Still, Nissan's ultimate success will continue to rest on its willingness to change and adapt to meet the turbulent challenges ahead.

The meaning of leadership

An age-old debate in the management community involves the difference between management and leadership as concepts that are central to determining organizational effectiveness. For example, is Carlos Ghosn a leader, a manager, or both? To some, there are very stark differences between the two constructs of leadership and management; to others, these differences are negligible. Why? Some people see management as focusing on operational issues involved in getting things done through people (e.g., planning, decision making, controlling, coordinating, etc.), while leadership involves the influence processes through which managers accomplish this (i.e., "lead"). One is mundane; the other is sexy. Others see management and leadership as being so closely intertwined that it becomes almost impossible to separate the two: Good managers are good leaders, and vice versa.

There are two ways to view this ongoing debate. The first view (the academic approach) involves attempts to tease out structural and behavioral differences between these two constructs. That is, what do leaders do compared to what managers do? How does each contribute to organizational success or failure? And how do we train leaders? The second view (the managerial approach) involves recognizing that for global managers, the integration of these two issues is probably more important than differentiation. That is, on the street and in the workplace, managers must, in fact, do both if they are to succeed (one requires the other), and if they fail, all of this becomes moot.

Hence, the critical question becomes: How do we train managers, including their leadership capabilities?

Our approach here assumes the latter view; that is, we view leadership as an integral and inseparable part of good management. Some managers may be charismatic; others may not. Some situations or locations may suggest participative managers; others may not. And some cultures may value team-oriented managers; others may not. In our view, in the end what matters most is how individual managers can see and understand the on-the-ground situational and cultural realities and then capitalize on their own unique personal skills and abilities (including their approaches to leadership) to get the job done. With this in mind, we turn to a recent model of leadership that works towards this objective.

What is leadership?

More books have been written about leadership than any other management topic. Many of these books review the various (and numerous) theories of leadership, comparing the advantages and disadvantages of each. Others represent serious empirical studies of actual leader behavior. And still others offer the equivalent of a secret elixir designed to transform ordinary managers into extraordinary leaders. What most of these books fail to do, however, is recognize that the leadership construct can vary significantly across geographic regions. That is, much of what is written discusses or proposes a particular leadership model that has been constructed based on Western (most often American) beliefs, values, and cultures, and then offers this model to the world as a precursor to managerial and organizational effectiveness.

If we are in doubt about the systematic variability in what constitutes an effective leader, we need look no further that the observations by various leaders and managers from multiple countries:[6]

- In Mexico, everything is a personal matter. To get anything done here, the leader must be more of an instructor, teacher, and father figure than a boss.
- Malaysians expect their leaders to behave in a manner that is humble, modest, and dignified.
- Peruvian employees look for decisiveness and authority in their leaders, even to the point of strongly resisting attempts to introduce employee participation programs.
- Egyptians treat their leaders as heroes and worship them so long as they remain in power.
- Chinese leaders are expected to establish and nurture personal relationships, practice benevolence towards subordinates, be dignified and aloof but sympathetic, and treat the interests of employees like their own.

- Nigerians expect leaders to replicate within their organizations the same social patterns that are found in local villages and tribes.
- The French expect their leaders to be cultivated – highly educated in the arts and mathematics.
- Japanese leaders are expected to focus on developing a healthy relationship with their employees where employees and managers share the same fate. Top managers must have an ability to manage people by leading them. In addition, *symbolic leadership* is also frequently seen in Japan, where an executive or manager will take public responsibility for the failures or inadequacies of the group or company (as when a CEO resigns over a corporate scandal).
- Americans are generally schizophrenic in their choice of leaders; some like leaders who empower and encourage their subordinates, while others prefer leaders who are bold, forceful, confidant, and risk-oriented.
- The Dutch stress egalitarianism and are skeptical about the value and status of leaders. Terms like "leader" and "manager" can carry a stigma to the point that Dutch children will sometimes refuse to tell their schoolmates if their father or mother works as a manager.

So what is leadership? The difficulty in answering this question lies in differing meanings of the construct itself in different cultures. That is, leadership means different things to different people. In most Anglo-Saxon countries (e.g., the UK, the US, Australia) leadership generally has a positive connotation. Leaders tend to be respected, admired, and, indeed, sometimes revered, whether they are in the political or business arena. Clearly, this is not a universal truth, however, as the opposite view of leaders can also be found in these same countries, consistent with their individualistic values. However, a direct translation of the word "leader" into other languages can invoke a variety of images, including dictator, parent, expert, and "first among equals." Some of these terms have strong connotations of highly directive or authoritarian styles of leadership that many people reject. Leaders are not necessarily to be trusted. We wonder about their motives and true goals or of other potentially undesirable behaviors and characteristics.[7] At the same time, in many egalitarian societies terms like "followers" or "subordinates" are also seen as being inappropriate. For example, subordinates in the Netherlands are frequently referred to as "co-workers" (*medewerkers*), not subordinates.

With such a diversity of opinions concerning the characteristics of effective leaders, how is it possible to reach agreement on even a simple definition of leadership? Moreover, what does this diversity of views suggest about our ability to apply largely

Western-based leadership theories across borders? What does this say about our ability to develop leadership development programs that can be used effectively in various regions of the world? And what does this say about so-called leadership "gurus" who travel the world with their packaged leadership programs?

To make matters even more complex, not only does the term "leader" translate differently across various language groups, but the meanings that are construed from these translations can also differ, sometimes significantly. Daniel Etounga-Manguelle, a management consultant from Cameroon, observed that "culture is the mother; institutions are the children."[8] As cultures vary, so too do the institutions within those cultures. Since leadership represents a critical component of institutional and organizational functioning, it obviously also varies. For example, in individualistic societies, leadership typically refers to a single person who guides and directs the actions of others, often in a very visible way. In more collectivistic societies, however, leadership is often less associated with individuals and more closely aligned with group endeavors. In hierarchical societies, leaders are often seen as being separate and apart from their followers, while in more egalitarian societies, leaders are often seen as more approachable and less different. Visiting the royal palaces of the kings and queens of Denmark and Norway, for example, visitors are surprised to see small signs on the surrounding grounds that ask visitors to keep a respectable distance from the front or back entrance. Indeed, these grounds are open to the public. Compare this with a visit to palaces, royal and otherwise, in the US and the UK, where high fences and numerous armed guards signal that someone important – "different" – lives within. Indeed, the rather common Anglo-American celebration of the accomplishments of various leaders stands in stark contrast to Lao Tzu's ancient but still widely cited observation that "A leader is best when people barely know he exists, who talks little, and when his work is done and his aim fulfilled, people will say, 'We did this ourselves.'"

Leadership: East meets West

Why is this? According to French philosopher François Jullien, the different foundations of strategy, leadership, and decision making in Eastern and Western traditions can be traced to ancient Chinese and Greek thought. These foundations are based on the separate paths these two ancient civilizations followed in their efforts to make sense out of human behavior.[9]

Ancient Greece developed the concept of *eîdos* as an ideal form that humans should aspire to and achieve as *télos* (goal). In this scheme, the work of a leader or strategist consisted of bridging the gap between *télos* as an ideal state and reality (or actual practice), with a goal of achieving perfection. By contrast, this concept of an ideal or archetype that would serve as a model for action and a desirable final state of affairs never developed in ancient China. Instead, reality in China was seen as a process emanating from the interaction between opposing and complementary forces, or *yin* and *yang*. Order did not result from an ideal to be accomplished, but rather from a natural propensity of processes already in motion. Because the emphasis was on current processes evolving here and now, Chinese thinking focused on very concrete and specific situations of everyday life, rather than abstractions of the essence of an ideal form. And because Chinese thinking did not abstract and generalize in the search for the ultimate *eîdos*, traditional Chinese language did not include words for "essence," "God," "being," "ethics," and the like. Indeed, today's modern Chinese language only incorporates these concepts out of a need to translate concepts from Western languages. This helps explain the separate paths of social thought and practice in these two divergent regions of the world. In many cases, Western thinking is difficult to understand or interpret without reference to concepts like "the ideal." In the arts, for instance, the pursuit of the perfect canonical form lies behind the drawing and modelling of the nude human body in the West, while nudes are absent in Chinese traditional arts since, lacking a sense of ideal or essential form, they could only be seen as pornography.

In many ways, current management thought is based on the originally Greek concepts of the ideal and purposeful action. Strategy appears as the art of arranging means towards desired end states. Corporate vision and mission make for a concrete definition of organizational ideals. Executives manage by objectives, and leaders strive to actively move the firm closer to achieving business goals and ideals that are carefully and publicly defined and implemented. The Chinese tradition, on the other hand, emphasizes positioning oneself in the flow of reality in a more passive way, so that we can discover its coherence and benefit from its natural evolution. Rather than establishing a set of objectives for action, one has to flow within the potential of each situation and the dynamics that the situation affords. This metaphor continually appears in traditional Chinese texts of the general and his soldiers as benefiting from a given evolution of events rather than behaving with particular heroism or bravery. As such, leaders must locate themselves in such a position that the desired path of events becomes the only viable alternative, the same way that they do not force the enemy (militarily or commercially) into a situation where their only alternative is to behave bravely against us.

In this regard, consider the ancient writings of Sun Tzu, the famous Chinese warlord during the fourth century BCE. Sun Tzu was a military general known for his battlefield prowess and continual victories. He is reputed to be the author of *The Art of War*, a classic book on the art of warfare that some Westerners believe provides significant insights into corporate strategy and successful management in competitive global markets.[10] Sun Tzu suggested three basic principles of leadership. First, it is important for leaders to have moral influence over their followers, controlling their hearts, not just their bodies. Second, leaders must be well rounded, instead of merely having technical knowledge. And finally, leaders must understand that everyone – both friends and enemies – has strengths and weaknesses, and it is paramount to know when and where one has a competitive advantage. He is reputed to have said that when you know your enemy (i.e., competitors) as well as you know yourself, you will always win.[11] Somewhat ironically, Sun Tzu and Confucius, coming from about the same time period, shared many common beliefs. They both believed in order and hierarchy, self-control, a sense of moral justice, a holistic approach to organized life, and behavior directed towards a common good.

The leader in the Chinese tradition does not begin by delineating an action plan based on a particular set of agreed upon objectives (the *logic of application*). Instead, he or she assesses the favorable and unfavorable elements in the surrounding situation so that the favorable elements can be appropriated as the situation evolves (the *logic of exploitation*). There is no sense of goal or finality, but a constant benefiting from the natural evolution of events. The result is assumed to be somehow preordained in the situation that contains it, and again we see the metaphor of battles already won or lost before actually being fought, for the winner benefits from the internal propensity of the situation rather than from some particular course of action that was wisely planned and implemented. As a result, while leaders in the West often follow a *logic of means and ends* hierarchically arranged through an action plan, leaders in China tend to follow a *logic of process* where the evolution of the situation leads naturally to the desired end state, practically without the need for action.[12]

At the same time, achievement or performance in the Western tradition results from minimizing the gap between the goal and the achievement, the planned and the attained. Action in the West is seen as a separate entity, an external disruption to the natural order of things. In China, by contrast, achievement or performance results from a minimization of action itself, leaving the situation to achieve its full potential in terms that benefit the organization. Chinese leaders thus focus on continual processes following their own internal dynamics, uninterrupted. Western action is seen from a Chinese perspective as being extemporaneous, quick, direct, and costly, while the Chinese "effortless action" is slow, indirect, progressive, and natural. Western leaders act; Chinese leaders transform. Transformation as opposed to action extends itself through time, as if without a beginning and end, imposing itself albeit in natural ways. Because it comes from the inside of the situation, it imposes itself softly, without resistance. Changes emanate by themselves and do not require heroic efforts and determination, in a continuous progression that is barely noticed. This does not mean that the concept of action is not present in traditional Chinese thought. But it is a subdued type of action: slow, subtle, anticipatory, naturally inserted in the natural flow of events. Rather than sudden action, occasions are anticipated, providing for the outcome of what will naturally appear. As a result, Chinese leaders pursue objectives in modest ways, silent and almost anonymous, *vis-à-vis* the grandiloquent apparatus and appearance of the heroic decision maker often seen or imagined in the West. Action is freed from activism and becomes discrete and subtle, confounded in the course of events, ignorant of particular protagonists. Confucius addressed this issue when he suggests that an ideal sovereign lets order reign by itself, without the need for action. And Confucian disciple Mencius (or Meng Ke; 372–289 BCE) talks of the need to clean and water around the plant rather than pulling from its sprouts in order to help its growth, not unlike the Japanese concept of *nemawashi*.

As a result of these differences and traditions, François Jullien suggests that leadership in parts of the East (China in particular) and the West (notably Western Europe as envisioned by Julien, but perhaps also including North America) follow different patterns of behavior. We see, for instance, a differential appreciation for action that is modest rather than grandiloquent, for leaders that prefer the naturalness of process and evolution to the abruptness of radical change. Of course, this naturalness and modesty is also expected to translate into specific personal behaviors of those at the top of the organization. This view on action and performance also tells us about the origins of particularly Chinese modes of attribution, accentuating the force of situations and circumstances over the behavior of isolated individuals. If one pursued other distinctive cultures, such as those of the Middle East or Sub-Saharan Africa or South America, other notable differences would likely be found until we reached the inescapable conclusion that cultural differences play a critical role in both leader behavior and decision strategies.

Leadership: West meets West

In one of Europe's more curious laws, in 1949 France banned children's books and comic strips from presenting cowardice in a favorable light, and backed up the law with a penalty of one year in prison for errant publishers.[13] The law also made it illegal to make laziness or dishonesty look attractive. The law further created an oversight committee to watch for positive depictions of these ills, along with various crimes, theft, hatred, debauchery, and other acts that were "liable to undermine morality" among the young. Taken literally, the law suggested that an ideal comic-book hero would resemble an overgrown boy scout, whose adventures involve pluck, fair play, restrained violence, and no sex. And the law still stands today.

Enter Tintin, a Belgian comic-book hero who enjoyed spectacular success in post-war Europe, and who remains very popular today. Tintin's slightly priggish character suited the times. His simple ethical code – seek the truth, protect the weak, and stand up to bullies – appealed to a continent waking up from the darkness of war. His wholesome qualities help explain the great secret of his commercial success – that he was, and remains, one of the rare comic books that adults are happy to buy for children. But probity alone cannot explain why Tintin became a cultural landmark in much of Europe, as important on his side of the Atlantic as Superman is on the other. There were many wholesome comics in post-war Europe, most of whom have long been forgotten. Something else in Tintin spoke to children and adults in continental Europe. Even in the straitened years of post-war reconstruction, he was soon selling millions of books a year.

Admirers of this local hero point to the quality of the drawing in Tintin, and the tense pacing of the plots, and they are right. It is all there: the dangerous glamour of cities at night; the terror of a forced drive into the forest; a world of tapped hotel telephones and chain-smoking killers in the lobby downstairs. But this alone fails to explain Tintin's success in Europe. For, despite his good qualities, Tintin never made a big hit in the Anglo-Saxon world. In Britain, he is reasonably well known, but as a minority taste, bound within narrow striations of class: his albums are bought to be tucked into boarding school trunks or read after Saturday morning violin lessons. And in the US, Tintin is largely unknown.

All societies reveal themselves through their children's books, and Europe's infatuation with Tintin is more revealing than most. An exploration of Tintin's hold on continental affections begins not with culture, but with history. For all the talk about morality, France's law on children's books had ideological roots. It was initiated by an odd alliance of Communists, Catholic conservatives, and jobless French cartoonists, determined that French children should be reading works imbued with "national" values, not Anglo-Saxon ones.

Unlike the US comic character Spiderman, Tintin is not an outsider or a rebel against the established order. He defends monarchs against revolutionaries (earning a knighthood in one book). His first instinct on catching a villain is to hand him over to the nearest police chief. He does not carry a weapon. Though slight in stature, he has a very gentlemanly set of fighting skills, including knowing how to box, sail, drive racing cars, pilot planes, and ride horses. He has few chances to rescue damsels in distress, moving in an almost entirely male world, but is quick to defend small children from unearned beatings. In this endeavor, his quick wits compensate for his lack of brawn.

Now, filmmaker Steven Spielberg is considering making a movie of Tintin. Spielberg first secured an option to film Tintin shortly before its creator's death in 1983, but no progress has been made. Why? The delays seem to have been caused by American puzzlement with the film's main character. The *Hollywood Reporter*, a trade publication, described the film as being about a young Belgian reporter and world traveler who is aided in his adventures by his faithful dog, and explained that this storyline is hugely popular in Europe.

Not so in America, it seems. To many European observers, the story of Tintin is more nuanced than American comic strips (or movies). A leader? Yes. A terminator? No. The American style of telling a story can at times threaten European sensibilities. They tend to be more violent and are much more aggressively paced. As a result, few in Europe seem to be awaiting an American version of a European hero. Meanwhile, Tintin has never fallen foul of the 1949 French law. He is not a coward, and his comics do not make that vice appear in a favorable light. But he is a pragmatist, albeit a principled one. Perhaps Anglo-Saxon audiences want something more from their fictional – and real – heroes. They want them imbued with the power to change events, and inflict total defeat on the wicked. But Tintin cannot offer something so unrealistic. In that, he is a very European hero.

GLOBE leadership study

So, what can we conclude from these examples about the meaning of leadership? For starters, we learn to be cautious about a one-size-fits-all portrait of successful leaders. A leader is not always a leader. And recent research seems to back this up. One of the more intriguing modern studies of leadership behavior across borders was conducted by a multicultural team of researchers who led the Global Leadership and Organizational Behavior Effectiveness Project, or GLOBE for short. This project examined the relationship between culture and successful leadership and management patterns in sixty-two countries around the world. For purposes of the study, *leadership* was defined as the ability of an individual manager to influence, motivate, and enable others within the organization to contribute toward the effectiveness and success of the enterprise.[14] Leadership is seen as an integral part of a manager's responsibilities. Their initial research led them to propose the nine GLOBE cultural dimensions, discussed in Chapter 3.

Based on this, the researchers then identified twenty-two leadership attributes that were widely seen as being universally applicable across cultures (e.g., encouraging, motivational, dynamic, decisive, having foresight) and eight leadership dimensions that were seen to be universally undesirable (e.g., uncooperative, ruthless, dictatorial, irritable). But several other attributes were found to be culturally contingent; that is, their desirability of undesirability was tied to cultural differences. These included characteristics like ambitious and elitist.[15] Here it was found that people in some cultures favored traits in leaders that people in other cultures rejected. For example, some cultures (e.g., the UK, Germany, France, the USA) often romanticize their leaders and give them exceptional privileges and prestige; they are held in high esteem. At the same time, however, others cultures (e.g., the Netherlands, Switzerland) denigrate the very concept of leadership and are often suspicious of people in authority. They worry about abuse of power and rising inequality.

Finally, the GLOBE researchers distilled their findings into six relatively distinct leadership dimensions: autonomous, charismatic/value-based, humane, participative, self-protective, and team-oriented (see Exhibit 8.1). Two of these leadership styles (charismatic/value-based leadership and team-oriented leadership) were strongly endorsed in all regional country clusters used in the study. Even so, the magnitude of this endorsement varied across regional country clusters. For example, both charis-matic/value-based and team-oriented leadership styles were most widely accepted in the Anglo, Asian, and Latin American clusters. They were still accepted in other regions of the world, but with less intensity.

Meanwhile, the other leadership styles were found to be more culturally contingent. Humane leadership was strongly endorsed in the Asian, Anglo, and Sub-Saharan African clusters, and less strongly endorsed in the Latin American and Nordic clusters. Autonomous leadership was generally seen as neither facilitating nor inhibiting a leader from being effective. However, within the Eastern European and Germanic clusters, this leadership style was considered to be more positively related to outstanding leadership than in other culture clusters. Finally, for self-protective leadership and participative leadership, there was substantial variability in the degree to which they were endorsed within the different country clusters.

Exhibit 8.1 GLOBE leadership dimensions

GLOBE leadership dimensions	Characteristics of dimensions	Regions where leadership dimensions are widely endorsed
Autonomous leadership	Individualistic, independent, unique.	Endorsed in Eastern European and Germanic clusters; weaker endorsement in Latin American cluster.
Charismatic/value-based leadership	Visionary, inspirational, self-sacrificing, decisive, performance-oriented.	Endorsed in all regions, but particularly in Anglo, Asian, and Latin American clusters; weaker endorsement in Arab cluster.
Humane leadership	Modest, tolerant, sensitive, concerned about humanity.	Endorsed particularly in Anglo, Asian, and Sub-Saharan African clusters; less so elsewhere.
Participative leadership	Active listening, non-autocratic, flexible.	Wide variations in endorsements across all regions, but less so in Arab and Latin American clusters.
Self-protective leadership	Self-centered, procedural, status-conscious, face-saving.	Wide variations in endorsements across all regional clusters.
Team-oriented leadership	Collaborative, integrating, diplomatic.	Endorsed in all regions, but particularly in Anglo, Asian, and Latin American clusters; less so in Arab cluster.

Source: Adapted from House *et al., Culture, Leadership and Organizations.*

Thus, the GLOBE study provides some evidence that acceptable managerial behaviors – including leader behaviors – are to some degree culturally contingent. To see how this works in actual practice, consider two examples.

A good example of charismatic or value-based leadership can be seen in British entrepreneur Richard Branson, best known for his Virgin brand. Branson's first successful business venture came at the age of 15, when he published a magazine called *Student*. He later set up a mail-order record business in 1970, followed shortly thereafter with a chain of record stores, Virgin Records (later called Zavvi). With his flamboyant and competitive style, Branson's Virgin brand rapidly grew to include 360 different companies. Ever the opportunist, Branson recently registered the business name "Virgin Interplanetary" in case space travel becomes commercially viable. Today, he is estimated to be worth close to US$8 billion. Branson is passionate about life and living every minute to its fullest. He continues to get adrenaline rushes through his world record-breaking attempts by boat and hot air balloon. Several distance and speed records have been attempted and achieved, but his attempt to be the first person to circumnavigate the world in a hot air balloon failed. Branson makes each record attempt a media event, with his Virgin logo prominently displayed during every launch, which has been an excellent source of free advertising and brand placement for the Virgin Group. He was awarded a knighthood for his contribution to entrepreneurship. Why is Virgin one of the world's most recognized brands around the world? The answer is simple: Branson strives to be the best rather than the biggest, working towards making profits in small pieces of large markets. Now able to use the success of his brand to attract investors and negotiate controlling shares and the management of the company, Branson leaves his partners to supply the majority of the capital. A flamboyant, charismatic character, Branson believes in self-promotion, having fun, and risking it all to achieve his goals. This has, however, meant that he has also experienced failure, as his ventures in vodka, computers, and magazines demonstrate. Still, his positive attitude and ability to apply large amounts of enthusiasm to each project allows him to attract both investors and followers who seek to be part of his exciting – and Anglo-centric – world. For Branson, charisma works.

By contrast, a good example of humane leadership can be seen in the management and leadership style of Konosuke Matsushita, founder of the Matsushita Business Group (now Panasonic Corporation).[16] True to his culture, Matsushita encouraged his employees at all levels to think long term and to visualize the results of any projects, not just to ask how to build something. Indeed, he once challenged his employees to develop a business plan for the company "that would last a thousand years." Obviously, he had no intention of the plan lasting so long; rather, he wanted to encourage his employees to focus on competing for the future. And Matsushita's management style was just as unusual as his approach to strategic planning. He stressed what he called the seven spiritual values of his company: national service through industry; fairness in all things; harmony and cooperation in social relations; struggle for betterment; courtesy and humility; adjustment and assimilation; and gratitude to those who participate. To develop these spiritual values, Matsushita established a management training school for his employees based on Buddhist principles, something not seen in the West. In doing so, he placed his personal reputation behind his company's determination to achieve greatness on behalf of both company and country.

Culture and leadership: a model

Building on the foregoing discussion and other available research on culture and leadership, it is possible to create a general framework to describe the interactive relationships between leaders, followers, and their environments as influenced by cultural differences (see Exhibit 8.2).[17] Normative beliefs and values concerning leaders' behavior emerge as a result of a society's unique cultural characteristics (e.g., individual

Exhibit 8.2 Cultural influences on leadership

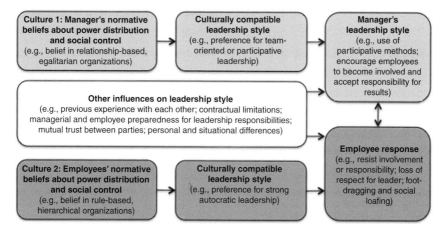

characteristics, environmental characteristics, and unique work norms and values – see Chapter 3). These beliefs include appropriate leader behaviors and subordinate responsibilities, key situational variables that must be attended to, and prevailing practices in terms of how leaders are selected and trained. These beliefs, in turn, influence the selection of culturally consistent leadership strategies (e.g., use of appropriate leadership style, rewards, and so forth) and preparedness (e.g., leadership training, lessons from previous efforts) that ultimately influence leadership behaviors, as well as the outcomes of leadership efforts (e.g., employee ownership of leader goals, increased goal-directed effort, increased organizational performance, etc.).

While this is occurring, team members or other targets of leadership efforts are also viewing the world and workplace based on their own normative beliefs. As with the leader, team members also determine what strategies and preparedness they require to respond to any leader behavior. These responses, acted out at a cultural crossroads, can include support or opposition to a leader's initiatives, a degree of common agreement on future courses of action, increased group cohesiveness, and possible conflict with the team leader.

Finally, individual and organizational learning on both sides feeds back to influence future preparedness and action. Once again, while this may look like a fairly simple linear series of actions, in real life such interactions are obviously more complex and interactive. Even so, the diagram is meant to highlight several of the more common factors that are involved in this process.

Thus, the GLOBE study discussed above represents a popular and useful approach to understanding cultural differences as they relate to leadership effectiveness. In addition, the discussion here on leaders, followers, and the exchange process goes one step further by outlining a process by which culture can influence leader efforts and effectiveness. Beyond this, however, is a large and reasonably rigorous body of research on the culture-leadership relationship by some of the best management scholars around the world. Their collective findings indicate some general, but certainly not universal, trends in this relationship relating to the use of leadership strategies.

For example, leaders in mastery-oriented cultures like those in North America and parts of Western Europe can often demand excellence from their employees and establish a competitive work environment to encourage greater effort, while such efforts may, in fact, fail to produce the desired results in other countries that stress harmony, like Mexico or China. Here, successful leaders tend to build a mutually supportive work environment and stress a balance between accomplishing key business goals and maintaining social harmony. Likewise, leaders in monochronic cultures, again like those found in North America, often try to establish clear task-directed goals and specific deadlines for task accomplishment, while leaders in more polychronic cultures like France or Italy more frequently expect delays in meeting goals and must accommodate greater interactions between work goals and non-work activities.

Considering the important influence of culture in determining what is expected of leaders, how can a leader be successful across cultures? In many cases, successful managers develop an awareness of cultural differences and adapt their leadership styles to the extent possible to match local conditions. However, this strategy is not always the best. In some cases, a manager is sent abroad to promote change, and not fitting the local culture may be the manager's most important competitive advantage. In these circumstances, "going native" may not be the best alternative. Consider again the example of Carlos Ghosn. When confronted with the challenge of leading Nissan, Ghosn had to make an important decision: Should he adapt to the Japanese style of management and leadership, should he impose his own culturally based views of management, or should he do something else?

Rob Goffee and Gareth Jones suggest that the key to leadership success lies in the ability to conform just enough to the local environment so as not to be rejected by the local culture.[18] However, conforming too much can undermine the leader's potential to make important changes in the organization. Indeed, some claim that Ghosn's success in changing Nissan was due – in part – to his position as an outsider to the culture. Goffee and Jones suggest a leader's behavior when facing a new culture falls into three main categories: freeze, please, or tease. Some leaders are so in awe of their destination that they *freeze*, they lose their ability to act and be themselves, and lose the very leadership attributes that took them there in the first place. Others are so eager to fit the new culture that they *please*; they go native and adopt wholeheartedly the new culture and miss the opportunities to make a contribution by promoting change. Frequently, managers are sent abroad or charged with global operations because of some personal characteristics and particular way of doing things that is linked to his or her cultural background. Losing these abilities may not be in the organization or followers' best interests. Finally, successful leaders *tease*. That is, they conform enough to the key aspects of the cultural context, allowing them to engage and gain leverage, which is then used to promote change.

The idea here is that leaders must conform enough to the new cultural milieu, gaining acceptance as a member in order to make the necessary connections to make changes. As Goffee and Jones put it, "Leaders who succeed in changing organizations challenge norms – but not all of them, all at once."[19] Instead, effective leaders understand what about the culture can be changed and what cannot – and operate within those constraints. Carlos Ghosn did just that. He studied Japanese and respected the Japanese culture at the same time that he implemented important changes to the organization that were at odds with Japanese culture.

Leading across borders can be a daunting task. Consider the experience of British-born Howard Stringer. Since being promoted from president of Sony's US operations to become Sony Corporation's first foreign chief executive, he has been slammed by Japanese financial analysts and Sony employees for being disconnected from the company's daily operations, especially during two big crises. Investors in the US, meanwhile, have put him under constant pressure to fix Sony's financial and techno-logical problems more quickly. And he has consistently received conflicting advice from both sides. "Look, in America, I was told to cut costs, but in Japan, I was told not to cut costs. Two different worlds. In this country (Japan), you can't lay people off very easily. In America, you can," observed a frustrated Stringer. He bristles at criticism – mostly from Japan – that he lives in a hotel when in Tokyo and spends too much time in New York and London to run the company effectively. "If I'm not running the company, who the hell is?"[20]

Fixing this iconic Japanese company represents a major challenge, regardless of who is in charge. Stringer's dilemma is that he is caught between different management styles and cultures. He says he recognizes the risk of falling behind amid breakneck changes in electronics. But he also says there's an equal risk in moving too aggressively. "I don't want to change Sony's culture to the point where it's unrecognizable from the founder's vision," he says. "That's the balancing act I'm doing."

Whether he can pull off a successful turnaround is still an open question. For the Welsh-born executive, the task is complicated by having to navigate a sea of obstacles, from uncommunicative top executives to poor public-relations advice. The risk to Sony from his management-through-persuasion is that the company could fall further behind nimbler and more aggressive rivals. He has already shifted gears once, adopting a more assertive stance after his softly-softly approach faltered.

When he became CEO, Stringer started cautiously. He knew that, despite its global brand name, Sony remained a traditional Japanese company, full of employees with lifetime tenure who were suspicious of change. Japan had opened up to the idea of having foreign managers run Japanese companies, notably Carlos Ghosn at Nissan (see above), but it hadn't necessarily embraced the Western style of management. Stringer, 65 years old, was stuck with the executive team he inherited. He tried gently persuading managers to cooperate with one another and urged them to think about developing products in a new way.

The risks inherent in that approach quickly became clear. Two major missteps – a delayed launch of the PlayStation 3 videogame console and an embarrassing battery recall – tarnished his first few years in charge. In both cases, managers tried handling problems in the traditional Sony way: quietly and without informing top executives. Stringer counseled patience to his critics, noting that his turnaround of Sony's US operations took five years to complete. "You can't go through a Japanese company with a sledgehammer." Even so, his forbearance seems to be wearing thin. "I'm going to do what I want to do now. I'm not going to be following everybody's suggestions. I've got to be true to myself in some ways."

Stringer says nothing has changed in his management style since his arrival in Tokyo. The perception of him as a hands-off manager was fueled by his decision to live in a Tokyo hotel. The CEO says he now regrets that decision, but also rejects as "insane" the notion that he wasn't firmly in control. He says his response to the crises wasn't a change of heart but a quickening of his long-term plans. He adds that his record has been obscured by the battery crisis, "which took too long for bizarre Japanese reasons that I don't want to spend the rest of my life discussing."

Global teams

Most large firms make use of teams to manage and operate many aspects of their global operations. Sometimes these teams consist of groups of employees from one country or culture who join forces to work on an issue of local or global nature (e.g., developing a business strategy for the Baltic region, launching a new product or service in Southeast Asia, etc.). Other times, teams are made of individuals from different parts of the world who work together to achieve a common goal. In this chapter, we focus on the latter; that is, teams consisting of sometimes highly diverse members from different countries or cultures who work together either co-located (at the same physical location) or virtually (from different locations and mediated through information technology).

A *global team* is a group of employees selected from two or more cultural contexts and sometimes two or more companies who work together to coordinate, develop, or manage some aspect of a firm's global operations.[21] Companies usually turn to such teams either when they need specific cross-cultural expertise on some aspect of the business (e.g., developing a new product marketing strategy for a particular geographic region) or when they partner with a foreign firm (e.g., form a strategic alliance or international joint venture). Many firms prefer using such teams because they can often do a better job than "local" teams consisting exclusively of either home or host country nationals. Multicultural global teams can provide an opportunity to integrate widely differing social, cultural, and business perspectives into key decisions affecting the success of international operations.

Global teams come in a variety of shapes, forms, and sizes. Some companies use multicultural or transnational development teams or product launch teams to help develop or refine products that are aimed at multiple international markets. Other firms use multicultural functional business teams in such areas as international marketing or core R&D technology development. Multicultural teams bring cultural diversity to help solve specific challenges, and exist naturally in both regional and global headquarters of many transnational firms, and in various international strategic alliances and joint ventures.[22] Multicultural teams also bring international expertise to decision making and managerial actions that can otherwise be missing in less diverse teams. These benefits – and some disadvantages – are summarized in Exhibit 8.3.

Recruiting and staffing global teams is only the first challenge faced by global firms. Beyond this, strategies and mechanisms must be developed to create truly effective work teams – to get members from divergent cultures to actually work together as a team. Global teams face two fundamental challenges in order to accomplish their mission.

Exhibit 8.3 Global teams: functions, advantages, and drawbacks

Team functions	Advantages and drawbacks of global teams
Creativity and problem solving	Frequently more creative in developing ideas and solutions.
Group cohesiveness	Often more difficult to develop closely knit groups.
Understanding foreign markets	Often increases understanding of global markets.
International marketing	Often more effective in working with international customers.
Decision-making effectiveness	Frequently takes longer to make decisions or reach consensus, but resulting decisions are often more comprehensive, realistic, and acceptable to all.
Time to implementation	Action plans can take longer to implement.
Work habits	Different work habits can lead to conflicts and misunderstandings.
Managing employees	Often better understanding of multinational employees.

First, they must identify their areas of responsibilities and organize their members. Second, they must develop productive group processes to facilitate collective efforts towards goal attainment. Managing tasks involves making sure that all team members understand why the group was formed. This includes clarifying the mission and goals of the team, setting a clear agenda and operating rules for team management, clarifying individual roles and responsibilities, clarifying how decisions will be made, and identifying who is responsible for task accomplishment (see Exhibit 8.4). By contrast, managing group processes include developing and completing team-building activities, understanding communication flows and patterns among group members, facilitating participation across team members, specifying methods of conflict resolution, and clarifying how and when performance will be assessed.[23]

Working with global teams

Despite their name, most multinational corporations probably have more national (or single-nation) teams than they do multinational teams. This is not surprising since, in many ways, multinationals are collections of multiple companies with multiple local operations. Hence, if we look at marketing teams within Velux America, a division of the Danish manufacturer of skylights and solar water heaters, it is not surprising that most of these teams are comprised exclusively of Americans. The same can be said for Velux Company Ltd., the division covering the UK and Ireland. Team members are almost exclusively English, Irish, Scottish, or Welsh. Indeed, within this sphere, all of the local marketing teams in Ireland are specifically Irish. This practice makes sense in terms of understanding and serving local markets. However, within the larger Velux

Exhibit 8.4 Challenges to global team effectiveness

Management issues	Challenges to global team effectiveness
Managing tasks	
Mission and goal setting	Identifying team mission, goals, and objectives; identifying performance expectations.
Task structuring	Agenda setting; creating operating rules and procedures; time management procedures.
Roles and responsibilities	Division of labor; responsibility charting; team interdependencies; role of leader.
Decision making	Delegation of authority; selection and role of a leader; how decisions should be made.
Accountability	Identifying who is responsible for task accomplishment.
Managing group processes	
Team building	Team-building activities; trust building; opportunities for social interaction.
Communication patterns	Selection of a working language; challenges of language fluency; appropriate use of information technologies.
Participation	Guaranteeing everyone a voice; balancing quiet and more vocal members; getting the best from everyone.
Conflict resolution	Accommodating legitimate differences of opinion; managing constructive conflict; eliminating destructive conflict; strategies for compromise.
Performance evaluation	How and when to evaluate performance; one-way vs. two-way evaluations; role of feedback; who evaluates performance.

Source: Based on Schneider and Barsoux, *Managing Across Cultures*.

operations, *global* marketing strategies and coordination across various local divisions requires teams composed of people from across the company's marketing regions.

Co-located and virtual global teams

Not only do teams vary in their degree of heterogeneity and tasks, but they also vary regarding the location of their team members. At one extreme, team members are all located in the same place and meet face to face to accomplish most of the tasks. (This is sometimes referred to as a traditional team.) At the other extreme, teams are dispersed around the global and seldom – or never – meet face to face. Instead, tasks are accomplished virtually, with the help of information and communications technologies such as email, telephone, and video conferencing (see Chapter 7). Exhibit 8.5 illustrates the types of teams found in global organizations, according to the degree of heterogeneity and geographic dispersion.

In real life, however, teams may not always fit neatly into these boxes. Both virtuality and heterogeneity are a matter of degree. For instance, a co-located team may meet face

Exhibit 8.5 Types of national and global teams

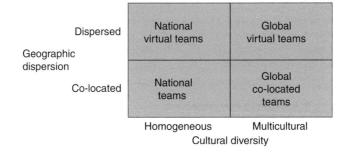

to face periodically but accomplish a significant amount of tasks independently and communicate primarily through email and telephone, even though they are working in the same building. Likewise, so-called local teams may include members from different cultural backgrounds even though they may live in the same town. However, our principal focus here is with the right-hand side of this exhibit, dealing with both forms of global teams: *co-located global teams* and *virtual global teams* (see Exhibit 8.6).

Special challenges of working with virtual global teams

An increasingly popular approach to global teams today is the *virtual global team*. The virtual global team takes advantage of technology to draw knowledge and resources from different parts of the organization and different geographical locations without relocating workers. Virtual global teams are characterized by a collaborative network of people dispersed across spatial, temporal, cultural, and organizational boundaries, working together to achieve common ends. In other words, while co-located teams emphasize time, virtual teams emphasize space.

While culture does play a role in the acceptance and use of technologies and work arrangements, technology also influences culture and norms of behavior in a reciprocal fashion. As people incorporate technologies into their lives, they develop new ways of dealing and relating to tasks and people. For example, a few years ago, when people needed information, they went to the nearest library. Today, most people go first to Google or some other internet search engine. The way – and frequency – we get information has changed. Similarly, the persistent use of technology may very well shape the way individuals work and relate, changing the way cultures interact.

For managers, this means great opportunities but also challenges. As technology changes the way work is organized, managers need to help members to make sense of new ways of working and relating to the organization.[24] Not only is our relationship

Exhibit 8.6 Characteristics of co-located and virtual teams

Global team characteristics	Co-located global teams	Virtual global teams
Team location and working patterns	Team members work regularly in close proximity; strong reliance on face-to-face interactions.	Team members work separately from various locations; strong reliance on virtual communications technology.
Team composition	Heterogeneous; multicultural.	Heterogeneous; multicultural.
Required skills for interaction	Emphasis on interpersonal and intercultural skills.	Emphasis on interpersonal, intercultural, and also technical skills.
Principal uses	When face-to-face discussions are important and possible, building trust and relationships are important, and decision time horizons can vary.	When key players are unable to co-locate, when contextual information from different locations is important, when tasks are well defined and can be accomplished independently, when ambiguity is low.
Principal team challenges	Communicating, making decisions, and taking actions in a largely face-to-face environment, where interpersonal styles can differ significantly (e.g., non-verbal communication; language subtleties, preserving or losing face).	Communicating, making decisions, and taking actions in a largely distributed and often computer-mediated environment, where interpersonal style, communication, and body language are largely unseen. Developing cross-cultural understanding and sensitivity from a distance. Developing productive working relationships from a distance. Understanding communications and reaching decisions in a largely computer-mediated environment.
Principal leadership challenges	Sensitivity to cross-cultural differences. Accommodate divergent viewpoints. Coordinate interpersonal group dynamics and keep members on-task. Master intercultural communications by listening for contextual messages behind content messages. Lead group efforts to achieve targeted objectives.	Sensitivity to cross-cultural differences. Accommodate divergent viewpoints. Coordinate computer-mediated group dynamics and keep members on-task. Master intercultural communications by reading between the lines on written messages and video-conferencing. Lead group efforts to achieve targeted objectives.

with technology likely to change, but our relationship with work and with each other will have to be adjusted. Managers will be in charge of keeping it together, preventing dispersed forces from pulling organizations apart, and holding the organization together through effective communication, clear goals, and shared meaning.

Exhibit 8.7 Special challenges facing virtual global teams

Challenges	Explanation
Lack of mutual knowledge	Lack of understanding of team members' personal or cultural environment (lack of mutual knowledge) may hinder the ability to interpret perspectives, positions, behaviors, and information.
Lack of contextual information	Contextual information, particularly in high-context cultures, may not be available to observe or interpret, leading to erroneous assumptions of cultural similarities.
Over-dependence on technology	Technological failures may cause information leaks garbled messages, and communication gaps.
Loss of detail	Loss of detail due to the increased brevity of messages when compared to face-to-face messages and conversations.
Lack of shared understanding	Lack of back channel communication can lead to an over-simplification of messages that can make information difficult to interpret.

Successful global managers understand that technology alone will not do the trick. It does not matter how good the technology is, and how effectively the task may get done; it is important to remember that individuals are behind the computer. As such, human dynamics and relational issues are just as important – or more so – than the technology and the task-related issues at hand.[25] In other words, the leader in a virtual team is a social problem solver and needs to create the conditions for workers to succeed in a virtual environment.

Perhaps the biggest challenge of working with virtual teams is that members, spread across different boundaries, have to learn a completely different way of interacting, overriding age-old human preferences for social interaction. Virtual teams can be classified in terms of two dimensions: their members' geographic dispersion and the extent of utilization of information and communications technology.[26] Each of these dimensions presents potentially beneficial and detrimental influences on the perform-ance of virtual teams (see Exhibit 8.7).

Lack of mutual knowledge

When team members are dispersed across distance, they typically work in different contexts, live in different time zones, and have access to different information.[27] Geographically dispersed teams are able to take advantage of these differences to obtain and use knowledge from multiple contexts. Whereas co-located teams must search for and may miss important market, cultural, and contextual information, teams with greater geographic reach have access to diverse knowledge. While greater geographic reach provides access to more diverse information, dispersed team members lack mutual knowledge, which can lead to an obstruction of information flow. Also known as common ground, mutual knowledge is the knowledge individuals have in common and are aware that they share.[28] In other words, mutual knowledge refers to the common basis of information that does not have to be repeated when communicating.

Lack of contextual information

When communicating across distance, people also have a tendency to omit *context* or *contextual information* from their messages and discussions, erroneously assuming similarities between locales. This is particularly important in high-context cultures, as discussed in Chapter 7. To make matters worse, when contextual information is communicated, it is frequently ignored or forgotten. It is difficult to imagine remote partners' contexts, and even harder to update our mental picture of their contexts as their situation changes.[29] This difficulty in understanding the other's situation also hinders our ability to identify which aspects of our own situation need to be explained. This lack of mutual knowledge frequently creates conflict, as remote partners fail to understand why others fail to honor deadlines, insist on particular points, or drop out of communication without warning.[30] For example, if you have an onsite meeting at 8:00 a.m. on a particularly bad weather day and a colleague is late, you quickly infer that your colleague must be stuck in traffic or is having difficulties arriving because of the weather. However, when your online colleague does not show up at the scheduled time and has no way of contacting you, you do not have any contextual information to make sense of the absence and may erroneously attribute his or her absence to a lack of interest or responsibility. Similarly, while we do not expect an answer during an important local holiday, we may not be aware of other countries' holidays and may misinterpret the other side's silence.

Global virtual teams are also likely to face important cultural differences. While a wealth of academic and practitioner literature recognizes and discusses the challenges of working abroad and working with people from different cultures, much less is known about how we deal with other cultures without the benefit of "seeing" how different things are abroad. In face-to-face cross-cultural situations, managers are advised to rely on contextual information in order to make sense of the communication. However, in virtual communications, such contextual information is not available, and we may not be looking for it, despite the fact that it is still there. For example, if we arrive by plane in South Africa, we quickly notice we are not home. The architecture, the smells, the way the people dress and talk, the accents, and the gestures remind us that we are in a foreign environment and therefore should suspend judgment, pay attention, and assume nothing. However, when we receive an email from someone in South Africa, we are likely to be in the comfort of our own environment, we do not hear any accent, we do not see anything different, and we may fail to realize that we are in a cross-cultural situation. However, chances are our South African counterpart has been influenced by his or her culture while writing the email and has embedded meaning in his or her communication that we may be unable to uncover.

Over-dependence on technology

Likewise, technology brings both beneficial and detrimental influences to virtual teams. Information technology has made virtual teams possible by allowing instantaneous information exchange regardless of geographic location. Teams transmitting information electronically may benefit from the fact that information is recorded prior to transmission, providing a record of transactions. Additionally, the ability to hand off work to teammates across time zones allows work to continue around the clock.

However, technological dependence for communication may lead to some problems. For instance, emails may not reach their final destination, attachments may not go through, and different versions of documents may be erroneously circulated. Sometimes members send information to one team member but assume everyone had access to that information. Even when messages get through, members can't control how the others will read or interpret their messages. When communicating face to face, we indicate what we consider to be important through changes in the tone of voice, facial expressions, and non-verbal gestures. Likewise, receivers signal their understanding by nodding their heads, gesticulating, or making brief verbalizations such as "yeah" and "m-hmmm". These signaling activities are more time and energy consuming in technology-mediated communication. Most of the time, people do not write emails checking their understanding of message context, saying something to the effect of "I read your email, and this is what I understood. Is that what you meant?"[31] These shortcomings curtail understanding, experimentation, and creative problem solving.

Loss of detail

Moreover, when communicating via text-based media such as email and electronic chat, not only is less information richness transmitted (e.g., body language or facial expressions), but less is explained as well. Writing down details tends to be laborious, so individuals do not write as much as they would say, hence oversimplifying communication and omitting important information.[32] For instance, a study found that in similar circumstances, individuals communicating via text-based technology exchanged an average of 740 words, while individuals communicating verbally exchanged an average of 1,702 words.[33] This, of course, is understandable as it is very difficult to know what information is important, and it takes a lot of work to write down details of our everyday reality, not knowing which parts of it may be relevant to our dispersed team members.

Lack of shared understanding

Frequently, virtual teams are spread across different time zones. In such cases, it may be difficult to arrange conversations with all members simultaneously, and there is an over-reliance on asynchronous communication such as email. The over-reliance on emails may result in a vast amount of information exchange but little shared understanding. Shared understanding requires more than information exchange; it requires people to learn together, relate to one another, and develop mutual expect-ations about the nature of the goal, task, and processes to accomplish the goals.[34]

Leadership and global teams

So, what can we conclude about leadership processes in general and the leadership of global teams in particular? First, there has been considerable progress in recognizing that theories of leadership are not universal – even within single countries – and that culture is one of many influences on leadership effectiveness. If this is correct, logical questions arise about how leaders can make the most of their work environments in ways that further the goals of an organization's various stakeholders, including customers, stockholders, and employees. (The stakeholder's model discussed in Chapter 5 is particularly relevant here.) From what has been discussed here, we can identify at least three sets of recommendations for global managers as they relate to leadership and global teams: the role of team leaders, leading co-located teams, and leading virtual teams.

The role of global team leaders

The role of a team leader is critical in helping global teams developing the foundations for high group cohesions and job performance (see Exhibit 8.8). As might be expected, leaders need to create the right context for teams to succeed, rather than try to

Exhibit 8.8 Management challenge: focusing global team efforts

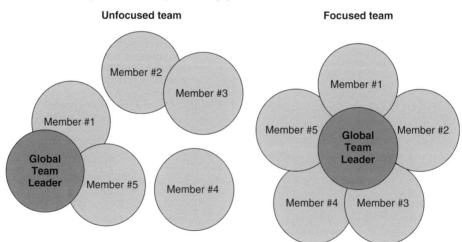

intervene and manage group behavior. To this end, managers may productively focus their efforts on the following areas:

- *Provide clear direction.* Provide global teams with direction, purpose, and clear performance goals: Team members must believe they have a worthwhile purpose to accomplish and have common expectations regarding their performance goals.[35]
- *Select members based on skills.* Select members for their skills and invest in global team members' development: Teams need the skills to accomplish their tasks and to work together. Team members should be carefully selected to make sure all necessary skills are available, and if not, are developed.
- *Build a positive team culture.* Help nurture a positive team culture: As discussed above, groups develop cultures based on their first experiences and the solutions they find to the problems they encounter.[36] For this reason, the creation of a global team must be carefully managed, as members are monitoring each other and the leader's behavior carefully to infer rules that will inform future behavior. Clear rules of behavior need to be developed at the outset of team formation, with the team purpose in mind.
- *Build team camaraderie.* Encourage global teams to take time to know one another. Teams need to develop a sense of trust and camaraderie that will facilitate creative exchanges. Teams need to spend time together, not only on-task but also building relationships and getting to know each other.
- *Use performance-reward contingencies.* Develop milestones and provide feedback and rewards throughout the project duration, and not just at the end of it. It will help global teams to reflect on their performance, celebrate small wins, and take action to deal with shortcomings.

To this end, University of Michigan professor Paula Caproni suggests that teams in general achieve synergy by building on five foundations or facilitators: purpose, performance measures, people, process, and practice.[37] These same facilitators apply to a wide variety of global teams, as described in Exhibit 8.9.

Global teams that make use of such techniques to manage both tasks and processes typically have an easier time completing their assigned responsibilities in a creative and productive manner. Group objectives, responsibility tasking, and ground rules are clearly understood by members. By contrast, groups that fail to manage these activities tend to do less well because they spend needless time assessing and reassessing goals and objectives and reinventing solutions to recurring problems that could have been dealt with more easily had a structure and process been squarely in place to guide behavior.

Exhibit 8.9 Management strategies for leading global teams

Facilitators of team performance	Team leadership strategies
Clear, engaging purpose	• Provide direction, inspiration, and motivation to team members. A clear purpose keeps the team together in difficult situations. • A powerful purpose should be consistent with organizational values and missions, create a sense of urgency, be positive and inspiring, be easily understood and remembered, be performance-based, flexible, attainable, but challenging.
Performance goals and measures	• Provide specific and measurable performance goals to evaluate the team's progress, focus the team's efforts on results, enable team members to see how they contribute to the team's goals, and create milestones that build team commitment, confidence, and competence.
People	• Team members need to have complementary skills and together have all the skills needed to accomplish a task. • Team members should also be committed to the team's purpose, have a specific expertise or skill set to contribute to the team, possess problem-solving, decision making and implementation skills. • They should also have relationship skills, including the ability to develop trust, deal with conflict, and communicate effectively, be adaptive, and aware of their own strengths and weaknesses.
Results-driven processes	• To accomplish complex tasks, teams need processes in place to identify problems and opportunities, generate solutions, make trade-offs, agree on decisions, implement solutions, evaluate the consequences of their decisions, and coordinate their efforts. • Teams also need relationship processes to help them deal with conflict and develop trust, that a sense of cohesiveness, and commitment. • These processes rest on norms of behaviors that can be implicit and well assimilated in the team's culture or explicit and well documented in a team contract.
Preparation and practice	• One of the most critical aspects of team success – and one frequently neglected – is preparation and disciplined practice. • High-performing teams routinely reflect on their performance, identify skills they need to succeed, and make efforts to acquire them.

Working with co-located global teams

Working with global co-located teams bring important advantages. They are usually more creative and innovative than less diverse teams, and can draw on different sources of information as members bring both understanding of different locales and relationships with different stakeholders. The co-location facilitates trust development and the sharing of information. However, making such teams work effectively is not an easy task. Former ABB CEO Percy Barnevik observed, "When we sit together as Germans, Swiss, Americans, and Swedes, with many of us living, working, and traveling in different places, the insights can be remarkable. But you have to force people into these situations."[38] It is often more difficult and requires more time to develop group cohesiveness when team members' backgrounds are highly diverse. Moreover, if often takes more time to both reach decisions and implement them, again due to differences in how decision-making processes are viewed. Finally, people's work habits – they way the approach even simple tasks at work – cannot only differ significantly across cultures, but can lead to considerable misunderstandings, conflict, and mistrust.

Consider, for example, what happened when three electronics giants – IBM, Siemens, and Toshiba – tried to form a strategic alliance to develop a new computer chip. Scientists from all three companies were brought to a state-of-the-art research facility in upstate New York to design the next generation semiconductor. The idea was to pool their knowledge to beat the competition. Unfortunately, each group of scientists quickly identified problems with the joint venture. German scientists from Siemens were shocked to find their Toshiba colleagues closing their eyes and appearing to sleep during meetings. They failed to understand that such behavior is a common practice in Japan for concentrating on what is being said. At the same time, the Japanese scientists from Toshiba, who were used to working in groups, found it uncomfortable to sit in small individual offices all day and speak English. And the American IBM managers complained that the Germans planned too much and that the Japanese wouldn't make clear and decisive decisions. Inter-group trust evaporated as suspicions began to circulate that some researchers were withholding information from the group. Finally, the alliance melted away.[39]

McGill professor Nancy Adler argues that cultural diversity in work teams provides the biggest asset for teams when team members are engaged in difficult discretionary tasks requiring innovation.[40] Under such circumstances, the differing perspectives provided by having people from different cultures around the table frequently leads to greater insights and a wider array of possible problem solutions. However, according to Adler, when teams are working on simple tasks or are working on implementation problems as opposed to creative or strategic problems, multicultural teams may be of less value. Indeed, they may slow the process. Thus, a multicultural team's greatest asset appears to be during the planning and development (or analysis) stage, not the implementation (or action) stage.

Working with virtual global teams

Working with, or indeed leading, a virtual team with workers distributed around the globe suggests a need to carefully select members with the right skills, abilities, and motivation to work in a highly complex and oftentimes ambiguous environment. It also suggests a need to provide these individuals with extensive training in technology use, virtual communication, virtual work, and cultural sensitivity. Also, expectations and reward systems ought to be consistent with the goals and nature of virtual work. Managers can't control the behavior of virtual team members and members are not "seen" while at work. Clear expectations, and measurable goals, are a better way of judging employees' performance and assigning rewards.

Not all tasks can be accomplished virtually, and successful virtual managers understand this. Some tasks are very difficult to accomplish using lean media and may require members to meet face to face, at least for an initial phase so participants get to know each other and negotiate ways to interact. As a rule of thumb, the higher the level of decision process or the more complex the message, the richer the communication medium required.[41] In other words, simpler tasks can easily be accomplished through lean media, while some tasks are better saved for co-located teams. In cases where insights from several regions are required, multicultural teams may be assigned temporarily to a location to work co-located in a task.

Once managers identify the right tasks, the right people, the right technology, and the right reward systems, they must work on processes to enable coordination, shared understanding, and trust. Managers can ease the challenges caused by lack of common context by actively working in disseminating information. For example, periodic face-to-face meetings may be arranged when possible. If it is impossible or too costly to have all members visit each other, one member of each location may visit remote locations and share information. Additionally, video and teleconferences should be utilized for information sharing, where each member is invited to tell how they are doing. This will create the conditions for contextual information to emerge, as members have the opportunity to mention things that are important parts of their reality, such as other projects or pressures they are facing.[42]

Managers must also facilitate communication among members. They can help members' communication by making communication norms explicit, providing intercultural communication training, and developing team-building interventions that help participants to develop communication rules and build mutual understanding.[43] Managers also need to make sure individual members do not feel isolated in remote locations. The key word here is *communicate!* Frequent short messages may go a long way to making members feel valued and feel they belong to the team.

Exhibit 8.10 summarizes the key issues managers must take into consideration when managing virtual teams.

Exhibit 8.10 Management strategies for leading virtual global teams

Team components	Leader responsibilities
People	• Selection of members with right skills, abilities, and motivation. • Provide training on technology use, virtual communication, and cultural sensitivity. • Align reward systems with nature of distributed work. • Set clear expectations and measurable goals for performance appraisal purposes.
Tasks	• Select tasks that are appropriate for virtual work. • Use richer media for complex problems.
Processes	• Disseminate information among team members. • Arrange periodic face-to-face meetings when possible. • Allow time for information sharing in video and teleconferences. • Make communication norms explicit. • Provide intercultural communication training. • Develop team-building interventions. • Make sure individuals do not feel isolated. • Communicate frequently with all members.

Source: Based on Maznevski and Athanassiou, "Designing the knowledge-management infrastructure for virtual teams."

Working virtually requires learning a new way of relating and interacting. Success in working virtually as a manager or collaborator requires learning to communicate information that maybe we would not have communicated in a face-to-face interaction. Members must communicate task-related information (details about what has to be done), social-related information (personality, styles, and reputation of those directly or indirectly involved in the task), and context-related information (type of support available, equipment, competing responsibilities, cultural norms, holiday schedules, office layouts, local rules, expectations and regulations).[44]

The conundrum facing virtual teams is that, while they need more information than co-located teams, they usually share less because members do not realize what information is important, take their own context for granted and assume similarity between locations, and have a difficult time imagining what is different for other members because it takes a lot of time and effort to write down or communicate everything. Yet, context affects behavior in ways we may not anticipate. For example, one member may feel pressured to finish a task quickly because he or she is under pressure to tackle another task. Yet, another member may be experiencing technological problems that may be slowing her down. In summary, succeeding in a virtual environment requires taking the time to communicate in a variety of ways all elements that may be affecting the work and work environment. It may include details about progress on the task, how you and others team members work, upcoming holidays, planned construction on your building, or server shutdowns. In short, everything you know that helps you to do your job is likely to help your counterpart to do his or her job as well.

As technology continues to evolve and globalization pressures increase, it is likely that organizations around the world will continue experimenting with new work arrangements and new ways to take advantage of resources available in different locations.[45] The challenge for global managers is to keep up with these changes and adapt their management styles accordingly.

Notes

1 See www.wipro.com.
2 Personal communication, Atsushi Kagayama, Panasonic Corporation, formerly Matsushita Business Group, Osaka, Japan.
3 Warren Bennis, *On Becoming a Leader.* Reading, MA: Addison-Wesley, 1989, p. 1.
4 "Face value: tough Ghosn," *The Economist*, September 15, 2007, p. 82; Arran Scott and Norihiko Shirouzu, "Nissan's chief to steer US operations," *The Wall Street Journal*, March 24, 2004, p. A2; "Nissan's boss," *Business Week*, October 4, 2004, pp. 50–60.
5 David Pearson, "Ghosn suggests splitting Renault-Nissan CEO post," *The Wall Street Journal*, May 3, 2008, p. A3.
6 These observations come from a variety of sources, including Robert J. House, Paul J. Hanges, Mansour Javidan, Peter W. Dorfman, and Vipin Gupta, *Culture, Leadership and Organizations: The GLOBE Study of 62 Societies*. Thousand Oaks, CA: Sage, 2004; Shejina Michailova, "When common sense becomes uncommon," *Journal of World Business*, 2002, 37, pp. 180–187; and comments made to the authors by local managers attending MBA and executive programs.
7 Peter W. Dorfman and Robert J. House, "Cultural influences on organizational leadership," in House *et al.*, *Culture, Leadership, and Organizations*, p. 56.
8 Daniel Etounga-Manguelle, "Does Africa need a cultural adjustment program?," in Lawrence E. Harrison and Samuel P. Huntington (eds.), *Culture Matters: How Values Shape Human Progress*. New York, NY: Basic Books, 2000, p. 75.
9 François Jullien has devoted several books to these issues, and we recommend the following three: *Penser d'un dehors (la Chine): Entretiens d'Extrême Occident*. Paris: Seuil, 2000; *Un sage est sans idée; ou L'autre de la philosophie*. Paris: Seuil, 1998; and *Traité de la efficacité*. Paris: Seuil, 1996.
10 Samuel Griffith (ed.), *Sun Tzu: The Art of War*. New York, NY: Oxford University Press, 1971. *The Art of War* (Chinese: 孫子兵法; pinyin: *Sūn Zǐ Bīng Fǎ*) is a Chinese military treatise that was written during the sixth century BCE by Sun Tzu. Composed of thirteen chapters, each of which is devoted to one aspect of warfare, it has long been praised as the definitive work on military strategies and tactics of its time. It was the first and most successful work on strategy and has had a huge influence on Eastern and

Western military thinking, business tactics, and beyond. Sun Tzu was the first to recognize the importance of positioning in strategy, and that position is affected both by objective conditions in the physical environment and the subjective opinions of competitive actors in that environment. He taught that strategy was not planning in the sense of working through a to-do list, but rather that it requires quick and appropriate responses to changing conditions. Planning works in a controlled environment, but in a competitive environment competing plans collide, creating unexpected situations. The book was first translated into the French language in 1782 by French Jesuit Jean Joseph Marie Amiot, and possibly influenced Napoleon, and even the planning of Operation Desert Storm in Iraq in the 1990s. Leaders as diverse as Mao Zedong, General Vo Nguyen Giap, and General Douglas MacArthur have claimed to have drawn inspiration from the work.

11 John Cullen and K. P. Parboteeah, *Multinational Management: A Strategic Approach.* Cincinnati, OH: Southwestern College Publishing, 2005, p. 27.

12 See, for instance, Edgard Slingerland, *Effortless Action: Wu-Wei as Conceptual Metaphor and Spiritual Ideal in Early China.* Oxford, UK: Oxford University Press, 2003.

13 "A very European hero," *The Economist*, December 18, 2008, pp. 45–46.

14 Dorfman and House, "Cultural influences on organizational leadership," p. 15.

15 House *et al.*, *Culture, Leadership, and Organizations*, p. 5.

16 John Kotter, *Matsushita Leadership: Lessons from the 20th Century's Most Remarkable Entrepreneur.* New York, NY: Free Press, 1997.

17 Rabi S. Bhagat and Richard M. Steers (eds.), *Cambridge Handbook of Culture, Organizations, and Work.* Cambridge, UK: Cambridge University Press, 2009; Peter Smith, Mark Peterson, and David Thomas (eds.), *Handbook of Cross-cultural Management Research.* Thousand Oaks, CA: Sage, 2008.

18 Rob Goffee and Gareth Jones, *Why Should Anyone be Led by You? What It Takes To Be an Authentic Leader.* Cambridge, MA: Harvard Business School Press, 2006, pp. 109–133.

19 *Ibid.*

20 Yukari Kane and Phred Dvorak, "Howard Stringer, Japanese CEO," *The Wall Street Journal*, March 3, 2007, p. A1.

21 Anil Gupta and Vijay Govindarajan, *Global Strategy and Organization.* New York, NY: Wiley, 2004.

22 Charles Snow, "Types of transnational teams," in Transnational Teams Project, *Transnational Teams Resources Guide.* Lexington, MA: International Consortium for Executive Development Research (ICEDR), 1993.

23 Susan Schneider and Jean-Louis Barsoux, *Managing Across Cultures*, 2nd Edition. London: Prentice Hall, 2003.

24 *Ibid.*

25 Martha Maznevski and Nicholas Athanassiou, "Designing the knowledge-management infrastructure for virtual teams," in C. B. Gibson and S. G. Cohen (eds.), *Virtual Teams that Work: Creating Conditions for Virtual Team Effectiveness.* San Francisco, CA: Jossey-Bass, 2003, pp. 196–213.

26 Christina B. Gibson and Jennifer L. Gibbs, "Unpacking the concept of virtuality: the effects of geographic dispersion, electronic dependence, dynamic structure, and national diversity on team innovation," *Administrative Science Quarterly*, 2006, 51(3), pp. 451–495.

27 Catherine D. Cramton, "The mutual knowledge problem and its consequences for dispersed collaboration," *Organization Science*, 2001, 12(3), pp. 346–371.

28 Cramton, "The mutual knowledge problem," p. 346.

29 *Ibid.*

30 *Ibid.*

31 *Ibid.*

32 Catherine D. Cramton and Kara L. Orvis, "Overcoming barriers to information sharing in virtual teams," in Gibson and Cohen, *Virtual Teams that Work*, pp. 214–232.

33 Susan G. Strauss, "Getting a clue: the effects of communication media and information distribution on participation and performance in computer mediated and face-to-face groups," *Small Group Research*, 1996, 27, pp. 115–142.

34 Pamela J. Hinds and Suzanne P. Weisband, "Knowledge sharing and shared understanding in virtual teams," in Gibson and Cohen, *Virtual Teams that Work*, pp. 21–36.

35 Jon R. Katzenbach and Douglas K. Smith, "The discipline of teams," *Harvard Business Review*, July–August 2005, pp. 162–171.

36 Edgar Schein, *Organizational Culture and Leadership*. San Fransisco, CA: Jossey-Bass, 2004.

37 Paula Caproni, *Management Skills for Everyday Life: The Practical Coach*. Upper Saddle, NJ: Prentice Hall, 2005, pp. 316–320.

38 Cited in David Thomas, *Cross-cultural Management: Essential Concepts*. Thousand Oaks, CA: Sage, 2009, p. 1.

39 E. S. Browning, "Computer chip project brings rivals together, but the cultures clash," *The Wall Street Journal*, May 3, 1994, p. A1.

40 Nancy Adler, *International Dimensions of Organizational Behavior*. Cincinnati, OH: Southwestern, 1997.

41 Martha Maznevski and Katherine Chudoba, "Bridging space over time: global virtual team dynamics and effectiveness," *Organization Science*, 2000, 11(5), p. 473.

42 Cramton and Orvis, "Overcoming barriers to information sharing," p. 229.

43 *Ibid.*

44 *Ibid.*

45 John Battelle, *The Search: How Google and Its Rivals Rewrote the Rules of Business and Transformed Our Culture*. New York, NY: Penguin Group, 2005.

CHAPTER 9

Culture, work, and motivation

- The world of work   284
- Work and leisure   290
- Culture, motivation, and work behavior: a model   292
- Culture and the psychology of work   295
- Incentives and rewards across cultures   299
- MANAGER'S NOTEBOOK: Culture, work, and motivation   310

To motivate employees, you must bring them into the family and treat them like respected members of it.

Akio Morita[1]
Founder and former CEO, Sony Corporation, Japan

We need the fork on employees' necks in Russia, not all these nice words and baby techniques.
Snejina Michailova[2]
University of Auckland, New Zealand

People in the workplace obviously come in different shapes and sizes, abilities and skills, ages and genders, educational and income levels, and so forth. They may be colleagues, managers, subordinates, advisors, customers, clients, and personal friends. They may speak different languages, approach problem solving in different ways, and sometimes seek different rewards and outcomes for doing the same job. What most of these people have in common, though, is a collective need to make useful contributions to those around them (as they define "useful"). That is, save for a few social loafers and free riders, most people seek to belong somewhere and to be recognized for their own personal worth. They seek to add value to their group or society and to be recognized and respected. When this drive is framed within the context of organizations, it becomes a question of work motivation. That is, what is it within people and their environments that influence them to work hard (or not), contribute their skills and expertise (or not), and continue to be a contributing member (or not)? And how do these motivational influences vary, if at all, across national boundaries?

Consider: Managers in both Russia and Japan make use of a variety of motivational strategies and techniques to facilitate employee performance, but, in terms of central tendencies, they could not be more different. One stresses a top-down autocratic approach to control subordinates, while the other stresses a cooperative and supportive approach to empower them. Both can be highly successful at times, but not so at others. Both have the power to enhance employee commitment to the organization and both have the power to drive employees away. The unanswered question here is why two fundamentally different approaches to work motivation can both be successful.

Observations by experts on work values and employee motivation around the world echo this dilemma. In Thailand, "the introduction of an individual merit bonus plan, which runs counter to the societal norm of group cooperation, can result in a decline rather than an increase in productivity from employees who refuse to openly compete with each other."[3] Likewise, in the Netherlands, "you can't get the Dutch to compete with one another publicly."[4] In the US, "to get the best people, you have to continually refine the gene pool; you must grade on a curve."[5] In Mexico, "everything is a personal matter; but a lot of [foreign] managers don't get it. To get anything done, the manager has to be more of an instructor, teacher, or father figure than a boss."[6] And in England and France, "efforts to improve managerial performance in the UK should focus on job content than on job context. Job enrichment programs are more likely to improve performance in an intrinsically oriented society such as Britain, where satisfaction tends to be derived from the job itself, than in France, where job context factors, such as security and fringe benefits, are more highly valued."[7]

The conclusion here is inescapable: Different countries often use different motivational strategies to get work done. The organizational goals may be similar, but the psychology and concomitant behaviors can be very different. This leads us to a fundamental question facing all managers, global and domestic: How can we best motivate employees?

To understand the complexities underlying these disparities, consider the very real problems encountered by the Lincoln Electric Company when it decided to expand internationally. Lincoln Electric is a small manufacturing company founded in Cleveland, Ohio in 1895.[8] Today, it manufactures arc-welding equipment and continues to prosper year after year in a highly competitive environment. Forty years ago, there were over fifty manufactures in this industry; today there are only six, and Lincoln has 40 percent of this market. By any measure, this company is a success story. Indeed, the most popular case study ever written by the Harvard Business School – still in use after thirty years – is about Lincoln Electric.

The company's business strategy is simple: Sell high-value, high-quality products at competitive prices and provide outstanding customer service. Within the US, it has a broad-based and well-respected reputation for quality, service, and competitiveness. It has maintained this reputation continuously since the 1930s. Technology has changed little in the industry over the years, and most competitors have access to the latest developments. Price, dependability, and quality represent critical success factors in sales and marketing.

The key to Lincoln Electric's success is its stable, hard-working, and highly skilled workforce. In a country that lavishes sizable executive bonuses on CEOs and other senior managers who can squeeze maximum productivity out of workers, Lincoln was founded – and continues to be run – on the twin principles of self-determination and equal treatment of all workers. And, above all, it stresses pay for performance. When James Lincoln assumed control of the company in 1929, he set about clarifying his management philosophy. Lincoln had an abiding respect for the ability of the individual and believed that, correctly motivated, ordinary people could achieve extraordinary results. He felt his company should be a meritocracy where people were rewarded based on their individual performance. He called it "intelligent selfishness." He also worked to remove all barriers between workers and managers and created one of the first "open door policies" in the US. All employees – including executives – ate in the same company cafeteria and there were no reserved parking spaces.

James Lincoln believed firmly that gains in productivity should be shared with consumers in the form of lower prices, with employees in the form of higher pay, and with shareholders in the form of higher dividends. This philosophy was reinforced by the creation of an incentive system that continues unchanged to this day, more than seventy years after its introduction. Following the turn-of-the-century principles of Frederick Taylor and scientific management, all workers at Lincoln are paid on a piece rate system. That is, they are paid for each unit they produce and do not receive either a salary or an hourly wage. There is no paid vacation, no paid sick leave, and no bonuses or job security for seniority. This principle applies to all employees up to and including the company president, with minor adjustments for the nature of managerial work.

In addition to receiving piece rate pay, workers can earn substantial bonuses based on their individual job performance and company profits. Bonuses are paid twice each year based on performance. Each employee is evaluated on four factors: quantity of work, quality of work, dependability, and cooperation. The first two criteria focus on individual job performance and productivity, while the second two focus on teamwork and cooperation in helping the company attain its corporate objectives.

Under this system, employee bonuses have been paid each year since 1934, and the company claims that its workers are the highest paid blue-collar workers in the world.[9] Indeed, employee bonuses often exceed annual wages, thereby more than doubling their income. There have been no layoffs in the company's long history, and absenteeism and turnover rates are the lowest in the industry. Indeed, it is said that when a severe snowstorm shuts Cleveland down, Lincoln employees make it to work. And despite its high employee compensation, Lincoln Electric's workers are so productive that the company has a lower cost structure than any of its competitors.

Lincoln Electric runs its operation like a cottage industry. It assumes that its workers are the best in the industry and can work independently. It therefore spends far less than its competitors on supervision; Lincoln Electric has a 100:1 supervisory ratio, compared to the industrial average of 25:1. The money saved is plowed back into company operations or given out in employee bonuses.

It takes a certain kind of employee to survive at Lincoln Electric. They must be skilled in their craft, physically strong and healthy, capable of working independently, highly moti-vated, and, above all, mercenary. Money, not job satisfaction, is the principal motivator here. People who do not fit this description soon leave or are forced out. Older workers sometimes leave because they find they can't keep up with the fast pace and begin losing income. People who become ill often leave for the same reason. Critics have called it social Darwinism, but for many workers it seemed to fit with America's highly individualistic culture.

In the late 1990s, Lincoln Electric decided to expand its operations internationally and become a bigger player in the emerging global economy.[10] It first set its sights on Germany, buying a small German arc-welding equipment manufacturer called Messer Griesheim. None of the American executives involved in the acquisition decision had any international experience, but they believed that because they had been so successful in the US, success would likewise follow elsewhere. John Gonzales, Vice President of Engineering, was assigned to be managing director of the new acquisition. Like the other executives, Gonzales also lacked international experience and, in addition, deci-ded to run the venture from Lincoln Electric's home office in Cleveland.

One of his first decisions was to retain the local German managers, since they best understood local customs and work practices. It was assumed that the Lincoln Electric compensation system would be adapted to fit local conditions, leading to increased productivity through heightened individual motivation. As Lincoln Electric's CEO observed several years later, "Our managers didn't know how to run foreign operations, nor did they understand foreign cultures. Consequently, we had to rely on the people in our foreign companies – people we didn't know and who didn't know us."[11]

Once the purchase had been completed, it quickly became apparent that the local German managers were either unable or unwilling to introduce Lincoln Electric's individualistic incentive plan among workers used to a somewhat more collectivistic work culture. Finally, out of exasperation, US headquarters ordered it done.

The response of the employees was quick and decisive. Employee grievances and even lawsuits arose challenging the newly imposed system, which was seen by many as being exploitative and even inhumane. Workers were being asked to work ever harder with little consideration for their quality of living. Many workers rejected the piece rate concept on principle, while others preferred extra leisure time over higher wages and were not prepared to work as hard as their US counterparts.

After a visit to the German facility to see first hand what was happening, Lincoln Electric's president observed,

> Even though German factory workers are highly skilled and, in general, solid workers, they do not work nearly as hard or as long as the people in our Cleveland factory.
> In Germany, the average factory workweek is thirty-five hours. In contrast, the average workweek in Lincoln's US plants is between forty-three and fifty-eight hours, and the company can ask people to work longer hours on short notice – a flexibility that is essential for our system to work. The lack of such flexibility was one of the reasons why our approach would not work in Europe.[12]

At the same time, a major recession was hitting Europe and sales declined sharply. Between the "poor work attitude" of the German workers and the decline in sales, Lincoln Electric had to make a decision that would satisfy the shareholders and employees back home who were subsidizing the German venture. It closed the Messer factory and decided to export US-made products to Germany instead.

Looking back over their German misadventure, Lincoln Electric executives drew what for them was a surprising conclusion:

> We had long boasted that our unique culture and incentive system – along with the dedicated, skilled workforce that the company had built over the decades – were the main sources of Lincoln's competitive advantage. We had assumed that the incentive system and culture could be transferred abroad and that the workforce could be quickly replicated.[13]

Lincoln Electric's disappointment in Germany was soon replaced with optimism following its experience with a Mexican subsidiary that occurred about the same time.

The company had purchased a unionized manufacturing plant in Mexico City. Despite the fact piece rate systems are generally rejected by Mexican workers (like their German counterparts), Lincoln introduced their system gradually and only following discussions with workers in the plant. Initially, when employees expressed reservations about the Lincoln plan, executives asked for two Mexican volunteers to test-drive the system. They were guaranteed that they would not lose money under the system during the trial period, but could keep any additional income they earned. Two employees reluctantly agreed to try the system. Soon, as the two workers began making more than their colleagues, other employees asked to join the plan. Over the next two years, everyone in the plant gradually asked to join. Today, the Mexican facility continues to prosper under the Lincoln incentive system.

From its experience in Germany and Mexico, Lincoln Electric concluded that moving across borders must be done slowly and only after a thorough understanding of local cultures. Moreover, they learned that transplanting ideas – whether they relate to incentive systems, management practices, or anything else – could only succeed after a thorough dialog with the workers that are directly involved. As we look back on this example, one wonders why the Lincoln Electric incentive program that had worked so well for decades in the US was so soundly rejected in these two other countries? Could this rejection be attributed exclusively to cultural differences or were there other factors in play here? And if so, what are these other factors?

Subsequent to these experiences, Lincoln Electric opened a manufacturing facility in Shanghai, China.[14] Using what they had learned about cross-cultural challenges, this time, management was more sensitive to local differences and demands. They spent considerable time getting to know both the employees and their families. They held open discussions with employees and sought their input on developing a culturally sensitive compensation system. In the end, management decided to move slowly towards some form of a merit-based compensation system, but perhaps with a Chinese flavor. At the same time, Lincoln management discovered that many younger Chinese workers were moving towards a more general acceptance of such systems (see Chapter 6).

The world of work

To see how and why Lincoln Electric succeeded, then failed, and then learned from its mistakes to again succeed, we must begin by asking a basic question: Why do people work? This question lies at the heart of the topic of personal work values. What is it about work, if anything, that people genuinely value? What motivates them to go to

Exhibit 9.1 Personal work values and employee behavior

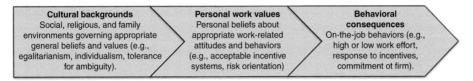

Cultural backgrounds	Personal work values	Behavioral consequences
Social, religious, and family environments governing appropriate general beliefs and values (e.g., egalitarianism, individualism, tolerance for ambiguity).	Personal beliefs about appropriate work-related attitudes and behaviors (e.g., acceptable incentive systems, risk orientation)	On-the-job behaviors (e.g., high or low work effort, response to incentives, commitment ot firm).

work? *Personal work values* reflect individual beliefs about desirable end states or modes of conduct for pursuing desirable end states. As such, they serve a useful function by providing individuals with guidelines and standards for determining their own behavior and evaluating the behavior of others. Personal work values are important because they signal what individuals and groups of employees see as being most important about their work efforts. They also influence the actual quality and focus of employee endeavors and the ways in which various employees may respond to work motivation strategies and tactics (see Exhibit 9.1). Throughout, the focus here is on understanding how personal values influence employee willingness and preparedness to contribute towards the attainment of organizational goals.

From a cross-cultural perspective, questions emerge concerning how variations across cultures may or may not affect employee behavior in the workplace, as well as what managers might do to accommodate such variations where they exist. For example, values concerning the relative importance of individualism versus collectivism can influence the manner in which employees work together. Thus, many Anglo-Americans tend to assert their individuality and revel in their differences, while many Japanese tend to emphasize harmonious interdependence with others and shun the spotlight.[15] Such values can represent an important influence on work-related behaviors.

Consider just one example: What happens when Korean managers supervise Mexican assembly workers in *maquiladora* plants in northern Mexico? Views on work values can differ sharply. As noted by Loyola Marymount professor Yongsun Paik and Yonsei professor Yong Suhk Pak, Korean managers tend to believe that Mexicans work not as a sacred duty as in Korea but as a means to an end or a necessary evil. Their Mexican subordinates routinely make commitments they have little intention of keeping.[16] They also fail to distinguish between work and play. They play loud music and talk excessively during work, wasting time. Korean managers are dumbfounded by such a lack of commitment.

Needless to say, Mexican workers have a different point of view.[17] To many of them, Korean managers evaluate all people and work situations using to their own philosophy and standards. The Mexican workers felt that their Korean supervisors should not use Korean cultural values as a criterion when comparing work ethics between countries. To the Mexicans, their Korean supervisors established unrealistic goals and then blamed the workers for being lazy when these goals were not achieved. Moreover, while Korean employees may be willing to work fifteen hours a day, this is Mexico, not Korea. Finally, first-line Mexican supervisors in these plants suggested that the reason for poor plant performance had less to do with work ethics and more to do to with an unwillingness on the part of Korean managers to allow Mexican participation in the production planning process. Who is right in this conflict may depend more on where you live than what you believe.

Work values across cultures

Personal work values have been studied systematically from a cross-cultural perspective for many years. One of the earliest studies was conducted by George England.[18] He and his colleagues focused on the impact of such values on employee behavior and found significant differences across managers in the five countries they studied. US managers tended to be high in pragmatism and achievement orientation and demanded competence. They placed a high value on profit maximization, organizational efficiency, and productivity. Japanese and Korean managers also valued pragmatism, competence, and achievement, but emphasized organizational growth instead of profit maximization. Indian managers stressed a moralistic orientation, a desire for stability instead of change, and the importance of status, dignity, prestige, and compliance with organizational directives. Finally, Australian managers tended to emphasize a moralistic and humanistic orientation, an emphasis on both growth and profit maximization, a high value on loyalty and trust, and a low emphasis on individual achievement, success, competition, and risk.

This initial work by England and his colleagues formed the basis for a subsequent international study of managerial values called the Meaning of Work Project.[19] This study sought to identify the underlying meanings that individuals and groups attach to work in six industrialized nations: Belgium, Germany, Israel, Japan, the UK, and the US. In this study, Japan was found to have a higher number of workers for whom work was their central life interest, compared to both Americans and Germans, who placed a higher value on leisure and social interaction. A high proportion of Americans saw work as a duty, an obligation that must be met. Japanese workers showed less interest in individual economic outcomes from work than their European and American counterparts.

As part of this survey, employees were asked to rank a list of common work goals in order of importance in their lives. These rankings illustrate that while differences can obviously be found across cultures, such differences may not be as diverse as is commonly believed. In fact, some perhaps surprising commonalities can be found. Interestingly work and pay consistently ranked at or near the top of the list for all countries. By the same token, promotion opportunities and convenient working hours ranked near the bottom of all lists. However, Japan ranked job-person fit first, while Belgium ranked it eighth, and job security was ranked high in every country except Israel. Finally, it is important to note that all of the countries included in this study represented highly industrialized and technology-rich nations and all are essentially from the Northern Hemisphere. One wonders if these rankings would be different if developing or underdeveloped nations were included.

In a second University of Michigan survey that did include some non-industrialized nations, results again shows some – although not a great deal of – convergence (see Exhibit 9.2). In this survey, conducted in the late 1990s, workers routinely sought more time off from work. Beyond this, however, differences were found across countries (e.g., Turkey, Peru, India, and Nigeria) in job preferences. Some preferred interesting work, while others preferred job respect or good working hours. A possible problem with this and similar surveys is that, while rigorously done, these surveys were conducted some time ago. Whether these same trends would hold today in the light of increasing globalization remains open for question. In addition, survey research routinely raises questions about central tendencies and the distribution of results around the mean.

Exhibit 9.2 Top four work preferences for employees in select countries

Preferred work characteristics	China	Germany	India	Japan	Nigeria	Peru	Russia	Turkey	United States
Achieve something				3		4			
Generous holidays	1	1	1		1	1	3	1	1
Good hours		3	4	4	2	3	4	4	3
Interesting job	4		3			2		2	
Respected job		2		1	4				2
Responsibility	2	4					1	1	
Use initiative	3		2	2	3		2		4

Source: Data reported in John Cullen and Praveen Parboteeah, *Multinational Management*. Mason, OH: Thompson/Southwestern, 2008, pp. 694–696.
Note: These numbers represent aggregate mean scores for each country, and considerable variations can be expected within cultures.

In other words, it can be difficult at times to determine what mean scores actually mean. This can be especially difficult for managers who find themselves working with particular sectors of the workforce (e.g., technology workers), whose work preferences may differ sharply from a national sample of employees. Still, surveys such as this can provide some important insight into what managers should look for when initiating assignments in various countries.

A very different example of personal values can be seen in the African concept of *ubuntu*.[20] This concept is perhaps best described as a clan value that requires members to serve the needs of other group members even at their own expense.[21] It is communal in the sense that it requires people to share what they have when someone else is in need, regardless of who worked to acquire it. As such, it is a manifestation of collectivism. It is a clan obligation that overrides any sense of ownership or concerns over inequity in input-output ratios. If your neighbor needs food, for example, it is your responsibility to feed him, even if you are also poor. This concept has no Western equivalent, except possibly compassion. When white Afrikaners began settling in South Africa to operate farms, factories, and mines, they quickly discovered that the incentive systems that they offered the local African population failed to have the desired effect. These systems were based on European values of individual achievement and competition, and failed to recognize the communal values inherent in many tribal cultures. Even today, as South Africa emerges from apartheid, the new African Government faces the same challenge: how to instill a will to achieve in a country that is rich in natural and human resources but sometimes lacking in a competitive spirit. This is not modern or traditional; it is simply different.

Changes in work values

While personal work values as described here are reasonably stable attributes, they are not set in concrete and can evolve over time. We can witness this in recent allegations that younger workers in many countries (e.g., Canada, Japan, France, the US, etc.) are losing their historical work ethics. Instead, they seek more balance between work and family or work and leisure. And at times, they seek simply less work. Their commitment and dedication to their employers have decreased, while their job expectations in terms of compensation and responsibility have increased. Whether these trends are accurate, universal, or reversible is open to debate. The point to be made here is that managers have a dual responsibility to both avoid stereotypes (e.g., "Koreans are all hard workers") and to learn to adapt where necessary to changing conditions. Flexibility and awareness is the key here.

At the same time, work environments and managerial expectations are also chang-ing, however slowly. For example, employees in some countries are increasingly demanding greater participation in major organizational decisions that affect them and their colleagues. And new labor legislation in some countries (e.g., Korea) often reinforces this trend. At the same time, however, other governments are seen to be moving in the opposite direction by attempting to reduce employee benefits, work rules, and security (e.g., France, the US)

Work values and the psychological contract

Finally, an increasing disparity seems to be emerging between organizations and their managers with respect to how they value or fail to value their employees. This issue centers on the continuing debate over whether employees – particularly those at lower levels in the hierarchy – should be considered fixed costs or variable costs. That is, are rank-and-file (and even managers) considered to be valued members of an organization for which management is responsible, or are they contingent factors of production to be retained or discharged depending upon current economic conditions? (This issue was discussed earlier in Chapter 6.) Many years ago, managers spent considerable time and resources trying to encourage employees at all levels to enhance their commitment to their employers. This involved a *psychological contract* in which employees gave their skills and efforts to an organization in the expectation of an equitable exchange from their employer in terms of compensation and job security (see Exhibit 9.3). In recent years, however, these contracts in many countries have broken down, as has mutual trust and commitment. An increasing number of countries now seem to live in a "free agent nation," where all employees are – or are at least treated as though they are – individual entrepreneurs, managing their own careers and well-being and seeking jobs where they can get the best return. This trend is based on a decidedly individualistic culture, yet it is emerging in some of the world's most collectivistic nations. How this plays out for both managers and employees remains to be seen.

Exhibit 9.3 The psychological contract

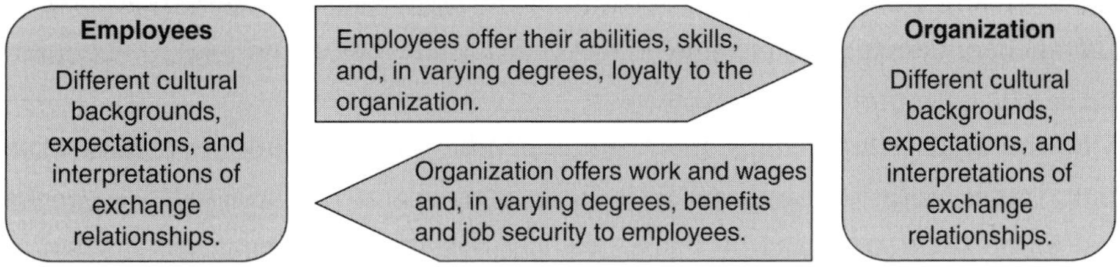

Work and leisure

A second question we must ask here in order to better understand Lincoln Electric's global experiences is how central is work in the lives of employees? Put more bluntly, do people live to work or work to live? We saw one example of this with Korean and Mexican employees (see above). Another example comes from Europe. A Danish colleague of one of the authors often points out that the fundamental difference between Danish and German managers is that the Germans live to work while the Danes work to live. (One wonders what the response of German managers might be.) Moreover, we sometimes hear that Americans work harder than Europeans – a comment more likely to be heard in New York than in London or Berlin. We hear, too, that Japanese and Koreans work harder than anyone else – a comment heard in many places, East and West. Indeed, everyone seems to have an opinion about who works the hardest.

Consider some additional "facts" as far as they will take us: According to one study by *The Economist*, US and Japanese employees work an average of 1,800 hours annually.[22] However, these data ignore the fact that many employees in both countries often work considerable overtime. In Japan, this is called "free overtime" (it is required but not compensated). Indeed, it is estimated that almost one-half of Japanese employees between the ages of thirty and forty work over sixty hours per week but are compensated for just forty hours. Meanwhile, according to this same study, the average German employee works 1,440 hours annually, significantly less than either their Japanese or American counterparts. While many factors play into decisions about workloads, work hours, and vacation policies, culture is certainly one of these.

Several EU countries now have a standard thirty-five-hour workweek, while the norm in the US is closer to fifty. Many Europeans can retire at the age of sixty, while most Americans must work until sixty-five or later. We see wide variations in official vacation policies across countries, ranging from one or two weeks in much of Asia to four or five weeks in much of Europe (see Exhibit 9.4 for examples). The unanswered question throughout this debate, however, is whether working harder than someone else is a badge of honor or a sign of necessity or, worse still, some deep psychological malfunction. Perhaps the question on the table should not be who works the hardest, but who is most productive and efficient.

In this regard, the findings of a *Business Week* study are informative. This survey looked at the number of vacation days actually taken (instead of official vacation policies) and found that Americans now take less vacation time than even the Japanese or

Exhibit 9.4 Vacation policies in select countries

Country	Typical annual vacation policy
France	Two-and-a-half days' paid leave for each full month of service during the year.
Germany	Eighteen working days' paid leave following six months of service.
Hong Kong (China)	Seven days' paid leave following twelve months of continuous service with same employer.
Indonesia	Twelve days' paid leave after twelve months of full service.
Italy	Varies according to length of service, but usually between four and six weeks' paid leave.
Japan	Ten days' paid leave following twelve months of continuous service, providing that employee has worked at least 80 percent of this time.
Malaysia	Varies according to length of service but usually between eight and sixteen days' paid leave.
Mexico	Six days' paid leave.
Philippines	Five days' paid leave.
Saudi Arabia	Fifteen days' paid leave upon completion of twelve months of continuous service with the same employer.
Singapore	Seven days' paid leave following twelve months of continuous employment.
United Kingdom	No statutory requirement. Most salaried staff receive about five weeks' paid leave; paid leave for workers based on individual labor contracts.
United States	No statutory requirement. Typically varies based on length of service and job function, usually between five and fifteen days' paid leave annually.

Source: Based on V. Frazee, "Vacation policies around the world," *Personnel Journal*, 1997, 75, p. 9; Arvind Phatak, Rabi S. Bhagat, and Roger Kashlak, *International Management*. New York, NY : McGraw-Hill/Irwin, 2004, p. 125.

Koreans.[23] Specifically, the study found that, on average, employees took the following vacation times (including public holidays): forty-two days in Italy; thirty-seven days in France; thirty-five days in Germany; thirty-four days in Brazil; twenty-eight days in the UK; twenty-six days in Canada; twenty-five days in South Korea; twenty-five days in Japan; and thirteen days in the US. Obviously, these are averages, and considerable variations can be found across the workforce. Even so, consider the effects of such long hours on home life, personal relationships, and even health. In the US, the average employee gives back almost two unused vacations days annually, worth US$20 billion to employers. Some companies, like SAS Institute, the world's largest privately held software company, are bringing the world to the workplace. Employees can consult nutritionists and doctors in their on-site medical facilities, and bring their kids to on-site day camps, day care centers, and kindergartens. Again, the question arises: Are such long hours necessary to get or stay ahead – either as an individual or a corporation – or are they a sign of something else?

At least in theory, since labor costs are such a large portion of a company's overall cost structure, time away from the job detracts from productivity and the inevitable bottom line. However, is this always the case? For example, a study by the Organization for Economic Cooperation and Development (OECD) found that the average European worker produced only two-thirds of the goods and services of their American counterparts on an annual basis.[24] Add to this the relatively higher labor costs and it can be concluded that European companies are at a significant competitive disadvantage in the global marketplace. Among other things, their goods and services will likely cost more due to operational inefficiencies.

However, there is a second *Business Week* study that discovered something very different. The vacation-loving French and Belgians out-produce Americans on an hourly basis.[25] That is, while they typically work fewer hours than their American counterparts, they seem to make each hour count more. Searching for an explanation of these findings, the authors of the study suggested that at some point across the course of a workday, there appears to be a declining rate of return as employees become increasingly inefficient or inattentive from working too long.

Consider: how should we calculate productivity – annually or hourly? Americans work longer hours on average and are more productive on an annual basis, while many of their European counterparts take more time off from work but are more productive on an hourly basis. Which is better for companies? Which is better for employees? And which is better for national economic development?

Culture, motivation, and work behavior: a model

Working with a global workforce is clearly no easy task. Even so, the task can be made somewhat easier if managers have a frame of reference or toolbox that can provide some structure for observation, understanding, and action. We suggest that work motivation theory can provide this structure. As such, we examine in this section the challenges of working with employees from different countries and cultures through the lens of work motivation. In doing so, we intend to raise three questions. First, on a general level, what is it that motivates (or fails to motivate) employees on the job? Second, on a more specific level, do these motivational drivers differ across cultures? And third, what is the role played by managerial efforts to involve employees in work-related decisions in securing employee motivation and performance? Throughout this analysis, the underlying question here relates to the utilization of human capital; that is, how can organizations maximize their return on their human resources, and is this goal best accomplished through direction or participation?

As noted in Chapter 4, Honda's Takeo Fujisawa observed that while Japanese and American managers may appear on the surface to behave similarly, in fact they frequently approach similar situations in very different ways.[26] And it's not just in Japan and the US. Differences in employee behavior can be found around the world. British and Canadian companies motivate their employees primarily through financial incentives, while Germany and Dutch companies focus on providing employment stability and employee benefits. Indonesian and Korean companies prefer rigid and often autocratic organizational hierarchies where everyone knows their place, while Swedish and Norwegian companies stress informality, power sharing, and mutual benefit in the workplace. Some countries, such as Germany, even combine formality and rigid hierarchies with power sharing and an emphasis on securing mutual gain for all employees.

Even so, managers involved in international business must recognize that if employee behavior is critical for the success of an organization, and if culture influences such behavior, then it represents a major influence on the ultimate competitiveness of the firm. Knowledge of this fact, as well as an understanding of how culture influences employee behavior and performance, represents a critical strategic asset for global managers in a highly competitive world.

For our purposes here, *work motivation* is defined as that which energizes, directs, and sustains human behavior in the workplace.[27] Without a highly motivated work-force that uses its brains, and not just its backs, competitive advantage becomes highly problematic. This is particularly true as we move further into an era where technology and knowledge often determine winners and losers. Simply put, competitive organiza-tions need all of their employees striving on behalf of the organization's goals and objectives, not just the people at the top. The challenge for the global manager is to accomplish this within a work context where behavior is often determined by cultural variations beyond their control. The question for managers, then, is how to use this knowledge to further the organization's competitive edge. This was the challenge faced by Lincoln Electric in its forays into Germany, Mexico, and China, and it is the challenge faced by most managers in their overseas assignments.

To understand how and why motivation affects work behavior, it may be useful to begin with a general examination of how cultural drivers create both the opportunities and constraints on efforts by managers and organizations to motivate their employees through various incentive and reward systems (see Exhibit 9.5).

Exhibit 9.5 Cultural influences on work motivation and performance

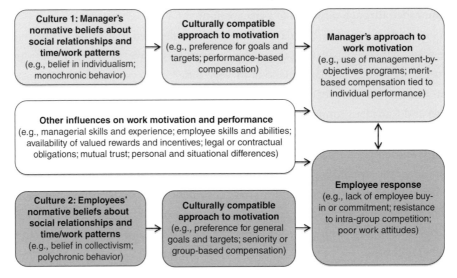

According to this model, normative beliefs about appropriate social relationships (e.g., individualism or collectivism) and performance-reward contingencies on each influence managerial and employee behavior. In addition, norms concerning the appropriateness of such factors as risk tolerance and social loafing are also an issue here (see below).

These cultural drivers, in turn, influence both managerial and employee strategies and preparedness for motivation – at times in opposite directions. Included here are cognitions, expectations, and possibly reactions of these strategies, along with routine or habitual motivational behavior and perceptions of equity. Each side has predispositions concerning what constitutes a fair day's work and a fair day's pay. The resulting managerial and employee behaviors play themselves out at the cultural crossroads, where both parties can either determine that the wage-effort bargain is or is not fair.

Presumably, where both sides perceive this to be fair, employee effort and performance would be expected to increase, as might mutual trust and commitment. Where perceptions of unfairness emerge or remain, however, motivational expectations or employee motivations would likely decline. In this equation, however, it is important to remember that both managers and employees can have very different perceptions of what fairness means, and at least to some extent this is influenced by culture and experience. Finally, feedback from these interactions to both managers and employees would typically provide useful learning for all sides as they prepare for future interactions.

Culture and the psychology of work

Going one step deeper, it is possible to discuss in a general way how certain social psychological processes found both within individuals and their particular cultural backgrounds can influence motivational processes and work behaviors as discussed above. While this can become a highly complex topic, we focus here on just four such processes as they influence work behavior across cultures: cognitions and expectations, causal attributions, risk and uncertainty, and social loafing and team performance.

Cognitions and expectations

Cultural influences on individuals' *cogitations and expectations* were discussed in Chapter 4. We return to this subject here because such processes play a critical role in motivational decisions and subsequent actions. Indeed, cognitive approaches to motivation remain a dominant force in the study of organizational behavior today.[28] These theories are based largely on the assumption that people tend to make reasoned choices about their behaviors based on their expectations and culturally based worldviews. These choices, in turn, influence job-related outcomes and work attitudes. While the majority of cognitive theories, as well as much of the empirical work relating to them, derive from North American efforts, a number of studies have also been conducted to test the external validity of these models in other regions of the world.

For example, research has long demonstrated that people's cultural surroundings can frequently influence their hopes and expectations.[29] One explanation that has been offered for such findings can be found in cognitive theories and reinforcement theories, including social learning theory, behavior modification, and behavioral management theory.[30] Critical to much of this research is the role played by *self-efficacy* in helping determine behavior. Stanford Psychology professor Albert Bandura has argued that incentives and reinforcements can be particularly meaningful if the employees have a high self-efficacy; that is, if they genuinely believe they have the capacity to succeed. Self-efficacy is important because it helps individuals focus their attention on tasks, commit to challenging goals, and seek greater feedback on task effort.[31] But, once again, factors that can enhance or reduce self-efficacy can vary by local environments.

Likewise, what people expect or prefer as rewards for hard work are also culturally based to some degree. Research has also identified an *equity principle* in many Western countries, in which people are motivated to achieve or restore equity (i.e., fairness) between themselves and others they compare themselves to. However, some international researchers have suggested that the equity principle may be somewhat culture bound.[32] Notably in Asia and the Middle East, examples abound concerning individuals who apparently readily accept a clearly recognizable state of inequity in order to preserve their view of societal harmony.

For example, men and women frequently receive different pay for doing precisely the same work in countries like Japan and Korea.[33] One might think that equity theory would predict that a state of inequity would result for female employees, leading to inequity resolution strategies such as those mentioned above. Yet, in many instances, no such perceived inequitable state has been found, thereby calling the theory into question. A plausible explanation here may be that women workers view other women as their referent other, not men. As a result, so long as all women are treated the same, a state of perceived equity could exist. This is not to say that such women feel "equal"; rather, compared to their female reference group, they are receiving what others receive. A state of equity – if not equality – exists.[34]

These cultural idiosyncrasies create at least two cultural limitations on the acceptable actions of both managers and employees. The first limitation focuses on problem analysis. That is, cultural drivers can, at times, affect in no small way how problems are identified and understood by both managers and employees. Indeed, they can even sometimes help determine whether something is seen as a problem at all. For example, while managers in one culture (e.g., Singapore) may focus very seriously on problems of employee absenteeism, managers elsewhere (e.g., Sweden) may see such behavior as more of a personal employee issue and as acceptable within broader limits. The issue in these two cultures is not whether absenteeism is good or bad; rather, it is the magnitude or severity of the problem compared to other behaviors and actions.

In addition, cultural drivers can influence the variety of possible solutions or preferred outcomes that are acceptable on the part of organizations, managers, and employees. Using the employee absenteeism example again, managers in some cultures (again, Singapore) may see strict punitive actions (e.g., financial penalties or termination) as either acceptable or even desirable when employees fail to come to work. In other cultures (again, Sweden), this may seem overly harsh and lacking in understanding of the underlying causes of the absences; such cultures may accept counseling but not termination. In still other cultures (e.g., Saudi Arabia), no action may be taken at all in the belief that absences are largely beyond the control of individuals and, as such, should not be a legitimate issue for managers.

Causal attributions

A significant area where Western theories of management and motivation are limited involves the role of *causal attributions* in the process of individual judgment. Attribution theory was largely developed in North America based on laboratory experiments using predominantly white college undergraduates.[35] This theory focuses on how individuals attempt to understand and interpret events that occur around them. One aspect of this theory that has been repeatedly demonstrated in US studies is the so-called *self-serving bias*, which asserts that in group situations, leaders will tend to attribute group success to themselves and group failure to others. Hence, a manager might conclude that her work team succeeded because of her leadership skills. Alternatively, this same manager may conclude that her team failed because of group negligence and despite her best efforts.

Evidence from one study, however, suggests that this process may be influenced by cultural differences.[36] In a comparison of Koreans and Americans, this study found support for the self-serving bias among his American sample but not in his Korean sample. Following Confucian tradition, Korean leaders accepted responsibility for group failure and attributed group success to the abilities of the group members – just the opposite of the Americans. Clearly, work motivation theories, regardless of their theoretical foundations, must account for cultural variations before any assertions can be made concerning their external validity across national boundaries.

Risk and uncertainty

Issues related to *risk and uncertainty* focus on the extent to which people at all levels of an organization either seek to avoid or embrace uncertainty. As noted in Chapter 3, Geert Hofstede identifies "uncertainty avoidance", his term for a lack of risk tolerance, as a key variable in differentiating between cultures in an aggregate sense. Like personal work values, expectations, and causal attributions, risk and uncertainty can be influenced – at least to a degree – by cultural differences. For example, cultural differences have been found to affect employee preferences for fixed versus variable compensation. For example, more risk-oriented American managers are frequently prepared to convert 100 percent of their pay to variable compensation, while more risk-averse European managers would seldom commit to more than 10 percent.[37]

Similarly, cultural variations can influence employee preferences for financial or non-financial incentives. Thus, Swedes will typically prefer additional time off for superior performance instead of additional income (due in part to their high tax rates), while, if given a choice, Japanese workers would prefer financial incentives (with a distinct preference for group-based incentives). Japanese workers tend to take only about half of their sixteen-day holiday entitlement (compared to thirty-five days in France and Germany) because taking all the time available may show a lack of commitment to the group. Japanese workers who take their full vacations or refuse to work overtime are frequently labeled *wagamama*, or "selfish").[38] As a result, *karoshi* ("death by overwork") is a serious concern in Japan, while Germans, Swedes, and Norwegians see taking time off as part of an inherent right to a healthy and happy life.

Social loafing and team performance

Finally, consider the challenge of *social loafing* (also called the *free rider effect*). A key concern in job performance is maximizing the collective contribution of group members towards the attainment of challenging goals.[39] In a competitive global economy, such collective action becomes a strategic advantage that can differentiate winners from losers. As such, the tendency of select group members to restrict output in the belief that others will take up the slack represents a serious impediment to organizational effectiveness. Free riders and social loafing as social phenomena have been scrutinized in a small but important set of studies.[40] Similar studies have found that individuals may loaf in a group setting because they assume that the actions of others will ensure the attainment of the collective good, thereby freeing them up to redirect their individual efforts towards the attainment of additional personal gains.

Social loafing can only be successful when individual behavior can be hidden behind group behavior. To accomplish this, group norms must support, or at least tolerate, a high level of individualism. It is therefore not surprising that such behavior tends to be more prevalent in organizations in America and Western Europe than in East Asia.[41] For example, studies found that Japanese and Taiwanese workers performed better in groups than alone.

Management researcher Christopher Earley specifically tested this hypothesis among Chinese and American managers and found that individualistic-collectivist beliefs moderated the tendency towards social loafing.[42] Specifically, he found that more social loafing occurred in the individualistic American group than in the more collectivist Chinese group. Building on these results, he posited that while individualists would consistently perform better when working individually rather than in a group, collectivists would perform better either when working in an in-group – as opposed to in and out-group condition – or working individually.[43] Since the basis of collectivism is rooted in allegiance to the group, such individuals would only exhibit this allegiance and subsequent effort when working with members with whom they have had a long and mutually supportive relationship. Working in groups where members were relative strangers would not engender the same cohesiveness or motivational pattern. Earley tested this hypothesis using a sample of US, Chinese, and Israeli managers. Results supported the hypothesis.[44] Collectivists anticipated receiving more rewards and felt more efficacious, both alone and as group members (and thus performed better) while working in an in-group situation than while working in either an out-group situation or working alone. Individualists, on the other hand, anticipated receiving more rewards and felt more efficacious (and thus performed better) when working alone than while working in either an in-group or out-group situation.

In conclusion, cultural differences have a strong influence on work motivation and performance. Culture can influence cognitive processes governing effort determination, interpretations of and responses to various forms of incentives, and output restriction mechanisms such as social loafing. What is perhaps surprising here is not so much the magnitude of this influence, but its breadth. Based on available findings, cultural differences seem to permeate many aspects of both the decision to participate and the decision to produce, the two fundamental decisions facing organizational members.[45] In view of these findings, it is surprising how few studies of work motivation have intentionally incorporated cultural variables into either their models or their research designs.

Incentives and rewards across cultures

What do people expect to happen – and, indeed, what do they wish to happen – as a result of their work efforts? Performance consequences can vary widely, as can reward structures. In general, when people are offered incentives to perform or rewards for good performance (or even punishment for poor performance) such actions are obviously viewed and evaluated by employees as being appropriate or inappropriate, acceptable or unacceptable, with corresponding attitudinal and behavioral consequences. If these positive or negative consequences are important to managers, then, clearly, care must be taken in developing incentives and reward systems.

There are many ways to see how this works. Let's begin with the negative side of this question. Specifically, what happens to employees when companies are experiencing either financial exigency or over-production and wish to reduce their labor force to save costs? Surprisingly, significant differences emerge across countries and regions. In North America, for example, such a situation leads logically – and culturally consistently – to lay-offs. While widely recognized as causing hardships on people, lay-offs are often deemed to represent a prudent response to a financial crisis. In the Netherlands, by contrast, long-standing social legislation makes it much more difficult – and more costly – to downsize employees. As a result, Dutch organizations will often seek other remedies, such as highly lucrative employee buy-outs. Finally, in Japan, lay-offs are rare (although still possible) since the organization risks losing its public reputation which can affect its business and future hiring opportunities. As a result, Japanese organizations frequently decide to transfer redundant employees to other parts of the organization or its subsidiaries. Thus, the same problem can lead to very different outcomes based on where the action occurs.

On the more positive side, consider the variety of outcomes and rewards offered to employees in exchange for their efforts on behalf of the organization. Generally, we refer to two types of incentives and rewards:

(1) *Extrinsic rewards* are rewards (or punishments) that are provided to employees as a result of good (or poor) performance, and usually include such items as salaries, bonuses, benefits, and job security. They are largely "administered" by the firm, not the employee, as a consequence of his or her performance.

(2) *Intrinsic rewards* are rewards that arise from doing one's job in a satisfactory way. They are largely "self-administered"; that is, employees may feel pride or satisfaction from a job well done or they may enjoy the holiday time they receive as a consequence of hard work.

Looking across cultures, it readily becomes apparent that reward preferences are, to a degree, culture-bound. Some cultures emphasize security, while others emphasize harmony and congenial interpersonal relationships, and still others emphasize individual status and respect. For example, a study examined employees of a large multinational electrical equipment manufacturer operating in forty countries around the world and found important similarities as well as differences in what rewards employees wanted in exchange for good performance.[46] Interestingly, in all countries, the most important rewards that were sought involved recognition and achievement. Second in importance were improvements in the immediate work environment and employment conditions such as pay and work hours. Beyond this, however, a number of differences emerged in terms of preferred rewards. Some countries, like the UK and the US, placed a low value on job security compared to workers in many nations, while French and Italian workers placed a high value on security and good fringe benefits and a low value on challenging work. Scandinavian workers de-emphasized "getting ahead" and instead stressed greater concern for others on the job and for personal freedom and autonomy.

Germans placed high on security, fringe benefits, and "getting ahead," while Japanese ranked low on personal advancement and high on having good working conditions and a congenial work environment.

Extrinsic incentives and rewards

As already noted, *extrinsic motivation* involves the exchange of organizational rewards for employee performance. These "concrete" rewards have received considerable attention in the research literature. We briefly examine four such rewards: financial incentives, executive compensation, gender and compensation, and employee benefits.

Financial incentives

Many merit-based (or pay-for-performance) incentive systems in use, particularly in the West, attempt to link financial compensation (and to some extent promotional opportunities) directly to individual, group, or even corporate performance. They view this as a statement of equity, if not equality. That is, the higher one's performance, the greater the rewards – a simple performance-reward contingency. Other cultures believe compensation should be based on group membership or group effort, thereby emphasizing equality. Everyone is deserving of more or less the same rewards. To understand the logic underlying such differences, it is helpful to understand the concept of *distributive justice* across cultures, especially as it relates to individualism or collectivism. One example of this can be seen in an effort by a US multinational corporation to institute an individually based bonus system for its sales representatives in a Danish subsidiary. The sales force rejected the proposal because it favored one group over another. The Danish employees felt that all employees should receive the same amount of bonus instead of being given a percentage of one's salary, reflecting a strong sense of egalitarianism.[47]

Similar results were found for Indonesian oil workers; individually based incentive systems created more controversy than results. As one manager commented: "Indonesians manage their culture by a group process, and everybody is linked together as a team. Distributing money differently amongst the team did not go over that well; so, we've come to the conclusion that pay for performance is not suitable for Indonesia."[48] Similar results were reported in studies comparing Americans with Chinese, Russians, and Indians. In all three cases, Americans expressed greater preference than their counterparts for rewards to be based on performance instead of equality or need.[49]

It is interesting to note that the basis for some incentive systems has evolved over time in response to political and economic changes. China is frequently cited as an example of a country that is attempting to blend quasi-capitalistic economic reforms with a reasonably static socialist political state. On the economic front, China's economy has demonstrated considerable growth as entrepreneurs are increasingly allowed to initiate their own enterprises largely free from government control. And within existing and former state-owned enterprises, some movement can be seen towards what is called a reform model of incentives and motivation. In this regard, a distinction can be made between the traditional Chinese incentive model, in which egalitarianism is stressed and rewards tend to be based on age, loyalty, and gender, and the new reform model, in which merit and achievement receive greater emphasis and rewards tend to be based on qualifications, training, level of responsibility, and performance. However, some researchers have suggested that the rhetoric in support of the reform model far surpasses actual implementation to date.

In Japan, meanwhile, efforts to introduce Western-style merit pay systems have frequently led to an increase in overall labor costs. Since the companies that adopted the merit-based reward system could not simultaneously reduce the pay of less productive workers for fear of causing them to lose face and disturb group harmony (*wa*), everyone's salary tended to increase.

Similar results concerning the manner in which culture can influence reward systems as well as other personnel practices emerged from a study among banking employees in Korea.[50] The two Korean banks were owned and operated as joint ventures with banks in other countries, one from Japan and one from the US. In the American joint venture, US personnel policies dominated management practice in the Korean bank, while in the Japanese joint venture a blend of Japanese and Korean human resource management policies prevailed. Employees in the joint venture with the Japanese bank were significantly more committed to the organization than employees in the US joint venture. Moreover, the Japanese-affiliated bank also demonstrated a significantly higher financial performance. Anyway you look at it, employees do not always seek the same rewards and outcomes for job performance.

Executive compensation

Much has been written about excessive executive compensation, particularly in the US. From a motivational standpoint, compensation is seen as the key to hiring and retaining the best executive leadership available. While it is true that incentive systems work, the question that many people are asking is how much money is necessary to hire and motivate the right CEO? In the US, we hear increasing concerns about the "imperial CEO," referring to what many consider to be excessive rewards that in many cases are not even tied to executive or corporate performance (see Chapter 6). In many cases, they

Exhibit 9.6 Ratio of average CEO compensation to average employee compensation

Country	Pay ratio	Country	Pay ratio	Country	Pay ratio
United States	475	United Kingdom	24	Netherlands	16
Venezuela	50	Thailand	24	France	14
Brazil	49	Australia	23	New Zealand	13
Mexico	47	South Africa	22	Sweden	12
Singapore	44	Canada	20	Germany	12
Argentina	44	Italy	20	Switzerland	11
Malaysia	42	Belgium	18	Japan	11
Hong Kong	41	Spain	16	South Korea	8

Source: Based on Richard M. Steers and Luciara Nardon, *Managing in the Global Economy*, Armonk, NY: M.E. Sharpe, 2006.
Note: numbers express the ratios between the average CEO compensation and the average compensation received by industrial and service workers in the same country.

are tied to the manipulation of stock prices, sometimes by illegal or certainly unethical means. Issues of fairness abound.

What has many people upset is that while executives in many countries are making increasing amounts of money, rank-and-file workers are increasingly seeing their real wages decreasing. Twenty years ago, the average American CEO made roughly forty times the salary of the average factory worker in his or her company. Today this figure is well over 400 times the salary! Worse still, the US seems to be way out in front of other nations in terms of this imbalance between workers' and executives' pay. Another way to understand this is to look at average CEO compensation compared to the average industrial and service worker on a country-by-country basis, as shown in Exhibit 9.6. While aggregate data always contain some systematic errors (e.g., the data for South Korea do not include owner-CEOs, who can become incredibly wealthy even if they are officially paid very little), it is difficult to believe that the magnitude of these results is far from accurate.

These data raise serious questions: Why are CEOs in the US paid so much compared to their counterparts in other parts of the industrialized world? Are they worth it? What is fair compensation for such work and responsibility? What is motivational and what is overkill or even abuse? Finally, from the standpoint of social policy, what should be the relationship, if any, between executive compensation and the income of rank-and-file employees?

Gender and compensation

Similar to the case of executive compensation, significant differences can also be found in pay levels between men and women across national boundaries. This can be a difficult topic to explore because it can very quickly turn into disagreement over beliefs and values irrespective of cultural differences. Put another way, should this discussion focus on what companies across borders do in their compensation policies or on what they should do? And who gets to determine the definition of "should?" Moreover, in making pay comparisons between genders, are we discussing disparities between the pay of men and women in similar jobs (e.g., assembly-line workers, marketing representatives, health care providers, etc.) or in different jobs that someone has determined to be on a par with each other in terms of the skills or qualifications required (e.g., a teacher and a manager – the issue of comparable worth)?

Our focus here is on basic statistical differences between what men and women make by job category in different countries. To accomplish this, we turn to a recent OECD study of gender wage gaps, as summarized in Exhibit 9.7. As can be seen, gender-based wage gaps can be found in all of the countries studied, ranging from a low of 6 percent wage disparity in New Zealand to a high of 40 percent disparity in Korea. Some of these disparities can be explained by the fact that women are more likely to be found in contingent labor categories, which typically pay less than permanent job status. Other disparities can be explained by differing sex role expectations and norms in some countries. And some can be explained by simple job discrimination. In this regard, it is interesting to note that in no country do men on average make less than women, disputing the notion that such wage differences are random in nature.

From both a managerial and a motivational standpoint, this issue can become intractable for the following reason. When global managers are assigned abroad, what is (or should be) their philosophy on compensation policies? Should they abide by

Exhibit 9.7 Wage gaps between men and women across nations

Country	Wage gap (%)	Country	Wage gap (%)	Country	Wage gap (%)
New Zealand	6	Sweden	15	Finland	20
Belgium	9	Spain	17	United States	21
Poland	11	OECD Average	18	Canada	22
Greece	12	Czech Republic	19	Switzerland	22
France	12	Portugal	19	Germany	24
Hungary	12	Ireland	20	Japan	32
Denmark	14	United Kingdom	20	Korea	40
Australia	15				

Source: Date derived from OECD, *Women and Men in OECD*. Paris: OECD 2007, pp. 15–18.
Note: Numbers are expressed as a percentage of the average wage gap between men and women by country.

prevailing local wage patterns (e.g., paying women lower salaries than men doing similar work) or should they apply the equal-pay-for-equal-work policies that may prevail in their home countries. Simply put, should global managers strive to play by local rules as defined by local cultures (particularism) or be agents of change as defined by their home country beliefs and values (universalism)? This value conflict illustrates another challenge facing managers at all levels of the organization, and is discussed more in greater detail in the next chapter.

Employee benefits

Finally, as human resources (HR) executives know all too well, employee benefits and prerequisites represent a sizable portion of overall labor costs for any operation. These costs typically range from 33 to 50 percent of salaries. These same executives also understand that such benefits can vary significantly across cultures, not just in their magnitude but also in their nature. As expatriate packages decline and global growth increasingly seeks to attract local talent from around the world, employers that ignore local quirks and customs do so at their own risk.[51] Companies that extend their stock options plans abroad often discover that the local tax systems substantially reduce any income – or motivational – advantages. The trick for managers here is to study local customs and work to match corporate benefits to local conditions.

To understand the extent to which these customs can vary, consider several examples. Indian firms frequently pay the expenses for the aging parents of employees. Companies in much of China are required to chip in to housing funds, usually on a matching basis, so that employees can buy their own houses. Likewise, companies in India and Russia often arrange for home mortgages for their employees and sometimes even pay part of the monthly mortgage expenses.

Employers in both Japan and the Philippines traditionally receive a monthly family allowance (called "rice allowances" in the Philippines and *kazoku teiate* in Japan) in addition to their wages. Many Mexican firms offer "pollution-escape trips" to allow employees to escape from polluted Mexico City and other cities to holidays in either the Pacific or Gulf coasts. Also in Mexico, Mother's Day is on a weekday, and employees often receive the entire day off to take their mothers to lunch. Executives in both Brazil and Mexico are often given chauffeur-driven cars with bulletproof windows to protect them against kidnapping.

In recognition of the litigious nature of American society, many US companies pay for employee legal services insurance just as they do employee health care insurance. Also in the US, most company health care insurance policies pay for Viagra (considered to be medication for a "medical condition"), but not birth control pills (not considered to be a "medical condition"). Finally, many French and German companies offer the use of company-owned ski chalets or beach houses for a nominal fee.

Intrinsic incentives and rewards

Next, consider *intrinsic motivation and rewards*. Here the issue is the job satisfaction, organizational commitment, self-fulfillment, or meaning that results from task performance. We consider just two examples here: employee involvement and work-related attitudes.

Employee involvement

One of the most common strategies to improve work quality, if not necessarily work quantity, is to get employees to take ownership in corporate outcomes. High-quality products depend heavily on high-quality employees. And high-quality employees are usually those who are not just well trained but also well informed. They are contributing members of the organization. The extent to which companies share information, knowledge, and power throughout the organization in an effort to maximize their return on human capital is generally referred to as *employee involvement* (see also the discussion on participation in organizational decision making in Chapter 5).

The assumption underlying most employee involvement programs is that rank-and-file workers are often best able to understand work processes – and how to improve these processes – and that involving all employees is the surest way to get everyone on board for any organizational effort to improve quality or productivity. Employee involvement reduces resistance to change and often sparks creativity among those people best able to facilitate such change. To be truly effective, however, these efforts must go well beyond allowing workers to have control over their own jobs and include attempts by firms to allow employees to influence decisions affecting work groups and sometimes the entire organization. To succeed, rank-and-file employees need information, support, and power to become genuine partners with managers in running the organization.

Research on employee involvement consistently suggests that it leads to several desirable organizational outcomes, including improved decision quality, increased commitment to implementing the chosen decision, enhanced employee development as a result of being allowed to participate in key decisions affecting their jobs, and increased job satisfaction and self-efficacy (see discussion below).[52]

Employee involvement takes many different forms both within and between cultures. As discussed in Chapter 5, Japanese culture and traditions dictate that managers consult with their employees on many aspects of individual and departmental perform-ance, and everyone is encouraged – even pressured – to contribute. At the same time, German law requires employee participation in most operational decisions within a firm. And in Canada and the US we see a wide mixture of strategies in which some firms support genuine employee participation and others do not.

Employee involvement efforts frequently include the use of self-managing teams. Self-managing teams exist when managers designate a whole project or work process to a team of employees, and then allow the team to determine how best to design and implement the assigned task. This is job enrichment in action. These groups require both autonomy and managerial support. They also frequently require considerable information pertaining to the background of the task and how it fits into the larger organizational purpose (something senior managers are often reluctant to provide in some cultures), as well as training in managing group processes.

Work-related attitudes

Work-related attitudes, like job satisfaction or employee commitment to organizations, can also represent a significant intrinsic reward for employees. These outcomes are generally viewed within the structure of a *psychological contract*, as discussed below. Under such contracts, employees (as well as employers) expect certain outcomes in exchange for their inputs. In the case of job satisfaction, it is generally thought that people become satisfied on the job to the extent that they perceive that the rewards they receive are fair – as seen by them – compared to their level of effort or input. This determination is obviously a personal thing, and is influenced heavily by perceptions and cognitions.

As a result of such comparisons, we would generally expect that positive or negative job attitudes would result from the employee's interpretation of the fairness of the rewards received (see Exhibit 9.8).

Because of this, we would expect that variations in job satisfaction levels would vary considerably within each country. This is only logical in view of the differences that are

Exhibit 9.8 Expectations, rewards, and job attitudes

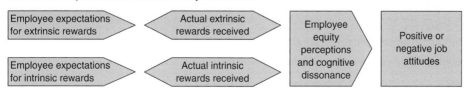

Exhibit 9.9 Average job satisfaction levels for select countries

Countries	Percent of employees reporting high job satisfaction	Countries	Percent of employees reporting high job satisfaction
Denmark	61	Argentina	38
India (middle class only)	55	Austria	36
Norway	54	Israel	33
United States	50	Brazil	28
Ireland	49	France	24
Canada	48	Japan	16
Germany	48	South Korea	14
Australia	46	China	11
Mexico	44	Czech Republic	11
Slovenia	40	Ukraine	10
United Kingdom	38	Hungary	9

Source: Adapted from Matthew Boyle, "Nothing is rotten in Denmark," *Fortune*, February 19, 2001, pp. 242–243.

normally found across individuals, jobs, and organizations. Even so, it is possible on an aggregate level to ask where employee job satisfaction tends to be higher or lower on a country-by-country basis. As shown in Exhibit 9.9, the results are not unpredictable. The most satisfied employees are not found in richer countries or the countries of a particular continent. They are not found in countries that claim certain religious affiliations. Nor are they found exclusively in either large or small countries. Instead, the most satisfied employees tend to be found in those countries where the prevailing management systems and motivational programs are compatible with and supportive of local cultures. These findings caution against a presumed "best practices" approach to management across diverse cultures or a one-size-fits-all approach to motivation. Ignoring cultural influences on employee work behavior is clearly done at a manager's – and an organization's – peril.

Furthermore, a recent poll of US workers found that, given a choice between two weeks of extra pay and two weeks of vacation, employees preferred the extra vacation by a 2:1 margin. Moreover, consider the effects of work on employee well-being. It might be suggested that while many Europeans load up on vacation time, many Americans load up on consumer products charged to their Visa cards. As the work pace quickens, health-related problems are rising, most notably heart problems among both men and women resulting from increasing job-related stress. However, the pressure to succeed and concern about the economy and job security frequently lead American workers in the opposite direction towards more work and less play.

While perhaps overly simplistic, the work versus leisure conundrum provides an easy conceptual entry into cultural differences, especially as they relate to the world of work. It indicates how central work is in some people's lives. However, this debate is only part of a larger debate over the social and economic consequences of increasing globalization. As noted earlier, many people believe – correctly or incorrectly – that the quickening pace of globalization and the competitive intensity of the new global economy are changing how people live, in ways not imagined earlier. The open question is whether these changes are for the better or for the worse.

MANAGER'S NOTEBOOK

Culture, work, and motivation

It is important for managers to understand that no culture or country has an absolute preference for one incentive system over the other. That is, almost all cultures make use of a combination of both extrinsic and intrinsic incentives. What does differ, however, is the relative balance between the two. Some cultures place greater emphasis on concrete, typically financially based, incentives in the belief that, at the end of the day, money matters. Others obviously recognize the importance of money as a motivator but prefer to emphasize and support improvements in such areas as work design and employee involvement in the belief that challenging and interesting work will maximize individual and collective contributions to organizational goal attainment. In any case, managers must discover, understand, and respond to work environments as they are influenced by cultural differences (see Exhibit 9.10).

As noted above, variations in managerial approaches to work motivation can be traced to cultural differences, as illustrated by the core cultural dimensions discussed in Chapter 3. So, what does this tell the manager faced with motivating employees and teams in different settings? Several suggestions can be offered here, based on a manager's assessment of local conditions on the ground.[53]

Exhibit 9.10 Management challenge and strategies: motivating a global workforce

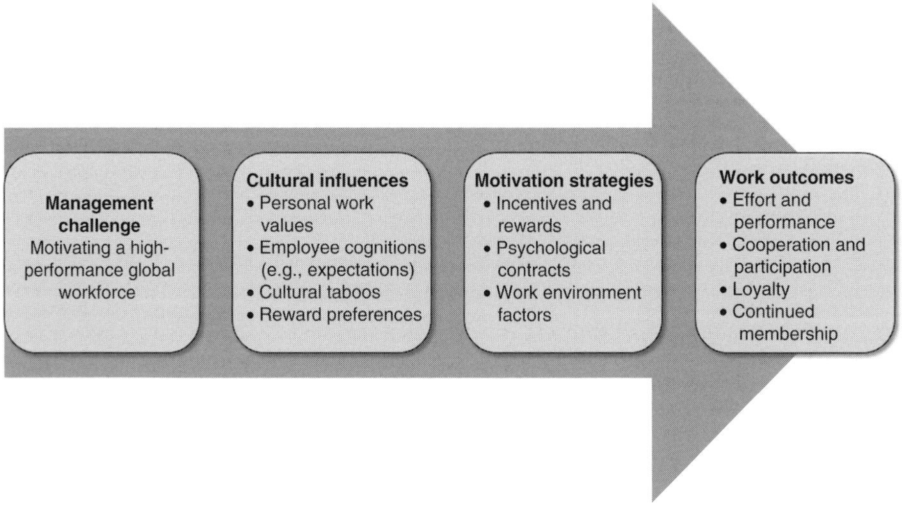

Management challenge	Cultural influences	Motivation strategies	Work outcomes
Motivating a high-performance global workforce	• Personal work values • Employee cognitions (e.g., expectations) • Cultural taboos • Reward preferences	• Incentives and rewards • Psychological contracts • Work environment factors	• Effort and performance • Cooperation and participation • Loyalty • Continued membership

Role of hierarchy in work motivation

Managers in hierarchical cultures, where power is centralized at the top, often empha-size extrinsic rewards over intrinsic ones. Job requirements and directives to employees are usually direct and clear. Decisive and powerful leaders typically run most organ-izations. In many African societies, for example, leaders are often compared to parents, while in many Western societies leaders are compared to athletes. Finally, managers in such cultures often prefer unquestioning subordinate compliance with their directives. Participation in decision making is typically low. Managers in highly egalitarian cultures, on the other hand, often emphasize the use of power equalization models, with an emphasis on intrinsic rewards and minimal salary differentials between groups of employees. Money is often less of a motivator than it can be in more hierarchical societies. Decision making is frequently based on widespread employee participation and involvement. And leaders are often flexible and collaborative, even if their stand-ards remain high.

Individual and group-centered action

Managers in individualistic cultures often emphasize extrinsic rewards (e.g., pay, pro-motion) tied to personal achievement, individual-based incentives, personal responsi-bility for task accomplishment, and the ability of employees to work independently. At the same time, managers in highly collectivistic cultures often emphasize intrinsic rewards tied to organizational commitment and loyalty (e.g., group camaraderie), group-based incentives, group norms and moral persuasion as motivators, and team-building focused on collective task accomplishment.

Defining relationships with the surrounding environment

Managers in mastery-oriented cultures often encourage competitive work environ-ments within the organization to stimulate employees' best efforts. Moreover, performance-based incentives using largely monetary and symbolic rewards (e.g., impressive job titles) are frequently seen. Showcasing high performers and encouraging employees to "think big" and overcome obstacles are also common strategies in such cultures. Finally, employee retention is often selective and based on superior perform-ance. By contrast, managers in harmony-oriented cultures often encourage cooperation and team effort for collective results instead of competition. Seniority or membership-based incentives are also common within work groups and departments, as is show-casing team efforts and organization-wide accomplishments. Respect for tradition, heritage, and the environment in general are common. Finally, management approaches to employee retention is typically universal, applying to all employees.

Time and work patterns

Managers in monochronic cultures often emphasize the use of simple and straightforward (step-by-step) directions for employees. Predictability and sequencing are important. There is often a preference for performing one task at a time. Each project should have specific time limits or deadlines, along with intermittent written progress reports. The job itself – quality, quantity, and timeliness – emerges as the central focus of work, and employees are encouraged to separate their work life from their personal life. At the same time, managers in polychronic cultures often emphasize flexible time limits for various tasks, or at least an acknowledgement that deadlines will often be missed. Intermittent progress reports through face-to-face personal discussions are common. Employees at all levels are encouraged – or required – to perform multiple tasks simultaneously. Finally, there tends to be a greater integration or acceptance of personal relationships intertwined with work activities.

Uncertainty, predictability, and social control

Managers in rule-based (or universalistic) cultures often encourage strict adherence to clearly publicized rules, regulations, and policies. These are applied uniformly to all employees regardless of their status or connections. Rewards are at least partly tied to rule compliance, not just performance, and performance evaluations are based largely on objective criteria. Meanwhile, managers in relationship-based (or particularistic) cultures often allow for extenuating circumstances or the nature of personal relationships in rule enforcement. Building personal relationships and trust between superiors and subordinates is important, as is showing patience to first-time rule breakers where possible. Influential people (e.g., the CEO or a high achiever) are often used as role models of success to help motivate others, and performance evaluations are often based to some degree on subjective criteria and incorporate loyalty as a key factor.

It is important to remember here that these are only general trends, and that variations around these trends obviously occur. Even so, they can provide a starting point for managers who are looking for some kind of conceptual entry for understanding the motivational bases of employee behavior in different regions of the world. The challenge for management here is knowing when and where to readjust the mix of motivators. At the same time, it must be remembered that companies that stress either extrinsic or intrinsic rewards can be found in all cultures. Part of this is tied to particular industrial sectors and particular job descriptions, while a part is also tied to cultural beliefs about the role of employees in organizations. Are employees widely considered to be factors of production or intellectual capital? Are employees at the top of the hierarchy valued differently than those towards the bottom? And underlying all of these questions is the fundamental HR challenge: how to get the most out of an organization's human capital. Perhaps the most a global manager can hope for here is the time and patience to develop an understanding of local practices in employment relations prior to a need to take action.

Notes

1 Akio Morita, Edwin M. Reingold, and Mitsuko Shimomura, *Made in Japan: Akio Morita and Sony*. New York, NY: Morrow, 1988.
2 Cited in Snejina Michailova, "When common sense becomes uncommon," *Journal of World Business*, 2002, 37, p. 180. This comment comes from Russian workers referring to local motivational practices.
3 F. Rieger and D. Wong-Rieger, "A configuration model of national influence applied to Southeast Asian organizations," *Proceedings of the Research Conference on Business in Southeast Asia*, May 12, 1990, p. 87.
4 Paul Thorne, quoted in Richard Hill, *EuroManagers*. Brussels: Europublications, p. 160.
5 Carol Hymowitz and Matt Murray, "General Electric's Welch discusses his ideas on motivating employees," *The Wall Street Journal*, June 21, 1999, p. A-1.
6 "Detroit South," *Business Week*, March 16, 1992, p. 64.
7 Rabindra Kanungo and Robert Wright, "A cross-cultural study of managerial job attitudes," *Journal of International Business Studies*, 1983, 13, p. 115.
8 James O'Connell, "Lincoln Electric: venturing abroad," *Harvard Business School Case #9-398-095*, April 1998; Charles Hill, *International Business*. New York, NY: McGraw-Hill/Irwin, 2003; Donald Hastings, "Lincoln Electric's harsh lessons from international expansion," *Harvard Business Review*, May–June 1999, pp. 163–178; Randall Schuler, Susan Jackson, and Yadong Luo, *Managing Human Resources in Cross-Border Alliances*. London: Routledge, 2004.
9 Hastings, "Lincoln Electric's harsh lessons," p. 164.
10 O'Connell, "Lincoln Electric: venturing abroad"; Hastings, "Lincoln Electric's harsh lessons."
11 Hastings, "Lincoln Electric's harsh lessons," p. 166.
12 *Ibid.*, p. 174.
13 *Ibid.*, p. 178.
14 Ingmar Bjorkman and Charles Galunic, "Lincoln Electric in China," in Dennis Briscoe and Randall Schuler, *International Human Resource Management*. London: Routledge, 2004, pp. 420–436.
15 Hazel R. Markus and Shinobu Kitayama, "Culture and the self: implications for cognition, emotion, and motivation," *Psychological Review*, 1991, 98(2), pp. 224–253.

16 Yongsun Paik and Yong Suhk Pak, "The changing face of Korean management of overseas affiliates," in Chris Rowley and Yongsun Paik (eds.), *The Changing Face of Korean Management*. London: Routledge, 2009, pp. 165–188.

17 *Ibid.*, p. 168.

18 George England, *The Manager and His Values*. Cambridge, MA: Ballinger, 1975.

19 George England, *National Work Meanings and Patterns: Constraints on Management Action*. Norman, OK: Center for Economic and Management Research, University of Oklahoma, 1986; David Thomas, *International Management: A Cross-Cultural Perspective*. Thousand Oaks, CA: Sage, 2002, pp. 210–212.

20 *Ubuntu* is a social norm governing people's allegiances and relations with one other. It helps define individuals based on their personal and family relationships. Within these relationships, commonwealth or communal norms often exist in which "what's mine is yours, and what's yours is mine." The term has its origin in the Bantu languages of Southern Africa. While the Zulu maxim *umuntu ngumuntu ngabantu* ("a person is a person through other persons") may have no apparent religious connotations in the context of Western society, in an African context it suggests that the person one is to become by behaving with humanity is an ancestor worthy of respect or veneration. Those who uphold the principle of *ubuntu* throughout their lives will, in death, achieve a unity with those still living.

21 Mzamo Mangaliso, "Building competitive advantage from *ubuntu*: management lessons from South Africa," *Academy of Management Executive*, 2001, 15(3), pp. 23–35.

22 "Jobs for life," *The Economist*, December 22, 2007, pp. 68–69.

23 *Ibid.*

24 Gregory Viscusi, "US production still tops Europe's," *Register Guard*, August 27, 2002, p. B-1.

25 Diane Brady, "Rethinking the rat race," *Business Week*, August 26, 2002, p. 143.

26 Takeo Fujisawa, cited in David Thomas, *Cross-cultural Management*. Thousand Oaks, CA: Sage, 2008, p. 145.

27 Lyman Porter, Greg Bigley, and Richard Steers, *Motivation and Work Behavior*. New York, NY: McGraw-Hill, 2003.

28 Terrence Mitchell and D. Daniels, "Motivation," in Walter C. Borman, Daniel R. Ilgen, and Richard J. Klimoski (eds.), *Comprehensive Handbook of Psychology: Industrial and Organizational Psychology*, 5th Edition, vol. XII. New York, NY: Wiley, 2002; W. Van Eerde and H. Thierry, "VIE functions, self-set goals, and performance: an experiment," in M. Erez, U. Kleinbeck, and H. Thierry (eds.), *Work Motivation in the Context of a Globalizing Economy*. Mahwah, NJ: Lawrence Erlbaum Associates, 2001, pp. 131–147; Porter *et al.*, *Motivation and Work Behavior*.

29 Porter *et al.*, *Motivation and Work Behavior*.

30 Albert Bandura, *Social Foundations of Thought and Action*. Englewood Cliffs, NJ: Prentice Hall, 1986; Albert Bandura, *Self-efficacy: The Exercise of Control*. New York, NY: Freeman, 1996; Fred Luthans and Robert Kreitner, *Organizational Behavior Modification*. Glenview, IL: Scott Foresman, 1985.

31 Bandura, *Social Foundations of Thought and Action*; Ruth Kanfer and P. L. Ackerman, "A self-regulatory skills perspective to reducing cognitive interference," in Irwin G. Sarason

and Barbara R. Sarason (eds.), *Cognitive Interference Theories: Methods and Findings*. New York, NY: Erlbaum, 1996; Edwin Locke and Gary Latham, *A Theory of Goal-Setting and Task Performance*. Englewood Cliffs, NJ: Prentice Hall, 1990; Anne Tsui and Susan Ashford, "Adaptive self-regulation: a process view of managerial effectiveness," *Journal of Management*, 1994, 20, pp. 93–121; A. Stajkovic and Fred Luthans, "Social cognitive theory and self-efficacy: implications for motivation theory and practice," in Porter *et al.*, *Motivation and Work Behavior*, pp. 126–140.

32 Gert Hofstede, *Culture's Consequence: International Differences in Work-related Values*. Beverly Hills, CA: Sage, 1980, rev. 2001; C. F. Fey, "Opening the black box of motivation: a cross-cultural comparison of Sweden and Russia," *International Business Journal*, 2005, 14 (3), pp. 345–367.

33 James Abegglen and George Stalk, *Kaisha: The Japanese Corporation*. New York, NY: Basic Books, 1985; Kae Chung, Hak C. Lee, and Ku H. Jung, *Korean Management: Global Strategy and Cultural Transformation*. Berlin: Walter de Gruyter, 1997.

34 Ken Kim, Hun-Joon Park, and Nori Suzuki, "Reward allocations in the US, Japan, and Korea: a comparison of individualistic and collectivistic cultures," *Academy of Management Journal*, 1990, 33(1), pp. 188–198.

35 H. Kelley, "The process of causal attributions," *American Psychologist*, 1973, 28, pp. 107–129; Barnard Weiner, *Human Motivation*. New York, NY: Holt, Rinehart and Winston, 1980.

36 Sang Nam, "Culture, control, and commitment in an international joint venture," *International Journal of Human Resource Management*, 1995, 6, pp. 553–567.

37 Richard M. Steers and Carlos Sanchez-Runde, "Culture, motivation, and work behavior," in Martin J. Gannon and Karen L. Newman (eds.), *Handbook of Cross-cultural Management*. Oxford, UK: Blackwell, 2002, pp. 190–216.

38 "Jobs for life," *The Economist*, December 22, 2007, pp. 68–69.

39 Edward Lawler, *The Ultimate Advantage: Creating the High Involvement Organization*. San Francisco, CA: Jossey-Bass, 1992.

40 B. Latane, K. D. Williams, S. G. Harkins, "Many hands make light the work: the causes and consequences of social loafing," *Journal of Personality and Social Psychology*, 1979, 37, pp. 822–832.

41 P. Christopher Earley, "Social loafing and collectivism," *Administrative Science Quarterly*, 1989, 34, pp. 565–581; J. George, "Extrinsic and intrinsic origins of perceived social loafing in organizations," *Academy of Management Journal*, 1992, 35, pp. 191–202; P. Christopher Earley, "East meets west meets mideast: further explorations of collectivistic and individualistic work groups," *Academy of Management Journal*, 1993, 36(2), pp. 319–348; T. Matsui, T. Kakuyama, and M. L. Onglatco, "Effects of goals and feedback on performance in groups," *Journal of Applied Psychology*, 1987, 72, pp. 407–415; W. Gabrenya, B. Latane, and Y. Wang, "Social loafing on an optimizing task: cross-cultural differences among Chinese and Americans," *Journal of Cross-Cultural Psychology*, 1985, 16, pp. 223–242.

42 Earley, "Social loafing and collectivism."

43 Earley, "East meets west meets mideast"; P. Christopher Earley, *Face, Harmony, and Social Structure: An Analysis of Organizational Behavior Across Cultures*. New York, NY: Oxford University Press, 1997.

44 Earley, "East meets west meets mideast."

45 James March and Herbert Simon, *Organizations*. New York, NY: Wiley, 1958.

46 Steers and Sanchez-Runde, "Culture, motivation, and work behavior."

47 *Ibid.*

48 *Ibid.*, p. 205.

49 *Ibid.*

50 Sang Nam, "Culture, control, and commitment in an international joint venture," *International Journal of Human Resource Management*, 1995, 6, pp. 553–567.

51 Jena McGregor, "The right perks," *Business Week*, January 28, 2008, pp. 42–44.

52 Steven Shane and Mary Ann von Glinow, *Organizational Behavior*. New York, NY: McGraw-Hill, 2003.

53 Carlos Sanchez-Runde, Sang Myung Lee, and Richard M. Steers, "Cultural drivers of work behavior: personal values, motivation, and job attitudes," in Rabi S. Bhagat and Richard M. Steers (eds.), *Cambridge Handbook of Culture, Organizations, and Work*. Cambridge, UK: Cambridge University Press, 2009, pp. 334–371.

CHAPTER 10

Negotiation and global partnerships

- Seeking common cause   321
- Culture and negotiation: a model   328
- The negotiation process: strategies, concessions, and contracts   330
- Negotiation patterns across cultures   337
- Building global partnerships   342
- Managing global partnerships   346
- MANAGER'S NOTEBOOK: Negotiation and global partnerships   350

> *When negotiating in Russia, the slower you go, the further you'll get.*
> *Don't hurry to reply, but hurry to listen.*
>
> Traditional Russian proverbs[1]

> *When Arabs give a "yes" answer to a request, they are not necessarily certain that the action*
> *will or can be carried out. Etiquette demands that your request have a positive response.*
> *A positive response to a request is a declaration of intention and an expression of goodwill –*
> *not more than that…If an action does not follow, the other person cannot be held responsible*
> *for failure.*
>
> Margaret Omar Nydell[2]
> University of Alexandria, Egypt

Initiating and building global partnerships can be a perilous enterprise. The stakes are often very high, both for the firms and the negotiators. Indeed, problems often begin as soon as negotiations are opened, with each side trying to gain an advantage at the other's expense (e.g., cheaper prices, royalty distributions, proprietary technology, market access, and so forth). If and when a contract is signed, the problems only multiply. How do we manage the partnership? Who is in charge? How do we build trust between the partners? How do we harmonize our long-term interests? Indeed, what is the meaning of the contract on which the partnership itself is based? And throughout the process, the personalities and private agendas of both the initial negotiators and alliance managers often play a significant role in determining success or failure.

To illustrate this point, consider the case of a failed negotiation. While General Electric had long dominated the market for basic electrical supplies, recent competition from Asia and Europe had begun to seriously erode its market share, and the company was determined to reestablish itself in this lucrative global market.[3] In its Asian markets, General Electric had a long-standing partnership with Japan's Fuji Electric Corporation, but this alliance failed to produce the results General Electric sought. Perhaps it was time to find a new partner. Jeff Depew, an aspiring young manager at General Electric, was assigned the task of laying the groundwork to make this happen. Fluent in Japanese, he was sent to Japan with instructions to cultivate a new relationship with Mitsubishi Electric, one of Japan's premier electrical equipment manufacturers and a possible partner for General Electric's new strategy. It was made clear to him by his boss that success in this assignment would position him well for continued career progression upon his return to the US.

As Depew tells the story, upon his arrival in Tokyo he began a carefully orchestrated effort to nurture relationships with his counterparts at Mitsubishi and, over time, won their respect and trust. What he envisioned was a quantum leap of the sort that would catch the attention of General Electric's then-CEO Jack Welch. Welch valued managers who could take control and make deals happen. He wasted little time on the niceties of negotiation and preferred to work with people who thought as big as he did. To Depew, a possible alliance between General Electric and Mitsubishi was just such a venture. The partnership would catapult them into a position of dominance in the global market, with combined annual sales of US$3.5 billion. As Depew saw it, the partnership made strategic and economic sense for both partners. The combined company would be the world leader in six of its eight product lines and would allow General Electric to establish a working relationship with a leading Japanese conglomerate.

After lengthy and promising discussions with Mitsubishi, Depew was finally ready to invite General Electric's CEO to come to Japan to meet Moriya Shiki, Welch's counterpart at Mitsubishi. The visit (called an *aisatsu*, or formal ceremonial greeting) would be a brief get-acquainted meeting to demonstrate General Electric's commitment to the project and begin to establish a working relationship between the two CEOs.[4] A date was set for the official meeting.

When Welch arrived, Depew briefed him on the progress that had been made, as well as the tasks that remained to be done. While many details of the agreement remained to be negotiated, everything looked good to Depew and he estimated that a deal could be reached after approximately five months of further cultivation and negotiation. Welch was obviously pleased and excited about the prospects. A meeting was scheduled for the next morning with Mitsubishi.

The official meeting between the two companies was a standard protocol session – a mating dance that preceded most major alliances. Not only did Welch understand this, but he had participated in several such rituals in the past. In these initial meetings, specific discussions about business were studiously avoided. Instead, only general issues were discussed, such as the state of the US electronics industry and Japanese competition. It was only later in private meetings that the details of any partnership would be discussed. The meeting between Welch and Shiki would proceed along a similar path. The two CEOs would exchange pleasantries, declare their mutual respect for one another, and withdraw. It was too early to discuss details; subordinates would handle this later.

When Jack Welch and his colleagues arrived at the Mitsubishi building for the scheduled meeting, he was both well prepared and enthusiastic. He was ushered into the conference room and formally introduced to Mr. Shiki and his subordinates. To Depew, both executives were impressive. Shiki was the epitome of the Japanese executive: dignified, elegant, smooth, and very much in control. As they exchanged business cards, both executives began with a profuse exchange of thanks along with the expected expressions of mutual admiration.

But then without notice, Welch quickly ended the pleasantries and launched into a discussion of why a deal was attractive to General Electric: the product lines were impressive, the cultures could work well together, and everything seemed to be a good fit. The venture would be a powerful force in the marketplace, one that would allow both Mitsubishi and General Electric to smash the competition. Mr. Shiki nodded his head quietly while Welch went on to point out that in the past, General Electric had tried to do deals with other big Japanese companies, but had always had troubles. Maybe this time would be different, he observed. He noted that both firms had large bureaucracies, but that this should not get in the way. Then he surprised everyone by suggesting that the two companies should agree to a deal then and there.

Depew was surprised, but couldn't betray his emotions in the meeting. He sat quietly but nervously. General Electric had crossed the protocol line. Perhaps they could have gotten away with this in the US, but not in Japan where protocol was religiously observed. It was highly inappropriate to press for an immediate commitment when negotiating with the Japanese – especially when Mitsubishi had already agreed to General Electric's proposed five-month timetable for closure of the deal. Shiki looked over at Depew as if to say, "What's going on here?," but Depew didn't have the slightest idea. After a long period of silence, Shiki reiterated his desire to go ahead with the plan – a subtle yet significant indication of how badly his company wanted to finalize the agreement. However, he was not about to conclude a final agreement on the spot.

It was well understood by both parties, although not discussed, that Mitsubishi Electric was trying to extricate itself from a long-standing agreement with General Electric rival Westinghouse. Mitsubishi was aware that Westinghouse was quietly preparing to abandon its business in Japan, and Shiki needed a new US partner on whom he could depend for the foreseeable future. General Electric suited his goals perfectly. However, Japanese etiquette required Mitsubishi to inform Westinghouse of its intentions to change partners before signing a formal agreement with General Electric. But when Shiki mentioned this obligation to Welch, Welch questioned why this was necessary. Shiki tried without success to explain the nature of the relationship, but Welch concluded that his counterpart was trying to play him off against Westinghouse. He reiterated that he didn't want to move forward unless Mitsubishi was unequivocally committed to the partnership. Shiki assured him that this was the case and that the agreement would be completed in due time.

With that, the meeting broke up amicably and Welch and his colleagues returned to their hotel. Later that evening, Welch stated that he had pressed Shiki because he had decided that if the agreement was not concluded quickly, it would not be concluded at all. He was convinced that Shiki's reluctance to quickly agree to the proposal meant that he was not serious about it. The next morning, while Welch made a courtesy call to the Ministry of Trade and Industry, Depew returned to Mitsubishi. This meeting went better than the previous one, and a consensus was soon reached concerning how negotiations should proceed and how the agreement should be structured. The deal was back on track. Welch returned to New York and Depew was assigned the task of moving things forward.

Several weeks later, however, Depew received a call from his boss in New York telling him that Welch was leaning against signing the agreement. He felt he had been sandbagged and embarrassed by one of the most prominent leaders of the Japanese business community. The only way to save the deal now, Depew was told, was for Shiki to write a personal letter of apology to Welch in which he stated unequivocally that he would agree to the proposal. Depew dutifully approached Mitsubishi with his orders. After some negotiation, it appeared that Mitsubishi was on the verge of complying with Welch's demand when Depew received another call from his boss notifying him to break off all negotiations with Mitsubishi. Instead, he was to return to General Electric's former partner, Fuji Electric, and attempt to rebuild relationships so that a new joint venture could be developed.

Two months later, Jeff Depew was recalled to New York headquarters. His boss explained that General Electric had decided to take a different approach to the Asia/Pacific region, focusing more on sales than business development. As a result of the change, General Electric was eliminating his position.

Seeking common cause

The question here is: What went wrong and why? Did one side – or both sides – commit errors that caused the failure of a potentially mutually beneficial partnership? Would they recognize these errors as errors? Or was this partnership an idea that was just not going to happen and neither side could do much about it? One way to seek an answer to these questions is to examine this case study from the standpoint of cross-cultural negotiation: goals, strategies, tactics, and, most of all, mistakes.

One lesson from the example of the General Electric and Mitsubishi executives above is that people tend to hear what they want to hear, and nowhere is this adage more accurate than when communicating across borders. People's frames of reference and individual situations – and even their worldviews – can all work to filter message reception by screening in/out what the receiver will likely attend to and by attaching meanings to how messages are interpreted.

While the problems encountered between General Electric and Mitsubishi Electric may appear to be extreme, it is, in fact, fairly common in today's complex business environment. Promising partnerships fail to get off the ground due to conflicts and misunderstandings during the negotiation process. Others flounder shortly after the ink on the contract is dry, again due to conflicts and misunderstandings and promises between partners that are not delivered.

Benefits of global partnerships

If we are looking for an example of a country that has benefited considerably over the decades from building and nurturing strategic partnerships, we need look no further than South Korea. Korean companies (traditionally referred to in Korean as *chaebols*) initiated a myriad of strategic alliances early in their economic development in order to gain needed technologies from both Japan and the West.[5] Many of these alliances continue today and new ones are added frequently. Beginning in the early 1970s and continuing through the mid 1990s, Korea was routinely mentioned as a textbook example of economic development, largely through successful international joint ventures. Aggressive Korean companies captured an increasingly larger share of key global markets, including automobiles, electronics, semiconductors, ship building, construction, and textiles. With a highly motivated and disciplined workforce, borrowed technology, government funding, corporate entrepreneurial talent, and protected local markets, Korean industry thrived.

Then, in 1997, the bottom fell out of the Korean financial markets, as it did in several other Asian countries, and a decade of economic progress disappeared overnight. To regain their status as a key player in the global economy, Korean companies needed a new approach to strategic management, particularly as it related to technology. If they were going to come back, their strategic partners would again play an important, albeit somewhat different, role. Companies like Samsung Electronics and Hyundai Motors had always used strategic partners. Indeed, this is how both companies initially gained the technologies necessary to enter global markets. In the past, however, their international partners held the upper hand and frequently sold the Koreans dated technologies. The Koreans then used this knowledge to manufacture inexpensive products for low-end markets.

But by the beginning of the twenty-first century, as Korea was climbing out of its financial crisis, the world of business had changed. The new global markets the companies now faced were not as forgiving as those in the past. Korea could no longer compete with countries like China at the low end of the market. Nor could Korea retain its protected local markets. Now they would have to compete based on technological sophistication (not cost), and for this they would need to leapfrog the competition. To succeed, they needed to redefine their relationships with their strategic partners from that of subordinate to equal partner. The turnaround began in earnest in the early 2000s.

In the case of Hyundai Motor Company, the company capitalized on its alliance first with Daimler to build increasingly technologically sophisticated cars for the global marketplace.[6] Four key strategies were used. First, Hyundai purchased competitor Kia Motors to increase its size and scope in the marketplace and its bargaining position with suppliers. Then, learning from its German partner, Hyundai focused relentlessly on improving product quality. At the same time, it opened design studios and research centers in the US, Europe, and Japan, and invested over US$5 billion in developing new models. Finally, it began opening new production facilities overseas (including in the US, India, and Eastern Europe), with a targeted global output of 5 million cars. As a result of these efforts, Hyundai Motors has been repeatedly recognized in J. D. Powers customer satisfaction surveys for making some of the best quality cars sold in the world. Today, it is the sixth largest car company in the world and growing.

In the case of Samsung Electronics, the story was much the same. Samsung capitalized on its alliances with Sumitomo Chemical, Dell Computer, Microsoft, Nokia, T-Mobile, and Sprint PCS and its distribution alliances with Best Buy and Circuit City to develop and sell products for higher-end markets.[7] Samsung made extensive use of vertical integration in developing and capitalizing on four key technologies: semiconductors, telecom, digital appliances, and digital media. As a result, today Samsung Electronics is a global leader in a wide variety of forward-looking technology-based industries, including cell phones, plasma and LCD displays, flash memories, DRAMs, MP3 players, and DVRs. In past years, Samsung Electronics acquired technology from its strategic partners; now it sells its own technologies to these same partners.

Other examples from Korea tell the same story, whether it is LG, GS, or SK. Korean firms learned from their strategic partners and went on to become equal, if not superior, partners in the alliance.[8] Today, these companies are widely respected for their product innovation, locally developed technologies, and manufacturing quality. For such companies, the future looks bright.

These examples from successful Korean firms illustrate how, in today's turbulent business and technological environment, many contemporary global firms from around the world often have no choice but to seek, secure, and successfully manage various international joint ventures and strategic alliances if they intend to survive and succeed over the long haul. Indeed, there are many reasons for this, most of which are based on corporate responses to opportunities and threats in the global business environment.[9] In particular, global partnerships allow companies to:

- Promote growth and development, as when a firm wants to serve a new market or achieve economies of scale in operations.
- Acquire new technologies for market applications. This includes technology transfer or sharing R&D costs and outputs.
- Respond to new government policies or restrictions. This is really an issue of political risk, and might include efforts to circumvent tariffs or quotas or satisfy indigenization laws in some countries. This may also help protect a company from the threat of nationalization by a hostile country.
- Take advantage of exchange rates between countries. This, in turn, allows firms to reduce their costs of doing business abroad and possibly reduces the impact of government repatriation policies on profits generated from local operations.

- Respond to changes in the economic environment, including staying ahead of inflation or gaining better access to capital.
- Reduce operating costs and/or increase productivity through lower labor costs, fewer labor policy restrictions, and access to a skilled workforce.
- Get closer to new clients. For example, when a company receives a contract to provide supplies or services to another company (e.g., supply assembly parts or enterprise software), having a local service center right next to the main producer can help provide better service and thereby build confidence and hopefully future business.
- Diversify operations and markets in other regions of the world where a firm wants to be.
- Open opportunities for increasing vertical integration or for simplifying or strengthening supply chains.

What does this long list of reasons have in common? Collectively, these actions serve the long-term interests of the partner firms by providing growth opportunities, operating efficiencies, protection from external threats, and, at the end of the day, increased revenues and profits. No wonder strategic partnerships have become so popular in recent years. As management expert Peter Drucker observed, "alliances, joint ventures, minority stakes, know-how agreements, and contracts will increasingly be the building blocks" of successful firms in the future.[10]

Challenges of global partnerships

Failures abound in the realm of global partnerships. Indeed, here is where many of the most important lessons for success can be learned. Consider two more failed examples.

First, consider a promising joint venture between Spanish and Japanese firms in the telecommunications industry. When Japan's Fujitsu joined forces with Spain's newly privatized national telephone company, *Telefónica*, and several local banks to create *Sociedad Espanola de Comunicaciones e Informatica SA* (or simply Secoinsa), everyone knew that it would be a challenging alliance. But few realized just how challenging.[11] The Japanese managers that arrived to help run the new partnership seemed totally unprepared for Spanish culture or ways of doing business. At the same time, their Spanish partners were equally perplexed about how to work with the Japanese. Problems began almost immediately.

The first notable problem in the partnership involved language. Both partners had to rely on English since few Japanese partners could speak Spanish and none of the

Spaniards could speak Japanese. The Japanese soon became frustrated because they could not express their true feelings in English, while the Spaniards were equally frustrated with what they considered to be the Japanese's "all business all the time" approach to inter-personal relations. The Spaniards concluded early on that their Japanese counterparts were not well rounded because all they talked about was business. They also felt that the Japanese were looking down on their local Spanish traditions and customs. The Japanese, in turn, questioned the work ethic of their Spanish counterparts because of their exces-sively long meals and time away from work. Neither side had an easy time building rapport, and numerous misunderstandings emerged. Stress levels increased on both sides.

Differences in decision-making styles also created problems. Substantial disagree-ments arose over the ways in which decisions were made at the new company. The Japanese side tried to use a consensual decision process that required considerable time but led to broad-based support for final decisions. The Spaniards preferred to have senior managers make decisions more autocratically and lost patience with the endless rounds of discussions requested by their partners. Compounding the problem was a significant difference in manufacturing quality-control strategies. Fujitsu managers insisted on maintaining strict controls over production processes to ensure quality control and prevent imitation by their competitors. They wanted all components used in the manufacturing process to be manufactured in Japan. If this proved to be unfeasible, they at least wanted all the parts to be tested in Japan at Fujitsu's testing facilities. Their Spanish partners preferred using components manufactured in Spain (or at least the EU), and saw no reason to ship them to Japan for testing. Fujitsu finally agreed to this so long as the components were manufactured by Secoinsa and not by any outside vendor. Both sides came to see the other as difficult, narrow-minded, inflexible, and overly nationalistic, but the venture continued because Fujitsu wanted access to the Spanish (and European) market and the Spanish wanted access to Japan's cutting-edge technology. But neither side was happy, and problems continued to mount. After several years of conflicts and tense relationships, the partnership was dissolved and Fujitsu assumed ownership and control over the entire enterprise.

Second, consider a merger between two pharmaceutical firms, one from Sweden and the other from the US. The merger was negotiated with the aim of making their combined assets better positioned in this highly competitive arena. Somehow, the focus got lost. When US-based Upjohn and Sweden's Pharmacia decided to merge to create a larger and hopefully more competitive enterprise, a central question for the executives of both companies was where to locate their new corporate headquarters.[12] Upjohn had long been headquartered in Kalamazoo, Michigan, and suggested that the new venture be run from there. Not surprisingly, Pharmacia, headquartered in Stockholm, had a different idea and suggested Sweden as its preferred location. After considerable negotiation, neither side would yield so it was decided to move the new headquarters and its 100-person executive staff to London instead. The new venture would be known as Pharmacia Corporation. Principal manufacturing centers for the new 30,000-employee company would remain in Kalamazoo, Stockholm, and Milan, and division managers from these operations would fly back and forth to London as needed. It was an inauspicious beginning.

Clashes between the parties began almost immediately. The hard-driving, mission-oriented Americans from Upjohn routinely clashed with the more consensus-oriented Swedes from Pharmacia. The Americans wanted more cost cutting and accountability, while the Swedes wanted to keep their employees informed and sought feedback on how to move the company forward. American managers scheduled meetings throughout the month of August, a common holiday time for the Swedes. At the same time, the more internationally experienced Swedes were surprised by the parochial manner and lack of sophistication of their American counterparts. Swedish managers had long worked with people from across Europe and tended to be more adaptable and flexible than their American counterparts. Upjohn's culture had banned smoking and required drug and alcohol testing of its employees, while Pharmacia's culture served liquor in the company cafeteria and provided ashtrays in each conference room. Finally, the Upjohn-based CEO kept his managers on a tight leash and required frequent reports, budgets, and staffing updates. Swedish members of the executive team considered this detail of reporting to be a waste of time, and soon simply stopped complying until the CEO finally resigned. Meanwhile, the Swedes concluded that the Americans were trying to take over the partnership and began resisting calls for cooperation. No one was happy.

To put the conflict into perspective, a Swedish executive observed, "I see in America a more can-do approach to things. They try to overcome problems as they arise. A Swede may be slower on the start-up. He sits down and thinks over all the problems, and once he is reasonably convinced he can tackle them, only then will he start running."[13] Another Swedish executive added, "The Swedish approach is more the engineering approach: 'Tell me why and how this thing works.' The American approach is much more direct. Their attitude is: 'Don't teach me to be an expert, just tell me what I need to know to do my job.'"[14]

The original impetus behind the merger was the compatibility of product lines of the two companies. Together, the new company was well placed in the global marketplace with a broad range of highly competitive pharmaceutical products. However, the

ongoing cultural conflicts between members of the executive team led to lost opportunities and less than anticipated sales and profits. Shortly thereafter, New York-
based Pfizer acquired Pharmacia, closed its London headquarters, and fired most of
its former executives.

These two examples illustrate how some of the more subtle aspects of culture can
influence the activities of global companies and their managers. Different perceptions
regarding how things should be done can jeopardize partnerships and create conflicts
that can be difficult to resolve. At Secoinsa, mistrust arose because of culturally based
perceptions about appropriate topics for conversation when building relationships,
work values, the place of work in life, and decision-making styles. Compounding
the problems, language differences also made communication difficult, and an
"us-versus-them" climate quickly emerged. Similar issues were present in Pharmacia's
merger: management and problem-solving styles were dramatically different and conflicts ensued.

Thus, while numerous advantages of global partnerships can be readily identified,
it is equally important to recognize some potential drawbacks.[15] Unfortunately, this is
relatively easy to do. Consider the following specific reasons for failed partnerships:

- In the haste to create a global partnership, long-term objectives and aspirations can
  sometimes remain ill defined, leading eventually to an incompatibility of goals as the
  partnership gets down to managing details. For example, General Electric's alliance
  with Germany's Siemens struggled because General Electric's management stressed
  financial management while Siemens stressed engineering. Such incompatibilities
  can result from differences in corporate or national cultures, disagreements over
  goals and objectives, personality conflicts between key players, and so forth.

- Partnerships can also fail because of a lack of long-term commitment by one or both
  partners. The question here is how much a partner is willing to invest in time and
  resources to ensure success. As Wharton professor Howard Perlmutter observes, "If
  you [a typical Western company] have a joint venture with a Japanese company, they
  will send twenty-four people here to learn everything you know, and you will send
  one person there to tell them everything you know."[16] This hardly sounds likes a
  strategy for success.

- Partnerships can flounder because one or more partners resist providing key – and
  often proprietary – information relating to the operations of the venture to their
  partners. A joint venture between Ford and Mazda stalled for several years when
  Mazda refused to allow their Ford engineering counterparts access to their research
  laboratory, despite the fact that Ford owned 33 percent of Mazda. The conflict was

finally resolved by allowing Ford engineers into the Mazda labs, but only for short periods of time.

● Conflicts can emerge over how earnings are distributed. Some partners may wish to reinvest earnings in research on future products, while others may wish to return all earnings to stockholders or equity partners. This happened when US-based Rubbermaid broke off an alliance with Dutch DSM Group to manufacture and distribute its products throughout Europe, Africa, and the Middle East because DSM refused to reinvest earnings in future product development, a key to the long-term success of the venture as Rubbermaid saw it.

● A major pitfall to successful partnerships is the threatened loss of local control by one partner to another. In point of fact, any partnership involves some loss of autonomy, and in many cases a partner realizes – sometimes too late – that it has lost control over decisions that it values. One partner may wish to continually introduce new products, while the other partner may wish to push older products as long as possible. In other cases, partnerships can lead to one partner buying out the other. One study found that of 150 terminated joint ventures involving Japanese firms, three-fourths ended because the Japanese partner bought out the other partner.[17]

● Finally, some partnerships falter because the business conditions change, suggesting more productive strategies for one or both partners. Economic conditions or customer tastes require companies to reassess their business practices, and, at times, previous cooperative arrangements no longer serve the needs or objectives on the firm. Ford and Volkswagen once created Autolatina, which became the largest car manufacturer in Latin America. The two companies believed that by working together they could surmount both the poor economic conditions and government import restrictions throughout Latin America. However, within a few years, import tariffs in Latin America had been reduced and the economy had improved. In the light of these changes, both auto firms decided that they were better off trying to capture market share in the region working individually rather than collectively. The partnership disbanded and the two companies went their separate ways.

Culture and negotiation: a model

These examples illustrate how cultural differences can play a major role in how partnerships are negotiated and managed once they are created. Indeed, like many other social processes, negotiation is heavily influenced by culture. Negotiators bring to the table expectations, ways of communicating, strategies, tactics, and preferences that are

Exhibit 10.1 Cultural influences on the negotiation process

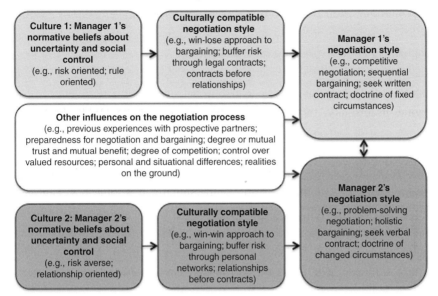

culturally based, and misinterpreting these differences may put an end to an otherwise promising partnership.

In order to provide a simple heuristic outlining of how normative beliefs can influence the negotiation process, consider Exhibit 10.1. Here we see that cultures can play an important – although certainly not exclusive – role in setting the limits and creating the opportunities on the actions of both parties throughout the process. Cultural differences and their subsequent normative beliefs influence such factors as: what objectives will or will not be sought; the degree to which each partner is risk-oriented or risk-averse; the characteristics of a good partner; and the preferred (and sometimes required) negotiating climates. In addition, culture can place other limitations on communication styles, emotional sensitivity and face-saving during the negotiation process, the basis for making decisions about whether a partnership should be formed, and views about how disputes should be resolved. Remember, however, that there are a number of other non-cultural drivers that can also affect this process, such as financial necessity, hostile takeovers, shareholder revolts, government-initiated partnerships, and so forth.

These normative beliefs, in turn, influence such negotiation strategies and behaviors as: how prospective partners are selected; how much advance preparation each party seeks; and whether the parties use a competitive or a problem-solving negotiation strategy. Additional parts of an overall negotiating strategy – also influenced by culture – include communication tactics (verbal versus non-verbal), the amount of information offered and sought, approaches to bargaining and concession making, and views on the final agreement and the nature of the final contract.

Finally, the interplay between culture, goals, and negotiation patterns and practices ultimately leads to several targeted negotiation outcomes. Perhaps the most important outcome here is whether the new venture or partnership is actually created. As we saw in the case of General Electric and Mitsubishi at the beginning of the chapter, cultural and personality differences were sufficiently strong enough to stop the partnership before it had even begun. In addition, other consequences include: how the organization is organized and managed; which operating processes will be used; how conflict will be resolved if it emerges; how trust will be built and then maintained over time; and how (or if) the corporate cultures of the two new partners will work to support or inhibit future success. The case studies of General Electric and Mitsubishi and Secoinsa and Phamacia illustrates what can happened when these factors, and their cultural precedence, are ignored.

The negotiation process: strategies, concessions, and contracts

In many cultures, business is built on long-standing personal relationships. This is as true in France and Mexico as it is in China and India. People do business with partners they know, people they can trust. As such, many international negotiations begin with both sides trying to establish a personal bond. This does not necessarily mean they plan to become life-long friends; rather, each side needs to determine if the other party is sufficiently trustworthy to conclude an agreement and stick with it. In many countries, it is insulting (as well as unproductive) to begin a business discussion until after such relationships have been firmly established. In these cultures, it is often said that business relationships must be "warmed up" before getting down to serious negotiations. This is a good principle to remember.

Ironically, the one place where such relationships, while important, are not necessarily critical to a successful negotiation is the US, where legal contracts are frequently seen as a substitute for personal relationships (see below). As a result, US negotiators are notorious for wanting to immediately get down to business, a practice that frequently leads to frustration and failure. More successful US negotiators understand the critical importance of subtleties and patience, not brashness and drive. As a result, most successful international managers – regardless of their home country – invest

Exhibit 10.2 Competitive and problem-solving bargaining strategies

Stages in negotiation	Competitive bargaining	Problem-solving bargaining
(1) Preparation	Identify current economic and other benefits your firm seeks from the deal. Prepare to defend your firm's position.	Define the long-term strategic interests of your firm. Prepare to overcome cross-cultural barriers to defining mutual interests.
(2) Relationship building	Look for weaknesses in your opponent's position. Learn about your opponent, but reveal as little as possible.	Adapt to the other side's culture. Separate the people involved in negotiation from the problems and goals that need to be solved.
(3) Information exchange and first offer	Provide as little information as possible to your opponent. Make your position explicit. Make a hard offer that is more favorable to your side than you realistically expect to receive.	Give and demand to receive objective information that clarifies each party's interests. Accept cultural differences in speed of response and type of information needs. Make firm but reasonable first offer.
(4) Persuasion	Use dirty tricks and pressure tactics where appropriate to win.	Search for new creative options that benefit the interests of both parties.
(5) Concessions	Begin with high initial demands. Make concessions slowly and grudgingly.	Search for mutually acceptable criteria for reaching accord. Accept cultural differences in starting position and in how and when concessions are made.
(6) Agreement	Sign only if you win and then ensure that you sign an ironclad contract.	Sign when the interests of your firm are met. Adapt to cultural differences in contracts where necessary.

considerable time and effort in getting to know their prospective partners. This frequently includes a variety of social activities (dinners, golf, etc.), where it is often inappropriate to discuss any business whatsoever. The stage is being set.

Competitive versus problem-solving strategies

Focusing initially on implementing an agreement instead of just securing one implies a problem-solving approach to negotiations. Generally speaking, there are two basic strategies for negotiation: competitive negotiation and problem-solving negotiation. The competitive approach views negotiations as a win-lose game, while the problem-solving approach seeks to discover a win-win solution where both sides can benefit, if at all possible. Exhibit 10.2 illustrates how these two different strategies are played out during negotiation.

   In *competitive negotiation*, each side tries to give as little as possible. They frequently begin with unrealistically high demands and make concessions only grudgingly. Competitive negotiators will, at times, use dirty tricks or other tactics that allow them to win. Little thought is given to building a long-term relationship between the parties. And since starting from inflexible positions often leads to outcomes that satisfy neither side, each side often develops negative attitudes towards the other. As a result, losers in the agreement often seek revenge, such as reneging on parts of the contract at a later date or substituting inferior-quality materials in production orders.

By contrast, *problem-solving negotiation* begins with the basic tenet that negotiators must separate positions from interests. Instead of defending a company's position as a major goal in the negotiation process, problem-solving negotiators begin by seeking a mutually satisfactory ground that is beneficial to the interests of both sides. Dirty tricks are avoided because they poison the development of long-term mutually advantageous relationships. Objective information is preferred wherever possible as a basis for discussion and problem-solving efforts, instead of unrealistic sales pitches or hyperbole. Oftentimes, problem-solving negotiation facilitates the identification of creative new ways to provide both parties with what they want to achieve. And even when mutually advantageous solutions are not found, both sides leave the table believing that sincere efforts were made on both sides of the table. This leaves open the possibility of returning to the bargaining table in the future when another opportunity presents itself.

There are three important points to remember regarding the choice between using either competitive or problem-solving bargaining strategies. First, it is very easy in cross-cultural negotiation to misread the intentions of the other party. Hence, a detailed understanding of the cultural backgrounds of one's opponents becomes critical in determining whether he or she is stating a highly inflexible position or offering a genuine opportunity to strike a deal. This is why many successful international negotiators always have advisors at their side who are intimately familiar with the culture and traditions of the other party. Second, culture sometimes predisposes negotiators to select one approach over the other. For example, observers note that some US managers believe there must be a winner and a loser, while many Japanese managers prefer a problem-solving approach. The smart bargainer understands this and adjusts his or her strategy accordingly. Finally, where possible, most experts on international negotiation recommend a problem-solving approach, because it tends to lead to better long-term solutions and relationships. This is particularly true in negotiating global partnerships. Winning now may mean big losses later. It is important to remember that the failure of the partnership is more expensive than small concessions given during the negotiation process.

Information exchange and initial offers

Exhibit 10.3 illustrates how culture can influence the specific issue of information sharing and making first offers. That is, managers in some cultures seek seemingly inexhaustible technical details about a product or service being discussed, while

Exhibit 10.3 Information exchange and initial offers by culture

Cultures	Information exchanged	First offer
East Asians	Extensive requests for proposal details and technical information. Assumption that all details of the proposal must be discussed before agreement can be reached.	10–20% below their desired end result.
Latin Americans	Focus more on information about the relationship and less on technical details of the proposal. Preliminary discussions focus on why we should do business together, not how we should do it.	20–40% below their desired end result.
Middle Easterners	Focus more on information about the relationship and less on technical details of the proposal. Preliminary discussions focus on why we should do business together, not how we should do it.	20–50% below their desired end result.
North Americans	Information is provided directly and briefly, often through multimedia presentations. Assumption that if an agreement can be reached in principle, details can be resolved later.	5–10% below their desired end result.
Russians	Extensive requests for proposal details and technical information. Assumption that all details of the proposal must be discussed before agreement can be reached.	50–60% below their desired end result.

Source: Based on Lillian Chaney and Jeannette Martin, *International Business Communication*. Englewood Cliffs, NJ: Prentice Hall, 1995, pp. 183–84.

managers in other cultures often ignore most of the product details and continue to focus on relationship building. In any event, at some point in the process, each side will make its first offer, their initial bargaining position. In some cultures (e.g., Russia, Saudi Arabia), first offers are often totally unrealistic, whereas in other cultures (e.g., Japan, Korea) they are often close to the final bargaining position. This first offer initiates the negotiating process that, hopefully, will culminate in a final agreement.

Bargaining and concessions

Clearly, the ultimate goal of a negotiation is to arrive at a mutually agreed-upon contract that is legally binding in both countries. To achieve this, concessions must be made. What is interesting here is that culture can, at times, influence how these concessions are determined. In North America, for example, companies frequently use what is called a *sequential approach* to concession making (see Exhibit 10.4). That is, they prefer to go through a proposed contract item by item and get agreement on each item as they go sequentially through the proposed contract.

By contrast, and popular throughout much of Asia, is the *holistic approach* to concession making. Here, the two parties work their way through the entire proposed agreement but do not agree to anything until they have completed their review. They then discuss the contract in its entirety and make final proposals and counter-proposals aimed at reaching a complete agreement. The holistic approach frequently perplexes

Exhibit 10.4 Sequential and holistic bargaining strategies

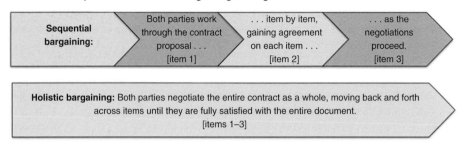

novice North-American negotiators when they learn that a point they thought was already agreed upon resurfaces to be discussed later by their Asian counterparts.

Final agreement and contracts

If countries often approach negotiating strategies so differently, it is not surprising that other aspects of building and managing partnerships can also be quite different. Consider contracts. In most Western countries, a contract – especially a written contract – represents a company's most effective tool against uncertainty and risk. This is not surprising in view of the largely monochromic orientation of these countries, where message content is often far more important than message context. Every dictionary in the world gives roughly the same definition of a contract: an agreement between two or more parties that establishes rules governing their business transactions.[18] Contracts typically spell out levels of investment, areas of responsibility and accountability, cost data where appropriate, control over proprietary technology, and procedures for sharing the benefits (and losses) of the enterprise. As such, most managers from most countries believe that written contracts are far superior to the proverbial handshake among honorable people. Or, as legendary MGM co-founder Louis B. Mayer observed long ago about negotiating with screen actors, "A handshake is only as good as the paper it's written on."

Mutual trust and forum shopping

Even so, in many regions of the world, much of the business is conducted on the basis of personal relationships and mutual trust, as in the case of *guānxi* (see Chapter 6). In these regions, prospective partners often see written contracts as a sign of distrust; contracts are unnecessary among trusted friends. This divergence across cultures obviously often creates a dilemma for global managers. What do they do when trying to develop a secure business relationship in countries where written securities are not commonplace? Again, how much can you trust a handshake?

In theory, a contract is a legally binding instrument that guarantees all parties to a contract what will happen and when (e.g., what each item or product will cost, when materials will be delivered, costs of technology transfer, etc.). Also, in theory, certain penalties are stipulated for non-compliance with the contract (e.g., financial penalties for late payments, criminal penalties for fraud or theft, etc.). Good negotiators are adept at capturing the essence, as well as the details, of contacts in clearly understandable writing. Moreover, experienced negotiators typically use specialized attorneys to ensure that contracts are internally consistent (i.e., there are no vague or conflicting clauses within the contract) and comply with local and international laws. They will also often have contracts translated into all of the languages of the parties to it so that the details and provisions are clear to everyone.

Unfortunately most experienced managers also know that there can be a sharp difference between what a contract says and what it actually means. At times, local governments will refuse to implement a contract for various reasons or will support the local partner to an agreement. Two important lessons seem to follow from this experience.

First, there is a critical need for all parties to a contract to trust each other's personal integrity and corporate intentions. Here is where culturally based practices such as *guānxi* come into play. A written contract between strangers represents a conflict waiting to happen in much of the world. This is why successful global negotiators invest so much time in getting to know their partners and nurturing this relationship after the contract is signed and implemented. Hence the importance of doing business with long-term and trusted partners should not be underestimated.

The second important lesson concerns where and how contract disagreements are resolved. This raises the issue of *forum shopping*. Forum shopping deals with where contract disputes are adjudicated. For example, if a contract between a Vietnamese and a French company is in dispute, conventional wisdom suggests that the Vietnamese partner would likely receive a more favorable hearing if the dispute is resolved in Vietnam, while the French partner may feel the same about his or her chances in France. Because of this potential conflict, many contracts now stipulate where and how disputes will be resolved, including stipulations requiring third-party oversight. In such cases, our Vietnamese and French partners may stipulate in advance that conflicts will be resolved through binding arbitration by a legal arbitrator located in Switzerland.

Exhibit 10.5 Contracts and the doctrine of changed circumstances

Typical contract under the doctrine of fixed circumstances	Typical contract under the doctrine of changed circumstances
Personal relationships generally follow from contracts.	Contracts generally follow from personal relationships.
Contracts summarize specific details of a binding agreement that will typically remain unchanged throughout its duration, regardless of changing circumstances.	Contracts typically summarize general details of an agreement that reflect current state of affairs and that may evolve or change over time depending upon changing circumstances.
Long, detailed, legalistic.	Short, less detailed, less legalistic.
Contracts backed largely by courts and judicial system.	Contracts backed largely by personal integrity and relationship of partners.

Note: It is important to note that contracts using some form of the doctrine of changed circumstances are far more prevalent around the world than typical and more legalistic "Western" contracts.

Doctrine of changed circumstances

One of the principal reasons for contract disputes around the world is the cultural variation in the meaning of a contract. To many Westerners (e.g., the UK, Australia, Germany, Canada, the US), a contract is a legal document that spells out the obligations of all parties. It is the culmination of a successful negotiation process. In the West, where people tend to have an internal locus of control (i.e., they believe that they largely control their own fate), a contract is a contract. It can be renegotiated upon expiration, but not until then unless otherwise specified in advance. As a result, Western negotiators must anticipate and prepare for every conceivable future problem, leading to rather lengthy business contracts.

Elsewhere in the world, where people tend to have a more external locus of control (i.e., they believe that the future is largely influenced by fate or karma), many businesses accept something called the *doctrine of changed circumstances* (see Exhibit 10.5). This doctrine holds that when circumstances beyond the control of a business partner change (e.g., hurricane damage, changes in government policies, price increases for raw materials), both partners are obliged to renegotiate the original contract so neither party loses materially. Under this doctrine, which can be found throughout much of Asia, Africa, and Latin America, a contract is thought of as a written recognition of a personal relationship between the two parties. As such, it is the beginning, not the end, of the process of mutual benefit as a result of working together.

As former US Secretary of State Henry Kissinger once observed about his negotiating experiences in China, "The Chinese think in terms of a process that has no culmination. Westerners think in terms of concrete solutions to specific problems."[19] Indeed, many

Asian, African and Latin American companies prefer to have only very brief general contracts (perhaps two or three pages in length) in the belief that it is impossible to anticipate all future circumstances that may affect the contract. As circumstances change, it is often expected that the contract will be modified to fit the new situation. After all, an honorable person would not take advantage of his or her partner if changes occur that were not caused by the two partners. Honorable people look after the interests of each other.

In the East, the doctrine of changed circumstances is designed to maintain harmony among partners; in the West, it violates the pursuit of mastery over one's environment. This difference underlying both contract negotiations and contract implementations between global partners often represents a major threat to the long-term prospects of global partnerships. Consider: If written (or even unwritten) contracts in one part of the world often mean something very different in another part, and two parties are negotiating an international joint venture, how can either side have confidence, predictability, and trust in their agreements? And what happens to the rookie manager who fails to understand this?

Negotiation patterns across cultures

To better understand how this process works, it is useful to review an interesting and well-crafted study among Japanese, Brazilian, and US managers. In this study, managers from the three countries were put in twenty-minute negotiation sessions and the investigators simply counted the number of times managers from each country used either a verbal or non-verbal negotiation tactic. Significant differences in both verbal and non-verbal bargaining tactics were found during bargaining sessions between managers (see Exhibit 10.6). Notice, for example, how often negotiators in each country interrupted the opponent, said "no," or touched the opponent. What does this say about cultural variations in negotiations?

Negotiation patterns in Japan

Going a step further, consider what cultural anthropologists and management researchers have discovered when analyzing some of the cultural drivers underlying negotiating strategies of the three groups (see Exhibit 10.7). These findings illustrate clearly some of the principal challenges of negotiating and building successful global partnerships across cultures. One key factor in determining whether to do business with someone in Japan is *shinyo*.[20] *Shinyo* refers to the mutual confidence, trust, and honor that are

Exhibit 10.6 Negotiating tactics in Japan, Brazil, and the US

Negotiating tactics	Number of times used in twenty-minute bargaining session		
	Japanese managers	Brazilian managers	US managers
Verbal negotiation tactics			
Offering rewards or incentives	1	2	2
Making promises	7	3	8
Making threats	4	2	4
Normative appeals to higher goals	1	0	1
Giving orders or commands	8	14	6
Interrupting opponent	13	29	10
Rejections (saying "no")	6	83	9
Non-verbal negotiation tactics			
Silent periods	6	0	4
Facial glazing or staring into space	1	5	3
Touching opponent	0	5	0

Source: Adapted from John Graham, "The influence of culture on the process of business negotiations," *Journal of International Business Studies*, 1983, pp. 84–88.

required on both sides for a business relationship to succeed. Unless you trust your partner implicitly, it is not wise to pursue a business relationship. This concept, while easy to understand, is nonetheless difficult for some foreigners to implement. This is in part because of many Westerners' fervent belief in the power of the legal contract over the importance of a personal relationship. In addition to *shinyo*, other differences can be identified between Japanese negotiators and their Brazilian and American counterparts.

Negotiation patterns in the US

Adding a touch of humor to this comparison, John Graham and Yoshihiro Sano, in their book entitled *Smart Bargaining*, describe a "typical" American negotiator as someone who is typically high on both self-confidence and independence.[21] This bargaining strategy is characterized by the following kinds of personal beliefs on the part of the highly individualistic negotiator: "I can do this by myself; I don't need any help"; "I am who I am. If you don't like me, too bad"; "Let's talk on a first name basis; formality just gets in my way"; "Of course, we'll speak in English; why would you expect me to speak your language?"; "Get to the point; don't waste my time"; "Put your cards on the table"; and "A deal is a deal; if you signed it, you own it." Clearly not all US negotiators behave in this manner, but the examples give us food for thought.

Exhibit 10.7 Negotiating strategies in Japan, Brazil, and the US

Negotiating strategies	Japanese firms	Brazilian firms	US firms
Ultimate goal	Long-term profitability, usually without personal benefit.	Long-term mutually beneficial relationships.	Short-term profitability, often with personal benefit for negotiator.
Ideal negotiating climate	Oblique and at times personal.	Impromptu; difficult to generalize.	Straightforward and impersonal.
Risk orientation	Risk averse.	Risk averse.	Risk-oriented.
Communication style	High context; talks indirectly; seldom blunt; extensive use of technical language.	High context; talks indirectly; frequently emotional; frequently exaggerates.	Low context; talks directly; frequently blunt; sometimes exaggerates.
Emotional sensitivity	Emotional sensitivity avoided; strong personal relationships critical for success.	Emotional sensitivity highly valued; strong personal relationships critical for success.	Emotional sensitivity avoided; negotiators often avoid close personal relationships.
Basis of decisions	Decisions usually made on cost-benefit basis for the long term.	Decisions often tied to emotional or family considerations.	Decisions usually made on a cost-benefit basis for the short term.
Importance of face-saving	Face-saving critical; embarrassing either party to the negotiation should be avoided at all costs.	Face-saving critical; embarrassing either party to the negotiation should be avoided, if possible.	Face-saving not critical; embarrassing opponent may lead to an advantage in negotiations.
Dispute resolution	Preference for conciliation and contract re-negotiation over litigation.	Preference for conciliation and contract re-negotiation over litigation.	Preference for contract language and litigation over conciliation for dispute resolution.
Conflict	Seldom argumentative; uncomfortable with serious conflict.	Argumentative, but uncomfortable with serious conflict.	At times argumentative, especially when put on the defensive.

Negotiation patterns in Brazil

Not surprisingly, Brazil's culture – and its approach to negotiation – differs from that of Japan. In contrast to Japan's position as a long-established industrial power, Brazil is often described as one of the world's most attractive emerging markets. Multinationals from various countries are increasingly establishing subsidiaries or doing business in Brazil in one way or another. In this environment, knowing how to negotiate with Brazilians is crucial for any serious global manager. In other words, international negotiators dealing with Brazil are more likely to succeed if they know a little about the country and understand its culture, its way of doing business, and its negotiation style.

The typical negotiating style of Brazilian managers reflects the country's cultural characteristics and business environment. This is summarized in Exhibit 10.7 above, as it compares to typical Japanese and US approaches. At the heart of Brazilian negotiating style is its emphasis on building, maintaining, and capitalizing on one's personal relationships. Brazilians are often seen as being highly engaged with their opponents or prospective partners during negotiation. They tend to believe that regardless of what happens during and after the negotiation, making friends and enjoying life is important. This focus on relationships leads Brazilians to avoid conflict and attempt to please the other party to the extent possible. There is also a tendency to use indirect language, hide unpleasant information, make false promises, and at times embellish the truth.[22]

The Brazilians' focus on personal relationships has been attributed to a need to deal with what some observers describe as a national inferiority complex.[23] Brazilians tend to be sensitive about their identity. They do not like to be compared with their neighbors and prefer to call themselves South Americans rather than Latin Americans. Brazilians need to feel accepted and become impatient when there is a conflict. When dealing with conflicts, aggressiveness is not a good alternative. Rather, a solution is most likely to emerge through active but friendly engagement.

The Brazilian tendency towards improvisation and flexibility is clear in their negotiation style as well. Many Brazilians do not follow logical steps in a negotiation, and instead may jump back and forth between topics. At times, they may not have a clear goal in mind. Risk-averse, Brazilians are likely to focus on seemingly irrelevant details, bargaining and negotiating for long periods of time. They enjoy the process of negotiating and are not in a hurry to make a deal. And they seldom make decisions based solely on analysis. Most likely, they consider emotions as well. In a recent article, a prominent Brazilian magazine interviewed successful Brazilian managers about their views on negotiation.[24] Among other things, the managers agreed that successful negotiations are typically conducted informally and with spontaneity. They are guided by intuition, and not by reason alone. And finally, real negotiations seldom happen at the negotiation table. Instead, they take place in parallel informal meetings, where the relationship is developed. To be successful in negotiating with Brazilians, foreigners need to be both friendly and patient.

Finally, it is interesting to consider differences between Brazilian and Japanese negotiating styles. The above review suggests that both cultures would have few problems negotiating with each other. Both emphasize building strong personal relationships, emotional sensitivity, trust, pride, confidence, and a personal sense of honor. In addition, both communicate indirectly, using context as much as content. And both are uncomfortable with high degrees of conflict.

However, these characteristics are very general and allow for important variations. Brazilians develop relationships by clearly expressing emotions, hugging, and touching the other party, often using exaggerations and euphemisms, and behaving in informal and open ways. By contrast, the Japanese are often hesitant to display emotions, remain silent and physically distant from others, and stress respect and formality when dealing with others. Thus, while both cultures' values are similar (e.g., strong personal relationships), they are expressed in different ways. Moreover, while both Brazilians and Japanese communicate indirectly and expect the other party to understand innuendos and subtleties, this does not guarantee that both sides will understand each other. Indirect communication relies on culturally established codes that communicate difficult information without causing embarrassment. However, since these codes are culturally embedded, two indirect communicators from different cultures may have a hard time understanding each other.

Successful (and unsuccessful) negotiators can be found in all countries and cultures. In this section, we focused on typical bargaining behavior in Brazil, Japan, and the US. Similarities and differences were noted as an illustration of how culture may influence negotiating behavior. However, it is important to remember that not all Japanese or Brazilians necessarily fit this pattern. People are complex and do not necessarily follow the rules of their culture all the time. Besides, cultural norms are cued more strongly in some situations than others. For instance, a US negotiator is more likely to behave according to American negotiation norms when working in the US with other Americans than when negotiating in Japan with Japanese counterparts. People adjust – more or less successfully – their behavior depending on the context in which they find themselves.

A recent study of bicultural Chinese Americans illustrates this point. The participants in this study were randomly assigned to one of two groups. The first group was shown a set of pictures reflecting centrist American culture, while the second group was exposed to pictures reflecting centrist Chinese culture. Next, the participants were asked to interpret a social conflict. The study found that the individuals displayed cultural biases in their interpretations that were consistent with the culture to which they were exposed at the beginning of the study. In other words, individuals that viewed Chinese pictures used Chinese cultural lenses to interpret the conflict, while the ones that viewed American pictures used American lenses. Yet all were, in actuality, Chinese Americans, raising the question of social influence that may transcend ethnic boundaries.[25]

Similarly, negotiation is a dynamic process of reciprocity. The action of one party will result in actions of the other. When all negotiators are from the same culture, this process is likely to reinforce cultural norms. But when negotiators are from different cultures, this process is likely to create behaviors that diverge from the original cultural script.[26] As such, successful managers tread cautiously in their international negotiations until they sufficiently understand the particular (and often unique) environment in which they find themselves. Based on this understanding, the global manager is better prepared to succeed.

Building global partnerships

So what have we learned about successful global negotiations and conflict resolution? And what have we learned about relationship building and working with global partners? British management researcher Charles Handy has observed that the most important skills that will be needed in the organizations of the future will be "the ability to win friends and influence people at a personal level, the ability to structure partnerships, and the ability to negotiate and to find compromises. Business will be much more about finding the right people in the right places and negotiating the right deals."[27] If this is correct, what can managers do to prepare themselves? From the materials presented, we can suggest seven basic lessons.

Criteria for selecting global partners

In view of the high "divorce rate" among international joint ventures and strategic alliances, a key question emerges concerning how and where to find the right partners and then negotiate a workable partnership. This challenge faces many, if not most, global partnerships today. In this regard, consider what it is that a company most requires in partners in order to expand its business in ways that are both efficient and effective and support its overall mission. Five key success factors can be identified:

(1) *Solid compatibility of strategic goals and tactics.* First and foremost among these factors is ensuring that prospective partners have goals and objectives that mutually reinforce one another's long-term objectives and short-term tactics. Without this congruence, organizational and managerial efforts are likely to dissipate while each partner expends time and resources trying to go its own separate way. We saw this problem with both the General Electric-Siemens and the Rubbermaid-DSM alliances above.

(2) *Complementary value-creating resources.* In addition, partners' approaches to methods, systems, inputs, and distribution channels should be similar and therefore understandable and comfortable to each partner. Moreover, ideally, each

partner would contribute assets to the partnership that the other partner may not have in abundance. The long-standing alliance between Samsung Electronics and Corning Glass is a case in point. When Samsung decided to enter the television market, it had little understanding of critical glass technologies that were essential to manufacturing success. At the same time, Corning was looking to expand its overseas ventures in East Asia based on its previous success in Japan. Both needed partners. As a result of the partnership, Samsung provided a highly educated workforce and capital to match Corning's highly sophisticated glass technology. Both learned from each other and complemented one another through their particular resource contributions to the enterprise.

(3) *Complementary corporate cultures.* Successful partners typically have complementary corporate cultures. Partnering with a firm that has a secretive corporate (or organizational) culture is likely to be unsustainable for a company that thrives on openness. As noted above, Ford and Mazda had this problem in the early years of their alliance. This is not to say that successful partners must have open and cooperative cultures, although this certainly makes partnerships more likely to succeed. Rather, it is to suggest that, at the very least, whatever the cultures are, they should be compatible in their characteristics.

(4) *Strong commitment to the partnership.* A major factor in selecting successful partners is the degree to which both partners have a strong interest and commitment to creating and managing a successful partnership. In the case of General Electric and Siemens, discussed above, we saw that both partners had only a tepid interest in making the venture succeed, with predictable results.

(5) *Strong philosophical and operational compatibility.* Finally, successful partnerships tend to share a common philosophical outlook, as well as strong operational capabilities. They share things in common and, as organizations, often look alike in many ways. At the same time, they frequently share basic philosophies of operational and human resource management. For example, when US-based Davidson-Marley was looking for a British partner, they sought (and found) a viable partner who shared many common characteristics that they felt would be required in order for the venture to succeed.[28] Both used consensus-style management. Both were part of a larger organization that was highly decentralized. Both desired to move to the Continent with a manufacturing presence. Both had similar views on how to grow the business. Both had similar philosophies about running the business and managing human resources. Both sought an open and fair relationship. As a result, the two partners got off to a good start and began business well along on the learning curve.

Preparing for global negotiations

Once a potential partner has been identified, companies next turn their attention to the negotiation process aimed at building a useful partnership. The negotiation process is the first step in relationship building, and represents an opportunity for both parties to determine the nature, scope, and ground rules for the partnership. As discussed above, despite the many benefits of a global partnership, there are several drawbacks, and partners must obviously work hard to make it work. During the negotiation process, partners have an opportunity to learn about each party's organizational and national cultures, their interests, commitments, and potential synergistic opportunities to create value.

Unfortunately, when negotiating such a partnership, negotiators frequently commit the mistake of focusing exclusively on signing the deal, assuming that once the contract is signed, everything else will follow smoothly. In reality, however, signing a contract is just the beginning of most partnerships. Given the high rate of failure in global partnerships, the real challenge is not signing the contract but putting the deal into practice. Companies that are able to use the negotiation process to get to know their future partners can often foresee and prevent future problems and avoid undue hardships. For these situations, negotiations expert Danny Ertel suggests that negotiators need a new mindset focused on implementation. He notes that:

> [T]he product of a negotiation isn't a document; it's the value produced once the parties have done what they agreed to do. Negotiators who understand that prepare differently than dealmakers do. They don't ask, "What might they be willing to accept?" But rather, "How do we create value together?" They also negotiate differently, recognizing that value comes not from a signature but from real work performed long after the ink has dried.[29]

To this end, he suggests five approaches toward an implementation mindset:
(1) *Start with the end in mind.* Think about how the deal will work twelve months after it is signed. How will you know when it is successful? What can go wrong? These questions focus negotiations on the implementation phase, making the partnership work after the deal has been signed.
(2) *Help the other side to prepare.* Surprising the other party in order to win concessions is likely to backfire, as the other party will not be able to deliver on its promises and both sides will lose.
(3) *Treat alignment as a shared responsibility.* If your interests are not properly aligned, problems will likely emerge at some time in the future. It is worthwhile investing in

time to gain acceptance by all those involved in the deal, who will have to make the deal work later on.

(4) *Send one clear message.* Share information with everyone involved in the deal. Withholding information may create early wins, but will cause problems in the implementation phase if one of the parties feels deceived.

(5) *Manage negotiations like a business process.* Signing a contract is just the first step; the implementation of the deal brings with it important associated costs. To ensure that the implementation will be smooth, negotiators use careful preparation and post-negotiation reviews.

Managing the negotiation process

Successful international negotiators are comfortable in multicultural environments and are skilled in building and maintaining interpersonal relationships. But a career in this arena is not for the faint of heart; this is a difficult job that requires a number of very specific skills, as well as an ability to handle significant amounts of conflict and stress. Successes come slowly and failures are commonplace. Even so, it is possible to identify a number of personal factors that often differentiate between successful and unsuccessful negotiators: a tolerance for ambiguity; patience, patience, patience; flexibility and creativity; a good sense of humor; solid physical and mental stamina; cultural empathy; curiosity and a willingness to learn new things; and a knowledge of foreign languages.

Among these recommendations, the one suggesting knowledge of a foreign language is perhaps the most controversial. Specifically, how important is it to speak two or more languages? Moreover, when negotiating with a foreign partner, which language should be used? And when should it be used? Consider, for example, the perils when someone is only monolingual and uses an interpreter for negotiations. A British manager was recently on a business trip to Mexico City and her local host took her to visit the famous Teotihuacán pyramids outside the city. Near the great pyramid of the sun, they ran across a Mexican peasant who was selling trinkets. The manager found something she liked and her Mexican host offered to help her negotiate. The peasant made an initial offer and the Brit's host translated and then suggested a low counter offer. "If we counter with this, he will then counter with that …," said the host. Not surprisingly, the peasant rejected the counter offer and offered only a slightly lower price. The host then suggested a higher counter offer, again explaining that if she offered x, the peasant would likely come back with y. Bidding and counter bidding went on like this for several minutes. Finally, the frustrated British manager, who had made little headway in gaining an advantageous price, gave in and agreed to pay almost full price for the item. At that, the poor Mexican peasant looked at the British manager and asked, in near-perfect English, "Would you like to charge it on American Express?" The lesson here is very simple: If you do not understand the local language, at least know whom you are bargaining with – and who is doing your translation.

One last question here about language: Has English replaced all other languages as the required language for global trade today? If so, why should anyone study another language? Or is there still a competitive advantage in having an ability to negotiate in a partner's home language?

Beyond these personal qualities, experts suggest several general strategies that have been found to facilitate successful negotiations, including the following:[30]

- *Concentrate on building long-term relationships with your partner, not short-term contracts.* Long-term partners usually yield greater long-term results for both parties.
- *Focus on understanding the organizational and personal interests and goals behind the stated bargaining positions.* The Latin *cui bono* ("Who benefits?") is certainly appropriate here.[31] What do the various parties to the negotiation hope to gain from an agreement?
- *Avoid over-reliance on cultural generalizations.* While there may be cultural trends within specific countries, no nation is monolithic and people can vary widely in their personal characteristics.
- *Be sensitive to timing.* Some cultures – and some negotiators – require considerable patience in working towards an agreement, while others demand prompt resolution of all issues or they will go elsewhere.
- *Remain flexible throughout the negotiations.* Circumstances, available information, and opportunities often change, and success sometimes hinges on both being prepared and being alert.
- *Plan carefully.* Nowhere is the old adage that "knowledge is power" more apt than in understanding international negotiations. Solid preparations can make all the difference.
- *Learn to listen, not just to speak.* Develop good listening skills to understand both the content and the context of the message. Use body language and facial expressions to identify informal or subtle cues to intentions.

Managing global partnerships

Global partnerships are typically organized and managed in one of three ways, based on where fiscal and operating responsibilities are assigned (see Exhibit 10.8). In some cases,

Exhibit 10.8 Management arrangements for global partnerships

Management arrangements	Responsibility and control	Potential problems
Shared arrangements	Partners share responsibilities for managing the venture, often through a joint management committee.	Keeping the partnership from growing stale; continual communication challenges, particularly across divergent cultures.
Assigned arrangements	One partner is assigned responsibility for managing the venture, while the other partner retains oversight rights.	Managing partner may inadvertently ignore its non-management partner or may put its goals ahead of others, thereby creating suspicion and mistrust.
Delegated arrangements	Control of operations delegated to managers specifically hired or assigned to operate the venture, while partner retains oversight responsibility.	Maintaining independence of the joint venture and ensuring that co-partners stay out of day-to-day operations and decisions. Three-way communication between partners and 'the international joint venture' can be difficult.

alliances use what is called a *shared management agreement*, where all partners to the venture actively participate in the management of the alliance. This is the case with the Samsung-Corning Glass partnership discussed earlier, where Corning brought its cutting-edge glass technologies and matched it with Samsung's manufacturing prowess. Under such arrangements, managers in the joint venture frequently have little serious operating autonomy since the partner companies are continually looking over their shoulder and actively participating in the management of the venture. In addition, efforts are required here to keep the partnership from growing old or stale. Communication misunderstandings can also be a challenge, particularly across divergent cultures. In order to succeed here, all partners must be very skilled in making cooperative arrangements work.

A second approach to management is an *assigned management arrangement*, whereby one partner is assigned responsibility for running the venture. Here, the lead partner has significant control over the operating decisions of the venture, although there is still joint oversight of the venture by the other partners. NUMMI, the successful Toyota-General Motors joint venture, is an example of this. While such arrangements are commonplace, they can frequently create problems between the partners, often brought about because the assigned management inadvertently (and sometimes intentionally) puts its own interests and goals before those of its partner, thereby creating suspicion and mistrust.

Finally, some alliances are run using a *delegated management arrangement*. This applies only to joint ventures where the entity has legal status as a corporation. Here, the international joint venture managers are hired or assigned to run the venture and the partners to the alliance agree to delegate management control to these managers.

Venture managers are responsible for day-to-day decisions and for implementation of the strategic objectives of the firm. Even so, they are still accountable to the partners that own the joint venture. Frequent problems with this sort of management arrangement can occur when the two (or more) partner companies interfere – or attempt to interfere – with the day-to-day operations of the joint venture. Communication problems between the partners and the international joint venture can also be a frequent challenge.

US President Ronald Reagan said long ago when talking about a political adversary, "Trust, but verify." Perhaps the same can be said about global partnerships. Trust and relationship building are critical to venture success, but like all organizational systems so too are control systems. Decisions must be made and parties must be held accountable. Oversight is a central part of partnership. Control issues in joint ventures and strategic alliances arise from many places and include a wide variety of issues. These include hiring and firing decisions, sourcing raw materials, product designs, production processes, quality standards, product pricing, sales strategies, budgets, and capital expenditures, just to name a few. Dealing with these critical issues illustrates the importance of starting a partnership on the right foot and only after careful consideration and due diligence.

On the other hand, perhaps the phrase "trust, but verify" represents a contradiction in terms, or at the very least poor advice for global managers. That is, if partners truly trust one another, it can be argued that there should be no need to verify (see the discussion below on trust). Indeed, behavior aimed at verification could potentially derail trust that has been so carefully developed over time. Perhaps this contradiction can be explained in part by different culturally based interpretations of the word trust. Some cultures, most notably the US, are often quick to trust others (remember "my new best friend"?) and may be interpreting the word in superficial ways, while others, perhaps the Japanese, see trust as being deeply rooted in the social and cultural fabric of society.

Having said this, there are a number of control mechanisms that are commonly used by firms to ensure compliance with the original agreement and specified goals of the joint venture. These include the following:

- clearly stipulated and written management policies and procedures
- contractual stipulations and requirements for both parties
- up-front agreements on the key personnel to be involved in the venture
- oversight by company or subsidiary boards of directors
- budgetary controls and the use of approved accounting principles and procedures

- the development of open and honest interpersonal relationships among key players
- clear policies on resource allocation and utilization, with continual tracking by both parties.

Such control systems do not guarantee success. However, if fully developed and articulated (and agreed upon by both parties) they go a long way towards resolving minor conflicts, avoiding misunderstandings, and preventing major threats to the integrity of the venture.

Negotiation and global partnerships

Creating global partnerships is no easy task. But, in many ways, the real work commences after the partnership is established. The issue here is not just the partnering process, but also making the new venture successful for the long term. In this endeavor, four key challenges face global managers: rethinking what is involved in a global partnership, building mutual trust, aligning corporate cultures, and managing conflicts between partners.

Rethinking negotiation and partnerships

Returning to the opening example of General Electric and Mitsubishi Electric, what lessons can be drawn for the materials discussed here that might have made the negotiation process run more smoothly and led to better results? While the details behind this negotiation process are not fully known, and while the information presented comes from only one source, it is difficult to see inside the organizational mind of either company. Still, some observations towards developing theories-in-use for global managers are possible.

The first issue to be considered involves the motives of the two firms in pursuing the partnership. Both sides claimed that the partnership would be beneficial, yet neither side tried too hard to make it happen. Perhaps there were other motives or goals involved in this process that failed to surface. For example, perhaps General Electric or Mitsubishi (or both) were simply trying to put added pressure on its old partners to strike a more favorable deal. Perhaps the formal (and relatively public) negotiation may have been all for show. If both parties were serious about the proposed partnership, why did they act in ways that made such a goal unreachable.

In addition, we can look at the personalities of the two CEOs. Both had extensive experience in negotiating and implementing international contracts. Were these two CEOs really as inept as they might appear in this episode or were other things going on? (Perhaps it was just jet lag.) And speaking of personalities, we might also look at Jeff Depew, the reporter of this incident. Writing as a recently terminated General Electric employee, how impartial is his account? Since no one else who was involved chose to speak on this issue, caution is in order concerning what actually happened and how

events should be interpreted. This last point is particularly important for global managers in general, since the quality of information negotiators often receive in advance of
meeting their prospective partners is very often incomplete and laden with hidden
agendas. Hence, a key to successful preparation for negotiations is verifying the facts
and vetting the players on both sides of the table.

At the same time, assuming both sides were indeed serious about the prospects of
the partnership, how much thought went into the initial discussions about the value-
added prospects that might result from the partnership – on both sides? Were there, in
fact, good long-term reasons to form a partnership here? (Consider the criteria for
selecting global partners discussed above.) Solid research about prospective partners,
as well as economic, technical, and operations data are often overlooked in the pursuit
of an alliance with a high-visibility partner.

Also assuming that both sides were serious here, what efforts were made by either
side to understand differences in negotiating styles? Exhibits 10.6 and 10.7 briefly
highlight some major cultural differences here. Was this taken into account by the
well-traveled and experienced CEOs? Why did at least one side apparently use a
competitive bargaining strategy (See Exhibit 10.2, above) when a problem-solving
strategy may have proven to be more effective?

On the topic of relationship building, if the case details were reported accurately, it
might seem that the Japanese side was more serious about this starting the partnership
off on the right foot. This may have been because building long-term relationships are
more important to the Japanese side. This relationship building in Japan often begins
with a formal ceremonial greeting (*aisatsu*), and this did not go down well with the
General Electric side, possibly because typical American firms pay less attention to such
activities and focus instead on contract details. (Remember the difference between
contracts that are often, but not exclusively, found in the East and West.) In any case, the
initial meeting did not go well, leading to an unraveling of months of work by the junior
parties of both sides.

Finally, consider the issue of trust. In fact, both sides might have acted differently if
they were indeed interesting in developing a long-term relationship based on mutual
benefit and trust (see below).

In the end, the proposed partnership collapsed, with both sides blaming each other.
However, consider what happened next: Shortly after the failure, Fuji Electric dissolved
its partnership with General Electric. In accordance with the dissolution agreement, the
parties divided their assets on a regional basis: the joint venture manufacturing business in China became a wholly owned subsidiary of Fuji, while the manufacturing

Exhibit 10.9 Can people be trusted?

Country	Agreement (%)	Country	Agreement (%)	Country	Agreement (%)
Brazil	7	Austria	32	United Kingdom	44
Turkey	10	Mexico	34	Ireland	44
Romania	16	Korea	35	United States	47
Slovenia	17	Spain	35	Canada	52
Latvia	18	India	35	Netherlands	54
Portugal	23	Russia	37	Denmark	58
Chile	24	Germany	38	China	60
Nigeria	24	Japan	42	Finland	64
Argentina	24	Switzerland	43	Norway	67
France	24	Iceland	44	Sweden	68

Source: Data compiled from World Values Study Group, *World Values Survey*. Ann Arbor, MI: Institute for Social Research, University of Michigan, 2000.

business in Mexico became a wholly owned subsidiary of General Electric. Fuji then began selling products in North, Central, and South America under its own brand name. At the same time, the Mitsubishi-Westinghouse partnership has not only survived; it has indeed expanded and is thriving today.

Building mutual trust

Trust in global partnerships is both important and elusive. Experience tells us that without trust between venture partners, the likelihood of long-term success is significantly reduced. But how is trust developed between partners, especially across cultures? Management experts Randall Schuler, Susan Jackson, and Yadong Lou have suggested four key ingredients to successful partnerships: development of long-term trust between the partners; serious commitment of both partners to the success of the venture; creation of structural linkages between the new venture and its parent companies that link the partners together organizationally in ways that integrate the partnership to both parent companies; and the development of effective mechanisms to reduce conflicts as they arise.[32] Of these four variables, the absence of trust and a sense of a true and mutually rewarding partnership is often the most likely cause of failure.

It has long been said that successful marriages are built upon trust. This assertion applies with equal vigor to business "marriages" across borders: global partnerships and strategic alliances. Indeed, a review of the research on successful partnerships reveals clearly that trust represents one of the key success factors.[33] Exhibit 10.9 compares trust

Exhibit 10.10 Management challenge: developing mutual trust

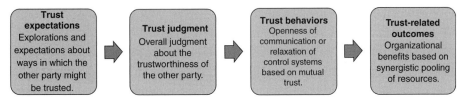

Trust expectations	Trust judgment	Trust behaviors	Trust-related outcomes
Explorations and expectations about ways in which the other party might be trusted.	Overall judgment about the trustworthiness of the other party.	Openness of communication or relaxation of control systems based on mutual trust.	Organizational benefits based on synergistic pooling of resources.

Source: Based on Buchman, "The complexity of trust"

levels by country. As can be seen, the belief that people can be trusted varies somewhat by region: Latin American countries in this study ranged from 7 percent for Brazil to a high of 34 percent for Mexico, while most – but not all – European countries were above this (between 23 and 68 percent). This was particularly true in the Scandinavian countries, where trust levels ranged from 58 to 68 percent. Canada and the US were in the third quartile, fairly trusting but also cautious.

Considering this disparity and the importance of trust raises two questions. First, what is the process by which trust between partners is developed? Second, what can strategic partners do to facilitate or enhance this trust over time? To answer the first question, consider a simplified model of trust development as shown in Exhibit 10.10. As shown here, a principal ingredient in the development of trust is the foundation upon which it is based. In this regard, three "trust expectations" can be identified: competence-based trust, the degree to which partners believe the other can deliver on his/her commitments; incentive-based trust, the extent to which each party believes the other is sufficiently motivated to deliver on his/her commitments; and benevolence-based trust, the extent to which each party believes the other is making a good-faith effort to meet his/her commitments.[34]

Following the model, parties to an agreement (or potential agreement) weigh each of these three expectations and calculate an overall expectation that the other party can be trusted. This "trust judgment" leads to trusting behavior (e.g., increased openness with partners, fewer demands for costly control systems or oversight, etc.) and subsequent trust-related outcomes (e.g., increased efficiency, cost reductions, joint goal attainment, etc.). While no model can capture the entirety of a complex process like developing trust, this model does serve to highlight several of the key factors in the process.

As might be expected, when trust development must occur between alliance partners from significantly different countries and cultures, the challenges of doing business can increase exponentially. Consider an international joint venture between a British and a Russian company. Both partners want to have a successful – and profitable – venture. But at the same time, both partners may have little experience or understanding of the other's culture and business practices, and none of the key players to the partnership may be particularly bilingual. Moreover, each partner is likely to have some perceptions or stereotypes about the other. For example, research shows that many Brits see Russian businesses (not necessarily Russians themselves) as being somewhat corrupt, dishonest, and self-serving, while many Russians see British businesses as being too idealistic and too close to their US neighbors. Moreover, data suggest that Russians may be more collectivistic, while the British are more individualistic. Russians may be more comfortable working in strictly hierarchical surroundings, while the British tend to prefer a more egalitarian environment. Brits may believe in building partnerships based on clear rules and detailed written contracts (in which language, however, English or Russian?), while Russians may prefer to base interactions more on personal relationships. Finally, both partners likely see the other as task-oriented, straightforward, direct, and controlling.[35]

Consider: How might two companies and their managers – one from Russia and one from the UK – build a partnership that benefits both parties? If trust between partners is a fragile commodity that is difficult to create but easy to destroy, what could these two strategic partners do to enhance the chances of building a long-term mutually rewarding relationship without jeopardizing their own self-interests?

In point of fact, a number of strategies can be identified that, while simple, can nonetheless be effective. For starters, partners must be open and candid in their communications with the other party. One misrepresentation of the facts can destroy years of stability and success. This is not to say that all proprietary information (e.g., trade secrets) must be shared; rather, it suggests that the other party must know when and why information is proprietary. If such information has little to do with the goals of the partnership, there is little reason that honest partners would push for answers in these confidential areas. On the other hand, when one partner keeps confidential information relating to the operation and success of the joint venture, this venture will likely begin to see its prospects as a partnership declines.

In addition, successful long-term partnerships are universally characterized by mutual benefit. No partner willingly remains in an inequitable relationship. However, when a partner sees the other party working diligently on behalf of the collective partnership and not just for his or her company, openness and trust will logically follow. Unfortunately, however, while this maxim appears to be obvious for managers, it can be difficult to follow in actual practice when a partner company faces a situation where it must choose between the welfare of its strategic partnership and its home company.

Aligning corporate cultures

Once a partnership has been formalized, partners will obviously have to work together. As discussed above, a key challenge in a global partnership is bringing together two or more organizations with different corporate cultures. In previous chapters we have discussed how national culture influences behavior. However, as discussed in Chapter 3, every organized group also develops cultural characteristics – be it a country, a region, an organization, a profession, or any other subgroup. Therefore, in a global partnership, the cultural challenges go beyond different national cultures. The culture of the organization and the specific units within that organization also need to be taken into account.

When we consider that individuals are culturally conditioned by the time they enter organizations, it is logical to consider that management practices within an organization are influenced to a large extent by the national culture in which it is located. Indeed, Hofstede's seminal work on cultural values (discussed in Chapter 3) was based on employee surveys in one organization, IBM, in a variety of countries, and revealed important variations among subsidiaries of the same organization. It is thus expected that organizations within a culture often share many of the same values and assumptions found in the national culture.[36]

However, this is not always the case. Many organizations adopt behaviors and assumptions that are at odds with the national culture, and these differences are at the core of their competitive advantage.[37] Organizations need to differentiate themselves from the environment in order to be competitive, and many times their source of competitive advantage lies in a unique corporate culture. For example, US-based Intel thrives by creating a driving "take no prisoners" organizational culture where competition and winning are center stage. At the same time, however, Hewlett-Packard, also a US-based global firm, thrives by creating a spirit of cooperation and team ownership of products and processes. Both high-tech companies are based in the same national culture (indeed, their corporate headquarters are very near each other), but each has created its own unique corporate culture that supports both its strategic plans and its partnering behavior.

A strong and unified corporate culture is important to implement the intangibles of business enterprise (e.g., high customer service, innovation, and teamwork) because no supervision can ever exercise sufficient control over employees. Under these circumstances, culture becomes one of management's most effective tools to influence

Exhibit 10.11 Management challenge: aligning corporate cultures

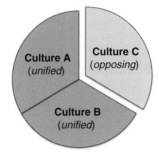

employees' behavior (see Exhibit 10.11). The success of organizations such as Southwest Airlines, Walt Disney, and Wal-Mart is frequently attributed to their strong corporate cultures. These service-oriented organizations were able to build cultures that emphasize high customer value and service. Culture influences how employees behave, which in turn shapes the value customers receive. By the same token, a divided (or worse yet, an opposing) corporate culture creates perpetual obstacles to the success of the joint venture or strategic alliance.

But herein lies a problem. Organizations with strong cultures may have important advantages because they differentiate themselves from others. However, they are likely to face important challenges when they acquire (or are acquired), merge, or engage in a joint venture with other organization with a different culture.

Consider, for instance, the partnership between AmBev and Interbrew. In 2004, these two brewing companies negotiated a partnership to create the largest beer company in the world.[38] The new alliance, called InBev, produced 15 percent of the beer sold worldwide. The new partnership between the two former rivals received considerable attention in the global business community, not just because of its size, but also because of its two partners. One is Brazilian; the other is Belgian. Some market analysts questioned whether the new venture could succeed in view of the wide disparity in the cultures of the two partners. In Brazil, AmBev's corporate culture was characterized by an informal approach to management, an emphasis on spontaneity and innovation, and a constant focus – some would say an obsession – with the bottom line. In contrast, Belgium's Interbrew was a very traditional firm originally founded in the fourteenth century and still run by a board of directors that includes barons, dukes, and marquises. Interbrew's corporate culture is formal, conservative, and – some would say – aristocratic. Long-term financial stability and security outweigh short-term profit considerations. In both cases, their strong corporate cultures were instrumental in their local market success.

How did these two very different companies from two very different cultures come together to form a partnership? With lots of help. Negotiations to create the partnership dragged on for five months and required more than fifty negotiation sessions to close the deal. The efforts of several international banks and legal experts from both countries, as well as from the US, were also required to close the deal. As a result of these lengthy negotiations, the two partners came to understand more about each other's culture, business objectives, and management style. Mistrust evolved into friendship and friendship evolved into partnership. The negotiations were difficult and time-consuming, but in the end they were successful.

Later, in 2008, InBev sought to add US-based Anheuser-Busch to its line-up. Again, after considerable negotiations – and US$52 billion – InBev announced that it had completed its acquisition of Anheuser-Busch following approval from shareholders of both companies. This merger created the global leader in beer and one of the world's top five consumer products companies. As part of the agreement, InBev changed its name to Anheuser-Busch-InBev to reflect the heritage and traditions of Anheuser-Busch, and St. Louis became the North American headquarters for the combined Brazilian-Belgian-American company. Consider the challenges – and the negotiation prowess – for a Brazilian company to first acquire a Belgian firm, followed by an American one.

Today, Anheuser-Busch-InBev has become a major player in the worldwide beer industry. However, creating a common culture is still a work in progress. The new organization has invested important time and resources into sensitizing its managers at various levels and locations to possible cultural differences among partners and subsidiaries around the globe. It has also launched an audacious program of culture transformation in which employees are constantly reminded of the commonalities, synergies, and benefits of working together.

Managing conflicts between global partners

Finally, despite well-intended efforts to develop a common culture and eliminate sources of conflict, chances are that conflicts are likely to emerge as the partnership develops. If and when that happens, what are managers supposed to do? A long tradition of studies on conflict management both within and across cultures points to several common strategies for dealing with conflict.[39] To begin with, consider five generic strategies for resolving conflicts, along with some factors that may

Exhibit 10.12 Management strategies: conflict resolution in global partnerships

help managers decide which one fits best the specifics of their situation (see Exhibit 10.12).

Conflict avoidance as a strategy consists on exiting the field so that the firm does not have to deal with the potential conflict. We will discuss in the following chapter how some firms have opted to leave markets where they would need to offer and/or receive bribes in order to stay in business. When a firm or its managers are not ready to leave the field, they may instead try to force their preferred strategies on the other party; we refer to this as *imposition* strategies. A third strategy, *accommodation,* is the opposite of an imposition strategy, and leads one party to give in to the preferred practice of the other party. A fourth strategy relies on *negotiation* in the expectation that a solution that is mutually satisfactory for all can be reached through common understanding, collaboration, and compromise. Finally, a long-term strategy of *education* seeks to publicize one party's perspective in the hopes of convincing other parties of the correctness of their approach.

Obviously, these five strategies are not always as clear-cut as they might first appear, and other approaches may combine a variety of strategies to make their case. Moreover, under certain conditions, some of their strategies may be preferable to others. Consider the following points:

- To begin with, how crucial is one specific practice for a party against the other party's alternative? If one practice is absolutely vital for a party, short-term imposition and long-term education are likely to make more sense than avoidance, negotiation, and accommodation. Of course, experienced international managers also need to understand that, other than the very issues themselves that operate at the core of the conflicting practices, other otherwise lateral considerations may also become critical if not properly managed. We know, for instance, that in many parts of Asia, losing and preserving face will easily taint the criticality of what is at stake, making for more difficult or easier resolutions.

- How much power does each party have *vis-à-vis* the other? Stronger parties, for instance, can afford imposition strategies to which weaker parties may have to acquiesce and accommodate, while similarly powerful parties may need to engage in collaborative forms of negotiation.
- The viability of a given strategy is also dependent of the timing with which a solution needs to happen. Urgent action may be easily compatible with avoidance and imposition, and not so with education and negotiation, for instance.
- Finally, parties need to account for the potential second-order consequences that derive from the current adoption of a given strategy. Accommodation by one party, for instance, may encourage future imposition attempts by the other party, and current investments in education by one party may pave the way for future accommodation and negotiation by the other.

Once managers account for criticality, power, and urgency, some strategies will at least appear as more convenient than others. In fact, some strategies may become clearly unfeasible while others appear as the only viable ones. This analysis is not always easy, but the better lines of action may begin to suggest themselves after all the above is considered. And through this process, most managers understand that culture will never leave the scene as an influence.

Taking a somewhat more applied viewpoint, conflict resolution expert Nike Carstarphen suggests a few things to consider when dealing with conflicts:[40]

- *Prepare people*. Preparing the people includes fostering a positive and open attitude towards dialogue, focusing on commonalities, not differences. People are central to any conflict, and in order to find a common ground, the attitude of "us versus them" must be replaced by an attitude of "we".
- *Prepare processes*. Preparing the process means fully assessing the situation, identifying the parties that should be present and the appropriate interventions to deal with the conflict. For instance, is it necessary to ask for outside help or can the conflict be solved in house? Is the conflict widespread or concentrated in a specific group?
- *Explore past and present*. Exploring the past and present, the origins of the conflict, and its current dynamics help uncover cultural assumptions and meanings that may be obstructing collaboration. By giving people the opportunity to explore how things were before and what frustrates them now makes it possible to identifying the real issues that may be causing the conflict.
- *Envision the future*. By asking individuals to imagine a common future, creativity and imagination may help to find solutions to the conflict. By envisioning a future

together, common values and needs are likely to become salient, and a common solution may emerge.

- *Create solutions.* Resolving conflicts is not only about envisioning possibilities; it is also about taking action. Here, parties must identify concrete actions to be taken to ease the conflict, and then take those actions, evaluating the effectiveness of those actions along the way and adjusting if necessary.

- *Rejuvenate and reflect.* Dealing with conflicts is an intensive, energy-consuming endeavor. It is important to pause from time to time, to reflect, regroup, and recover energies before the process may continue. It is also important to take time to celebrate successes and give a boost to morale.

- *Don't forget relationships.* Conflicts are typically about relationships between people. It is the very interdependence among people that creates conflict, and no solution will be found if this interdependence is not acknowledged and fostered.

Notes

1 Two old Russian proverbs cited by Yale Richmond, *From Nyet to Da*. Yarmouth, ME: Intercultural Press, 1992, pp. 39 and 139.
2 Margaret Omar Nydell, *The Acquisition of Egyptian Arabic*. Washington, DC, WA: Georgetown University Press, 2007.
3 Thomas O'Boyle, *At Any Cost: Jack Welch, General Electric, and the Pursuit of Profit*. New York, NY: Alfred Knopf, 1998.
4 *Aisatsu* is the Japanese word for greetings or giving a brief speech. It is formed from two *kanji*, both of which have the same literal meaning: to come up close to someone. Greetings in Japan are, like anywhere else, considered polite and preferable to not greeting, but, like most social interactions in Japan, they are more ritualized than in the West.
5 Kae Chung, Hak Chong Lee, and Ku Hyun Jung, *Korean Management: Global Strategy and Cultural Transformation*. Berlin: Walter de Gruyter, 1997; Gerardo Ungson, Richard Steers, and Seung-Ho Park, *Korean Enterprise: The Quest for Globalization*. Boston, MA: Harvard Business School Press, 1997.
6 Ihlwan Moon and Chester Dawson, "Building a Camry fighter," *Business Week*, September 6, 2004, pp. 62–63.
7 Cliff Edwards and Ihlwan Moon, "The Samsung way," *Business Week*, June 16, 2003, pp. 56–64.
8 Chris Rowley and Yongsun Paik, *The Changing Face of Korean Management*. London: Routledge, 2009.
9 Randall Schuler, Susan Jackson, and Yadong Luo, *Managing Human Resources in Cross-border Alliances*. London: Routledge, 2004. This is an excellent resource for people interested in the human resource management implications of global partnerships.

10 Peter Drucker, "The next society," *The Economist*, November 3, 2001, p. 5.

11 Schuler *et al.*, *Managing Human Resources*; Oded Shenkar and Yadong Luo, *International Business*. New York, NY: Wiley, 2004.

12 Based on Schuler *et al.*, *Managing Human Resources*, pp. 92–93.

13 *Ibid.*, p. 93.

14 *Ibid.*

15 *Ibid.*

16 Howard Perlmutter, cited in Andrew Kupfer, "How to be a global manager," *Fortune*, March 14, 1988, pp. 52–58.

17 Jeremy Main, "Making a global alliance work," *Fortune*, December 17, 1990, pp. 121–126.

18 Helen Deresky, *International Management*. Upper Saddle River, NJ: Pearson/Prentice Hall, 2008.

19 *Newsweek*, May 7, 2001.

20 One of the most important concepts in daily life in Japan is *shinyo*, which means "trust," and when the Japanese have dealings with individuals or businesses, choosing someone they can trust is extremely important. Of course, everyone wants to deal with people and companies they believe will do right by them, but in Japanese society the idea of only working with trustworthy entities is elevated to a much higher cultural level. One way to make sure you're working with people you can trust is the concept of *shokai*, a kind of introduction whereby someone who is already trusted by a third party will formally introduce you to them, in effect sharing the goodwill they've already established with both you and the third party. Because both parties have a trust relationship involved, they have an obligation to make sure everything goes smoothly to avoid "stepping on the face" (to use the Japanese phrase) of the person that brought you together. There is no single aspect of Japan that isn't improved by this trust-based relationship system, and time and time again managers have found themselves depending on people who have been formally introduced to them by someone else they trusted.

21 John Graham and Yoshihiro Sano, *Smart Bargaining: Doing Business with the Japanese*. New York, NY: Harper & Row, 1989.

22 Luis A. C. Junqueira, "The Brazilian way to deal with the crisis and recovery," available at the website of the Instituto MVC (www.institutomvc.com.br/english/articles.htm).

23 Leila R. Magalhaes, "Negociando no mercosul," available at www.rhportal.com.br/artigos/wmview.php?idc_cad=t2yf2_h_2.

24 Cynthia A. Rosenburg, "A arte do aperto de maos," *Revista Exame*, 2003, 37(8), pp. 106–118.

25 Michael Morris, "When culture counts – and when it doesn't," *Negotiation*, June 2005, 8, pp. 1–3.

26 Jeanne Brett, "Negotiation and culture: a framework," in Roy Lewicki, Bruce Barry, and David Saunders, *Negotiation: Readings, Exercises, and Cases*. McGraw-Hill, 2007, pp. 349–363.

27 Charles Handy, *Business: The Ultimate Resource*. London: Bloomsbury, 2002, p. 75.

28 Schuler *et al.*, *Managing Human Resources*., p. 44.

29 Danny Ertel, "Getting past yes: negotiating as if implementation mattered," *Harvard Business Review*, November 2004, pp. 60–68.

30 Gary Ferraro, *Cultural Dimensions of International Business*. Upper Saddle River, NJ: Prentice Hall, 2002.

31 *Cui bono* ("To whose benefit?" or "As a benefit to whom?") is a Latin adage from Roman times that is used today either to suggest a hidden motive or to indicate that the party responsible for something may not be who it at first appears to be. With respect to motive, a public works project that is purported to benefit the city may have been initiated rather to benefit a favored campaign contributor with a lucrative contract. Commonly, the phrase is used to suggest that the person or people guilty of committing a crime may be found among those who have something to gain, chiefly with an eye toward financial gain. The party that benefits may not always be obvious or may have successfully diverted attention to a scapegoat, for example.

32 Schuler *et al.*, *Managing Human Resources*.

33 Nancy Buchman, "The complexity of trust: understanding the influence of cultural environment on the nature of trust and trust development," in Rabi Bhagat and Richard M. Steers (eds.), *Cambridge Handbook of Culture, Organizations, and Work*. Cambridge, UK: Cambridge University Press, 2009.

34 *Ibid.*

35 Richard Steers and Luciara Nardon, *Managing in the Global Economy*. New York, NY: M. E. Sharpe, 2006.

36 Geert Hofstede, "The interaction between national and organizational value systems," *Journal of Management Studies*, 1985, 22(4), p. 347.

37 Reed Nelson and Gopalan Suresh, "Do organizational cultures replicate national cultures? Isomorphism, rejection and reciprocal opposition in the corporate values of three countries," *Organization Studies*, 2003, 24(7), p. 115.

38 "A formatacao do negocio," *Exame*, March 16, 2004, available from the magazine website (http://portalexame.abril.com.br).

39 We rely here on the work of Paul F. Buller, John J. Kohls and Kenneth S. Anderson, "When ethics collide: managing conflict across cultures," *Organizational Dynamics*, 2000, 28(4), pp. 52–66.

40 Nick Carstarphen, "A map through rough terrain: a guide for intercultural conflict resolution," in Michelle LeBaron and Venashri Pillay, *Conflict Across Cultures: A Unique Experience of Bridging Differences*. Yarmouth, ME: Intercultural Press, 2006, pp. 137–201.

CHAPTER 11

Managing in an imperfect world

- Rules of the game   364
- Bases of cross-cultural conflicts   367
- Ethics, laws, and social control: a model   373
- Ethical conflicts and challenges   374
- Institutional conflicts and challenges   384
- MANAGER'S NOTEBOOK: Managing in an imperfect world   395

There are truths on this side of the Pyrenees that are falsehoods on the other.

Blaise Pascal[1]
Seventeenth-century philosopher, France

The computer is on the dock, it's raining, and you have to pay a bribe to get it picked up and delivered.

William C. Norris[2]
Founder, Control Date Corporation, USA

Ethical standards reside within people, not organizations. In fact, organizations have no ethical standards; it is only their members – executives, managers, and rank-and-file employees – who determine whether or not a particular company will act ethically or responsibly at any given point in time, and even this determination lies in the eye of the beholder. Ethical standards are oftentimes amorphous, conflicting, and transitory, but their impact on local communities around the world can be profound.

Consider the challenges facing the petroleum industry in doing business in Nigeria. Global economists and political observers have long suggested that Nigeria has two attributes in abundance: oil and corruption. According to *The Economist*, Nigeria is one of the most corrupt nations in the world.[3] Indeed, bribery is so commonplace that they even have their own name for it: "chopping." If this is the case, how do global companies gain access to Nigeria's vast oil reserves to help supply an insatiable world demand for petroleum? Through bribery, of course. Companies that refuse to play – and pay – by the local rules risk being shut out of this lucrative market. But what happens if a company is bound by its home country laws not to engage in this form of bribery?

This is precisely the situation that confronted Houston-based Halliburton when it sought a lucrative contract to develop a natural gas project in Nigeria. In 2004, both the French and US Governments simultaneously launched investigations into whether an oil consortium led by Halliburton paid US$180 million in bribes and other illegal kickbacks to secure the contract.[4] If proven to be true, Halliburton and its officers would be guilty of violating the US Foreign Corrupt Practices Act (FCPA), a law that forbids US companies or their employees from making any kind of illegal payment to secure business (see below). Severe penalties, including sizable fines and jail time, await those convicted of violating this act. Halliburton's CEO initially refused to comment on the allegations, other than to say that this – and similar allegations of violating US trade sanctions with Iran – were the result of "personal bias" against the company. He asserted that Halliburton won its contracts because of "what we know, not who we know."[5] Later, the company acknowledged, "payments may have been made to Nigerian officials."[6] In 2009, however, just one month after former US Vice President Dick Cheney (the former CEO of Halliburton) left office, the company pleaded guilty to violating FCPA regulations by bribing Nigerian government officials to secure contracts totaling US$6 billion. In addition to paying major fines, Halliburton agreed to have independent monitors review and report on future company compliance with the FCPA.[7] It is somewhat curious that no one was brought to justice while the Vice President remained in office.

The example of Halliburton illustrates a fundamental dilemma in international business. If a company follows its home laws, but these laws do not bind its competitors from other countries, how does it compete in an environment characterized by corruption? How does it level the playing field? And how does it define – and then implement – appropriate ethical standards in a complex and turbulent multicultural world? Such questions get to the heart of the legal, political, and ethical challenges facing global business today.

Rules of the game

It is often said that in a perfect world (including the world of global business), there would be little conflict, no corruption, and justice for all. Companies and their managers would seek compromise and mutual benefit, and would ensure that all stakeholders (not just stockholders) to a venture benefited. Fairness and equality would abound and everyone would hold themselves accountable to the highest ethical standards. While everybody agrees on the desirability of such a perfect world, making it happen seems to most people to be impossible. Why is this? Poverty, class distinctions, competing social and political systems, social injustice, nationalism, and greed – to name just a few. We live and work in an imperfect world because people and social systems are different and local factor endowments vary considerably. But we need a deeper explanation here.

A relatively optimistic explanation of why we do not live in a perfect world cites research that suggests that poverty and corruption co-vary; that is, corruption and bribery, environmental degradation, and social injustice are most frequently found in poorer countries and regions, those with fewer social resources or educational opportunities. Thus, we find far more corruption in Nigeria than in Finland. Many of the people inhabiting poorer countries are more concerned with survival than success, the argument goes, and higher ethical standards are often considered a luxury people cannot afford. This is an optimistic view because it implies that improving socioeconomic conditions across the board will move us closer to that perfect world. And there is some truth to this position. For instance, most people will more easily expect – and possibly even condone – the stealing of food by a poor, starving person than the same behavior by a well-fed, wealthy individual. (This is why shoplifting by movie stars, for example, is always front-page news.) However, the fact that these two phenomena – corruption and poverty – co-vary does not necessarily mean that one leads to the other. Philosophers still ponder how the Holocaust, for instance, took place in one of the most cultivated and industrialized countries in the world.[8] Similarly, ratings of national corruption actually vary across equally poor nations in similar geographic regions (e.g., Indonesia and Malaysia, Nigeria and Kenya, Russia and Poland).[9] Hence, the causal relationship may be difficult to find.

On the other hand, a relatively pessimistic view of this situation concludes that we live in an imperfect world because of our imperfect human nature. Take greed, for instance. Some people seem overly driven to maximize their income and personal possessions at almost any cost. In this pursuit, ethical standards often take a back seat to the pursuit of profit. This line of reasoning has value in helping us understand how some people seem to behave, but it fails to address the ultimate motives behind that greed. An obsession with amassing income and possessions may actually mask a deeper, unbalanced obsession for security or status, for instance. This is relevant in order to attempt to build a world that gets increasingly closer to perfection because accounting for the more superficial obsessions and ignoring the deeper ones will not address the issue. The initial pessimism in this position, with its ring of "if someone is greedy, there is not much that can be done about it" may then turn into a more hopeful stance, because the anxiety and need for security or status has more to do with how one feels than with how one is, and the former is more malleable than the later. Moreover, as readers are well aware, culture has a strong effect on how one defines greed, security, or status, and we will have to account for these differences when dealing with ethical business or management behavior across societies.

Beyond optimism and pessimism, there may be a third explanation, one that is culture-based. For example, in more collectivistic societies, most people aspire to some form of socio-economic egalitarianism, where income and benefits are roughly evenly divided; no one is either too rich or too poor, and harmony prevails as an ultimate goal. By contrast, in more individualistic cultures, many people argue the benefits of competition between individuals, with market forces driving out inefficiencies and reducing consumer costs, and superior rewards going to those who demonstrate greater drive, initiative, and mastery. If this perspective is used, the key question becomes what we mean by a perfect world, not how to get there. Relating this to global business, is a perfect world characterized by an environment where everyone plays by the same rules on a level playing field or by an environment where everyone (or at least every group) creates their own rules? And if everyone plays by the same rules, who gets to determine what those rules are?

Behind these apparently simple and straightforward questions are a variety of complex issues, beginning with the various types or foci of cultural conflicts. A particular point of interest here is the ongoing conflict across cultures between what is moral or "culturally sanctioned" and what is "legal." What happens, or should happen, when these two powerful forces stand in opposition to each other? Consider the following example: The *Trique*, an indigenous native community in rural Mexico, has long had a tradition of parents arranging the marriages of their children, and doing so at an early age.[10] They also have a custom whereby the groom's family pays the bride's family a dowry, primarily to cover costs associated with the wedding ceremony. Such customs can be found in many communities throughout the world. In one such family, Marcelino de Jesus Martinez arranged to marry his 14-year-old daughter to a neighbor's son. Both young people apparently agreed to the wedding. In Mexico, this wedding would have gone unnoticed, as it follows long-standing customs. However, the wedding occurred not in Mexico but in the Californian farming community of Greenfield, where many Mexican farm workers live and work. As a result, Martinez was arrested on US felony charges of procuring a child under the age of 16 for sex and for recklessly endangering the health of a minor. To make matters worse, Martinez had accepted

US$16,000 in exchange for his approval of the marriage, considered a dowry in Mexico but as solicitation for financial advantage in California. As noted by the California prosecutor in the case, "This is not a traditional trafficking case, because there was no force or coercion in this. We are aware of the cultural issues here, but state law trumps cultural sensitivity." The final irony of this case is that none of this would have come to light had Martinez not sought police assistance in forcing a recalcitrant groom's father to pay the dowry.

Bases of cross-cultural conflicts

French philosopher Blaise Pascal and Control Data Corporation founder William Norris, both quoted above and coming from two very different time periods (and with two very different visions of globalization), come to much the same conclusion on the topic of ethics, albeit with a different focus. Pascal noted that the peoples of two different cultures (in his case, France and Spain) at times see the "facts on the ground" very differently from one another. We can either interpret this conflict in terms of who is right or wrong, or we can dig deeper and try to understand the bases for each point of view. In a nutshell, this is the primary tension underlying most cross-cultural conflicts: how to tease out the "real" facts and discover the "truth" as we are willing to accept it. At the same time, William Norris points out that transnational firms are subject to local conditions and "realities on the ground," whatever those may be. While such firms obviously have the option of withdrawal, remaining incurs obligations, commitments, and, many times, costs. Thus, the question for Control Data Corporation and others is how to run a successful transnational in an efficient and effective way while simultaneously accommodating differences of opinion regarding the facts on the ground across different locations.[11]

The difference here between Pascal and Norris is one of seeing versus doing. That is, Pascal makes an observation about differences in worldviews, while Norris focuses on differences in required behavior. Both are important to global managers confronted with conflicts. In fact, when we discuss conflicts, it is important to note that conflicts across borders most often involve one of three issues: What is ethical? What is fair? And what represents good stewardship of the resources controlled or impacted by the firm? All three of these issues deserve attention, not only because they relate to appropriate managerial behavior, but also because, at the very least, they can get managers and their firms into deep trouble very quickly. As Norris observes, ignoring the local environment comes with major risks.

Cultural conflicts like the example given above can appear in many different forms. Consider the example of a recent dinner discussion in London between a group of Chinese, French, and Ecuadorian business partners. As they began to order appetizers, they quickly fell into polite disagreement over whether to order rat soup, cooked snails, or fried ants. While this discussion was lively and contained ample room for disagreement over what to order, few would describe this as a heart-felt conflict. Imagine, however, if the French partner liked the fried ants so much that she decided to open a new restaurant on the fishermen's bay of the beautiful French village of Argenton. Chances are her new restaurant and its cuisine might face opposition from its Breton neighbors; it might even face challenges from French health officials who worry about food safety. On one level, different cultures can foster manifestly different tastes and practices (do you really like fried ants?). On another level, however, they can foster manifestly different laws and regulations (are fried ants safe?). As such, we need to differentiate between conflicts over matters of personal taste on the one hand, and conflicts between what some may consider acceptable ethical behavior and local legal or policy requirements on the other.

To represent the whole spectrum of cultural conflicts, we need to add a third and more delicate category: beliefs and values. Keeping with our illustration, imagine a culture that believed that rats, snails, and ants belonged to a higher group of beings that guided our human ancestors in their afterlife. In this context, eating ants may go beyond taste, practice, and the law and into the deeper waters of value conflicts. This is an arena where beliefs and values themselves collide.

Thus, when we consider how cross-cultural conflicts can impede global business and management success, we can readily summarize these challenges into three relatively distinct categories (see Exhibit 11.1):

(1) *Acceptance or rejection of different tastes and preferences.* Conflict between a person's or group's tastes or preferences and those of others. People must

Exhibit 11.1 Sources of cross-cultural conflict

determine which tastes or preferences will prevail or be tolerated. Impact can be influenced by the extent to which the parties are open to compromise.

(2) *Preference for ethical imperatives or legal requirements.* Conflict between what a person or group thinks is ethical and what they think is legal. People must make a decision between following their conscience or following prevailing laws and regulations. One has spiritual or moral implications; the other has enforcement or punishment implications.

(3) *Tolerance or intolerance of different beliefs and values.* Conflict between the beliefs and values of one individual or group compared to another. People must determine how tolerant or intolerant they are in relationship to the other party's beliefs and values. Is there room for compromise (or at least separation) or not?

Conflicts over tastes and preferences

People in different cultures obviously have different tastes and preferences. In their simplest form, these tastes and preferences are usually so personal and subjective that they can be easily ignored (e.g., being a vegan or vegetarian). As management writer David Cooper puts it, where tastes are concerned, we can simply agree to disagree.[12] However, when these tastes or preferences affect other people in fairly direct ways (e.g., being a vegan sales representative for a major meat processor like Tyson Foods but refusing to eat meat products with clients or customers), they are harder to ignore. In such cases, we often see increased pressures to think of ways to resolve the conflict or change personal behavior. Thus, knowing how and when to move beyond an "agree to disagree" strategy becomes crucial.

Consider the example of a small Dutch high-tech firm that was recently acquired by a major US electronics firm. Consistent with Dutch tradition, the small company had long provided many of its middle managers with company cars to offset the country's high tax rate on personal incomes. In the eyes of its employees, this was part of their compensation package. However, after the acquisition, the American executive overseeing the acquisition sought to rescind the local company's car policy since it was far more generous than that of the parent company back in the US. (Following a number of resignations, the parent company policy change was dropped.) This example illustrates the conflicts and challenges faced by many of today's global managers. From his or her standpoint, the American executive was seeking equality in their employee personnel policies across the two countries, but from the Dutch standpoint the company cars were part of this equality since their income tax rate was substantially higher than their US counterparts.

Conflicts between ethical versus legal imperatives

For millennia, societies have worked to separate the sphere of the legal from that of the ethical. To understand this, it might be helpful to look at the mediating role of religion. In Christian doctrine, for example, social relations emphasize the need to clearly separate the spheres of government (that which "belongs to Caesar") from the spheres of spirituality (that which "belongs to God"). Other religions and philosophies have tended to be somewhat less clear on how distinct this separation should be. For example, Confucianism (really more of a secular system of ethics than a religion) saw in the virtues of the emperor and public officials the ultimate model for everyone's behavior, and proposed that social relations generally mirror the relationships that ought to be established between rulers and the ruled. Hinduism, as revealed in one of the *Veda* hymns, reserves to members of the Kshatriya caste all military and governance duties. Islam, too, conflates the public and private spheres negating the separation of legal and religious duties and rulers, as, for instance, when discussing Islamic finance and banking (see Chapters 2 and 5).

With time, however, the doctrines and practices of many of these faiths have increasingly begun to separate the ethical and religious domains from the legal one, the exception being Muslim countries that continue to adhere to the Islamic legal-and-religious regulation known as the *sharia*. (It should be noted that some Western philosophers see this lack of separation of the legal and the ethical/religious in Islamic countries as transitory, with the expectation that Muslim societies will eventually move towards separating both spheres. Of course, many people in Islamic cultures disagree strongly with this assessment, sensing that this hypothetical evolution may be an attempt to interfere with a fundamental tenant of the Islamic faith and way of life.)

The major practical implication of this separation of the ethical and the legal is that only the most fundamental parameters of human behavior (e.g., major crimes against society) are mandated by the law and oftentimes punished, while the ethical is often seen as being largely self- or group-regulating and largely excluded from direct government intervention (e.g., freedom of religion). For this dichotomy to work in actual practice, however, few contradictions can exist between the mandates of the law and of ethics, and this is clearly not always the case.

Now we come to an interesting question: What should people (including managers) do, then, when confronted with a conflict between their ethical beliefs on the one hand, and local laws and regulations on the other? When all reasonable efforts to reconcile these conflicting forces fail, research shows that, in most cultures, precedence is most often given to the ethical over the legal.[13] That is, people will follow their conscience before they follow the law. This obviously does not suggest that doing so will be easy. In many cases, following one's moral conscience risks the penalties that breaking the law entails. Even so, most cultures most of the time reinforce the importance of doing what is right over doing what is legal. Indeed, this is how many local heroes are born. Moreover, many companies encourage their employees to adhere to this doctrine.

For example, in-house training programs at Motorola advise their global managers to check out whether the consequences of applying the law in various countries may violate basic principles of human rights or environmental protection prior to taking action.[14] Motorola's reasoning seems to be attractive to many people, yet it assumes implicitly that instances of conflict between ethical and legal prescriptions will take place only in foreign land, not inside the US. Far less training in this area is provided to many of its local managers.

Thus, people frequently become more apprehensive when what is at stake is the law of their home country than that of a foreign nation. For example, business travelers to Iran will often lie to Iranian authorities about ever having visited Israel, since this would automatically prohibit their entry. But when these same travelers are asked how they feel about similarly violating the immigration laws of their own country, their responses frequently become much more nuanced and they typically show a clear reluctance to break the law. The question for global managers, then, is when and where to place personal convictions above the law. Not an easy question, as we will see below.

Conflicts over beliefs and values

Finally, many managers see conflicts between values as almost natural and unavoidable in cross-cultural encounters. Such conflicts are obviously an important issue, but their relevance may, at times, be a bit overstated. First, much of this conflict also happens within cultures, especially in cultures that pride themselves on integrating different viewpoints or prize high levels of heterogeneity and diversity. Second, we have already noted that much of what appears to be conflicts between competing values from different cultures actually masks conflicting practices emanating from similar, non-competing values. Third, cross-cultural encounters certainly result from conflicting values at times, but they also result from instances where values that operate in one culture are also found in another, which results in value reinforcement rather than conflict. And finally, anthropologists consistently point out that entering another culture promotes awareness and understanding of values and practices already present in our own culture, but which are perhaps taken for granted and forgotten.

A principal issue here has to do with the weighting and harmonization of different values within, not across, cultures. Not all values are equally valuable at all times, and some values are not easily amenable to simultaneous implementation. On the one hand, because of increased globalization pressures, cultures may end up differing not so much in the values they espouse, but rather in how they weigh and combine these values for specific purposes through specific practices. On the other hand, with cultures becoming increasingly intermixed, value conflicts can become more salient within cultures than among them. Recent research on what it means to be an ethical leader in different cultures, for instance, is particularly illuminating. This point was also made earlier in Chapter 4 when discussing whether management styles and patterns of doing business would likely converge or not in the future.

Researchers in the GLOBE project (discussed in Chapter 8) examined the endorsement of ethical leadership across cultures by surveying the ethics and leadership literatures to find several key attributes that characterize ethical leadership.[15] These attributes included: character and integrity; ethical awareness; community and people orientation; motivating, encouraging, and empowering people; and managing ethical accountability. Using the GLOBE data, they derived four factors that matched closely four of the six attributes from the literature review, which they named "character and integrity," "altruism," "collective motivation," and "encouragement." The results showed that the endorsement of each of the four dimensions of ethical leadership differed significantly across the country clusters used in their study.[16] However, because the average endorsement of the attributes was beyond the midpoint average for all dimensions, the authors concluded that some degree of common agreement existed in the endorsement of the components of ethical leadership. This research suggests that the four dimensions of ethical leadership represent a somewhat universal principle according to which, while all cultures appreciate and value some common ethical leadership dimensions, they also allow for significant differences in their enactment.

To illustrate this situation, take, for instance, the "character and integrity" factor in the GLOBE study. This dimension received the highest endorsement by societies in the Nordic European cluster, and the lowest among the Middle Eastern cluster. Nordic and Middle Eastern countries, the authors pointed out, both value character and integrity in their leaders, but consistently rank very differently in international indexes of corruption (see below). The same Nordic European countries, however, show the lowest endorsement of the "altruism" dimension, while societies in Southeast Asia rank the highest. One could argue that this relates to the fact that Southeast Asians also rank higher than Nordic Europeans on in-group pride, loyalty, and a humane orientation.

Whatever the reason, however, a logical conclusion here would be that ethical values and acceptable or desired leadership roles vary across country clusters (see Chapter 8).

Ethics, laws, and social control: a model

Ethics, conflict, and culture are three of the most intractable words in the English language. Each concept is by itself both clear and fuzzy, dynamic and static, emotional and objective. Put them together and confusion and disagreements reign. And if ethical questions within a single homogeneous society are complicated, imagine how these challenges multiply when we look at the intersection of two or more cultures.

To begin this discussion on value-based conflicts, it is helpful to separate ethical or normative beliefs and values from institutional requirements (see Exhibit 11.2). *Ethical conflicts* represent disagreements that arise when two or more people (or groups) disagree on what is morally or philosophically correct. This disagreement is often posed in terms of right and wrong, moral and immoral, and each group gets to decide its own version of these two polar opposites. Cheating on income taxes is a case in point. While some societies believe that failure to pay one's share of corporate or personal taxes represents a theft from society and is morally reprehensible, other societies (and other people in the same society) merely pay lip service to their tax obligations and acknowledge – and, indeed, sometimes encourage – people's efforts to minimize or eliminate such a financial imposition. In 2008, for example, a major Italian city accidentally posted its tax rolls on a website, allowing everyone to see what every citizen paid in taxes. A moral eruption of outrage resulted, but with a curious twist: half of the city was morally outraged because so many of their fellow citizens flagrantly

Exhibit 11.2 Normative beliefs, institutional requirements, and social control

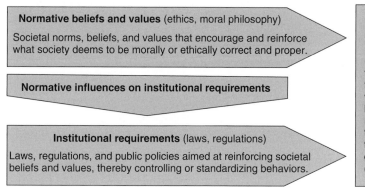

avoided their tax obligations, while the other half was equally outraged because the city's error caused embarrassment to its non-taxpaying citizens. Who is morally correct here?

By contrast, *institutional conflicts* represent differences over what is legal or consistent with legitimately determined public policy. The fundamental difference here is that, while ethical conflicts focus on what is moral, institutional conflicts focus on what is legal. For example, many governments adopt strong consumer protection laws to protect their citizens from unhealthy, unsafe, or poorly constructed products. Other governments take a more *laissez-faire* approach (or *caveat emptor* – "let the buyer beware"). And still others have laws on the books but seldom enforce them. In addition to laws, governments and public agencies also sanction a number of public policies, policies that are designed for the common good. For example, many governmental organizations issue edicts, recommendations, or targets on issues relating to social policy (e.g., automobile emissions, greenhouse gases, and sustainable development). Some of these public policies have various means of (usually mild) enforcement, while others are enforced only by social pressure.

What is interesting here is that many institutional requirements (laws, regulations) are implemented to reinforce a society's normative (moral) beliefs. For example, if social norms or religious beliefs forbid theft, laws are often enacted to back this up by making such actions illegal. As a result, normative beliefs and institutional regulations tend to correlate highly with one another in most societies, particularly those that are relatively homogeneous. Moreover, in some cultures, legal requirements are directly integrated into religious beliefs (e.g., Islam's *sharia*, often defined as a system of divine law governing beliefs and practices). Even so, what is moral or legal in one society may not necessarily be so in another. For example, while some Western countries consider insider trading (where corporate officers and others close to the executive wing use confidential information that is not publicly available to general stockholders to purchase or sell shares before adverse or unexpected news becomes public) to be both unethical and illegal, others see such behavior as inevitable (i.e., how can society expect executives not to act on future knowledge about their firms?) and do not attempt to proscribe it.

Ethical conflicts and challenges

Everyday, global managers are faced with *moral or ethical conflicts* relating to both personal and societal beliefs and values. This arena includes both societal norms in general about right and wrong, as well as religious beliefs about what people "should" or "must" do. As is the case with management theories in general, much of the readily accessible writings on business and managerial ethics have been developed by Western scholars educated in Western traditions of thought, and with an eye towards the specific circumstances of Western decision makers managing in largely Western environments. Efforts to broaden this analysis, even if only by incorporating the tensions faced by Westerners in contact with non-Westerners, are still in a somewhat primitive stage of development. From a Western perspective, things would be simpler if a Western approach to business ethics gained total consensus among the experts, but such is not to be the case. The work of current writers and philosophers on business and managerial ethics either examine the foundations of alternative schools of (Western) thought, with their differential and even opposing implications for practice, or directly proceed to discussions of specific issues at hand, assuming without discussion the validity of a tradition of thought favored by the authors. While these limited approaches may be interesting, the issues and challenges surrounding ethical behavior and conflict really need to be addressed from a global perspective, not a regional one, if we are to make progress in understanding the role of ethics in managerial behavior.

Writers on business ethics have generally acknowledged, at least on some level, that they have consistently been parochial in their conscious ignorance of other cultural traditions. Even so, this has seldom been a central issue for them because most writers have routinely assumed the universal validity of their approaches.[17] That is, most of these writers have assumed that business ethics represent a universal phenomenon and that the challenge is to discover (and then teach) the "correct" set of values and social norms. Obviously, this approach is both naïve and unsatisfactory, as most global executives already understand.

Levels of understanding of cross-cultural ethical conflicts

Before proceeding further with this discussion, it is helpful to clarify three points that relate to our levels of understanding of conflict processes across cultures (see Exhibit 11.3): What do we mean by the concept of "universal" values regarding ethical behavior? What is the interplay between principles and practices in cross-cultural ethical conflicts? How do individual and organizational ethical values relate to each other and to subsequent managerial action. Taken together, these three factors help explain why cross-cultural conflicts can be so intractable and challenging, especially for those who are trying to do the "right" thing.

Exhibit 11.3 Levels of understanding of cross-cultural ethical conflicts

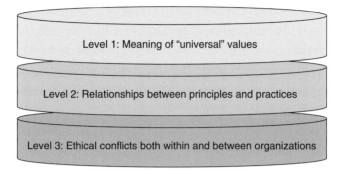

Level 1: Meaning of "universal" values

Level 2: Relationships between principles and practices

Level 3: Ethical conflicts both within and between organizations

Level 1: What is the meaning of "universal" values?

On a purely descriptive level, ethical mandates differ across both time and space.[18] Concepts such as "right" and "wrong" vary through time within any given culture, as well as through cultures themselves at any given time. What is significant here, however, is whether we think of the evolution of what people consider to be right or wrong, through time and space, in terms of a specific pattern of meaning or, to the contrary, whether no discernible pattern can be identified from the temporal and geographical evolution of ethical mandates. Moreover, regardless of whether people behave in more or less "ethical" ways, each generation often sees itself as being more advanced than its predecessors in the accuracy, completeness, and validity of its ethical awareness and understanding. When looking at how each society answers the basic questions of life, very few, if any, would want to renounce the intellectual advancements that their culture has achieved through time. For example, who would seriously want to return to the times when one man owned another, when women were not allowed to express themselves in social life, when caring for the environment did not systematically cross anyone's mind, or when "an eye for an eye" appeared as the most sophisticated inducement against disproportionate forms of revenge? Again, this does not necessarily mean that people behave better now than in the past, only differently. To the extent that people across cultures find this a reasonable argument when applied to their own traditions, we can conclude that some values and principles are, indeed, universal. However, beyond some presupposition of the continuous advancement of ethical standards, however defined, we suggest that no ethical standard that any tradition may hold at any point of time or space can genuinely be considered universal in the long run. If it could, we would be negating the possibility of further improving that standard across time and space.

In short, people and cultures evolve over time and space, as do their ethical beliefs and values. At times, these values seem to run somewhat in tandem across cultures. This can be seen in many commonly espoused beliefs to "respect one's neighbors" or "protect the defenseless" that can be found in various forms in such widely dispersed writings as the *Bible*, the *Dharma*, the *Koran*, the *Puranas*, and the *Talmud*. However, at other times, this convergence seems to disappear, as is sometimes the case with women's rights (e.g., Should women have equal rights? What does "equal" mean? And is "equal" better than "different?"), reinforcing the notion that ethical values are not universal over time or space. If this is correct, the global manager lives perpetually in a parallel universe of conflicting values and acceptable modes of behavior.

Level 2: What is the relationship between principles and practices?

A second issue that requires some clarification is the relationship between principles and practices in cross-cultural ethical conflicts. Many people believe that conflicting principles, as opposed to conflicting practices, are the root cause of most conflicts. Accordingly, it is argued that if people could only reach agreement on the principles from which contrasting practices emanate across countries, this would pave the way to ethical consensus. In our experience, however, the opposite is correct. Disagreement over practices, not principles, lies at the heart of most complex ethical conflicts.

Consider the example of Halliburton discussed above. Prevailing values in the parent country (in this case, the US) stress the undesirability – indeed, the immorality – of paying bribes to secure business. This helps explains the public outrage in the US when local news media unveiled what it described as unethical behavior. However, Nigerian news media reported no such alarms. While Nigerian cultures also have principles governing ethical behavior, the implementation of these principles – the practices – is quite different. In Nigeria, ethics has more to do with accepting responsibility to support one's family and clan than how such money is obtained. Perhaps working across cultures has more to do with seeking common ground than highlighting uncommon behaviors.

The fifth-century Greek scholar and historian Herodotus observed: "[I]f someone were to assign to every person in the world the task of selecting the best of all customs, each one, after thorough consideration, would choose those of his own people, so strongly do humans believe that their customs are the best ones."[19] He advised people not to interfere with the customs and practices of others as the principal way in which to avoid, or at least minimize, conflict. However, when this is not possible, perhaps the best course of action is to focus first on areas of agreement, where commonalities across cultures can be found. As such, rather than focus on objectionable practices, perhaps managers should direct more attention to how to build mutually acceptable practices that are based on common principles.

Level 3: How can we reconcile ethical conflicts both within and between organizations?

Finally, we need to differentiate the focus of cross-cultural ethical conflicts between organization-to-organization conflicts and organization-to-individual conflicts. In most cases, what is at stake is a conflict between the positions of a given company and some external party, such as consumers, suppliers, strategic partners, and so forth. In other cases, however, the conflict is internal, between the values that a firm espouses and those held by one or more of its employees. Consider the plight of the pharmacist who disagrees with selling certain drugs that his or her employer, as well as the medical community and pharmaceutical industry, support. Or consider the plight of a US Department of Agriculture employee who is asked to participate in promoting tobacco exports to foreign countries in spite of his (and his own government's) public opposition to smoking. (Indeed, the US Government subsidizes both local smoking abatement efforts and tobacco export promotion programs.) Such conflicts are as common as they are inevitable.

While it may be tempting to disregard such situations by saying that firms must uphold their principles as part of their culture, vision, and mission (and if employees disagree, they may always leave for another firm), things are seldom this simple. Controversial organizational values can seldom be imposed successfully on individual employees who disagree with them, even if these employees act publicly as if they agree. In Japan, for example, as discussed in Chapter 6, doing or saying the right thing according to what is expected of you (*tatemae*) can be quite different from what an individual actually thinks or prefers to do (*hone*). Thus, understanding conflicts requires an understanding of the parties to the conflict, as well as their respective roles (expected and preferred) within the organization.

The pursuit of "truth"

Communications consultant Richard Lewis has suggested, only partly in jest, "For a German and a Finn, the truth is the truth. In Japan and Britain, it is all right to tell the truth if it doesn't rock the boat. In China, there is no absolute truth. And in Italy, the truth is negotiable."[20] And British actor Peter Ustinov has observed, again only partly in jest, "In order to reach the truth the Germans add, the French subtract, and the British

Exhibit 11.4 Universalism, particularism, and truthfulness

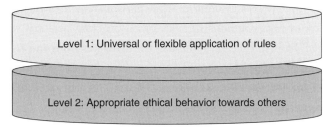

Level 1: Universal or flexible application of rules

Level 2: Appropriate ethical behavior towards others

change the subject. I did not include the Americans, since they often give the impression that they already have the truth."[21] To the extent that these observations have merit, it would appear that truth is clearly in the eye of the beholder. That is, the "truth" is not always the "truth." At the very least, we have to conclude that, at times, there are no universals when it comes to being truthful.

To understand the impact of culture on how people see right and wrong and try and make sense of their responsibilities both to themselves and others, we need to work on two different levels (see Exhibit 11.4). First, culture has an effect on whether groups of people might be treated differently based upon their cultural backgrounds – what might be called the "who" question and which relates to the parties to an exchange over ethics and the role that cultural memberships may play in that exchange. Second, culture can also affect the content of what one considers proper behavior towards oneself and others – the "what" question. This is an important distinction, and global managers who fail to understand this often end up characterizing acceptable behaviors as unethical, thus escalating tensions and conflicts in their relations with others.

Level 1: Should we hold everyone to the same or to different standards?

The answer to the "who" question is directly linked to where cultures stand in terms of universalism and particularism. This conflict can be illustrated in a classic confrontation between a driver and a pedestrian.[22] Imagine that you are riding in a car driven by a close friend and he hits a pedestrian. You know he was driving too fast in a limited speed zone. You know further that there are no other witnesses, and your friend's lawyer asks you to testify that he was actually driving more slowly. Indeed, if you testify honestly to his actual speed at the time of the accident, your friend will face serious legal consequences. What would you do?

When presented with this dilemma, people from "universalistic" and "particularistic" cultures tend to behave in different ways. (Remember from Chapter 3 that universalistic – or rule-based – cultures believe that everyone should he held accountable to the same rules that are equally applied, while particularistic – or relationship-based – cultures allow room for exceptions to rules based on close personal relationships or unique situations). In a typical case, about half the managers from universalistic cultures are likely to answer that friendship should play no role in their decision, objectivity should take precedence, and you should testify against your friend. The other half of this group first tries to escape, rather than resolve the dilemma, by refusing to testify one way or another. This is not always an easy position for them, since they realize that they fail in their fundamental duties of collaborating with both a friend and the administration of justice, but they see this as less morally onerous than either lying or somehow taking part in the imposition of serious consequences to their friend. Coming from universalistic cultures, they see the reasonableness of a system that rests on the assumption that people will either tell the truth (which they would favor in most circumstances) or refrain from testifying under special circumstances. They would clearly reject a system where people could either tell the truth or tell a lie, since they believe that life would then become excessively chaotic and unreliable. In other words, they need the predictability in their world, but retain for themselves an option not to participate.

At the same time, managers from particularistic cultures respond to the scenario in a very different way. They also tend to split into halves, with one group immediately stating that they would lie for their friend, and the other half asking for additional information before making a decision. Interestingly, they do not tend to avoid testifying as a way out of the dilemma, at least not as much as universalists do. This is less of an option for particularists either because they do not seem initially interested in anything else than theirs friend's welfare or because they feel like they should not abstain from contributing to restore some sort of "state of justice" or equilibrium that the accident has broken.

Thus, universalists tend to emphasize norms and value objectivism and predictability, while particularists tend to favor relationships, subjectivism, and ambiguity. There is nothing intrinsically ethical or unethical about those preferences, even if they obviously lead to contrasting, even contradictory, behaviors towards others. Performance appraisal in organizations, for instance, may be eventually practiced through objective, pre-established standards that will be equally applied to each employee. Not coincidentally, this is the preferred method in mostly universalistic Western countries, as well as in most HR management books. In other cultures, like particularistic ones, the specific circumstances regarding each employee may be given a more salient role in assessing performance and behavior. As a result, we see questions such as this: Why is it inherently wrong to award greater recognition and rewards to those who have worked harder to achieve the same results as their more able peers? The issue, then, is not so much who is right or wrong, but rather what frames of reference are used in making the assessment.

These are cultural choices that may make sense within their own cultural environments more than in foreign territories, but that does not speak of their ethical value. Columbia University anthropologist Lawrence Rosen notes, for instance, the differences between Western and Islamic countries with respect to the functioning of the legal system.[23] In the West, property is viewed for legal purposes in terms of ownership (who owns this land?); this is an objectivist approach. By contrast, under Islam, property is viewed in terms of its relationships to others (who is associated with this land?); this is a subjectivist approach. Because the idea of a divisible self is unimaginable in Islam, power is both institutional and personal, with the implication that judges (and managers, we may add) are expected to rule without consciously trying to exclude their personal feelings and attitudes. Judges, then, will open widely the bounds of relevance to ascertain ties of indebtedness of the various parties to a dispute, often getting people back to negotiate their own agreements within their kin rather than enunciating particular rights. Judges will assess witness reliability according to the nature and intensity of the witnesses' social ties rather than primarily relying on their objective expertise, and they will ascertain facts according more to their evaluation of the person and their past history than by observable circumstances. Rosen also stresses that because of their greater effect on their networks of relationships, educated and wealthier people are also held to higher legal standards in Islamic cultures. For managers, the ethical landscape looks very much the same. Business contracts make heavy use of both personal contacts and networks and are largely transitory when conditions change in more particularistic cultures than in universalistic ones.

Hence, from a purely objective standpoint, treating people "equally," regardless of who they are (as universalists propose), or "differently," based on group memberships (as particularists defend), is, strictly speaking, neutral in ethical terms. It only becomes correct or incorrect when we interject our own value systems into the picture.

Level 2: What is considered to be proper behavior towards others?

We have now seen that one aspect of an ethical exchange focuses on the particular cultural group to which the parties to the exchange belong – the "who" question – and the different implications that universalistic and particularistic viewpoints assume. Beyond this, we also need to look at how cultures view ethical demands in different ways and the implications that this holds for international management. In other words, we turn now to the "what" question. That is, how can cultures affect the content of what people consider to be proper or acceptable – ethical – behavior towards oneself and others? How should people be treated from an ethical standpoint across cultures?

It is said that truth is the first casualty when conflict escalates. We often hear managers complain that their counterparts across borders fail to keep their commitments, refrain from clearly explaining how they see the issues, and, at times, simply fail to tell the truth. In fact, viewed from the vantage point of only one culture, such behaviors would easily be defined as mendacious. The question, then, is whether we need to account for different cultural approaches to the idea of truth before simply concluding that one of the parties is behaving unethically.

Many instances in which someone says something that is believed to be false result from the different cognitive filters that cultures bring to their members, as we saw in Chapter 4. These are not necessarily instances of ethical conflict, just misunderstandings, and they are easily resolved once a miscommunication is detected and corrected. In other cases, however, one of the parties to an exchange is consciously making statements that are not formally true.[24] Of course, when this falsehood is discovered, the other party is likely to accuse the speaker of misrepresentation or worse. We are not interested here in the phenomenon of lying just because the liar belongs to a certain culture. In fact, misrepresentations of the truth can be found in all cultures, and most cultures agree in varying degrees that such behavior is improper. What interests us here is the issue of intentional misrepresentations when a cultural rationale underlies what is said. That is, in these instances, while one party may feel offended, the other party may consider this as a natural way of conducting an exchange. In such cases, serious conflicts are likely to follow.

Consider the following example: The Chinese HR manager of a Latin American multinational in Shanghai told one of the authors of this book how difficult it was for him to deal with half-truths and mistruths by expatriate employees of the firm. The expatriates would, for instance, approach their managers with a request for vacation time that the manager thought was inappropriate, largely because of work schedules. While in their own countries these managers would have openly answered "no" to these requests, such an approach is considered rude in a Chinese context. Therefore, the managers would answer something along the lines of "I will have to think about it and get back to you." Of course, some of the expatriates lacked the experience to understand that they had already been given a negative answer in a subtle way that spared either party any embarrassment, thus saving face. Instead, they kept waiting for the manager to get back to them and, since this never happened, they considered themselves cheated and the manager a liar. That this is not an issue regarding the global meaning of truth is demonstrated here by the fact that no Chinese employees ever misread the real answer behind the rather neutral response. Put another way, who gets to define whether evasive or non-verbal behavior is, on the surface, dishonest or misleading?

In another example concerning Russia and Eastern Europe, management ethicist Eileen Morgan argues that much of the conflict between Western and some of these former communist countries results from a misunderstanding about the concept and meaning of corruption.[25] That is, historically, "business" is not a concept that comes naturally in the Russian language. To begin with, there is no original Russian word for business. *Biznez*, as it is incorporated into the language, carries with it a strong cultural baggage dating from communist times, and it is still associated with ideas like exploitation and corruption. Unlike Westerners, Russians differentiate ethics from corruption. Corruption is seen as institutionalized, hierarchical behavior that falls out of the control of individuals. Ethics, on the other hand, is seen as the set of principles that should guide one-on-one relationships, between individuals. Corruption, then, refers more to the institutional environment in which individuals, like it or not, must operate. Individual behavior is not commensurate with the presence or absence of corruption. If one partner steals from another partner, there is a breach in ethical behavior, but not an incidence of corruption. The implications here are very important. If institutions systematically behave in a certain "corrupt" manner, alternative behaviors from individuals may become extremely unsustainable. Even more, when corruption becomes part of the business environment, concepts like guilt and shame lose some of their saliency because free will by individuals regarding corrupt behavior may have disappeared altogether. When corruption becomes part of the institutional fabric, it becomes something to be expected in the normal course of events. The only problem here is that all parties to a deal or partnership should understand how this works, and, not surprisingly, many global managers with little of no experience in this region can easily be taken in.

Next, look at bribery (discussed in greater detail below). Western countries tend to see bribery as an unfair practice that destroys the good will that is so fundamental in international business transactions. By contrast, in countries like Nigeria, as illustrated above, bribery is often an enabler of business relationships, not an inhibitor, thus losing some of its negative connotations. Bribery is also seen in many countries simply as the way things are, some peculiar trait of the social environment and not unlike the Russian example just noted. As a result, it is easy to suggest that personal accountability under such conditions could not be expected to operate in the same way it would in Western countries.

Finally, some have suggested that the basic problem with corruption and other forms of unethical behavior is that it introduces unreliability into social interactions. This may be correct in some places. However, in locations where corruption is part of the system, people often come to expect it, and its effects can be readily discounted. Corrupt systems, then, need not necessarily be unreliable, only corrupt. Under such circumstances, many corporations refrain from operating in those environments and pursue other alternative and honest alliances. This is understandable and may become the only sensible reaction to legal systems that will punish giving in to corrupt environmental pressures, or to decision makers that prefer not to engage in what they see as profoundly unethical behavior. But there is a side effect to such attitudes. First, only parties who feel more comfortable in the corrupt environments will operate there, thus compounding the problem for those who would rather change the way things are. Second, what happens to those with no alternative deals available, like most people living in the local environment? How is it possible to argue against the chorus from poorer families that are stuck in these environments that only if you are wealthy enough to flee the area can you afford to behave ethically?

Institutional conflicts and challenges

In contrast to the ethical (i.e., normative or moral) conflicts and challenges, *institutional conflicts* focuses on how people and societies view socially mandated laws, rules, regulations, and public policies. Here the focus is more on doing what is required by law or strongly encouraged by governmental or intergovernmental agencies (e.g., the OECD, the International Labour Organization (ILO), the UN). These policies focus on what is "legally" correct, as opposed to what is morally right or even culturally sanctioned. As a result, this discussion logically begins with a look at national and international laws and public policy guidelines that influence corporate and managerial behavior across borders.

In response to growing political and business corruption involving numerous corporate companies around the world, a number of governments over the years have begun – however slowly – to address the problem of bribery and corruption, as well as other "fairness" issues. One such effort is the US Foreign Corrupt Practices Act (or FCPA). Essentially, the FCPA prohibits US companies, their employees, or their agents from paying a bribe in any form to any foreign government official to help secure or retain business. Specifically, the act prohibits five categories of behavior:

(1) payments to a foreign official, foreign political party, or candidate for a foreign political office or for the purpose of influencing any act or decision to obtain, retain, or assist in obtaining business for a company

(2) the maintenance of off-the-books accounts or slush funds

(3) intentionally making false statements on company books, records, and supporting documents, such as payments for services or payments on expense accounts

(4) engaging in over-billing, under-billing, or similar practices for the purpose of effecting transactions or improper payments that will not be accurately reflected in the company's books

(5) making any payment that, in whole or in part, is used for purposes other than those designated by the documents supporting or authorizing them.

Following the passage of the FCPA, many US companies initially complained that the law placed them at a competitive disadvantage compared to other nations in securing business in countries widely known for corruption. This conflict was resolved when the OECD (whose principal purpose is to promote market-oriented economic growth and development around the world) brought its membership together and collectively agreed on standards for defining and proscribing bribery of foreign officials in international business.

While the US Government labeled bribery and corruption as illegal, the Paris-based OECD labeled it as unethical. That is, the *OECD Guidelines* represent a set of normative, yet voluntary, guidelines for global managers and their firms that are aimed simultaneously at developing the economies of less developed nations while protecting them from exploitation by large and rich companies from the industrialized world.[26] These guidelines aim to ensure that the operations of these enterprises operate in harmony with local government policies, to strengthen the basis of mutual confidence between global firms and the societies in which they operate, to help improve the foreign investment climate, and to enhance the contribution to sustainable development made by global companies.

While details of the *OECD Guidelines* are explored in Appendix B, we will focus here on just three of the guidelines, relating to bribery and corruption, employment relations, and environmental stewardship.[27] These three issues highlight the challenges faced every day by global managers. Here is the problem: Most moral philosophers, business ethicists, business instructors, and other writers on the subject of management ethics send a clear message that violations of ethical standards and fair practices such as those embodied in the *OECD Guidelines* represent a breach of moral integrity for which there is little or no excuse. That is, ethical doctrines are to be followed, period. However, as noted by twentieth-century British philosopher Alfred North Whitehead, people think in generalities, but they live in detail.[28] That is, the writers on managerial and corporate ethics have seldom been faced with the ethical dilemmas they write about. Instead, such challenges fall to on-site managers who often find themselves in isolated locations and cultures and face-to-face with a conflict of needs, demands, expectations, and laws. This is not abstract or theoretical to them; it is very real, and jobs can depend on it.

Moreover, experienced travelers note that ethical standards can vary from one culture to another, as discussed above. This raises an interesting question: Who gets to determine what is ethical? The fact that the *OECD Guidelines* were approved by a group of industrialized (and mostly wealthy) nations may help to illustrate this. Nigeria is not a co-signer, possibly because it loses more than it gains by agreement. In short, implementing these guidelines can be more difficult that it seems. Indeed, there are numerous pressures for both supporting and opposing these guidelines. And the global manager is caught in the middle. This isn't to suggest that the guidelines are not a sign of progress in international trade and management; rather, it is to highlight the difficulty of doing business in multiple and often conflicting environments.

Finally, there is the issue of enforcement. As noted above, while the US FCPA has some legal teeth, the *OECD Guidelines* really do not. This lax enforcement only adds to the managerial dilemma of what to do. With few penalties and ongoing corporate competitive pressures for results, it is little wonder that graft and corruption – however defined – is so prevalent. With these issues in mind, let us begin with a look at bribery and corruption.

Bribery and corruption

A major reason behind the myriad of laws and regulations governing international commerce is fear – real or perceived – that some companies will use underhanded tactics (by their definition) to gain competitive advantage or to exploit others. Many of these problems ultimately come down to issues of corruption and bribery. Corruption and bribery can obviously make it much more difficult to conduct business in a foreign country, not just because of the unethical nature of such activity and the unjustified increases in operating costs incurred, but also because of the resulting uncertainty surrounding future government actions or the actions of competitors. Several organizations have tried in recent years to classify countries based on the

Exhibit 11.5 Corruption index for various countries

Country	Corruption index	Country	Corruption index	Country	Corruption index
Argentina	2.8	Hungary	4.9	Portugal	6.3
Australia	8.6	India	2.7	Russia	2.7
Austria	7.8	Indonesia	3.1	Singapore	9.3
Azerbaijan	1.4	Ireland	7.1	Slovakia	3.7
Belgium	7.1	Israel	7.3	South Africa	4.8
Brazil	4.0	Italy	5.2	South Korea	4.5
Canada	9.0	Japan	7.1	Spain	7.1
Chile	7.5	Luxembourg	9.0	Sweden	9.3
China	3.5	Malaysia	4.9	Switzerland	8.5
Colombia	3.6	Mexico	3.6	Taiwan	5.6
Czech Republic	3.7	Netherlands	9.0	Thailand	3.2
Denmark	9.5	New Zealand	9.5	Turkey	3.2
Finland	9.7	Nigeria	1.2	United Kingdom	8.7
France	6.3	Norway	8.5	United States	7.7
Germany	7.3	Philippines	2.6	Venezuela	2.5
Greece	4.2	Poland	4.0		

Source: Data from *The Economist, Pocket World in Figures*, London, 2008. Note: This scale runs from 1.0 to 10.0, with a 10.0 representing high incorruptibility and highly ethical behavior.

degree to which political corruption represents a major problem in international business. One such effort is the Political Corruption Index, shown in Exhibit 11.5. Using this index, corruption is more likely to be found in Nigeria, Azerbaijan or Venezuela (with scores of less than 2.5 on a scale of 10.0) than in Finland, Denmark, and New Zealand (with scores of around 9.5). As with any index, however, rankings of corruption can be imprecise and are meant only to highlight the need for further investigation before making investment decisions. Moreover, such ratings can sometimes be surprising. For example, while many people repeatedly point to commonalities between Canada and the US, note that their ratings on corruption are significantly different.

The existence of underground economies around the world complicates this picture further. The *underground economy* involves business transactions that are essentially off the books or unrecorded. No public records are kept, no taxes are paid, and applicable laws are frequently ignored. Underground economic activities vary widely from paying under the table for a nanny or someone to mown the lawn to purchasing supplies for one's business outside of governmental regulations or oversight. Underground economies exist everywhere, but are more prevalent in certain countries. According to *The Economist*, the underground economy in the US accounts for less than 10 percent of the total GDP.[29] By contrast, in Brazil it is estimated that 40 million people out of a total population of 170 million are employed in the underground economy. Such differences have very clear implications for the conduct of business.

The *OECD Guidelines* place considerable emphasis on corruption and bribery. In brief, these guidelines include the following (see Appendix B for details):

- Managers (and their companies) must not make payments to public officials to secure contracts.
- Managers may only make remuneration to agents for legitimate purposes.
- Managers must promote public awareness and transparency of company activities in the fight against bribery and extortion.
- Managers must promote employee awareness of and compliance with company policies against bribery and extortion.
- Managers must adopt management control systems that discourage bribery and corrupt practices, and adopt financial and tax accounting and auditing practices that prevent the establishment of off-the-books or secret accounts.
- Managers must not make illegal contributions to candidates for public office or to political parties or other political organizations.

If these guidelines had been followed in the case of Halliburton, discussed above, events might have played out differently. Having said this, however, here is where and why the picture becomes somewhat less clear in such cases. Simply put, managers at Halliburton – and most companies, for that matter – faced a series of countervailing forces that made a clear picture fuzzy. One might suggest that the "right" answer lies in the eye of the beholder. That is, at times, questions of ethical behavior vary depending on people understanding the circumstances surrounding a potential dilemma.

One way to understand the countervailing pressures faced by managers is through the use of a *force field analysis*, a mechanism that simply identifies pressures for and against a value, belief, attitude, or action.[30] Such an analysis can be used productively to understand the dilemmas frequently faced by global managers in the field. As shown in Exhibit 11.6, the decision to remain ethical (as defined by one's culture) is at times challenged by several reasons not to be ethical. Herein is one of the major challenges facing global managers.

Exhibit 11.6 Management challenge: OECD bribery and corruption guidelines

Pressures to support guidelines	Bribery and corruption guidelines	Pressures to oppose guidelines
• Builds corporate reputation for honesty and integrity. • Avoids prosecution for illegal activities by local or home countries. • Protects employees from outside pressures. • Identifies illegal behaviors early through continual monitoring. • Supports corruption-free local governments.	• Prohibit bribes and illegal kickbacks. • Take a public stance against corruption. • Inform employees of corporate anti-corruption policies. • Monitor potential corrupt activities within firm. • Prohibit local campaign contributions.	• May threaten new local business opportunities. • Risks government retaliation for non-payment of bribes. • May fail to protect firm against corrupt or illegal actions by competitors. • Can ultimately threaten corporate revenues and profitability.

To see how this works, suppose you work for a New York-based company that wants to build a stronger business presence in China's fast-growing consumer markets. Suppose also that your promotion and future career with this company is heavily dependent upon your success in securing a China deal. Suppose you are aware that the Chinese Government has lax oversight regulations, poor inspections, and only minimal enforcement procedures across a wide range of the products it makes, including children's toys, prescription drugs, candy, milk products, and even dog food. Finally, suppose that your own government consistently turns a blind eye to such consumer abuses because it does not want to risk alienating an important trading partner. Question: How would you approach your company's objective – and your personal responsibility – to secure new business dealings in China? Where do you draw the line? What is an acceptable risk here? And would you be willing to jeopardize your job and take a strong position against any such deals?

In the final analysis, managers should remember two things about this ethical challenge. First, with different names and in different forms, bribery and corruption can be found throughout the global political and business environment; it is not the exclusive province of poor countries. Second, managers often have a choice in how they respond to corruption. In some cases, governments can help to minimize such practices. When this is not the case, companies can choose not to reinforce such behavior and hold their ground or do business elsewhere. While this may, at times, lead to short-term losses, it typically leads to long-term gains. The bottom line for managers and their companies is understanding what they stand for and not sacrificing principle for short-term promises.

Employment relations

A major reason why global firms build facilities overseas is to reduce operating costs. This typically takes the form of significantly lowering labor costs. Beyond this, however, do global firms have any obligations to provide these local workers with employee rights and benefits that are similar to those provided to their employees back home? What employee rights and benefits, if any, are inviolate and universal for all workers regardless of their location, and which are situationally determined by the various locations of the facilities? This question is addressed in the second set of *OECD Guidelines* focusing on the employment relationship.

These guidelines focus heavily on company responsibilities to local employees. Towards this end, they suggest that, within the framework of law, regulations, and prevailing labor relations and employment practices, global firms should do the following (see Appendix B):

- Managers (and their companies) must respect the right of their employees to be represented by trade unions and other bona fide organizations of employees, and engage in constructive negotiations.
- Managers must observe standards of employment and industrial relations no less favorable than those observed by comparable employers in the host country.
- To the greatest extent practicable, managers should utilize, train, and prepare for upgrading members of the local labor force in cooperation with representatives of their employees and, where appropriate, the relevant governmental authorities.
- In considering changes in their operations that would have major effects on employees, managers should provide reasonable notice of such changes to representatives of their employees and cooperate with the employee representatives and appropriate governmental authorities so as to mitigate to the maximum extent practicable adverse effects.
- Managers should implement their employment policies, including hiring, discharge, pay, promotion, and training, without discrimination.
- Managers may not threaten to transfer an operating unit or employees from the country concerned in order to influence unfairly those negotiations or to hinder the exercise of a right to organize.
- Managers must enable authorized representatives of their employees to conduct negotiations on collective bargaining with representatives of management who are authorized to make decisions on the matters under negotiation.

As with bribery and corruption, there are a number of forces both for and against heeding these guidelines, as seen in Exhibit 11.7. As such, we can see the managerial

Exhibit 11.7 Management challenge: OECD employee relations guidelines

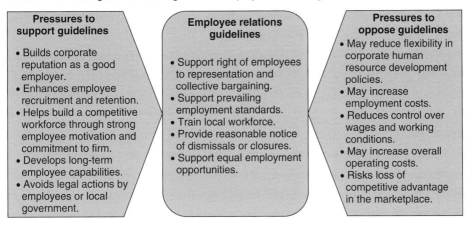

challenge. What is interesting here, however, is the decision point where HR policies are determined. Are these policies set in Berlin, Tokyo, or New York, by executives in corporate headquarters or by local and regional managers who are more sensitive to local conditions and requirements?

A good example of this issue can be found in the HR policies of Sony and Samsung in their electronic assembly plants in Thailand.[31] While Sony applies HR policies dictated largely from Tokyo and treats local employees largely as outsourced workers, Samsung takes a more local approach that is largely determined within Thailand and treats local employees more as members of the Samsung Group. Data suggest that subsequent employee commitment, job attitudes, and productivity are higher in the Samsung facilities. This is not to say that there is a universal conclusion here, since it is not always the case that higher adherence to ethical standards will necessarily lead to higher performance; rather, it highlights the need for local managers to monitor the impact of corporate HR policies as they relate to local conditions.

Environmental stewardship

Finally, consider what responsibilities global companies have to the local communities where they do business? What are their responsibilities to help with local economic development? What are their responsibilities with respect to protecting the environment? What are their responsibilities to help facilitate social justice? This general area often falls within the domain of corporate social responsibility and can be addressed in several ways. We begin with a look at how global companies can often impact local economic development for good or ill.

Global companies are often criticized for being insensitive to environmental needs, and, indeed, many companies choose to locate factories in countries that have lax pollution and environmental laws, like China and Mexico. By the same token, however, many other companies spend millions each year in reclaiming environmental lands and reducing air and water pollution. For example, Dow Chemical has been credited with making major investments to clean up toxic wastes sites in Eastern Europe.[32] Indeed, the list of environmentally responsible companies is longer than many people think or wish to believe.

Research suggests that in many industries, it may actually pay to be "green." That is, companies that are good environmental stewards also tend to be more profitable than their competitors, especially in more dynamic industries.[33] Such findings add substance to the assertion that socially responsible managers frequently find ways to support sustainability and environmental quality as part of their corporate strategies, not in spite of them, and that integrating environmental and sustainability perspectives into business practices can lead to improved overall corporate performance.

The *OECD Guidelines* focus here on the protection of the local environment from unsafe products and practices and help mitigation of any damage where it occurs. Global enterprises, within the framework of laws, regulations, and administrative practices in the countries in which they operate, are required to take due account of the need to protect the environment and avoid creating environmentally related health problems. In particular, companies, whether multinational or domestic, should do the following (see Appendix B):

- Managers (and their companies) must assess, and take into account in decision making, foreseeable environmental and environmentally related health consequences of their activities.
- Managers must cooperate with competent authorities by providing adequate and timely information regarding the potential impacts on the environment and environmentally related health aspects of all their activities and by providing the relevant expertise available in the enterprise as a whole.
- Managers must take appropriate measures in their operations to minimize the risk of accidents and damage to health and the environment, and to cooperate in mitigating adverse effects.

Once again, the ideal of environmental sensitivity and social responsibility is at times threatened by forces outside the control of the firm, which can turn good deeds into potential nightmares. Exhibit 11.8 highlights these threats. One of the principal liabilities here involves increased costs associated with increased regulation and reporting. Here,

Exhibit 11.8 Management challenge: OECD environmental stewardship guidelines

Pressures to support guidelines	Environmental stewardship guidelines	Pressures to oppose guidelines
• Supports corporate environmental stewardship goals. • Builds responsible corporate image in local communities. • Supports local economic development and local sustainability goals. • Avoids legal action by local governments, advocacy groups, and consumers.	• Consider public health implications of all products, transportation, and waste disposal activities. • Provide local authorities with information on environmental impact of corporate actions. • Take actions to prevent accidents and help mitigate damage where they occur.	• May increase costs associated with compliance and monitoring. • May increase reporting and accountability burdens on firm. • May reduce operating efficiencies, at least in the short term. • May reduce corporate revenues and profitability.

good intentions by local governments – or their distrust of multinational firms – has caused many global companies to pick and choose their local operating sites based upon who has the lightest regulations. This is not necessarily to say that such firms are socially irresponsible; rather, many firms seek to do the right thing (again, as defined by their own cultures), but see excessive regulations as being too limiting to guarantee the fulfillment of their corporate mission. In other words, the fundamental challenge here is a balancing act that both corporations and local governments must perform to seek mutual benefit: job creation and economic development versus corporate returns on their investments. Without both sides securing benefit, it is difficult to imagine a successful partnership.

This tension can be seen in the 2008 decision by India's Tata Motors to build an automobile plant to assemble its new *Nano*.[34] The *Nano* was designed to be the world's cheapest car, and was squarely aimed at developing nations. In searching for a suitable site, Tata was encouraged by local administrators in West Bengal to locate its new US$300 million factory in Singur. The new facility would help stimulate economic development in a very impoverished region by ultimately creating 10,000 new jobs, plus perhaps another 10,000 jobs for local suppliers. However, as the factory neared completion, local farmers began demanding that the company go elsewhere. In particular, they objected to losing farmland that had traditionally supported the local economy. Moreover, many farmers claimed that the local government had forced them to sell their lands. Despite government backing and Tata's reputation for social and environmental consciousness, local farmers continued to protest. As a result, Tata decided to close its near-completed factory and move everything to Sanand (near Ahmedabad) in Gujarat Province.

Looking back on the experience, company chairman Ratan Tata observed, "We lost a lot of time, unfortunately, but I think we can set out to do what we need to do on Gujarati soil."[35] While the company likely had the power, money, and influence to go ahead with its original plans, its concern for local environmental – and political – conditions led it to rethink its location decision. As a result, West Bengal remains a largely farming region (a local priority), while Gujarat moves closer to its ambition to lead India in economic development (also a local priority). Also as a result, and despite the added cost and lost time, Tata will likely benefit from the move over the long term by having a more supportive local community in which to operate.

Managing in an imperfect world

Much of what we do and say is related somehow to ideas – and ideals – of right and wrong, good and bad, and win and lose – whether it is in business, social activities, athletics, or our personal lives. Managers are no exception, as was observed in the opening case of Halliburton in Nigeria. Examples of exemplary, disappointing, and sometimes downright illegal managerial behaviors can be seen throughout the business environment. As a result, many experts in business ethics argue that all firms, but especially global ones, need an ethical compass to guide their organizational actions in ethical ways. Others, however, seem to make the opposite assertion: There is no such thing as right or wrong – they only exist in the eye of the beholder. This dichotomy of views suggests that either there are universal truths that transcend all cultures, or that concepts such as right and wrong are embedded within cultures and, as such, different cultures can define them differently. Where is the educated global manager in all of this? Probably caught somewhere in the middle. This conflict captures the essence of good management, nationally and globally. Managers must frequently act in the absence of concrete information and in the face of uncertain outcomes. Nonetheless, they must act, and they will be judged based on the outcomes. As such, in terms of ethical behavior, managers do require a moral compass, but one that is neither self-serving nor xenophobic.

This chapter did not focus on the fundamentals of business ethics in general; rather, we focused specifically on some of the particulars of business ethics as they relate to managers and organizations. Unfortunately, many of these discussions of managerial ethics focus on the negative – violations of trust, ethical standards, or the law. Seldom do these discussions take an optimistic tone. By overemphasizing the negative (some would call this the reality), many managers tend to avoid such discussions, not because they are dishonest but because they see such discussions as emphasizing the wrong thing. That is, for many managers, ethical behavior is not limiting or disempowering, but rather normal and even empowering at times. Ethical behavior represents the best of the human spirit, as well as an opportunity for companies and their managers to contribute in positive ways to "the betterment of the human condition," as Wharton professor Robert House observed (see Chapter 3).[36]

It should be clear from this discussion that working in diverse cultures allows managers to understand divergent foreign perspectives, as well as practices and behaviors that are not clear when issues are only seen from the home country perspective. For example, Japanese sales representatives travelling to Mexico may observe how business transactions differ from their home country. They may see behaviors and practices that are unusual – perhaps even illegal or at least unethical – compared to back home (e.g., an open solicitation of a bribe, or *mordida*). What they may not see, however, is that many of their Mexican counterparts are also seeing strange – and possibly unethical – behaviors when they visit Japan, or any other country (e.g., white envelopes filled with cash that pass between managers and associates). On both sides, are these cash exchanges bribes, commissions, gratuities, courtesies, or something else? In fact, the more widely traveled both the Japanese and Mexican managers become, the more likely they are to see patterns of questionable – and admirable – behavior that collectively develop their capacity to understand what is just unusual or different and what is truly unethical.

Distinguishing between personal (and organizational) tastes and preferences, ethical and legal mandates, and beliefs and values is important for understanding both national and international contexts. Within national contexts, however, some of those differences are not seen as clearly as they are when managers cross cultures. For example, Islamic cultures foster the integration of the legal and the ethical – and the religious – spheres. The religious and the secular are often integrated. Managers working in these regions expect this as a context or background for their business enterprise. At the same time, however, many Western managers work in cultures that are rooted in the separation of these spheres (e.g., separation of church and state). As a result, it is quite common for Western managers to forget the historical evolution that led to that separation and which explains how things stand in present times. But a Western manager's visit to Saudi Arabia or Iran will highlight some of these differences, and will add to the developmental process of the manager. The same can also be said for the Saudi or Iranian manager traveling to the West. The point here is simple: Travel is a great educator for managers who are willing to look, listen, interact, compare, and learn.

These differences in managerial behaviors across cultures are easier to understand when some of the heuristics discussed above are employed. For example, the meaning and role of universals and particulars are unlikely to come under scrutiny when managers and decision makers share the same basic cultural outlook (e.g., a group of Czech or Thai managers). Yet an understanding of what is core (or universal) and what is peripheral (or particular) can be critical in guiding ethical decision making from either the temporal or historical perspective (the idea of ethics across time), as well as from the spatial and cultural perspective.

Without these cultural frames, a manager's understanding of universals and particulars in ethics is likely to remain incomplete. Moreover, the universal-particular dynamics that the presence of different cultures underlines is at the heart of a more complete understanding of who the principal parties are to an ethical exchange and how they are to be treated. Finally, the full extent of ethical behavior around the practices of bribery and corruption, employment relations, technological transfer, environmental stewardship, and general business practices is also unlikely to unfold unless in the context of multiple cultures interacting with one another in the global arena.

Managing within ethical and moral constraints

With this in mind, we close by examining the managerial lessons that follow from both the ethical and institutional perspectives discussed here. More specifically, what can global managers learn here to enhance their ability to behave responsibly in the world of work? In our view, based on their ethical beliefs, as well as their tolerance for the beliefs of others, global managers and their employers have a responsibility to work to build a consensus regarding how they define ethical behavior across cultures and nations. In this pursuit, the following points may be germane:

- *Understand the core values of the firm.* It seems reasonable to expect that firms operating in different countries, with different tastes, practices, and values, will need to work diligently to preserve both a core set of beliefs that encourages unity and commonality, as well as clearly articulate spheres for variation, pluralism, and diversity in how to operate across countries. They need to know their limits and degrees of flexibility in doing business across borders.
- *Understand the limits of universalism.* Feelings of unity and commonality across cultures and business partners can (and perhaps should) rest on what and how people see and understand the concept of universal at different times and places (see above). Is there agreement across parties concerning what beliefs and values are indeed universal? And can all parties take a nuanced approach to universalism that never assumes that the universals have been completely and perfectly defined? To the contrary, what is seen as universal generally evolves (and hopefully improves) over time and space, and managers need to build on universals that are never final but which are in search for continual improvement. What this means for managers is that flexibility and tolerance are key to success across borders. Managers have to recognize that

while all of their partners may oppose company theft as a general principle, for example, their perspectives concerning what constitutes theft may vary. For example, is taking minor office supplies home theft or not? The question for managers is whether this is acceptable or, perhaps more importantly, to what extent it is acceptable.

- *Understand the cultural contexts underlying agreements.* Universals are seldom self-sustaining. They do not rest in thin air, and they require incardination at various points in time and space. As such, universals always need to be grounded in a given culture. Indeed, they cannot be understood, much less acted upon, in isolation from their cultural context. As such, any effort to seek agreement on a set of universal standards or principles first requires an understanding of the various cultures to the proposed agreement. Without this understanding and appreciation, the likelihood of reaching – or enforcing – agreements diminishes rapidly.
- *Understand the roles and backgrounds of the parties to a dispute.* Simply identifying the parties to a dispute is insufficient to move towards conflict resolution. In addition, we must understand something about the other party's roles and backgrounds. What does their company or their society expect from them? How much leeway might they have in bargaining? And what types of conflict resolution strategies may be appropriate or expected? (This issue was discussed in Chapter 10.) Such knowledge clarifies where the other parties to a dispute are, as well as how to deal effectively with them. This may require an ability on the part of managers to negotiate in a particularistic environment, instead of a universalistic one.
- *Understand the context or basis of the conflict.* The content of an ethical exchange also needs to account for cultural differences even at the initial phase of the interchange, when people are trying to discover what is right and wrong. What exactly is the basis of the conflict? Such bases are often masked in the guise of a different – often more superficial – issue. Without such knowledge, time is easily wasted discussing or debating things that really don't matter, while the root cause of the conflict remains.
- *Understand different types of cultural conflict.* Finally, managers must be able to distinguish between different types of cultural conflict in organizations. Conflicts involving tastes and practices, the legal system, and beliefs and values cannot be conflated in a single category. Instead, they can require different approaches to problem solving.

Managing within legal and institutional constraints

Since their publication, the *OECD Guidelines* have proven to be a respected point of reference for many companies (see Appendix B). Even though the guidelines are voluntary, they carry the weight of a joint recommendation of OECD governments. Alongside national laws, they form part of a legal, or at least quasi-legal, infrastructure that promotes responsible behavior by global firms. In addition, the guideline language has influenced other codes of conduct for global firms, such as the ILO's Tripartite Declaration and the Code of Conduct for Transnational Corporations of the UN. Still, there are several issues that global managers should be aware of prior to being placed in situations where such guidelines carry significant weight:

- *Understand the proper role of institutional guidelines.* There are many guidelines here and, taken together, they can serve to seriously constrain the activities of many honest companies. So, too, are there many questions. First, is it proper for national governments to come together to formulate such guidelines or is it better to allow companies to develop their own guidelines within the boundaries of national and international laws? And second, the *OECD Guidelines* are just that: guidelines. They have no legal standing. If these guidelines are important for global business, should they have some type of enforcement provisions behind them? If so, how would such provisions be enforced?

- *Understand the limitations of institutional guidelines.* We have attempted to overview one approach to encouraging ethical and socially responsible behavior on the part of global firms. As members of the OECD will affirm, it is not a perfect solution, but perhaps it is a major first step in securing responsible action on the part of highly diverse and competitive firms around the world. What remains to be seen is the degree to which the respective governments of OECD member states get behind these guidelines. To date, the response has been encouraging among many European members, but less so among other nation states.

- *Understand the controversies underlying institutional guidelines.* As with any internationally negotiated instrument, however, these guidelines have sometimes been criticized, either for being too general or too detailed. Some have argued, for example, that they do not go far enough in ensuring that global firms comply with various national laws and practices, while others have suggested that the guidelines go well beyond those standards in some areas so as to restrict legitimate business goals and strategies. Another area of debate involves the follow-up, which some say needs to be made stronger, while others argue that it is too juridical.

■ *Understand the tension created by forces both for and against "doing the right thing."* Indeed, in many situations, how do we know what is the right thing to do? Institutional guidelines attempt to set common rules to guide everyone. However, it is difficult to account for cultural differences and preferences when assembling one set of rules. Moreover, as with legal requirements, guidelines tend to state the specific when flexibility is sometimes needed. Finally, in view of the fact that only thirty countries have signed up for the *OECD Guidelines*, why should other nations bother with these since they have no bearing on local regulations or behavior?

■ *Understand where conflicts need to be settled.* When guideline issues arise, the onus of attempting a settlement is placed largely on the country where the "problem company" – a highly debatable term – is headquartered. As such, the effectiveness of the guidelines depends to a large degree on the commitment of the home and host countries to the principles of the OECD, the ILO, and so forth. This effectiveness, in turn, obviously differs from country to country.

■ *Understand the lack of education or awareness of institutional guidelines in the training of managers.* A final thought: The *OECD Guidelines* are seldom taught or even mentioned in the ranking business schools of most countries. Why is this? What are we teaching future generations of managers about the importance of behaving responsibly in global transactions?

Notes

1 Blaise Pascal, *Pensées: Thoughts on Religion and Other Subjects*. New York, NY: Washington Square Press, 1965, p. 90. This popular version of Pascal's quotation is a modern interpretation of the original translation from French, which reads, "Three degrees of latitude reverse all jurisprudence; a meridian decides the truth … A strange justice that is bounded by a river! Truth on this side of the Pyrenees, error on the other side."

2 William Norris, cited in Helen Deresky, *International Management: Managing Across Borders and Cultures*. Upper Saddle Creek, NJ: Pearson/Prentice Hall, 2008, p. 45.

3 *The Economist Pocket World in Figures*. London: Profile Books, 2008.

4 Russell Gold, "SEC investigates Halliburton unit over payments," *The Wall Street Journal*, June 14, 2004, p. A3; Russell Gold and Charles Fleming, "In Halliburton's Nigeria project, a search for bribes to a dictator," *The Wall Street Journal*, September 29, 2004, p. A1.

5 "Halliburton: a scandal-hit firm fights back," *The Economist*, February 19, 2004, p. A1.

6 Russell Gold, "Halliburton concedes possibility of payments to Nigerian officials," *The Wall Street Journal*, November 8, 2004, p. A5.

7   "Defense contractor pleads guilty to bribing officials," *Register-Guard*, February 12, 2009, p. D1.

8   George Steiner, *In Bluebeard's Castle: Notes Towards the Redefinition of Culture*. New Haven, CT: Yale University Press, 1971.

9   *The Economist Pocket World in Figures*.

10 "Police: father arranged marriage of 14-year-old girl," *Register-Guard*, January 14, 2009, p. A2.

11 For the record, partly as a result of Control Data Corporation's efforts to apply their US-based ethical standards to operations around the world, the company lost its competitiveness and is no longer in business.

12 David E. Cooper, *Ethics for Professionals in a Multicultural World*. Upper Saddle River, NJ: Pearson/Prentice Hall, 2004, p. 90.

13 Sometimes ethics will demand obedience to a law that contradicts an ethical mandate if, for instance, not doing so will cause unfair and disproportionate harms to third parties. Here, however, the legal is preferred over the ethical not because of it being legal, but because of the ethical mandate. In other cases of conflict, the ethical mandate may allow us to either follow or oppose the law (ethics, for instance, does not allow us to make injustices, but it allows us to suffer them if we so choose). Again, this is a case of eventually following the law not because the law should be given prevalence, but because ethics will allow it. The universal nature of the priority of the moral over the legal should not surprise us once we understand that the ultimate justification for a legal mandate – what the state should impose – always rests on a moral mandate – what people ought to do. Because of this, it is commonly argued that laws that violate ethics are not real laws to be obeyed, but are instead arbitrary impositions to be opposed.

14 This is one of the conclusions of the opening case ("Uncompromising integrity and egregian justice") in a textbook sponsored by Motorola for use in its internal training programs (R. S. Moorthy, Richard T. De George, Thomas Donaldson, William J. Ellos, Robert C. Solomon, and Robert B. Textor, *Uncompromising Integrity: Motorola's Global Challenge*. Schaumburg, IL: Purdue University Press, 1998). It is true that this case depicts an extreme situation where denouncing an instance of employee theft to the local authorities led to a criminal process that ended in the death penalty, and it may have actually been exaggerated for instructional purposes. But this only makes for stronger evidence of the path Motorola is willing to follow when preservation of a moral stance may require that its employees ignore a law that is deemed unfair.

15 Christian J. Resick, Paul J. Hanges, Marcus W. Dickson, and Jacqueline K. Mitchelson, "A cross-cultural examination of the endorsement of ethical leadership," *Journal of Business Ethics*, 2006, 63, pp. 345–359.

16 Empirically derived from the database, cultures were grouped along the following clusters: Anglo, Confucian Asian, Eastern European, Germanic European, Latin American, Latin European, Middle Eastern, Nordic European, and Southeast Asian.

17 Even situational approaches to ethics (of the type "when in Rome, behave as the Romans do") are not situational in the sense of mandating the applicability or non-applicability of their

provisos depending on whether one is in Rome or Romania, and they issue their "when in Rome" command both from Rome and Romania, universally.

18 Some authors differentiate between descriptive and normative ethics. Descriptive ethics would deal with how people are and act, while normative ethics would account for how people ought to be and act. Others argue that "descriptive ethics" is more about psychology and sociology than about ethics, strictly speaking. We are not interested in this polemic right now, but want to emphasize that when we talk about ethical mandates differing across cultures, we are only taking a descriptive stance, unless otherwise noted.

19 Carolyn Dewald and John Marincola (eds.), *The Cambridge Companion to Herodotus*. Cambridge, UK: Cambridge University Press, 2006.

20 Richard Lewis, *When Cultures Collide*. London: Nicholas Brealey Publishing, 1999, p. 8.

21 Peter Ustinov, quoted in Richard Hill, *EuroManagers*, Brussels: Europublications, 1998, p. 230.

22 Samuel A. Stouffer and Jackson Toby, "Role, conflict, and personality," *American Journal of Sociology*, 1951, 56(5), pp. 395–406.

23 Lawrence Rosen. *Law as Culture: An Invitation*. Princeton, NJ: Princeton University Press, 2006, pp. 98–100.

24 The concept of truth has been extremely difficult to pin down throughout history. Whatever the approach to truth, there are always two elements in its definition that are not easy to combine. On the one hand, truth refers to some external reality. On the other hand, truth talks about how one approaches that reality, so that when our internal mental model of reality basically agrees or disagrees with the external reality, we talk, respectively, of truth and falsehood. One set of issues, then, derives from the fact that mental models and reality are not co-extensive, and some degree of incommensurability will always be present. Another issue is that the same realities are often viewed differently across times and places. The quote at the beginning of this chapter by Pascal, for instance, refers to the reality of two contiguous countries, France and Spain, with different laws and judicial systems. The implications can be striking. For instance, someone may be considered a murderer in one country and not in the other. These conflicts are not really conflicts of truth but of a given set of incompatible practices. Only a few pages later, Pascal talks about the history of the Church as "the history of truth" (Pascal, *Pensées: Thoughts on Religion and Other Subjects*, p. 90), which shows that he did not hold a relativistic view of truth and was actually pointing at conflicting practices between the two neighbors. This is worth pointing out for two reasons: first, because it is becoming increasingly common to use this quote by Pascal as an example and justification of relativism, and nothing is actually further away from Pascal's thought: and second, because this type of misunderstanding is easily solved by distinguishing practices (legal and judicial practice in Pascal's mind) and values, as we propose in this chapter.

25 Eileen Morgan, *Navigating Cross-Cultural Ethics: What Global Managers Do Right to Keep from Going Wrong*. Woburn, MA: Butterworth-Heinemann, 1998.

26 OECD members include Australia, Austria, Belgium, Canada, Czech Republic, Denmark, Finland, France, Germany, Greece, Hungary, Iceland, Ireland, Italy, Japan, Korea, Luxembourg, Mexico, the Netherlands, New Zealand, Norway, Poland, Portugal, Slovakia,

Spain, Sweden, Switzerland, Turkey, the UK, and the US. In addition, there are a number of affiliate members who agree to support the group's activities and abide by its guidelines, including Argentina, Brazil, Chile, Estonia, Israel, Lithuania, and Slovenia.

27 See www.oecd.org/daf/investment/guidelines.

28 For more details concerning Whitehead's philosophy, see his book, *The Function of Reason*. Boston, MA: Beacon Press, 1929.

29 "Blinded by the dark," *The Economist*, April 2, 1998, p. 15.

30 A *force field analysis* is a management technique developed by Kurt Lewin, a pioneer in the field of social sciences, for diagnosing situations. It is useful when looking at the variables involved in planning and implementing a change program, as well as team projects when attempting to overcome resistance to change. Lewin assumes that in any situation there are both driving and restraining forces that influence any change that may occur. *Driving forces* are those forces affecting a situation that are pushing in a particular direction; they tend to initiate a change and keep it going. In terms of improving productivity in a work group, pressure from a supervisor, incentive earnings, and competition may be examples of driving forces. *Restraining forces* are forces acting to restrain or decrease the driving forces. Apathy, hostility, and poor maintenance of equipment may be examples of restraining forces against increased production. Equilibrium is reached when the sum of the driving forces equals the sum of the restraining forces.

31 Personal communication, Won Shul Shim, Hanyang University, Seoul, Korea, 2008.

32 Richard M. Steers and Luciara Nardon, *Managing in the Global Economy*. New York, NY: M. E. Sharpe, 2006.

33 Michael Russo and Paul Fouts, "A resource-based perspective on corporate environmental performance and profitability," *Academy of Management Journal*, 1997, 40(3), pp. 534–559.

34 Eric Bellman, "Tata to shift production of minicar after protests," *The Wall Street Journal*, October 8, 2008, p. A-14.

35 *Ibid*.

36 Robert J. House, "Introduction," in Robert J. House, Paul J. Hanges, Mansour Javidan, Peter W. Dorfman, and Vipin Gupta, *Culture, Leadership, and Organizations: The GLOBE Study of 62 Societies*. Thousand Oaks, CA: Sage, 2004, p. 1.

CHAPTER 12

Epilogue: the journey continues

■ Learning from the past 405
■ Looking to the future 407

When I want to understand what is happening today or try to decide what will happen tomorrow, I look back.

Omar Khayyám
Eleventh-century poet, Persia

If we are facing in the right direction, all we have to do is keep walking.

Siddhārtha Gautama
Fifth-century BCE founder of Buddhism, India

Futurists and their closely watched predictions abound in these changing times, and nowhere is this trend more prominent than with regards to future economic trends and the future of global business. Some experts predict that past competitors will become future partners, while other experts predict just the opposite. Some predict increased economic integration brought on by globalization, while others predict increased economic fragmentation and turmoil, also brought on by globalization. Even the opinions of great philosophers of the past apparently disagree. The eleventh-century Persian mathematician, astronomer, and poet, Omar Khayyám, suggests that in order to see the future we must study the past. Learn from history; the past is prologue. At the same time, the fifth-century BCE Hindu prince and founder of Buddhism, Siddhārtha Gautama (also known as *Śākyamuni*), suggests that if we want to see the future (indeed, if we want to be part of the future), we should step forward. If we are facing in the right direction, he notes, all we have to do is keep moving. Keep your eye on the ball; the future belongs to those who search it out and are prepared to capitalize on it. Two philosophers and two different opinions – again. And again, our challenge is to learn from such contradictions, past and present.

404

Learning from the past

Throughout this volume, an effort has been made to integrate issues of culture with those of management, in the belief that success in the global economy requires a detailed understanding of both. Successful global managers move with ease across international borders and adapt readily to local changes and challenges. They look for a competitive edge wherever they can find it. But most of all, they continually learn from their surroundings and apply these lessons to their work. In this regard, perhaps a good place to begin this learning process is with history. Spanish philosopher George Santayana once observed, "Those who fail to learn from the mistakes of their predecessors are destined to repeat them."[1] This may be true, but it is equally correct that one of the benefits of studying history – learning from the past – is that it alleviates the need to start from scratch. History provides lessons as building blocks upon which to build our own approach to management, as well as our own careers.

In this spirit, we offer three lessons from three very different time periods and involving very different people and circumstances. The first two examples, Christopher Columbus and Mahatma Gandhi, come from earlier generations, while the third comes from the very recent past. All speak to business managers, locally and globally.

Christopher Columbus is widely credited with being the first European explorer to "discover" America. Many Scandinavians disagree, and point out that the Vikings landed and actually colonized the northeastern tip of Canada centuries earlier. And many Native Americans and Inuits also disagree, and point out that they were actually there first; indeed, some of them met Columbus on the shore of Hispaniola when he arrived in the "New World," and paid a heavy price. Columbus is also widely, if incorrectly, credited with proving that the world is round instead of flat. The controversies surrounding Columbus aside, what many scholars have overlooked in this story is that Columbus succeeded in his quest of discovery because he was wrong, not because he was right.

Consider: Ancient Greek mathematicians demonstrated long before Columbus that the world was round. They even estimated with amazing accuracy that the earth was approximately 25,000 miles in circumference. Columbus and his maritime contemporaries understood this, if many peasants and less educated people did not. Most explorers of the time reasoned with moderate accuracy that India and the Spice Islands – their targeted objective – was roughly 8,000 miles to the west of Spain. They also reasoned, correctly, that in view of this distance, such a voyage was impossible.

Given prevailing technology of the time, no ship could travel so far without running out of water and supplies. Columbus studied available maps and charts of the time and concluded, incorrectly, that his contemporaries were wrong and that India was only about 3,000 miles away, a journey he considered possible, if difficult. Off he sailed in 1492. After his long voyage at sea and, ironically, just over 3,000 miles from Spain, Columbus sailed into the Caribbean and concluded, again incorrectly, that he had reached India.

The useful lesson from Columbus' voyage is simple. If Columbus had had more accurate information or had listened to local experts about the true distance to India, he might never have attempted the voyage. But he believed he was right and he initiated action based on his belief. As he continued his journey, he adapted his strategies and tried to learn from his mistakes. Indeed, many of today's managers have learned this same lesson: Some of life's greatest successes result from accidents, hunches, or simple luck. All managers make mistakes and miscalculate – some more than others. Managerial success is seldom linear; there are many bumps and detours along the way. What differentiates winners from losers, however, is both their steadfastness and determination and their ability to learn, adapt, and, where possible, capitalize on their mistakes.

The second lesson is more direct, and comes from the nonviolent Indian peace activist of the twentieth century, Mahatma Gandhi. Gandhi was fond of saying that "we must be the change we wish to see in others." That is, the real challenge for global managers is leadership, not followership. The challenge is how to build both a more prosperous company and a more prosperous world. To accomplish this, successful global managers must bring people together in both collaborative and symbiotic ways that create value for the organization and its surroundings. In this endeavor, an understanding of how cultures differ and how they influence both organizational and managerial processes emerges as an essential ingredient in a successful global manager's toolkit.

A final example comes from the global economic turmoil of the past several years. We have heard much recently about economic downturns, financial exigencies, bankruptcies, corporate bailouts, recessions, and unemployment. And we have seen a number of people and institutions blamed, including bankers, investors, mortgage lenders, manufacturers, offshore companies, and politicians. We see leaders from entire continents collectively blaming leaders from other continents. The finger of blame is pointing in an almost infinite number of directions. And finally, we have seen individual and collective greed like never before. In the world of business, regardless of geographic location, we have witnessed entrepreneurs and managers alike desperately trying to find a quick fix, a short-term competitive advantage that will allow them to become wealthier than their competitors and colleagues. Wealth is celebrated, even worshipped, in places. Meanwhile, millions of people around the world in both developing and industrialized countries lose their homes, jobs, security, health, and even education for their children.

What has been lost in all of this chaos is a fundamental premise of successful global (and local) business: mutual exchange and mutual benefit. Researchers and managers alike see successful global negotiations as being based on people and companies coming together to achieve their common objectives. Even in countries where legal contracts reign supreme, the role of personal relationships is not undervalued. Likewise, successful communication is typically seen as being best facilitated when all parties share a common understanding – and a common cause. Leaders are seen to be more effective when they strive to see that everyone involved wins. Work motivation and performance is best facilitated when employees at all levels see a reason for buy-in. And equity, fairness, and stewardship are seen by most people to be the most effective way to create a more ethical and sustainable world.

Certainly, these management processes get more complex and challenging when managers and their companies cross borders, yet the fundamental principles hold. The individual and corporate selfishness of the past few years has demonstrated quite clearly that greed is a short-term and non-sustaining strategy for future development and security, both at home and abroad. And breaking faith with one's stakeholders – whether they are customers, investors, or employees – is invariably suboptimal in the long run. Instead, global managers and their firms would be better advised to seek long-term global strategies and partnerships and to incorporate a genuine stakeholders model as part of their business plan. Inclusion rather than exclusion. Partnerships rather than lethal competition.

Looking to the future

We suggested early on in this book that culture and cultural differences represented a major key to understanding managerial thought and action, although it is certainly not the only key. We also suggested that a productive way to discover the utility of this key is to approach intellectual discovery and management development as part of an overall learning strategy. To understand how individuals learn, we introduced experiential learning theory, one of the most influential models of managerial development.[2] As will be remembered, following this theory, the learning process is composed of four stages: concrete experiences, observation and reflection, abstract concepts and generalizations, and testing implications of concepts.

By using this approach, managers still do not have the power to see into the future, but they do have an ability to better prepare themselves for it. Chung Ju Yung, the founder of the Korean conglomerate Hyundai, often said that the difference between winners and losers in a highly competitive business environment is the ability both to prepare for upcoming challenges and opportunities and to recognize such opportunities when they emerge.[3] Preparation *and* recognition – both are required. Seeing opportunities for the future without adequate preparation or preparing for the future without adequate study of emerging opportunities are both recipes for coming in second or third place. Chung also observed, "Two historic factors have served to slow human progress across the centuries. The first is a tendency to be overconfident about the future. The second is a tendency to underestimate the importance of the times in which we live."[4] This observation suggests that much of the future may be before our eyes right now; it must only be recognized and then pursued.

In the same manner, many have noted that the word *weiji* means "crisis" in Chinese and is typically expressed using two characters: one for danger and one for opportunity.[5] This interpretation of the concept suggests that crisis, or crises, are often related to two other variables: threats and opportunities. And in many cases, threats and opportunities can lead to productive changes in organizations to make them more nimble, quicker to respond, and more competitive. Again, however, this only occurs if and when managers realize what is happening and understand the surrounding environment to the extent that they are in a position to capitalize on the events as they unfold.

When the business environment is viewed in this manner, it may be that Omar Khayyàm and Siddhārtha Gautama are actually giving the same advice to global managers in the twenty-first century. Yes, the past is prologue, and we must understand the how's and why's about how we got to this point. But also, yes, if we believe we are headed in the right direction (we can "see" the future, at least metaphorically), all we need to do is to pursue it. So perhaps the focus of our principal attention right now should be on the present, as Chairman Chung suggested, so long as we see this present in dynamic or continuous terms: past > present > future. Most business opportunities are here now, not in the past and not in the future. So perhaps the wisest thing global managers can do is to understand this dynamic. What can we learn from the past that can help us in the future? And what can we do in the present that can help guarantee this success in the future?

To accomplish this, as we have discussed throughout this book, global managers must develop proficiencies in working across cultures, because this is where most future opportunities will be found. They must develop an ability to distinguish between cultural differences and similarities across borders, as well as differences within single countries. They must develop an ability to tease out the subtle contradictions and dualities that are rooted in various cultures, and not look for easy answers where none may exist. And they must develop an ability to adapt traditional management skills, such as leadership, motivation, negotiation, and communication, to fit cross-cultural or multicultural venues. Herein lies the essence of effective global management.

The prospects of dealing with people from different cultural backgrounds can be very challenging, but potentially it can also be very rewarding. But for many managers, it doesn't happen easily. Remember Percy Barnevik's dictum from Chapter 1 that "Global managers are made, not born. This is not a natural process."[6] Remember, too, Thomas Stewart's observation that "a global manager is set apart by more than a worn suitcase and a dog-eared passport."[7] To the extent that these observations are correct, the onus is clearly on managers to prepare themselves for success in the future. Engaging with managers and entrepreneurs from different cultures opens up considerable opportunities to learn more about ourselves, discover new ways of doing things, and find creative solutions to both old and new problems. It is clearly part of the developmental process for most managers. And in this pursuit, continual cognitive, analytical, and experiential learning plays a significant – and often under-appreciated – role.

Notes

1 George Santayana, *The Life of Reason or the Phases of Human Progress: Reason in Common Sense*. New York, NY: Charles Scribner and Sons, 1924, p. 284.

2 David A. Kolb, "Management and the learning process," *California Management Review*, 1976, 18(3), pp. 21–31; David A. Kolb, *Experiential Learning: Experience as the Source of Learning and Development*. Englewood Cliffs, NJ: Prentice Hall 1984.

3 Personal communication to author from Chung Ju Jung, cited in Richard M. Steers, *Made in Korea: Chung Ju Yung and the Rise of Hyundai*. New York, NY: Routledge, 1999.

4 *Ibid.*, p. 219.

5 The Chinese word *weiji* (危機 in traditional Chinese; 危机 in simplified Chinese) is typically translated as "crisis" in much of the world, and is said to be composed of the characters for "danger" and "opportunity," the implication being that in Chinese culture, a crisis is regarded not merely as a danger, but also as an opportunity. This translation is open to question, however. In fact, *wei* (危) can mean many things, including danger; dangerous; endanger; jeopardize; perilous; precipitous; precarious; high; fear; and afraid. And the polysemous *ji* (機) can mean machine; mechanical; airplane; suitable occasion; crucial point; pivot; incipient

moment; opportune, opportunity; chance; key link; secret; and cunning. Thus, while the word *jihui* (機會) can mean "opportune," "opportunity" in modern Chinese, its *ji* component has many meanings, of which "opportunity" is only one. In *weiji* (危機), *ji* means "crucial point," not necessarily "opportunity."

6 Percy Barnevik, cited in Philip Harris, Robert Moran, and Sarah Moran, *Managing Cultural Differences*, 6th Edition. Amsterdam: Elsevier, 2004, p. 25.

7 Thomas Stewart, cited in Harris *et al.*, *Managing Cultural Differences*, p. 1.

Models of national cultures

For many managers, the study of culture often begins with a comparison of different cultures or countries using several cultural dimensions (e.g., individualism-collectivism). For example, if a manager from France is traveling to Prague in the Czech Republic, it can be quite helpful to understand differences in cultural trends between the two locales prior to arrival. While such models clearly do not explain everything managers need to know to succeed, they can be a useful starting point.

A number of such models are available and have been widely adopted. These include the works of Clyde Kluckhohn and Florence Strodtbeck, Geert Hofstede, Edward T. Hall, Fons Trompenaars, Shalom Schwartz, and Robert House and his GLOBE project associates. Each attempts to capture the essence of cultural differences through the use of multiple dimensions or measures. In doing so, each model highlights different aspects of societal beliefs, norms, and/or values, and, as such, convergence across the models has been seen as being very limited. However, this may not be the case. Below, we briefly summarize each of the six models. This is followed by a brief comparison across the models in search of commonalities.[1]

Competing models of cultural dimensions

Based on the initial research by Clyde Kluckhohn, cultural anthropologists Florence Kluckhohn and Fred Strodtbeck suggested one of the earliest models of culture that has served as a principal foundation for several later models.[2] They proposed a theory of culture based on value orientations, arguing that there are a limited number of problems that are common to all human groups and for which there are a limited number of solutions. They further suggested that values in any given society are distributed in a way that creates a dominant value system. They used anthropological theories to identify five value orientations, four of which were later tested in five subcultures of the American Southwest: two Native American tribes, a Hispanic village, a Mormon village, and a farming village of Anglo-American

Exhibit A.1 Kluckholn and Strodtbecks' cultural dimensions

Cultural dimensions	Scale anchors		
Relationship with nature: Beliefs about the need or responsibility to control nature.	*Mastery*: Belief that people has a need or responsibility to control nature.	*Harmony*: Belief that people should work with nature to maintain harmony or balance.	*Subjugation*: Belief that individuals must submit to nature.
Relationship with people: Beliefs about social structure.	*Individualistic*: Belief that social structure should be arranged based on individuals.	*Collateral*: Belief that social structure should be based on groups of individuals with relatively equal status.	*Lineal*: Belief that social structure should be based on groups with clear and rigid hierarchical relationships.
Human activities: Beliefs about appropriate goals.	*Being*: Belief that people should concentrate on living for the moment.	*Becoming*: Belief that people should strive to develop oneself into an integrated whole.	*Doing*: Belief on striving for goals and accomplishments.
Relationship with time: Extent to which past, present, and future influence decisions.	*Past*: In making decisions, people are principally influenced by past events or traditions.	*Present*: In making decisions, people are principally influenced by present circumstances.	*Future*: In making decisions, people are principally influenced by future prospects.
Human nature: Beliefs about good, neutral or evil human nature.	*Good*: Belief that people are inherently good.	*Neutral*: Belief that people are inherently neutral.	*Evil*: Belief that people are inherently evil.

homesteaders. The five dimensions are identified in Exhibit A.1. Each dimension is represented on a three-point continuum.

Dutch management researcher Geert Hofstede advanced the most widely used model of cultural differences in the organizations literature.[3] His model was derived from a study of employees from various countries working for major multinational corporations and was based on the assumption that different cultures can be distinguished based on differences in what they value. That is, some cultures place a high value on equality among individuals, while others place a high value on hierarchies or power distances between people. Likewise, some cultures value certainty in everyday life and have difficulty coping with unanticipated events, while others have a greater tolerance for ambiguity and seem to relish change. Taken together, Hofstede argues that it is possible to gain considerable insight into organized behavior across cultures based on these value dimensions. Initially, Hofstede asserted that cultures could be distinguished along four dimensions, but later added a fifth dimension based on his research with Michael Bond.[4] The final five dimensions are illustrated in Exhibit A.2.

Edward T. Hall, a noted American cultural anthropologist, has proposed a model of culture based on his ethnographic research in several societies, notably Germany,

Exhibit A.2 Hofstede's cultural dimensions

Cultural dimensions	Scale anchors	
Power distance: Beliefs about the appropriate distribution of power in society.	*Low power distance*: Belief that effective leaders do not need to have substantial amounts of power compared to their subordinates.	*High power distance*: Belief that people in positions of authority should have considerable power compared to their subordinates.
Uncertainty avoidance: Degree of uncertainty that can be tolerated and its impact on rule making.	*Low uncertainty avoidance*: Tolerance for ambiguity; little need for rules to constrain uncertainty.	*High uncertainty avoidance*: Intolerance for ambiguity; need for many rules to constrain uncertainty.
Individualism-collectivism: Relative importance of individual vs. group interests.	*Collectivism*: Group interests generally take precedence over individual interests.	*Individualism*: Individual interests generally take precedence over group interests.
Masculinity-femininity: Assertiveness vs. passivity; material possessions vs. quality of life.	*Masculinity*: Values material possessions, money, and the pursuit of personal goals.	*Femininity*: Values strong social relevance, quality of life, and the welfare of others.
Long-term vs. short-term orientation: Outlook on work, life, and relationships.	*Short-term orientation*: Past and present orientation. Values traditions and social obligations.	*Long-term orientation*: Future orientation. Values dedication, hard work, and thrift.

Exhibit A.3 Hall's cultural dimensions

Cultural dimensions	Scale anchors	
Context: Extent to which the context of a message is as important as the message itself.	*Low context*: Direct and frank communication; message itself conveys its own meaning.	*High context*: Much of the meaning in communication is conveyed indirectly through the context surrounding a message.
Space: Extent to which people are comfortable sharing physical space with others.	*Center of power*: Territorial; need for clearly delineated personal space between themselves and others.	*Center of community*: Communal; comfortable sharing personal space with others.
Time: Extent to which people approach one task at a time or multiple tasks simultaneously.	*Monochronic*: Sequential attention to individual goals; separation of work and personal life; precise concept of time.	*Polychronic*: Simultaneous attention to multiple goals; integration of work and personal life; relative concept of time.

France, the US, and Japan.[5] His research focuses primarily on how cultures vary in interpersonal communication, but also includes work on personal space and time. These three cultural dimensions are summarized in Exhibit A.3. Many of the terms used today in the field of cross-cultural management (e.g., monochronic-polychronic) are derived from this work.

Building on the work of Hofstede, Dutch management researcher Fons Trompenaars presented a somewhat different model of culture based on his study of Shell and other managers over a ten-year period.[6] His model is based on the early

Exhibit A.4 Trompenaar's cultural dimensions

Cultural dimensions	Scale anchors	
Universalism-particularism: Relative importance of applying standardized rules and policies across societal members; role of exceptions in rule enforcement.	*Universalism*: Reliance on formal rules and policies that are applied equally to everyone.	*Particularism*: Rules must be tempered by the nature of the situation and the people involved.
Individualism-collectivism: Extent to which people derive their identity from within themselves or their group.	*Individualism*: Focus on individual achievement and independence.	*Collectivism*: Focus on group achievement and welfare.
Specific-diffuse: Extent to which people's various roles are compartmentalized or integrated.	*Specific*: Clear separation of a person's various roles.	*Diffuse*: Clear integration of a person's various roles.
Neutral-affective: Extent to which people are free to express their emotions in public.	*Neutral*: Refrain from showing emotions; hide feelings.	*Affective*: Emotional expressions acceptable or encouraged.
Achievement-ascription: Manner in which respect and social status are accorded to people.	*Achievement*: Respect for earned accomplishments.	*Ascription*: Respect for ascribed or inherited status.
Time perspective: Relative focus on the past or the future in daily activities.	*Past/present-oriented*: Emphasis on past events and glory.	*Future-oriented*: Emphasis on planning and future possibilities.
Relationship with environment: Extent to which people believe they control the environment or it controls them.	*Inner-directed*: Focus on controlling the environment.	*Outer-directed*: Focus on living in harmony with nature.

work of Harvard sociologists Talcott Parsons and focuses on variations in both values and personal relationships across cultures.[7] It consists of seven dimensions, as shown on Exhibit A.4. The first five dimensions focus on relationships among people, while the last two focus on time management and society's relationship with nature.

Taking a decidedly more psychological view, Shalom Schwartz and his associates asserted that the essential distinction between societal values is the motivational goals they express.[8] He identified ten universal human values that reflect needs, social motives, and social institutional demands.[9] These values are purportedly found in all cultures and represent universal needs of human existence. The human values identified are: power; achievement; hedonism; stimulation; self-direction; universalism; benevolence; tradition; conformity; and security. Schwartz argued that individual and cultural levels of analysis are conceptually independent.[10] Individual-level dimensions reflect the psychological dynamics that individuals experience when acting on their values in their everyday life, while cultural-level dimensions reflect the solutions that societies find to regulate human actions. At the cultural level of analysis, Schwartz identified three dimensions: conservatism versus autonomy, hierarchy versus egalitarianism, and mastery versus harmony,

Exhibit A.5 Schwartz's cultural dimensions

Cultural dimensions	Scale anchors	
Conservatism-autonomy: Extent to which individuals are integrated in groups.	*Conservatism*: Individuals are embedded in a collectivity, finding meaning through participation and identification with a group that shares their way of life.	*Autonomy*: Individuals are autonomous from groups, finding meaning in their own uniqueness. Two types of autonomy: Intellectual autonomy: (independent pursuit of ideas and rights) and Affective autonomy: (independent pursuit of affectively positive experience).
Hierarchy-egalitarianism: Extent to which equality is valued and expected.	*Hierarchy*: Cultures are organized hierarchically. Individuals are socialized to comply with their roles and are sanctioned if they do not.	*Egalitarianism*: Individuals are seen as moral equals who share basic interests as human beings.
Mastery-harmony: Extent to which people seek to change the natural and social world to advance personal or group interests.	*Mastery*: individuals value getting ahead through self-assertion and seek to change the natural and social world to advance personal or group interests.	*Harmony*: Individuals accept the world as it is and try to preserve it rather than exploit it.

summarized in Exhibit A.5. Based on this model, he studied school teachers and college students in fifty-four countries. His model has been applied to basic areas of social behavior, but its application to organizational studies has been limited.[11]

Finally, in one of the most ambitious efforts to study cultural dimensions, Robert J. House led an international team of researchers that focused primarily on understanding the influence of cultural differences on leadership processes.[12] Their investigation was called the "GLOBE study" for Global Leadership and Organizational Behavior Effectiveness. In their research, the GLOBE researchers identified nine cultural dimensions, as summarized in Exhibit A.6. While several of these dimensions have been identified previously (e.g., individualism-collectivism, power distance, and uncertainty avoidance), others are unique (e.g., gender egalitarianism and performance orientation).

Based on this assessment, the GLOBE researchers collected data in sixty-two countries and compared the results. Systematic differences were found in leader behavior across the cultures. For example, participatory leadership styles that are often accepted in the individualistic West are of questionable effectiveness in the more collectivistic East. Asian managers place a heavy emphasis on paternalistic leadership and group maintenance activities. Charismatic leaders can be found in most cultures, although they may be highly assertive in some cultures and passive in others. A leader who listens carefully to his or her subordinates is more valued in the US than in China. Malaysian leaders are expected to behave in a manner that is

Exhibit A.6 GLOBE project's cultural dimensions

Cultural dimensions	Scale anchors	
Power distance: Degree to which people expect power to be distributed equally.	*High*: Society divided into classes; power bases are stable and scarce; power is seen as providing social order; limited upward mobility.	*Low*: Society has large middle class; power bases are transient and sharable; power often seen as a source of corruption, coercion, and dominance; high upward mobility.
Uncertainty avoidance: Extent to which people rely on norms, rules, and procedures to reduce the unpredictability of future events.	*High*: Tendency to formalize social interactions; document agreements in legal contracts; be orderly and maintain meticulous records; rely on rules and formal policies.	*Low*: Tendency to be more informal in social interactions; reliance on word of people they trust; less concerned with orderliness and recordkeeping; rely on informal norms of behavior.
Humane orientation: Extent to which people reward fairness, altruism, and generosity.	*High*: Interests of others important; values altruism, benevolence, kindness, and generosity; high need for belonging and affiliation; fewer psychological and pathological problems.	*Low*: Self-interest important; values pleasure, comfort, and self-enjoyment; high need for power and possessions; more psychological and pathological problems.
Institutional collectivism: Extent to which society encourages collective distribution of resources and collective action.	*High*: Individuals integrated into strong cohesive groups; self viewed as interdependent with groups; societal goals often take precedence over individual goals.	*Low*: Individuals largely responsible for themselves; self viewed as autonomous; individual goals often take precedence over societal or group goals.
In-group collectivism: Extent to which individuals express pride, loyalty, and cohesiveness in their organizations and families.	*High*: Members assume they are interdependent and seek to make important personal contributions to the group or organization; long-term employer-employee relationships; organizations assume major responsibility of employee welfare; important decisions made by groups.	*Low*: Members assume they are independent of the organization and seek to stand out by making individual contributions; short-term employer-employee relationships; organizations primarily interested in the work performed by employees over their personal welfare.
Assertiveness: Degree to which people are assertive, confrontational, and aggressive in relationships with others.	*High*: Value assertiveness, dominance, and tough behavior for all members of society; sympathy for the strong; value competition; belief in success through hard work; values direct and unambiguous communication.	*Low*: Prefers modesty and tenderness to assertiveness; sympathy for the weak; values cooperation; often associates competition with defeat and punishment; values face-saving in communication and action.
Gender egalitarianism: Degree to which gender differences are minimized.	*High*: High participation of women in the workforce; more women in positions of authority; women accorded equal status in society.	*Low*: Low participation of women in the workforce; fewer women in positions of authority; women not accorded equal status in society.
Future orientation: Extent to which people engage in future-oriented behaviors such as planning, investing, and delayed gratification.	*High*: Greater emphasis on economic success; propensity to save for the future; values intrinsic motivation; organizations tend to be flexible and adaptive.	*Low*: Less emphasis on economic success; propensity for instant gratification; values extrinsic motivation; organizations tend to be bureaucratic and inflexible.
Performance orientation: Degree to which high performance is encouraged and rewarded.	*High*: Belief that individuals are in control of their destiny; values assertiveness, competitiveness, and materialism; emphasizes performance over people.	*Low*: Values harmony with environment over control; emphasizes seniority, loyalty, social relationships, and belongingness; values who people are more than what they do.

humble, dignified, and modest, while American leaders seldom behave in this manner. Indians prefer leaders who are assertive, morally principled, ideological, bold, and proactive. Family and tribal norms support highly autocratic leaders in many Arab countries.[13] Clearly one of the principal contributions of the GLOBE project has been to systematically study not just cultural dimensions, but also how variations in such dimensions affect leadership behavior and effectiveness.

Common themes across models

Taken together, these six culture models attempt to accomplish two things. First, each model offers a well-reasoned set of dimensions along which various cultures can be compared. In this regard, they offer a form of intellectual shorthand for cultural analysis, allowing researchers to break down assessments of various cultures into power distance, uncertainty avoidance, and so forth, and thus organize their thoughts and focus attention on what otherwise would be a monumental task. Second, four of the models offer numeric scores for rating various cultures. For example, we can use Hofstede's model to say that Germany is a thirty-five while France is a sixty-eight on power distance, suggesting that Germany is more egalitarian than France. Regardless of whether these ratings are highly precise or only generally indicative of these countries, they nonetheless provide one indication of how these countries might vary culturally.

As is evident from this review, there are many different ways to represent cultural differences. Unfortunately, the six cultural models available frequently focus on different aspects of societal beliefs, norms, or values, and, as such, convergence across the models seems at first glance to be limited. This lack of convergence presents important challenges both for researchers attempting to study cultural influences on management and for managers trying to understand new cultural settings.

Instead of advocating one model over another, we suggest that all of the models have important factors to contribute to our understanding of culture as it relates to management practices (see Chapter 3).[14] In order to navigate this culture theory jungle, we argue that the most productive approach is to integrate and adapt the various models based on their utility for better understanding business and management in cross-cultural settings. In doing so, we seek common themes that collectively represent the principal differences between cultures. While no single model can cover all aspects of a culture, we believe it is possible to tease out the principal cultural characteristics through such a comparative analysis.

Exhibit A.7 Common themes across models of national cultures

Common themes	Culture models					
	Kluckhohn and Strodtbeck	Hofstede	Hall	Trompenaars	Schwartz	GLOBE
Power distribution		1	1	1	1	2
Social relationships	1	1		1	1	2
Environmental relationships	2	1		1	1	3
Time/work patterns	1	1	1	1		1
Uncertainty and social control	1	1		1		1
Other (see text)			1	2		

Note: Numbers indicate the number of cultural dimensions from the various models that fit within each theme.

In our view, five relatively distinct common themes emerge from this comparison (see Exhibit A.7):

(1) *Power distribution: distribution of power and authority in society.* How are power and authority distributed in a society? Is this distribution based on concepts of hierarchy or egalitarianism? What are societal beliefs concerning equality or privilege?

(2) *Social relationships: centrality of individuals or groups as the basis of social relationships.* What is the fundamental building block of a society: individuals or groups? How does a society organize for collective action?

(3) *Environmental relationships: people's relationship with their environment.* On a societal level, how do people view the world around them and their relationship with the natural and social environment? Is their goal to control the environment and events around them or to live in harmony with these external realities?

(4) *Time/work patterns: use of time and work.* How do people in a society organize and manage their time to carry out their work and non-work activities? Do people approach work in a linear or non-linear fashion?

(5) *Uncertainty and social control: mechanisms of personal and social control to minimize uncertainty.* How do societies try to ensure predictability in the behavior of their members? Do they work to control people through uniformly applied rules, policies, laws, and social norms or do they rely more on personal ties or unique circumstances?

To achieve this clustering, we must recognize that in a few cases, multiple dimensions in the original models can be merged into a single more general or unifying cultural dimension (e.g., institutional and in-group collectivism in the GLOBE model), as discussed below. In addition, we need to look beyond the simple adjectives often used by the various researchers and seek deeper meaning in the various concepts themselves, also discussed below.

At first glance, these five themes seem to replicate Hofstede's five dimensions, but closer analysis suggests that the other models serve to amplify, clarify, and, in some cases, reposition dimensions so they are more relevant for the contemporary workplace. Indeed, we believe the commonality across these models reinforces their utility (and possible validity) as critical evaluative components in better understanding global management and the world of international business. As such, each model thus adds something of value to this endeavor.

Notes

1 Luciara Nardon and Richard M. Steers, "The culture theory jungle: divergence and convergence in models of national culture," in Rabi S. Bhagat and Richard M. Steers (eds.), *Cambridge Handbook of Culture, Work, and Organizations*. Cambridge, UK: Cambridge University Press, 2009, pp. 3–22.

2 Clyde Kluckhohn, "Values and value orientations in the theory of action," in Talcott Parsons and E. A. Shils (eds.), *Towards a General Theory of Action*. Cambridge, MA: Harvard University Press, 1951; Florence Kluckhohn and Fred Strodtbeck, *Variations in Value Orientations*. Evanston, IL: Row, Peterson, 1961.

3 Geert Hofstede, *Culture's Consequences: Comparing Values, Behaviors, Institutions, and Organizations Across Nations*. Thousand Oaks, CA: Sage, 1980, rev. 2001.

4 Michael Bond and Peter Smith, "Cross-cultural social and organizational psychology," *Annual Review of Psychology*, 1996, 47, pp. 205–235.

5 Edward T. Hall, *The Silent Language*. New York, NY: Doubleday, 1959; Edward T. Hall and Mildred R. Hall, *Understanding Cultural Differences*. Yarmouth, ME: Intercultural Press, 1990.

6 Fons Trompenaars, *Riding the Waves of Culture: Understanding Cultural Diversity in Business*. London: Economist Books, 1993; Fons Trompenaars and Charles Hampden-Turner, *Riding the Waves of Culture: Understanding Diversity in Global Business*. New York, NY: McGraw-Hill, 1998.

7 Talcott Parsons and E. A. Shills, *Toward a General Theory of Action*. Cambridge, MA: Harvard University Press, 1951.

8 Shalom Schwartz, "Universals in the content and structure of values: theoretical advances and empirical tests in 20 countries," in Mark Zanna (ed.), *Advances in Experimental Social Psychology*. vol. XXV. New York, NY: Academic Press, 1992, pp. 1–65.

9 Cigdem Kagitçibasi, "Individualism and collectivism," in Marshall Segal and Cigdem Kagitçibasi (eds.), *Handbook of Cross-Cultural Psychology*, vol. III. Boston, MA: Allyn & Bacon, 1997, pp. 1–49.

10 Shalom Schwartz, "Beyond individualism/collectivism: new cultural dimensions of values," in U. Kim, Harry C. Triandis, Cigdem Kagitçibasi, S. C. Choi, and G. Yoon (eds.), *Individualism and Collectivism: Theory, Methods and Applications*. Thousand Oaks, CA: Sage, 1994, pp. 85–122.

11 Bond and Smith, "Cross-cultural social and organizational psychology."

12 Robert J. House, Paul J. Hanges, Mansour Javidan, Peter W. Dorfman, and Vipin Gupta, *Culture, Leadership and Organizations: The GLOBE Study of 62 Societies*. Thousand Oaks, CA: Sage, 2004.

13 *Ibid.*

14 Nardon and Steers, "The culture theory jungle."

OECD guidelines for global managers

The principal goal of the Paris-based Organization for Economic Cooperation and Development (OECD) is to promote market-oriented economic growth and development around the world.[1] As part of its activities, and because of its moral force in the economic community, the OECD has long promoted ethical and socially responsible behavior by companies of its member states, as discussed in Chapter 11. The principal means through which this objective is pursued is through the promulgation and support of the *OECD Guidelines for Multinational Enterprises*. These guidelines represent a set of normative, yet voluntary, guidelines for global managers and their firms that are aimed simultaneously at developing the economies of less developed nations while protecting them from exploitation by large and rich companies from the industrialized world. These guidelines aim to ensure that the operations of these enterprises operate in harmony with local government policies, to strengthen the basis of mutual confidence between global firms and the societies in which they operate, to help improve the foreign investment climate, and to enhance the contribution to sustainable development made by global companies.[2]

The *OECD Guidelines* are divided into five categories: bribery and corruption; employment relations; technology transfer; environmental stewardship; and general business practices (see Exhibit B.1).

Bribery and corruption

The *OECD Guidelines* place considerable emphasis on corruption and bribery. In brief, these guidelines proscribe the following:

- *Payments to public officials*. Managers are not allowed to offer, nor give in to demands, to pay any portion of a contract payment to public officials or the employees of business partners. Nor should they use subcontracts, purchase orders, or consulting agreements as a means of channeling payments to public

Exhibit B.1 OECD guidelines for global managers

OECD guidelines	Principal emphasis
Bribery and corruption	Encourages companies to take a public position against bribery and corruption and discourage such activities in securing or operating a firm.
Employee relations	Encourages fair treatment of all local employees consistent with prevailing local conditions.
Technology transfer	Encourages technology diffusion and local licensing of technological processes and technology-based products and services.
Stewardship	Encourages protection of the local environment from unsafe products and practices and help mitigation of any damage where it occurs.
General business practices *Competition*	Encourages open and fair competition, particularly involving local firms; supports local government attempts to open markets.
Consumer protection	Encourages fair business, marketing, and advertising practices; promotes product safety and quality.
Transparency/disclosure	Encourages transparency and disclosure of locally required information about organization structure and corporate policies.
Finance and taxation	Encourages full compliance with local reporting requirements and fair payment of local taxes.

Source: See OECD Guidelines for details at www.oecd.org/daf/investment/guidelines.

officials, to employees of business partners, or to their relatives or business associates.

- *Remuneration of agents.* Managers should ensure that the remuneration of agents is appropriate and for legitimate services only. Where relevant, a list of agents employed in connection with transactions with public bodies and state-owned enterprises should be kept and made available to competent authorities.
- *Promotion of public awareness.* Managers should enhance the transparency of their activities in the fight against bribery and extortion. Measures could include making public commitments against bribery and extortion and disclosing the management systems the company has adopted in order to honor these commitments. The manager should also foster openness and dialogue with the public so as to promote its awareness of and cooperation with the fight against bribery and extortion.
- *Promotion of employee awareness.* Managers should promote employee awareness of and compliance with company policies against bribery and extortion through appropriate dissemination of these policies and through training programs and disciplinary procedures.
- *Management control systems.* Managers should adopt management control systems that discourage bribery and corrupt practices, and adopt financial and tax

accounting and auditing practices that prevent the establishment of off-the-books or secret accounts or the creation of documents that do not properly and fairly record the transactions to which they relate.

- *Campaign contributions.* Managers should not make illegal contributions to candidates for public office, or to political parties or other political organizations. Contributions should fully comply with public disclosure requirements and should be reported to senior management.

Employment relations

OECD Guidelines also focus heavily on company responsibilities to local employees. Towards this end, they suggest that, within the framework of law, regulations, and prevailing labor relations and employment practices, global firms should do the following:

- *Employee representation.* Respect the right of their employees to be represented by trade unions and other bona fide organizations of employees, and engage in constructive negotiations, either individually or through employers' associations, with such employee organizations with a view to reaching agreements on employment conditions, which should include provisions for dealing with disputes arising over the interpretation of such agreements, and for ensuring mutually respected rights and responsibilities; provide such facilities to representatives of the employees as may be necessary to assist in the development of effective collective agreements; provide to representatives of employees information that is needed for meaningful negotiations on conditions of employment; and provide to representatives of employees, where this accords with local law and practice, information that enables them to obtain a true and fair view of the performance of the entity or, where appropriate, the enterprise as a whole.
- *Employment standards.* Observe standards of employment and industrial relations not less favorable than those observed by comparable employers in the host country.
- *Employee training and development.* In their operations, to the greatest extent practicable, utilize, train, and prepare for upgrading members of the local labor force in cooperation with representatives of their employees and, where appropriate, the relevant governmental authorities.
- *Lay-offs and dismissals.* In considering changes in their operations that would have major effects upon the livelihood of their employees, in particular in the case

of the closure of an entity involving collective lay-offs or dismissals, provide reasonable notice of such changes to representatives of their employees, and, where appropriate, to the relevant governmental authorities, and cooperate with the employee representatives and appropriate governmental authorities so as to mitigate to the maximum extent practicable adverse effects.

- *Equal employment opportunity.* Implement their employment policies, including hiring, discharge, pay, promotion, and training, without discrimination unless selectivity in respect of employee characteristics is in furtherance of established governmental policies that specifically promote greater equality of employment opportunity.

- *Freedom from coercion.* In the context of bona fide negotiations with representatives of employees on conditions of employment, or while employees are exercising a right to organize, not threaten to utilize a capacity to transfer the whole or part of an operating unit from the country concerned, nor transfer employees from the enterprises' component entities in other countries in order to influence unfairly those negotiations or to hinder the exercise of a right to organize.

- *Right of collective bargaining.* Enable authorized representatives of their employees to conduct negotiations on collective bargaining or labor-management relation issues with representatives of management who are authorized to make decisions on the matters under negotiation.

Technology transfer

Member states of the OECD have also set forth clear guidelines governing technology transfer. These guidelines are aimed largely at sharing technological wealth by bringing developing nations into the *technology club* – those nations that collectively develop and control cutting-edge technologies that have commercial applications. These guidelines identify technology transfer as an important vehicle for global and regional economic development. Three guidelines have been adopted:

- *Consistency with national goals.* Endeavor to ensure that their activities fit satisfactorily into the scientific and technological policies and plans of the countries in which they operate, and contribute to the development of national scientific and technological capacities, including, as far as appropriate, the establishment and improvement in host countries of their capacity to innovate.

- *Technology diffusion.* To the fullest extent practicable, adopt in the course of their business activities practices that permit the rapid diffusion of technologies with due regard to the protection of industrial and intellectual property rights.
- *Licensing.* When granting licenses for the use of industrial property rights or when otherwise transferring technology, do so on reasonable terms and conditions.

Environmental stewardship

OECD Guidelines focus here on the protection of the local environment from unsafe products and practices and help mitigation of any damage where it occurs. Global enterprises, within the framework of laws, regulations, and administrative practices in the countries in which they operate, are required to take due account of the need to protect the environment and avoid creating environmentally related health problems. In particular, companies, whether multinational or domestic, should do the following:

- *Public health risks.* Assess, and take into account in decision making, foreseeable environmental and environmentally related health consequences of their activities, including plant location decisions, impacts on indigenous natural resources and foreseeable environmental and environmentally related health risks of products, as well as from the generation, transport and disposal of waste.
- *Environmental impact.* Cooperate with competent authorities by providing adequate and timely information regarding the potential impacts on the environment and environmentally related health aspects of all their activities, and by providing the relevant expertise available in the enterprise as a whole
- *Accident prevention.* Take appropriate measures in their operations to minimize the risk of accidents and damage to health and the environment, and to cooperate in mitigating adverse effects, in particular: by selecting and adopting those technologies and practices that are compatible with these objectives; by introducing a system of environmental protection at the level of the enterprise as a whole, including, where appropriate, the use of environmental auditing; by enabling their component entities to be adequately equipped, especially by providing them with adequate knowledge and assistance; by implementing education and training programs for their employees; by preparing contingency plans; and by supporting, in an appropriate manner, public information and community awareness programs.

General business practices

Finally, the *OECD Guidelines* seek to improve corporate social responsibility through promoting good business practices as seen through the eyes of the member states. Four areas of concern are discussed: competitive practices; consumer protection; transparency and disclosure; and finance and taxation. Taken together, these guidelines round out what the OECD sees as a socially responsible global manager.

Competitive practices

Competition is a double-edged sword for many under-developed nations. It holds out the possibility of facilitating economic development but also opens opportunities for exploitation. In this regard, the *OECD Guidelines* aim to facilitate open and fair competition, including a special regard for local industries and companies. According to the guidelines, global firms should support the following actions, while still conforming to official competition rules and established policies of the countries in which they operate:

- *Anti-competitive behavior.* Refrain from actions that would adversely affect competition in the relevant market by abusing a dominant position of market power, by means of, for example: anti-competitive acquisitions; predatory behavior toward competitors; unreasonable refusal to deal; anti-competitive abuse of industrial property rights; and discriminatory (i.e., unreasonably differentiated) pricing and using such pricing transactions between affiliated enterprises as a means of affecting adversely competition outside these enterprises.
- *Purchaser's rights.* Allow purchasers, distributors, and licensees freedom to resell, export, purchase, and develop their operations consistent with law, trade conditions, the need for specialization, and sound commercial practice.
- *Restraint of trade.* Refrain from participating in, or otherwise purposely strengthening, the restrictive effects of international or domestic cartels or restrictive agreements that adversely affect or eliminate competition and which are not generally or specifically accepted under applicable national or international legislation.
- *Cooperation with authorities.* Be ready to consult and cooperate, including the provision of information, with competent authorities of countries whose interests are directly affected in regard to competition issues or investigations. Provisions

of information should be in accordance with safeguards normally applicable in this field.

Consumer protection

When dealing with consumers, global firms should act in accordance with fair business, marketing, and advertising practices and should take all reasonable steps to ensure the safety and quality of the goods or services they provide. In particular, they should do the following:

- *Product standards.* Ensure that the goods or services they provide meet all agreed or legally required standards for consumer health and safety, including health warnings and product safety and information labels.
- *Product information.* As appropriate to the goods or services, provide accurate and clear information regarding their content, safe use, maintenance, storage, and disposal sufficient to enable consumers to make informed decisions.
- *Complaint resolution.* Provide transparent and effective procedures that address consumer complaints and contribute to the fair and timely resolution of consumer disputes without undue cost or burden.
- *Deceptive claims.* Not make representations or omissions, nor engage in any other practices that are deceptive, misleading, fraudulent, or unfair.
- *Consumer privacy.* Respect consumer privacy and provide protection for personal data.
- *Public safety.* Cooperate fully and in a transparent manner with public authorities in the prevention or removal of serious threats to public health and safety deriving from the consumption or use of their products.

Transparency and disclosure

With due regard to their nature and relative size in the economic context of their operations and to requirements of business confidentiality and cost, global firms should publish, in a form suited to improve public understanding, a sufficient body of factual information on the structure, activities, and policies of the enterprise as a whole, as a supplement, in so far as necessary for this purpose, to information to be disclosed under the national law of the individual countries in which they operate.

To this end, companies should publish within reasonable time limits, on a regular basis, but at least annually, financial statements and other pertinent information relating to the enterprise as a whole, comprising in particular: the structure of the enterprise, showing the name and location of the parent company, its main affiliates, and its percentage ownership – direct and indirect – in these affiliates, including shareholdings between them; the geographical areas where operations are carried out and the principal activities carried on therein by the parent company and the main affiliates; the operating results and sales by geographical area and the sales in the major line of business for the enterprise as a whole; significant new capital investment by geographical area and, as far as practicable, by major lines of business for the enterprise as a whole; a statement of the sources and uses of funds by the enterprise as a whole; the average number of employees in each geographical area; R&D expenditure for the enterprise as a whole; the policies followed in respect of intra-group pricing; and the accounting policies, including those on consolidation, observed in compiling the published information.

Finance and taxation

Finally, in managing the financial and commercial operations of their activities, and especially their liquid foreign assets and liabilities, global firms should take into consideration the established objectives of the countries in which they operate regarding balance of payments and credit policies. In this regard, they should focus on three responsibilities:

- *Balance of payments and credit policies.* In managing the financial and commercial operations of their activities, and especially their liquid foreign assets and liabilities, they should take into consideration the established objectives of the countries in which they operate regarding balance of payments and credit policies.
- *Accurate information.* Upon request of the taxation authorities of the countries in which they operate, provide, in accordance with the safeguards and relevant procedures of the national laws of these countries, information necessary to determine correctly the taxes to be assessed in connection with their operations, including relevant information concerning their operations in other countries.
- *Tax base.* Refrain from making use of the particular facilities available to them, such as transfer pricing that does not conform to an arm's length standard, for modifying in ways contrary to national laws the tax base on which members of the group are assessed.

Notes

1 OECD members include Australia, Austria, Belgium, Canada, Czech Republic, Denmark, Finland, France, Germany, Greece, Hungary, Iceland, Ireland, Italy, Japan, Korea, Luxemburg,

Mexico, the Netherlands, New Zealand, Norway, Poland, Portugal, Slovak Republic, Spain, Sweden, Switzerland, Turkey, the UK, and the US. In addition, there are a number of affiliate members who agree to support the group's activities and abide by its guidelines, including Argentina, Brazil, Chile, Estonia, Israel, Lithuania, and Slovenia.

2 See www.oecd.org/daf/investment/guidelines.

Index

accounting and finance practices, cultural differences 53–55
acculturation skills of global managers 38
Adler, Nancy 77, 165, 273
affirmations 216
aisatsu 318, 351
Amsden, Alice 87
analytic versus holistic thinking 98–100
Anglo cluster
  cultural trends 64–66
  organization and management trends 163–165
Anheuser-Busch-InBev 356–357
Arab cluster, cultural trends 64–66
Arab culture
  authority of elders 47
  consultation and consensus in decision making 47
  foreign manager's preparation for 46–49
  gender roles 47
  Hofstede's cultural model 48–49
  patriarchal societies 47
  role of the extended family 46–47
assessment and reasoning processes 94–96
assigned management agreement 347
asynchronous communication 227
automation 150

Barnard, Chester 126
Barnevik, Percy 1, 272, 409
Bavli, Talmud 45
beliefs and values
  cross-cultural conflicts 368–369, 371–373
  influence of culture 51
Bennis, Warren 241
Berkeley, George 90
BMW 151
body language 220
Branson, Richard 255–256
Brazil
  jeitinho concept 72
  negotiation patterns 339–341
bribery and corruption
  dilemmas for international business 363–367
  ethical conflicts and challenges 383–384
  OECD guidelines 386–389
Buchman, Nancy 353
bumiputra firms in Malaysia 110–112

business growth, evolutionary and strategic approaches 98–99
business success, consequences of ignoring global issues 1–2

Canadian firms, organization and management trends 163–165
Cannon-Brookes, Michael 85
categorization of information 92–93
categorization processes 98–100
causal attribution 94–96
  and work motivation 297
cause and consequences, perceptions of 100–102
centralized decision making 140–143
centralized stakeholder model 130
chaebols (Korean firms), benefits of global partnerships 321–324
change, in the global business environment 12–17
change and stability, views on 99–100
Child, John 164
Chinese cultural patterns 175–178
  Confucianism 175–177
  guānxi (social connections) 177
  importance of rank 178
  lian (face) 177–178
  mianzi (face) 177–178
  mien-tzu (face) 177–178
  renqing (personal obligations) 178
  responsibility for group harmony 178
Chinese *gong-si* (companies) 142, 175–181
  Chinese cultural patterns 175–178
  East Hope Group (Shanghai) 155–156
  family-run enterprises 179–181
  organization and management trends 179–181
Chung Ju Yung 408
Chung Mong Koo 86
CNN 35
codetermination 146, 182
co-located global teams 263–264, 272–273
cognitions and expectations, influence on work motivation 295–296
cognitive processes
  cognitive consistency 90–91
  cognitive dissonance 90–91
  cognitive evaluation 90–91
  cultural variations in 88–91

mental screens 88–89
    perceptual selection 90–91
    see also managerial thinking patterns
collaborative decision making 140, 145–148
Columbus, Christopher 405–406
communication across cultures
    appropriate behaviors 221–224
    appropriate formalities 221
    assumptions about mutual knowledge 226–227
    asynchronous communication 227
    challenges for "frequent flyer" managers 228–231
    challenges for managers 232–238
    cultural logic and shared meaning 208–210
    developing learning skills 228–231
    English as the *lingua franca* of global business 210–214
    enhancing message clarity 233–235
    enhancing message comprehension 235–237
    influence of language on thinking 205–208
    intercultural communications skills of global
        managers 38
    interdependent learning 228–231
    lack of contextual information 224–226
    language and linguistic structures 205–208
    learning the local language 207–208
    lingua franca and message comprehension 210–214
    message content 215–217
    message context 217–221
    minimizing communication breakdowns 237–238
    perceptual filters 201–202
    potential for misunderstandings 199–200
    protocols within cultures 221–224
    speed of communication 224
    technology breakdowns 227
    technology mediated communication 224–227
    varying meanings and interpretations 199–200
    virtual global teams 263–269
communication and culture (model) 202–204
communication protocols within cultures 221–224
    appropriate behaviors 221–224
    appropriate formalities 221
competitive negotiation 331–332
Confucianism 175–177
consultative decision making 140, 143–145
contextual information 224–226 *see also* message
    context
contracts 334–337
    cultural variations in meaning of 336–337
    doctrine of changed circumstances 336–337
    forum shopping 335
    method for resolving disagreements 335
    mutual trust 334–335
core cultural dimensions
    approach to power distribution 59
    approach to social relationships and organization 61
    approach to surrounding environment 61–62
    approach to uncertainty and predictability 62–64
    approach to work patterns and use of time 62
    country clusters 64–66
    culture theory jungle 55–57

five core dimensions 57–59
    hierarchical/egalitarian dimension 59
    individualist/collectivist dimension 61
    integration of existing models 57–59
    masculine/feminine cultural dimension 61–62
    mastery-oriented/harmony-oriented cultural
        dimension 61–62
    mechanism for comparing cultures 55
    models of cultural dimensions 55–57
    monochronic/polychronic cultural dimension 62
    potential problems for managers 55–57
    regional trends 64–66
    rule-based/relationship-based cultural dimension
        62–64
    social control 62–64
    universalistic/particularistic cultural dimension
        62–64
corporate governance, cultural influences 9–10
corporate social responsibility 391–394
corruption
    dilemmas for international business 363–367
    ethical conflicts and challenges 383–384
    Foreign Corrupt Practices Act (US) 364, 384–385
    see also bribery and corruption
cosmopolitan outlook of global managers 38
country clusters, cultural trends 64–66
cross-cultural communication strategies 214–215
cross-cultural conflicts 366–373
    beliefs and values 368–369, 371–373
    ethical versus legal imperatives 368–369, 370–371
    tastes and preferences 368–369
Crozier, Michael 155
cultural adaptation
    culture shock(s) 16
    dealing with multiple cultures 16–17
    developing global managers 16–17
    traditional approach 16
cultural complexities and contradictions 66–75
    cultural stability and change 69–71
    cultures and subcultures 74–75
    dualities perspective 69–75
    explanatory and predictive powers 73–74
    holistic and fragmented behavior 71–72
    Muslim businesswomen 66–69
    universal and idiosyncratic characteristics 72–73
cultural convergence versus divergence in
    globalization 8–10
cultural differences
    negative impacts of 12–13
    regional trends 64–66
cultural dimensions
    core cultural dimensions 57–64
    culture theory jungle 55–57
    mechanism for comparing cultures 55
    models 55–57
    potential problems for managers 55–57
cultural friction 78–79
cultural intelligence *see* multicultural competence
cultural logic and shared meaning 208–210

cultural pluralism versus plurality of cultures in
    globalization 10–11
cultural sensitivity of global managers 38
cultural stereotypes 76–77
cultural synergy skills of global managers 38
culture
    and normative behavior 50, 51, 52–55
    and personality 51–52
    definitions 49–52
    how culture is learned 50
    identifying what is universal and what is not 50–52
    influence on beliefs and values 51
    influence on socialization processes 51
    preparing to visit a different culture (example)
        46–49, 66–69
    shared nature of culture 50–52
    significance for managers 45–46
culture shock(s) 16
culture theory jungle 55–57
culture, values and world views 76–80
    avoiding cultural stereotypes 76–77
    influence on managerial behavior 76
    learning skills for managers 79–80
    preparing for the unexpected 79–80
    seeing cultural differences in neutral terms 77–79

Das, Gucharan 126
decision making see organizational decision making
delegated management agreement 347–348
digital nomads 30
distributed stakeholder model 130, 131–132
distributive justice concept 301–302
doctrine of changed circumstances 336–337
Drucker, Peter 324
dualities perspective
    cultural complexities and contradictions 69–75
    globalization 7–12

Earley, P. Christopher 298
East Hope Group 155
East/Southeast Asian cluster, cultural trends 64–66
"Eastern" and "Western" thinking compared 96–102
Eastern European cluster, cultural trends 64–66
economic and political interconnectedness 14–15
employee commitment to the organization 307–309
employee involvement 306–307
employee benefits 305–306
employment relations, OECD guidelines 390–391
England, George 286
English language
    as the lingua franca of global business 210–214
    different versions of 210–214
enterprise unions (Japan) 174
environment, mastery-oriented/harmony-oriented
        cultural dimension 61–62
environmental stewardship 391–394
equity principle 295–296
Ertel, Danny 344–345
ethical conflicts, definition 373–374

ethical conflicts and challenges 374–384
    bribery 363–367, 383–384
    conflicts within and between organizations 378
    corruption 363–367, 383–384
    cultural perspectives on honesty 381–384
    cultural perspectives on right and wrong 379–381
    limited Western perspective 374–375
    meaning of "universal" values 376–377
    need for a global perspective 374–375
    proper behavior towards others 381–384
    pursuit of "truth" 378–384
    relationship between principles and practice 377–378
    understanding in a cross-cultural context 375–378
    universalist versus particularist viewpoints 379–381
ethical leadership 372–373
ethical versus legal imperatives, cross-cultural conflicts
        368–369, 370–371
ethics, laws, and social control (model) 373–374
evolutionary approach to business growth 98–99
exclusion versus inclusion in globalization 11
executive compensation 302–303
expatriate managers
    long-term assignments 29–32
    regional myopia 34
experiential learning cycle 40–41
extrinsic incentives and rewards 300, 301–306
    distributive justice concept 301–302
    employee benefits 305–306
    executive compensation 302–303
    financial incentives 301–302
    gender and compensation 303–305
    merit-based incentive systems 301–302
    pay-for-performance systems 301–302
    value conflicts 303–305

face
    kao (Japan) 72
    lian (China) 177–178
    mianzi (China) 177–178
    mien-tzu (China) 177–178
facial expressions 219
fast-food industry, cultural influences 9
Fayol, Henri 26
Fellini, Federico 199
filial piety 175
financial incentives 301–302
financial practices, cultural differences 53–55
five cardinal virtues 175
flexible management style of global managers 38
force field analysis 388–389
Foreign Corrupt Practices Act (US) 364, 384–385
foreign direct investment, magnitude of 15
forum shopping 335
France, management patterns 106–110
free rider effects at work 298–299
"frequent flyer" managers
    communication challenges 228–231
    global myopia 34
    short-term assignments 29–30, 32–33

Friedman, Thomas 4
Fujisawa, Takeo 86, 293

Gandhi, Mahatma 406
Gautama, Siddhārtha 404, 408
Geertz, Clifford 50
gender and compensation 303–305
General Electric
    global partnership negotiations 350–352
    negotiations with Mitsubishi Electric 318–321
General Motors, centralized decision making 141–142
George, Claude 26
German cultural patterns 181–182
German *konzern* (firms) 181–186
    German cultural patterns 181–182
    industrial democracy 182–184
    Mittelstand firms 135–137
    organization and management trends 182–186
    technical competence 184–186
    technological complexity 151
Germanic cluster, cultural trends 64–66
Ghosn, Carlos 242–245, 258–259
global business environment
    economic and political interconnectedness 14–15
    effects of continual change 12–17
    from biculturalism to multiculturalism 15–17
    from intermittent to continual change 13–14
    from isolation to interconnectedness 14–15
    impacts of technological developments 13–14
    magnitude of foreign direct investment worldwide 15
    negative impacts of cultural differences 12–13
global frame of reference for managers 2–3
global issues, influence on business success 1–2
global management myopia 34
    global myopia 34
    regional myopia 34
    technological myopia 34
global managerial skills
    development of skills 39–43
    experiential learning 40–41
    learning strategies 42–43
    multicultural competence 36–38
global managers
    categorization 29–30
    challenges in the global economy 17–22
    definition of a global manager 28
    demands on managers and companies 35–36
    digital nomads 30
    distinction from traditional managers 28
    expatriates 29–32
    "frequent flyers" 29–30, 32–33
    inpatriates 30
    preparations to visit a different culture (example)
        46–49, 66–69
    requirements for success 17–22
    risk of short-sightedness 34
    telecommuters 30
    variety of 28
    virtual managers 29–30, 33–34

global mindset *see* multicultural competence
global myopia, "frequent flyer" managers 34
global partnerships
    aligning corporate cultures 355–357
    assigned management agreement 347
    benefits 321–324
    building partnerships 342–346
    challenges for managers 350–360
    conflict management 357–360
    criteria for selecting partners 342–343
    culture-related challenges 324–328
    delegated management agreement 347–348
    international joint ventures 347–348
    managing partnerships 346–349
    managing the negotiation process 345–346
    mutual trust 348, 352–355
    negotiation process 330–337
    preparing for global negotiations 344–345
    problems in negotiation across cultures
        318–321
    reasons for failed negotiations 350–352
    reasons for lack of success 324–328
    shared management agreement 346–347
    see also negotiation
global teams
    co-located teams 263–264, 272–273
    leadership 270–276
    location and composition of teams 262–269
    organizational challenges 261–262
    role of global team leaders 270–271
    types of teams 261
    virtual teams 263–269, 273–276
globalization
    challenges facing companies 5–6
    debate over merits or demerits 6–12
    definition 3–4
    drivers 5–6
    dualities approach 7–12
    historical development 4–5
    influence on management patterns 115–117
    phases of development 4–5
globalization dualities 7–12
    cultural convergence versus cultural
        divergence 8–10
    inclusion versus exclusion 11
    plurality of cultures versus cultural
        pluralism 10–11
GLOBE project 253–256
    ethical leadership 372–373
    model of cultural dimensions 55–57
gong-si see Chinese *gong-si*
Google
    developing global managers 24–25
    learning strategies for their managers 43
Graham, John 338
grupo see Mexican *grupo*
Grupo Carso, organizational structure 189–190, 192
guānxi (reciprocal exchange/social relationships) 135,
        142, 177, 334, 335

Håkansson, Anna, preparing to visit another culture (example) 46–49, 66–69
Hall, Edward T. 55–57, 107, 109, 181, 217, 411, 413
Halliburton, operations in Nigeria 363–364
Hampden-Turner, Charles 103
Handy, Charles 342
Henderson, Frederick 141
Herodotus 377
Hewlett-Packard 355
hierarchical/egalitarian cultural dimension 59
high-context cultures 218–219
Hoffer, Eric 24
Hofstede, Geert 126
    model of Arab culture 48–49
    model of cultural dimensions 55–57, 61, 411, 413
holistic versus analytic thinking 98–100
honesty, cultural perspectives on 381–384
honne 144, 219, 378
House, Robert J. 45, 116, 411, 415–417
Hyundai Motor Company 86–88, 132–133, 322–323

imperial CEO 162, 302
InBev 356–357
inclusion versus exclusion in globalization 11
independent self concept 100–102
Indian-English communications 212–214
individualist/collectivist cultural dimension 61
industrial democracy 184
information acquisition, retention, and recall 92
information processing 118–119
inpatriates 30
institutional conflicts, definition 373–374
institutional conflicts and challenges 384–394
    bribery and corruption 386–389
    corporate social responsibility 391–394
    environmental stewardship 391–394
    employment relations 390–391
    force field analysis 388–389
    Foreign Corrupt Practices Act (US) 364, 384–385
    OECD guidelines 385–394
    underground economies 387–388
institutional environment and strategic choice 132–134
Intel Corporation 35, 127–128, 355
interdependent learning 228–231
interdependent self concept 100–102
international joint ventures 347–348
intrinsic incentives and rewards 300, 306–309
    employee commitment to the organization 307–309
    employee involvement 306–307
    job satisfaction 307–309
    psychological contract 307–309
    work-related attitudes 307–309
Ishikawa, Junya 116
Islamic banking and finance practices 53–54
Islamic law 53
Iyengar, Adhira 32

Jackson, Susan 352
Japan
    approach to marketing 94–96
    cultural patterns 166–167
    kao (face) 72
    negotiation patterns 337–338, 340–341
Japanese kaisha (companies) 165–174
    consultative decision making 143–145
    enterprise unions 174
    human resource management systems 173–174
    influences on organizational strategy 133–134
    Japanese cultural patterns 166–167
    organization and management trends 167–174
    process simplification 150–151
    quality circles 174
Japanese keiretsu (business groups) 134
    Japanese cultural patterns 166–167
    keiretsu designs and operations 167–173, 243
    organization and management trends 167–173
job satisfaction 307–309
Jullien, François 248–251

Kagayama, Atsushi 241
kaisha see Japanese kaisha
kaizen 174
kanban (just-in-time) inventory system 172
kao (face) 72
keiretsu see Japanese keiretsu
Khayyám, Omar 404, 408
Kia Motors America 86–88
Kiggundu, Moses 114
Kirin Holdings Company (member of Mitsubishi keiretsu) 170–171
Kluckholn, Clyde 50, 413–414
konzern see German konzern
Korean chaebols (firms), benefits of global partnerships 321–324

language and linguistic structures 205–208
    influence on thinking 205–208
Lao Tzu 248
Latin American cluster, cultural trends 64–66
Latin European cluster, cultural trends 64–66
Latino culture, orgullo concept 72
Laurent, Andre 102
leadership
    and management 245–246
    ethical leadership 372–373
    of global teams 270–276
leadership and culture
    ancient Chinese traditions 248–251
    ancient Greek traditions 248–251
    characteristics of effective leaders 246–248
    cultural contingency of leadership styles 253–256
    differing definitions across cultures 246–248
    European cultural ideals 251–253
    foundations of Eastern and Western views 248–251

GLOBE study 253–256
  leading across cultures 258–260
  model 256–260
learning, influence of culture on 93–94
learning from the past 404–407
  Columbus, Christopher 405–406
  Gandhi, Mahatma 406
  Gautama, Siddhārtha 404, 408
  Khayyám, Omar 404, 408
  recent global economic turmoil 406–407
  Santayana, George 405
learning model 39–43
  experiential learning 40–41
  strategies for global managers 42–43
learning skills for managers
  facing cultural complexities 79–80
  preparing for the future 407–409
  recognising emerging opportunities 407–409
legal conflicts see institutional conflicts and challenges
Lewis, Richard D. 199, 378
LG electronics, expatriate managers 30–31
lian (face) 177–178
Lincoln Electric Company 280–284
lingua franca and message comprehension
    210–214
linguistic structures 205
logic of application 250
logic of exploitation 250
Lou, Yadong 352
low-context cultures 218

Machailova, Snejina 279
Malaysia, management patterns 110–112
management
  and leadership 245–246
  geographical bias of studies 28
  traditional views 26–28
management board (Germany) 182
management patterns
  comparison across cultures 106–115
  France 106–110
  influence of globalization 115–117
  Malaysia 110–112
  Nigeria 112–115
  question of convergence across cultures 115–117
management styles, cultural differences 85–88
Manager's notebook
  communication across cultures 232–238
  culture, values, and world views 76–80
  developing global management skills 39–43
  global teams 270–276
  inside the managerial mind 118–121
  inside the organizational mind 149–153
  leadership 270–276
  learning model 39–43
  managing in an imperfect world 395–400
  negotiation and global partnerships 350–360
  organizing frameworks 193–195
  work and motivation 310–313

managerial actions
  cultural differences 85–88
  ethical and moral constraints 397–398
  influence of culture and cognition 88–91
  legal and institutional constraints 399–400
  translating thought into action 88–91,
    119–120
managerial ethics 395–400 see also institutional
    conflicts and challenges
managerial mind 118–121
  actual versus idealized managerial roles
    120–121
  information processing 118–119
  translating thought into action 88–91,
    119–120
managerial roles
  actual versus idealized roles 102–106, 120–121
  culture-related expectations about 102–106
  influence of cultural differences 102–106
managerial thinking patterns 91–96
  approaches to business growth 98–99
  assessment and reasoning processes 94–96
  attributions of causality 94–96
  categorization of information 92–93
  categorization processes 98–100
  concept of self 93
  different philosophical traditions 99
  "Eastern" and "Western" thinking compared
    96–102
  holistic versus analytic thinking 98–100
  improving understanding between groups
    96–102
  independent or interdependent self concept
    100–102
  inferring mental states 94
  information acquisition, retention, and recall 92
  learning 93–94
  network maps 98–100
  norm of authenticity 94
  perceptions of cause and consequences 100–102
  self concepts 100–102
  views on stability and change 99–100
Mangaliso, Mzamo P. 85
maquiladora 285
masculine/feminine cultural dimension 61–62
mastery-oriented/harmony-oriented cultural
    dimension 61–62
Matsushita, Konosuke 256
McDonalds, local cultural influences 9
meister 185
Mencius 251
mental screens that separate people 88–89
mental states, inferring 94
merit-based incentive systems 301–302
message content 215–217
  affirmations 216
  appropriate topics for discussion 215–216
  openness to express opinions 216–217
  rejections 216

message context 217–221
  body language 220
  facial expressions 219
  high-context cultures 218–219
  low-context cultures 218
  non-verbal communication 217–221
  personal space 219–220
  secret communication 220–221
Mexican cultural patterns 187–188
Mexican *grupo* (business group) 186–192
  Mexican cultural patterns 187–188
  organization and management trends 189–192
mianzi (face) 177–178
mien-tzu (face) 177–178
Mintzberg, Henry 27, 105–106
Mitsubishi Electric
  global partnership negotiations 350–352
  negotiations with General Electric 318–321
Mittelstand firms (small to medium-sized firms),
    Germany 135–137
models of cultural dimensions 55–57
monochronic/polychronic cultural dimension 62
mordida 189, 396
Morison, Patricia 155
Morita, Akio 279
motivation *see* work motivation
multicultural competence 3
  components of 36–38
  cosmopolitan outlook 38
  cultural sensitivity 38
  cultural synergy 38
  flexible management style 38
  intercultural communications skills 38
  rapid acculturation skills 38
multicultural teams *see* global teams
multiculturalism 15–17
Munsterberg, Hugo 26
Muslim businesswomen 66–69

namaste 199
Nasrudin, Mullah 24
negotiation
  influence of normative beliefs 328–330
  problems with negotiation across cultures
      318–321
  see also global partnerships
negotiation and culture (model) 328–330
negotiation patterns across cultures 337–342
  Brazilian negotiators 339–341
  Japanese negotiators 337–338, 340–341
  reciprocal processes 341–342
  situational influences 341
  US negotiators 341
negotiation process 330–337
  bargaining and concessions 333–334
  competitive bargaining approach 331–332
  contracts 334–337
  establishing personal relationships 330–331
  final agreements and contracts 334–337

  getting to know prospective partners 330–331
  information exchange and initial offers
      332–333
  problem-solving approach 331–332
  strategies for negotiation 331–332
nemawashi 143
nenpo system 173
network maps 98–100
Nicholson, Nigel 163
Nigeria
  bribery and corruption 363–364
  management patterns 112–115
Nike 35
Nisbett, Richard 96
Nissan 242–245
non-verbal communication 217–221
Nordic cluster, cultural trends 64–66
norm of authenticity 94
normative behavior, and culture 50, 51, 52–55
normative decision model 139–148
Norris, William 363, 367
Nydell, Margaret Omar 317

OECD guidelines, institutional conflicts and
    challenges 385–394, 421–429
operational strategies
  automation 150
  cultural influences 150–151
  process simplification 150–151
  technological complexity 151
opinions, openness to express 216–217
organization, definition 126
organizational decision making
  centralized decision making 140–143
  collaborative decision making 140, 145–148
  consultative decision making 140, 143–145
  decision strategies across cultures 139–148
  employee involvement issues 152–153
  normative decision model 139–148
organizational decision making (model) 137–139
  analytical framework 138–139
  challenges for managers 138
  definition of employee participation 138
  extent of employee participation 137–138
organizational mind concept 149
organizational strategy 126, 128
  influence of the institutional environment
      132–134
  influences on Japanese firms 133–134
  influences on US firms 133–134
  Intel Corporation 127–128
  stakeholder power and influence 130–132
  strategic management cycle 129
  strategy-structure nexus 134–137
  structural determinism 135–137
  ways of understanding 149–150
  Wipro Technologies 127
organizational structure, ways of understanding
    149–150

organizing frameworks
    Chinese *gong-si* (companies) 175–181
    country comparisons 157–192
    East Hope Group (Shanghai) 155–156
    family businesses 155–157
    German *konzern* (firms) 181–186
    influences on organization design 157–159
    Japanese *kaisha* (companies) and *keiretsu*
        (business groups) 165–174
    managerial challenges 193–195
    Mexican *grupo* (business group) 186–192
    Sugar Bowl Bakery 156–157
    US corporations 159–165
Ouchi, William 39

Paik, Yongsun 285
Pak, Yong Suhk 285
Parker Follett, Mary 26
Pascal, Blaise 363, 367
pay-for-performance systems 301–302
perceptual selection 90–91
personal space 219–220
personal work values across cultures 284–289
personality, and culture 51–52
philosophical traditions, influence on managerial
        thinking 99
plurality of cultures versus cultural pluralism in
        globalization 10–11
pok chow (Chinese gang contracting) 112
Political Corruption Index 387
power distribution in different cultures 59
predictability, different cultural views of 62–64
Premji, Azim H. 241
problem-solving negotiation 331–332
process simplification, operational strategy 150–151
productivity 292
psychological contract, and work motivation 289,
        307–309
psychology of work 295–299
    attitudes to risk and uncertainty 297–298
    equity principle 295–296
    free rider effects 298–299
    role of self-efficacy 295
    social loafing and team performance 298–299
    variation in cognitions and expectations 295–296
    variations in causal attributions 297
public policy conflicts *see* institutional conflicts
        and challenges

quality circles (Japan) 174
Qur'an 94

recency effects 201
regional myopia, expatriate managers 34
regional trends and cultural differences 64–66
rejection 216
renqing (personal obligations) 178
rewards *see* work incentives and rewards
ringi-seido 143

ringi-sho 144
risk and uncertainty at work, attitudes to 297–298
Ronan, Simcha 64
Ruiz Gonzalez, Carlos 189
rule-based/relationship-based cultural dimension
        62–64

Samsung Electronics, strategic partnerships 323, 391
Santayana, George 405
Sapir, Edward 206
Schneider, Susan 116
Schuler, Randall 352
Schwartz, Shalom 411, 414
secret communication 220–221
selective perception 201
self concept 93, 100–102
self-efficacy and work motivation 295
self-serving bias 297
shared knowledge, assumptions about 226–227
shared management agreement 346–347
shared meaning and cultural logic 208–210
sharia 53, 370, 374
Shenkar, Oded 64, 78
shinyo 337
shunto, wage negotiations 174
shura 47
Slim Helú, Carlos 192
social control, differences across cultures 62–64
social loafing and work team performance 298–299
social relationships and organization across cultures 61
socialization processes, influence of culture 51
Sony Corporation 259–260
speed of technology-mediated communication 224
stability and change, views on 99–100
stakeholder models 130
stakeholder power and influence 130–132
stakeholders, influence on strategy and structure
        149–150
stakeholders and strategic choice (model) 128
strategic approach to business growth 98–99
strategic management cycle 129
strategy *see* organizational strategy
strategy-structure nexus 134–137
Stewart, Thomas A. 1, 409
Stringer, Howard 259–260
structural determinism 135–137
Sub-Saharan African cluster, cultural trends 64–66
subcultures, cultural complexity 74–75
Sun Tzu 250
supervisory board (Germany) 182
Sweden, Hofstede's cultural model 48–49
Swidler, Ann 50

Taher, Nahed 66–69
tastes and preferences, cross-cultural conflicts
        368–369
Tata Motors 393–394
tatemae 144, 219, 378
Taylor, Frederick 26

technik 185
technological complexity, operational strategy 151
technological developments, global impacts 13–14
technological myopia, virtual managers 34
technology, influences on operational strategies 150–151
technology-mediated assignments, virtual managers 29–30, 33–34
technology-mediated communication 224–227
  assumptions about mutual knowledge 226–227
  asynchronous communication 227
  lack of contextual information 224–226
  speed of communication 224
  technology breakdowns 227
  virtual global teams 263–269
telecommuters 30
Thurow, Lester 2
time use and work patterns, differences across cultures 62
Tintin character, European appeal 251–253
Toshiba, consultative decision making 144–145
total quality management (TQM), cultural influences on implementation 151–152
Toyota, process simplification 150–151
Toyota Production System 127
Trompenaars, Fons 50, 55–57, 103, 411, 413
trust, in global partnerships 334–335, 348, 352–355
"truth", pursuit of 378–384

UK firms, organization and management trends 163–165
US corporations
  comparison with Canada and the UK 163–165
  influences on organizational strategy 133–134
  organization and management trends 162–163
  organizing frameworks 159–165
  use of automation 150
US cultural patterns 159–161
US negotiation patterns 341
uncertainty, different cultural views of 62–64
underground economy 387
universalistic/particularistic cultural dimension 62–64
Ustinov, Peter 378

vacation time, national differences 290–291
value conflicts, incentives and rewards 303–305
values and beliefs
  cross-cultural conflicts 368–369, 371–373
  culture, values, and world views 76–80
  influence of culture 51
Velux America 262
virtual global teams 263–264
  challenges associated with 264–269
  impacts of cultural diversity 267–268
  lack of contextual information 267–268
  lack of mutual knowledge 266–267
  lack of shared understanding 269

  loss of details 268–269
  over-dependence on technology 268
  working with 273–276
virtual managers
  technological myopia 34
  technology-mediated assignments 29–30, 33–34
Volkswagen AG
  collaborative decision making 146–148
  stakeholder influence 131–132
  technological complexity 151
Vroom, Victor 139

Wagoner, Rick 141
Weber, Max 26–27
Welch, Jack 318
"Western" and "Eastern" thinking compared 96–102
Whorf, Benjamin 206
Wipro Technologies 127
work incentives and rewards 299–309
  distributive justice concept 301–302
  employee benefits 305–306
  executive compensation 302–303
  extrinsic rewards 300, 301–306
  financial incentives 301–302
  gender and compensation 303–305
  intrinsic rewards 300, 306–309
  merit-based incentive systems 301–302
  pay-for-performance systems 301–302
  performance consequences 299–300
  reward preferences 300–301
  value conflicts 303–305
work motivation
  attitudes to risk and uncertainty 297–298
  challenges for global managers 292–295
  changes in personal work values 288–289
  culture and the psychology of work 295–299
  definition 293
  equity principle 295–296
  extrinsic rewards 300, 301–306
  free rider effects 298–299
  incentives and rewards 299–309
  individual and group-centered action 311
  intrinsic rewards 300, 306–309
  managerial approaches 310–313
  model for culture and work motivation 292–295
  motivational strategies in different cultures 279–284
  performance consequences 299–300
  personal work values across cultures 284–289
  productivity 292
  psychological contract 289
  relationship with the cultural environment 311–312
  reward preferences 300–301
  role of hierarchy 311
  role of self-efficacy 295
  role of work in employees' lives 290–291, 292
  social control 312
  social loafing and team performance 298–299
  time and work patterns 312

uncertainty and predictability 312
vacation time 290–291
variation in causal attributions 297
variation in cognitions and expectations 295–296
working hours 290–291
work motivation theory 292–295

work patterns and use of time, differences
   across cultures 62
work-related attitudes 307–309
working hours 290–291

Yetton, Phillip 139